HARCOURT
Science

Harcourt School Publishers

Orlando • Boston • Dallas • Chicago • San Diego

www.harcourtschool.com

Cover Image
This butterfly is a Red Cracker. It is almost completely red on its underside. It is called a cracker because the males make a crackling sound as they fly. The Red Cracker is found in Central and South America.

Printed in the United States of America

ISBN 0-15-311206-9

6 7 8 9 10 032 2000

Authors

Marjorie Slavick Frank
Former Adjunct Faculty Member at Hunter, Brooklyn, and Manhattan Colleges
New York, New York

Robert M. Jones
Professor of Education
University of Houston-Clear Lake
Houston, Texas

Gerald H. Krockover
Professor of Earth and Atmospheric Science Education
School Mathematics and Science Center
Purdue University
West Lafayette, Indiana

Mozell P. Lang
Science Education Consultant
Michigan Department of Education
Lansing, Michigan

Joyce C. McLeod
Visiting Professor
Rollins College
Winter Park, Florida

Carol J. Valenta
Vice President—Education, Exhibits, and Programs
St. Louis Science Center
St. Louis, Missouri

Barry A. Van Deman
Science Program Director
Arlington, Virginia

UNIT A

LIFE SCIENCE
Plants and Animals

UNIT B

L I F E   S C I E N C E

Plants and Animals Interact

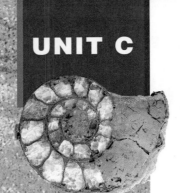

UNIT C

EARTH SCIENCE
Earth's Land

UNIT D

EARTH SCIENCE
Cycles on Earth and In Space

UNIT E

PHYSICAL SCIENCE

Investigating Matter

UNIT F

PHYSICAL SCIENCE
Exploring Energy and Forces

ix

Using Science Process Skills

When scientists try to find an answer to a question or do an experiment, they use thinking tools called process skills. You use many of the process skills whenever you think, listen, read, and write. Think about how these students used process skills to help them answer questions and do experiments.

Maria is interested in birds. She carefully observes the birds she finds. Then she uses her book to identify the birds and learn more about them.

Try This Find something outdoors that you want to learn more about. Use your senses to observe it carefully.

Talk About It What senses does Maria use to observe the birds?

Process Skills

Observe — use your senses to learn about objects and events

Charles finds rocks for a rock collection. He observes the rocks he finds. He compares their colors, shapes, sizes, and textures. He classifies them into groups according to their colors.

Try This Use the skills of comparing and classifying to organize a collection of objects.

Talk About It What other ways can Charles classify the rocks in his collection?

Process Skills

Compare — identify characteristics of things or events to find out how they are alike and different

Classify — group or organize objects or events in categories based on specific characteristics

Katie measures her plants to see how they grow from day to day. Each day after she **measures** she **records the data**. Recording the data will let her work with it later. She **displays the data** in a graph.

Try This Find a shadow in your room. Measure its length each hour. Record your data, and find a way to display it.

Talk About It How does displaying your data help you communicate with others?

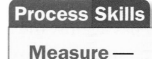

Process Skills

Measure — compare mass, length, or capacity of an object to a unit, such as gram, centimeter, or liter

Record Data — write down observations

Display Data — make tables, charts, or graphs

An ad about low-fat potato chips claims that low-fat chips have half the fat of regular potato chips. Tani **plans and conducts an investigation** to test the claim.

Tani labels a paper bag Regular and Low-Fat. He finds two chips of each kind that are the same size, and places them above their labels. He crushes all the chips flat against the bag. He sets the stopwatch for one hour.

Tani **predicts** that regular chips will make larger grease spots on the bag than low-fat chips. When the stopwatch signals, he checks the spots. The spots above the Regular label are larger than the spots above the Low-Fat label. Tani **infers** that the claim is correct.

Try This Plan and conduct an investigation to test claims for a product. Make a prediction, and tell what you infer from the results.

Talk About It Why did Tani test potato chips of the same size?

Process Skills

Plan and conduct investigations—identify and perform the steps necessary to find the answer to a question

Predict—form an idea of an expected outcome based on observations or experience

Infer—use logical reasoning to explain events and make conclusions

You will have many opportunities to practice and apply these and other process skills in *Harcourt Science.* An exciting year of science discoveries lies ahead!

Safety in Science

Here are some safety rules to follow.

① Think ahead. Study the steps and safety symbols of the investigation so you know what to expect. If you have any questions, ask your teacher.

② Be neat. Keep your work area clean. If you have long hair, pull it back so it doesn't get in the way. Roll up long sleeves. If you should spill or break something, or get cut, tell your teacher right away.

③ Watch your eyes. Wear safety goggles when told to do so.

④ Yuck! Never eat or drink anything during a science activity unless you are told to do so by your teacher.

⑤ Don't get shocked. Be sure that electric cords are in a safe place where you can't trip over them. Don't ever pull a plug out of an outlet by pulling on the cord.

⑥ Keep it clean. Always clean up when you have finished. Put everything away and wash your hands.

In some activities you will see these symbols. They are signs for what you need to do to be safe.

CAUTION

Be especially careful.

CAUTION

Wear safety goggles.

CAUTION

Be careful with sharp objects.

CAUTION

Don't get burned.

CAUTION

Protect your clothes.

CAUTION

Protect your hands with mitts.

CAUTION

Be careful with electricity.

Plants and Animals

UNIT A

LIFE SCIENCE

Plants and Animals

Unit Project | ## Naturalist's Handbook

Observe the plants and animals that live around you. Make notes and sketches about your observations. Use tools like a hand lens, ruler, and thermometer to help you make your observations. Use reference materials to identify and describe the living things. Organize the information you find in a handbook to share.

How Plants Grow

Plants grow almost everywhere on Earth. Plants come in many sizes. Some are tall, like oak trees. Others are smaller, like rosebushes. But each plant has the same basic needs. These needs must be met in order for the plant to live and grow.

Vocabulary Preview

root
stem
leaf
seed
germinate
seedling
photosynthesis
chlorophyll

FAST FACT

Duckweed floats on the tops of ponds and quiet streams. It is the smallest flowering plant in the world.

Sizes of Plants	
Plant	**Height**
Duckweed	0.6 mm (0.02 in.)
Saguaro	15 m (50 ft)
Bamboo	30 m (100 ft)
Redwood	113 m (370 ft)

Frog in duckweed

FAST FACT

The largest cactus is the saguaro. It can be 50 feet tall and can weigh 14,000 pounds! In fact, it would take about 200 8-year-olds to match the weight of one giant saguaro.

What Do Plants Need?

In this lesson, you can . . .

 INVESTIGATE plant needs.

 LEARN ABOUT how plants meet their needs.

 LINK to math, writing, art, and technology.

 **INVESTIGATE**

Needs of Plants

Activity Purpose Plants need certain things to live and grow. In this investigation you will **observe** changes in plants. Then you will **compare** your observations to find out some of the things plants need to grow.

Materials

- 6 young plants
- 6 paper cups
- potting soil
- marker
- brown paper bag
- water
- ruler

Activity Procedure

1 Put the plants in the paper cups and add soil. Make sure all six plants have the same amount of soil. Label two of the plants *No Water*. Put these plants in a sunny window. (Picture A)

◄ **The radishes you eat are roots.**

Plants	Day 1	Day 3	Day 5	Day 7	Day 9	Day 11
No Water						
No Light						
Water and Light						

2 Label two plants *No Light*. Place these plants on a table away from a window. Water the plants. Then cover them with a paper bag.

3 Label the last two plants *Water and Light*. Water these plants. Put them in a sunny window.

Picture A

4 Every other day for two weeks, **observe** the plants. Check to make sure the plants labeled *No Light* and *Water and Light* have moist soil. Add enough water to keep the soil moist.

5 Make a chart like the one shown. On the chart, **record** any changes you **observe** in the plants. Look for changes in the color and height of each plant. (Picture B)

Picture B

Draw Conclusions

1. Which plants looked the healthiest after two weeks? Why do you think so?

2. Which plants looked the least healthy after two weeks? What was different for these plants?

3. **Scientists at Work** Scientists often **compare** observations to reach their conclusions. Compare your observations of the plants to tell what things plants need to grow. Make a list.

What Plants Need

FIND OUT

- four needs of plants
- how roots, stems, and leaves help plants live
- some different shapes and sizes of leaves

VOCABULARY

root

stem

leaf

These bluebonnets and Indian paintbrush flowers get what they need to live from nature. ▼

Plant Needs

Plants are living things. They live in places all over the world. Plants grow in deserts, in rain forests, and in your back yard. But no matter where they grow, all plants need the same things to live. As you learned in the investigation, these things include water and light. Plants also need soil and air.

Most plants live and grow without human care. They get what they need from the sun, the air, the rain, and the soil. Different kinds of plants need different amounts of these things. For example, a cactus needs very little water. Other plants, such as water lilies, need a lot of water. This is why the kinds of plants in one place may be very different from those in another place.

✔ **What four things do all plants need?**

The sun provides plants with light. ▼

Rain gives plants the water they need. ▼

Plant Parts

A tall oak tree looks very different from a daisy. A rosebush looks different from a dandelion. Yet all these plants have the same parts.

The **roots** of a plant are underground, where you often don't see them. A **stem** connects the roots with the leaves of a plant and supports the plant above ground. You may have seen a thin green stem on a flower. The thick, woody trunk of a tree is also a stem.

Leaves are plant parts that grow out of the stem. Most plants have many leaves.

✔ **How does water in the soil get to a plant's leaves?**

Soil contains the minerals plants need. ▼

Roots, stems, and leaves are parts of a plant. They help the plant get what it needs to live.

The stem carries water from the roots to other parts of the plant.

Leaves take in the air and light a plant needs.

Roots hold a plant in the ground. They take in water and minerals from the soil.

A7

Leaf Shapes

Leaves help plants get the light and air they need. You may know that most leaves are green. But did you know that leaves have many shapes and sizes?

Many leaves, such as those from maple and oak trees, are wide and flat. Others, such as those from the jade plant, are small and thick. Leaves can be many different shapes. A leaf may have smooth or rough edges. Some leaf shapes may remind you of other things you have seen in nature. The way a leaf looks can help you tell what plant the leaf came from.

✓ **When you observe a leaf, what can help you tell what plant the leaf is from?**

▲ **The black oak leaf is long and wide, with rough edges.**

◄ **The leaf of the beech tree is oval and has rough edges.**

The leaf of the sweet-gum tree is star-shaped. Its edges are rough. ▼

The jade plant has leaves that are small and thick. The edges are smooth. ►

The ginkgo leaf is fan-shaped with smooth edges. ▶

Summary

Plants need water, light, soil, and air to live and grow. Roots, stems, and leaves help a plant get what it needs to live. Roots take in water from the soil. Stems carry this water to other parts of the plant. Leaves help the plant use light and air. Leaves have different shapes and sizes.

Review

1. Name four things a plant needs to live.
2. How does a plant take in water from the soil?
3. What plant part supports the leaves and branches of a tree?
4. **Critical Thinking** How might you care for an indoor plant?
5. **Test Prep** The plant parts that take in water and minerals from the soil are the —

   A flowers   **C** leaves
   B roots   **D** stems

LINKS

MATH LINK

Graphing Leaf Sizes Gather five to ten kinds of leaves. Use a ruler to measure the length of each leaf from the bottom of its stem to its tip. Make a bar graph to show the lengths of the leaves.

WRITING LINK

Informative Writing— Description Most states have a state tree and a state flower. What are these plants in your state? Write a description for your teacher of each.

ART LINK

Leaf Album Make drawings or crayon rubbings of your favorite kinds of leaves. Show the different shapes, sizes, and colors of the leaves. Label each drawing, and put it into a booklet.

TECHNOLOGY LINK

Learn more about plants and what they need by visiting the National Museum of Natural History Internet site.
www.si.edu/harcourt/science

 Smithsonian Institution®

What Do Seeds Do?

In this lesson, you can . . .

 INVESTIGATE what seeds need to sprout.

 LEARN ABOUT why seeds are important.

 LINK to math, writing, technology, and other areas.

INVESTIGATE

Sprouting Seeds

Activity Purpose Cucumbers, carrots, and apples come from very different kinds of plants. But as different as these plants are, they all started as seeds. Seeds need certain things to sprout and grow. In this investigation, you will **observe** seeds to find out what they need to grow into new plants.

Materials

- 3 kinds of seeds
- paper towels
- 3 small zip-top bags
- scissors
- water
- tape
- hand lens

Activity Procedure

1 Start with a small amount of mixed seeds. Use size and shape to sort the seeds into three groups.

◀ **These corn seedlings have roots, stems, and leaves.**

Seeds	Days				
	1	2	3	4	5
Group 1					
Group 2					
Group 3					

Picture A

2 Cut two paper towels in half. Fold the towels to fit into the plastic bags. Add water to make the towels damp. Do not use too much water or you will drown the seeds. (Picture A)

3 Put one group of seeds into each bag, and seal the bags. Label the bags *1*, *2*, and *3*. Tape the bags to the inside of a window.

4 Use a hand lens to **observe** the seeds every school day for 10 days. Use a chart like the one shown to **record** your observations. (Picture B)

Picture B

Draw Conclusions

1. What changes did you **observe** in the seeds?

2. How quickly did the changes take place in the different kinds of seeds?

3. **Scientists at Work** Scientists **observe** their investigations closely to get new information. How did observing the seeds help you understand more about seeds?

Investigate Further Repeat the investigation steps, but place the bags in a dark closet instead of in a window. **Predict** what will happen. **Record** your observations.

> **Process Skill Tip**
>
> When you **observe**, you use your senses to gather information. Observing sprouting seeds over time will help you understand more about how plants grow.

Growing Plants from Seeds

FIND OUT

- how plants reproduce
- what seeds need to sprout and grow
- four ways seeds are spread from one place to another

VOCABULARY

seed
germinate
seedling

What Seeds Are

Have you ever found seeds inside an orange or apple you were eating? Many plants reproduce, or make more plants like themselves, by forming seeds. The **seed** is the first stage in the growth of many plants.

Seeds may be large or small. They may be round, oval, flat, or pointed. Seeds may be many colors, too—they may even be striped. A seed looks very different from the plant that grows from it. But all seeds become plants that look like the plants they came from.

✔ **What does a seed do?**

This cone from a pine tree produces many seeds.

After a sunflower seed germinates, a new sunflower plant will grow.

A12

What Seeds Need

In the investigation, you observed that seeds began to grow into new plants when you gave them water. When the small plant breaks out of the seed, we say the seed **germinates**.

As a seed begins to sprout, a root grows from it. Next, the seed breaks open and a young plant, or **seedling**, appears. The seedling begins to form the parts it will need as an adult plant. The roots grow longer, and the stem begins to grow. Soon the seedling breaks through the soil. As the plant grows larger, leaves begin to form.

✔ **What do both seeds and plants need to grow?**

This summer squash is ready to eat. It is filled with seeds that could grow into new plants. ▼

How does the squash change as it grows from a seed to a young plant?

A13

Some Plants Make Seeds

Plants that reproduce by seeds usually form more than one seed at a time. These seeds carry the information needed to grow into plants that look very much like the adult plant they came from.

Two groups of plants form seeds. In one group are the plants that have flowers. You may have seen flowers growing on bushes, on trees, or on small plants.

In the other group of seed-forming plants are plants that have cones. Some evergreen trees, such as pine trees, have cones. The cones have hard scales that protect the seeds under them.

Some plants can be grown from other plant parts. For example, if you place a leaf or a piece of a stem in water, it may form roots. Once roots form, you can put the plant part in soil, and it will grow into a new plant. The leaf or piece of stem used to grow the new plant is called a cutting. Underground plant parts such as tubers and bulbs can also be used to grow new plants.

✔ **Name five plants that form seeds.**

A bulb is a part of the stem. Many flowers, such as this tulip, grow from bulbs.

◄ **Dandelions form many seeds that are easily blown by the wind.**

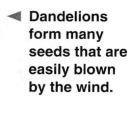

The seeds in a watermelon are protected by its fruit. ►

Seed Parts

Seeds may be many different shapes, sizes, and colors. But all seeds have the same parts. Seeds are like packages with tiny plants inside. The "package" is wrapped by the seed coat. Inside the seed coat is a seedling and food for the seedling.

✔ **What are the parts of a seed?**

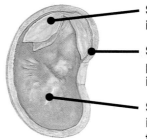

The Parts of a Seed

Seedling: A seedling lives inside every seed.

Seed coat: The seed coat protects the young plant inside the seed.

Stored food: Most of the inside of a seed is stored food. The young plant uses the food to grow when the seed sprouts.

THE INSIDE STORY

Sizes of Seeds

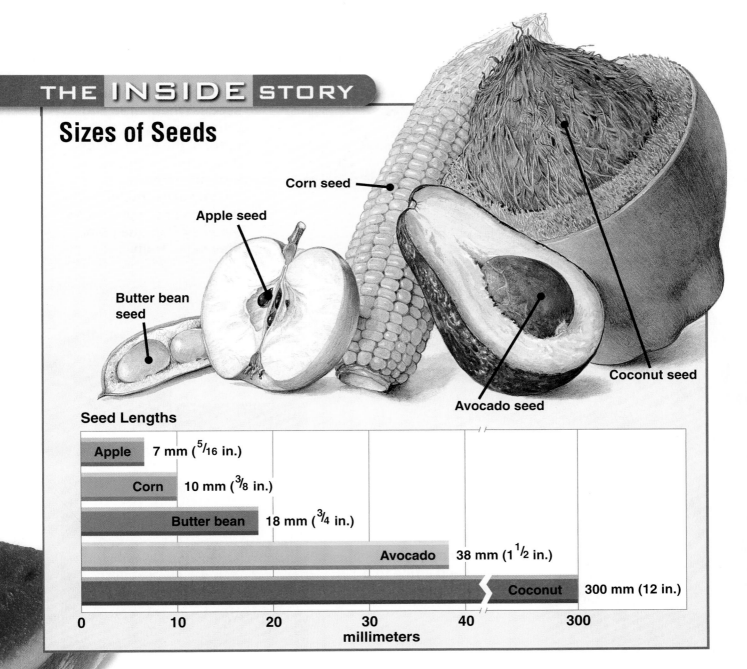

Corn seed

Apple seed

Butter bean seed

Coconut seed

Avocado seed

Seed Lengths

Seed	Length
Apple	7 mm ($^5/_{16}$ in.)
Corn	10 mm ($^3/_8$ in.)
Butter bean	18 mm ($^3/_4$ in.)
Avocado	38 mm ($1^1/_2$ in.)
Coconut	300 mm (12 in.)

0   10   20   30   40   300
millimeters

How Seeds Are Spread

Many seeds do not simply fall off the adult plants and sprout in the soil. Instead, they are scattered and moved to new places. Seeds are spread to new places in many ways. Some seeds are shot out of the adult plant like cannonballs from a cannon! Other seeds are spread by air, water, and animals.

✓ **What are some ways seeds are spread from one place to another?**

The fluffy parts of these milkweed seeds help them float away on the wind. ▶

Many berries contain seeds. When birds and other animals eat the berries, the seeds pass through their digestive systems unharmed. These seeds are later dropped onto the ground far away from the plant they came from.

◀ A cocklebur has hooks that grab onto fur or clothing. An animal or a person may give this seed a ride to a faraway place.

Water carries these mangrove seeds to new places. ▶

▲ Witch hazel plants shoot their seeds to spread them. This is called bolting.

Summary

Some plants form seeds to make new plants. Some plants also can be grown from plant parts. Seeds grow to look like the adult plants they came from. Although they may look different from one another, all seeds have the same parts and need water to sprout. Seeds are often spread to new places by air, water, and animals.

Review

1. What is a seedling?
2. What are some ways plants make new plants?
3. Describe some ways an animal can carry a seed from one place to another.
4. **Critical Thinking** If two seeds look alike, will they always grow into plants that look the same?
5. **Test Prep** What happens when a seed germinates?
   A The seed breaks open and a seedling appears.
   B The seedling breaks through the soil.
   C Leaves begin to form.
   D A root grows from the seed.

 LINKS

 MATH LINK

Counting Seeds Working with a partner, cut open an apple. Count the seeds inside. How many seeds in the whole class? Group the seeds by tens.

 WRITING LINK

Narrative Writing—Story Write a creative story for a younger child about the life of a seed.

 SOCIAL STUDIES LINK

Seeds Are Food Research the kinds of seeds people eat. Share with the class what you learn.

 ART LINK

Fruity Posters Collect seeds from your favorite fruits. Use them to make a poster that tells about each fruit and its seeds.

 TECHNOLOGY LINK

Visit the Harcourt Learning Site for related links, activities, and resources.
www.harcourtschool.com

A17

How Do Plants Make Food?

In this lesson, you can . . .

INVESTIGATE what plants need to make their own food.

LEARN ABOUT photosynthesis.

LINK to math, writing, language arts, and technology.

◄ Lemon trees make their own food.

INVESTIGATE

Food Factories

Activity Purpose
How do plants get food? They make it! To make food, plants must use the things around them. In this investigation, you will **observe** a plant making food. Then you will **infer** what plants need to make their food.

Materials

- scissors
- elodea
- dowel or pencil
- twist tie
- empty 0.5-L plastic bottle
- water
- brown paper bag
- watch or clock

Activity Procedure

1 **CAUTION** **Be careful when using scissors.** Use scissors to cut a piece of the elodea (el•oh•DEE•uh) as long as the bottle.

2 Wrap the elodea around the dowel. Use a twist tie to attach it to the dowel. (Picture A)

3 Put the elodea into the bottle, and fill the bottle with water. (Picture B)

4 Put the bottle in a place away from any windows. Cover the bottle with the brown paper bag. After 10 minutes, remove the bag. **Record** any changes you **observe.**

5 This time, place the bottle in bright sunlight and don't cover it with the brown paper bag. After 10 minutes, **observe** the bottle. **Record** any changes you observe.

Picture A

Draw Conclusions

1. Did the elodea and water in the bottle look different after Steps 4 and 5? If they did, tell how they were different.

2. What did you change between Steps 4 and 5? What remained the same in Steps 4 and 5?

3. **Scientists at Work** From what you **observed,** what can you **infer** about the bubbles you saw?

Picture B

Investigate Further Scientists often **measure** what happens in experiments. One way to measure what is happening in this experiment is to count the number of bubbles that appear. Put the bottle with the elodea in bright sunlight, and count the number of bubbles that appear in one minute. Then move the bottle out of the direct sun. Again count the number of bubbles that appear in one minute. How are the two measurements different? **Infer** why they are different.

Process Skill Tip

When you **infer,** you use what you have **observed** to form an opinion. That opinion is called an inference.

A19

How Plants Make Food

FIND OUT

- how plants make their own food

- why plants need chlorophyll to make their food

VOCABULARY

photosynthesis
chlorophyll

Making Food

Like other animals, you cannot make food in your body. You must get your food by eating. Plants, however, can make their own food. This food-making process is called **photosynthesis** (foht•oh•SIN•thuh•sis). A process is a way of doing something.

The leaves of most plants are green. Plants get their green color from **chlorophyll** (KLAWR•uh•fil). Chlorophyll helps the plant use energy from the sun to make food. Plants need light to make food. They also need water and carbon dioxide. Carbon dioxide is a gas in the air.

The sun provides light energy to plants.

◄ A plant that gets enough light (and soil and water) grows into a healthy plant.

▲ A plant that does not get enough light does not grow well, even though it has soil and water. It may die.

Photosynthesis

During photosynthesis, a plant takes in sunlight, water, and carbon dioxide. The chlorophyll in the leaves lets the plant use these things to make food. The plant makes sugar and gives off oxygen.

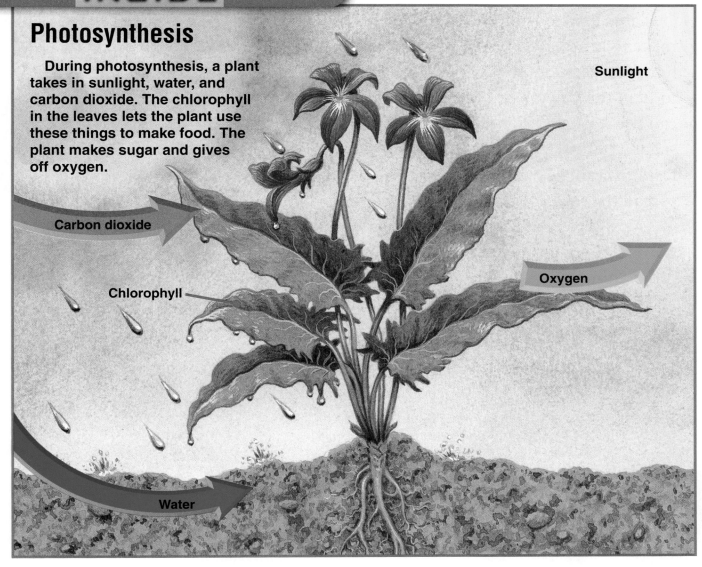

Sunlight

Carbon dioxide

Chlorophyll

Oxygen

Water

During photosynthesis, water and carbon dioxide combine inside a plant to make food. Sunlight provides the energy needed for this to happen. The food the plant makes is a kind of sugar. The plant uses some of the sugar right away and stores the rest.

During photosynthesis, plants also make oxygen. The oxygen is given off into the air through the plant's leaves. The bubbles you observed in the investigation were oxygen given off by the leaves into the water.

✔ **Name four things plants need for photosynthesis.**

How Plants Use Food

Plants use some of the food they make to grow larger. They also use it to make seeds. Some plants store food in their stems and roots so they can use it later. Other plants store sugar in fruits. This makes the fruit tasty to animals, who eat it and spread the seeds.

The stems, leaves, roots, seeds, fruits, and even flowers of plants are used as food by people and other animals.

▲ Bananas grow in bunches called hands.

✔ **What are three ways plants use the food they make?**

◀ People eat the red fruit of the strawberry plant.

◀ The stalks of celery plants contain fiber and water.

A potato is an underground stem that stores food made by the potato plant. ▼

▲ When you break open a pea pod you can see the pea seeds inside.

Summary

Photosynthesis is the process plants use to make their own food. Plants need chlorophyll, light, carbon dioxide, and water for photosynthesis. The sun provides the light energy that plants need to make food. Plants use the food they make to grow bigger and to make seeds. They store some of their food in roots, stems, and fruits. People and other animals eat many different plant parts.

Review

1. Describe what happens during photosynthesis.
2. Why are plants green?
3. How does chlorophyll help in photosynthesis?
4. **Critical Thinking** How does photosynthesis help make the food people and other animals eat?
5. **Test Prep** What do plants give off during photosynthesis?
   A carbon dioxide
   B water
   C oxygen
   D light

LINKS

MATH LINK

Plant Parts and Food Make a list of 20 foods you eat that come from plants. Identify how many of these foods come from roots, stems, leaves, fruits, seeds, and flowers. Make a bar graph from your list.

WRITING LINK

Informative Writing— Explanation Plants are like food factories. Use what you know about photosynthesis to write a paragraph for your teacher that explains how a plant is like a factory.

LANGUAGE ARTS LINK

Putting It Together The word *photosynthesis* is made up of the words *photo* and *synthesis*. Use a dictionary to find out what these words mean.

TECHNOLOGY LINK

To learn more about how people use the food that plants store, watch *Grocery Garden* on **Harcourt Science Newsroom Video.**

CNN®
Turner
Le@rning

Drought-Resistant Plants

Different kinds of plants live in different kinds of places. Water plants need lots of water. Plants that live in the desert need very little water. Plants that need little water are called drought-resistant plants.

What Makes Plants Drought Resistant?

Drought-resistant plants have traits that allow them to live successfully with little water. One trait is gray or white leaves or bark. Their light color reflects the heat of the sun rather than absorbing it. This keeps the plant cooler, so it doesn't dry out as much. Another trait these plants have is narrow leaves, which help the plant keep moisture in.

Many drought-resistant plants bloom early in the spring, when there is plenty of water. They develop seeds before the hot, dry months.

Some plants have underground bulbs or enlarged root systems that store food. When dry weather arrives, the plant has plenty of food it can use.

Who Needs Drought-Resistant Plants?

Some parts of the United States get little rain. Many of these places are warm and get lots of sun. More and more people are deciding to live in these warm, sunny places. These people often try to grow gardens with the kinds of plants they had where they came from. These plants need more water than they get naturally in dry areas, so people have to water them a lot. But this uses water that is needed for other things, such as farms, animals, and people.

One way to have pretty plants without using much water is to use a process called Xeriscaping (ZIR•uh•skayp•ing). Xeriscaping is the use of water-saving methods and drought-resistant plants in gardens and yards.

How Does Xeriscaping Work?

First the gardener analyzes the soil and the amount of water in the garden area. Then the gardener chooses plants that can grow well in those conditions. Often the gardener chooses plants that are native to the area because they have adapted to the local climate. The gardener puts a layer of mulch, such as leaves or wood chips, around each plant to help hold water in the ground. Xeriscaping saves water costs for the gardener and conserves water for the whole community.

Think About It

1. How can planting drought-resistant plants help the environment?

2. What are some native plants in your area?

WEB LINK:
For Science and Technology updates, visit the Harcourt Internet site.
www.harcourtschool.com

Careers | Agricultural Extension Agent

What They Do Extension agents often work for state or local governments. These people offer help and information to  farmers, gardeners, and teachers. They often travel to different areas to teach and train people in new technology used in agriculture.

Education and Training An extension agent must study agriculture and animal science. Training in computers and agricultural technology will be required for the agents of the future.

George Washington Carver

AGRICULTURAL CHEMIST

"I literally lived in the woods. I wanted to know every strange stone, flower, insect, bird, or beast."

How many ways can you think of to use a peanut? George Washington Carver found more than 300!

After completing college, Carver was invited to teach at the Tuskegee Institute in Alabama. For almost 50 years, he taught there and conducted experiments with plants. He experimented to solve many problems of farming. The problems included poor soil, amounts of sunlight and moisture, plant diseases, and ways of reproducing plants.

Carver persuaded farmers to rotate their crops so the soil would not lose all its nutrients. One year the farmers could plant cotton or tobacco, but the next year they planted peanuts or sweet potatoes. The land produced so many crops that Carver had to find new uses for them. Besides his work with peanuts, he found more than 100 uses for sweet potatoes and 75 for pecans.

Some of the plants that Carver worked with ▼

Think About It

1. George Washington Carver was interested in plants from his boyhood. Think about the things that interest you now. Which ones do you think will interest you when you grow up?
2. What qualities do you think a plant scientist ought to have?

What Stems Do

How does water move through a stem?

Materials

- 3 1-L plastic bottles
- water
- food coloring
- 3 freshly cut white carnations
- scissors

Procedure

1. Fill the plastic bottles with water. Add a few drops of food coloring. Put a different color in each bottle.

2. **CAUTION** **Be careful when using scissors.** Trim the end off the stem of each flower. Place one flower in each bottle.

3. Keep the flowers in the bottles overnight. Then observe the flowers.

Draw Conclusions

Explain your observations. Make a bouquet of flowers with the colors you like best.

Growing Plants

Can plant parts be used to grow a new plant?

Materials

- 1 plant with many stems and leaves
- scissors
- 1-L plastic bottle
- water
- ruler

Procedure

1. **CAUTION** **Be careful when using scissors.** Cut off a 15-cm piece of the plant.

2. Fill the plastic bottle with water. Place the cut part of the plant in the bottle.

3. Place the plant in bright sunlight.

Draw Conclusions

Observe the plant for ten days. Record any changes you observe.

Chapter 1 Review and Test Preparation

Vocabulary Review

Use the terms below to complete the sentences 1 through 7. The page numbers in ( ) tell you where to look in the chapter if you need help.

roots (A7)   **germinate** (A13)
stem (A7)   **photosynthesis** (A20)
leaves (A7)   **chlorophyll** (A20)
seeds (A12)

1. Many new plants grow from ____.

2. The plant parts that grow out of stems are ____.

3. ____ gives plants their green color.

4. A seed needs water to ____.

5. The underground parts of a plant that take in water from the soil are the ____.

6. The food-making process of plants is ____.

7. A ____ connects the roots and leaves of a plant.

Connect Concepts

Use the terms from the Word Bank to complete the concept map.

wind   chlorophyll   water   oxygen   animals

How Plants Grow		
What Plants Need	**What Seeds Do**	**How Plants Make Food**
Roots help a plant take in water from the soil.	Many plants can form seeds. Seeds need air and water to sprout. Seeds are spread in many ways.	Plants make their own food by a process called photosynthesis.
Leaves take in carbon dioxide from the air. They give off 8. ____.	Three ways seeds are spread are by 9. ____, 10. ____, and 11. ____.	12. ____ in plants helps take in light.

Check Understanding

Write the letter of the best choice.

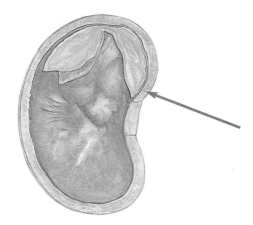

13. Look at the picture. Which part of the seed is the arrow pointing to?

   A stored food   **C** seed coat

   B young plant   **D** stem

14. Some plants are grown from bulbs. A bulb is a part of the —

   F root   **H** stem

   G seed   **J** leaf

Critical Thinking

15. What would happen to a farmer's crop if there were little or no rain for a long period of time?

16. How can a dandelion growing in the schoolyard be a parent to young dandelion plants growing miles from school?

17. If a plant reproduces by bulbs, does it make seeds, too? Explain.

Process Skills Review

18. You are growing two plants. You want to test one plant to find out how sunlight affects its growth. You will provide the other plant with everything it needs for growth. Explain how you will **observe** the plants and **compare** your results.

19. What can **observing** tree leaves help you learn?

Performance Assessment

Design a Garden

With a partner, design a garden to grow your favorite kinds of plants. Make a list of all the things you will need for your garden.

Types of Animals

How many different kinds of animals can you name? You probably listed animals such as cats, dogs, cows, and fish. But there are many more. Even though there are many kinds of animals, they all need the same types of things to live and grow.

Vocabulary Preview

inherit
trait
mammal
bird
amphibian
gills
fish
scale
reptile

FAST FACT

It's a trick! These butterfly fish have spots on their tails that look like eyes. The "eyes" scare away larger fish that might eat them.

FAST FACT

Types of Animals on Earth

75% insects

25% all other animals

Swat! Slap! Mosquitoes bite. Bees sting. Of every 100 types of animals in the world, 75 are insects.

1

What Is an Animal?

In this lesson, you can . . .

 INVESTIGATE animal homes.

 LEARN ABOUT how animals meet their needs.

 LINK to math, writing, literature, and technology.

 **INVESTIGATE**

Animal Homes

Activity Purpose Everyone needs a place to live—including animals. Animals live in many kinds of places that give them the things they need. In this investigation you will **observe** animal homes and use the homes to **classify** the animals.

Materials
- Animal Picture Cards

◀ **Ladybugs get food from this bluebonnet.**

A32

Activity Procedure

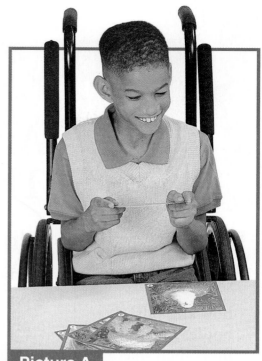
Picture A

1. Select six Animal Picture Cards or use the pictures on page A32. As you **observe** the cards, pay close attention to the types of homes the animals live in. (Picture A)

2. Describe each animal home you **observe. Record** your descriptions.

3. With a partner, discuss the different types of animal homes shown. Talk about the ways the animal homes are alike and the ways they are different. Then **classify** the animals by the types of homes they live in.

Draw Conclusions

1. **Compare** two of the animal homes you observed. Tell how each home helps protect the animal that lives there.

2. What did you **observe** about the home of a Canada goose and the home of an albatross?

3. **Scientists at Work** Scientists **classify** animals into groups based on what the animals have in common. How many groups did you classify the animals into? What were the groups?

Investigate Further Study the Animal Picture Cards again. This time, look at the body covering of each animal. Describe each covering. How can you use body coverings to **classify** the animals?

> **Process Skill Tip**
>
> When you **classify** things, you put them into groups. You put things into a group because they have something in common. For example, you could put into one group the animals that build nests.

Animals and Their Needs

FIND OUT

- what animals need so they can live
- how animals' bodies help them meet their needs
- how animals get their traits

VOCABULARY

inherit

trait

What Animals Need

Have you ever cared for a pet? If so, you know that a pet needs food and water. A pet also needs shelter, or a place to live. Wild animals have the same needs as pets. The difference is that wild animals must meet their needs on their own.

As you learned in the investigation, different animals make their homes in different surroundings. From their surroundings, they get all the things they need. This is something all animals have in common.

✔ **Name three things animals need.**

This reef is made up of tiny living animals called corals. Other animals, such as the dolphin shown here, look for food in the reef and use the reef for shelter. ▼

Animals Need Air

Have you ever thought about the air around you? Air contains a gas called oxygen. Animals need oxygen to live.

Animals that live on land, such as giraffes, have lungs that get oxygen from the air. Insects get oxygen from the air through tiny holes in their bodies. Many water animals, such as fish, get their oxygen from water. Other water animals, such as whales, must come to the surface and breathe air to get oxygen.

✓ **Name two ways animals get oxygen.**

▲ **An alligator comes to the water's surface to breathe the air it needs.**

Animals Need Water

The bodies of all animals contain water. Every day some of this water leaves the animals' bodies. For example, when an animal pants or sweats, it loses some water from its body. The animal must replace this water to stay alive.

Most animals get the water they need by drinking. The water they drink may come from puddles, streams, rivers, ponds, or lakes. Other animals get most of their water in the foods they eat.

✓ **How do animals get the water they need?**

At this water hole on the African plains, animals drink the water they need. ▼

Animals Need Food

All animals need food. Food gives animals the materials they need so they can grow and stay healthy. Animals also get energy from food.

Unlike plants, animals cannot make their own food. Instead, they get their food by eating plants or other animals. Some animals eat only plants. Some eat only animals. Some eat both.

How do animals get the food they need? Many of them have body parts that help them get their food. For example, an elephant uses its trunk to grab leaves from trees. A hawk can use its sharp claws to catch a mouse.

✔ **What do animals eat?**

▲ **This chameleon uses its tongue to catch insects.**

Brown bears live in forests, where they eat many kinds of plants and animals. They often eat fish they catch in streams. They also eat grass and other plants.

A panda eats only bamboo plants. ▼

Beavers Build Shelters

1. Beavers cut down trees to build a dam in a stream.

2. The dam makes a pond. In the pond, the beavers build their home, called a lodge.

3. To build their lodges, beavers use trees they have cut down and rocks that they cover with mud.

4. Young beavers, called kits, stay warm and dry inside the lodge.

Animals Need Shelter

Most animals need shelter, or a place to live. Shelters protect animals from other animals and from the weather. Some birds build shelters called nests high in tree branches. They build their nests out of twigs, grass, and mud. Other animals, such as deer mice, build their homes in hollow logs or in spaces under rocks. Turtles use their own hard shells as their homes. Many other animals dig tunnels and make their homes in the ground.

✓ **Why do animals need shelter?**

Animal Traits

Jellyfish, polar bears, and snakes don't look much alike, but they are all animals. Different animals have many different shapes and sizes. They also have many different body parts. For example, a bird has wings and feathers. A lion has paws and fur. All these features are important to the way an animal lives.

How do animals get their features? Young animals inherit their features from their parents. **Inherit** (in•HAIR•it) means "to receive from parents." The body features an animal inherits are called **traits**. Traits also include some things that animals do.

✔ **What are traits?**

▲ **A sea horse is a type of fish. This male sea horse has the trait of carrying its young inside a pouch.**

These young cheetah cubs will grow to look like their parents. They will stay with their mother for several years and will learn to hunt for their food. ▼

▲ **A mother duck watches her young ducklings carefully.**

▲ These young snakes will grow to look very much like the adult snake.

Summary

Animals need air, water, food, and shelter. Different animals have many different shapes and sizes and many different body parts. These traits help the animals get the things they need. All animals inherit their traits from their parents.

Review

1. How do animals that live in water get air?
2. Describe how beavers change their surroundings to meet their needs.
3. What are four things that animals need?
4. **Critical Thinking** Why will a young lion cub grow to look like an adult lion and not like a sea horse?
5. **Test Prep** Which of the following is **NOT** a need of all animals?

   A food   C air
   B water   D soil

LINKS

MATH LINK

How Many? Suppose that there are 15 duck families that live at a pond. If each of the families has 8 ducklings, how many ducks would live at the pond?

WRITING LINK

Informative Writing— Compare and Contrast Birds make many sounds. Listen to birds that live in your area. If possible, record their sounds with a sound recorder. Write a paragraph for your teacher that compares and contrasts the bird songs.

LITERATURE LINK

A Wolf Pup Diary You can learn about the life of a young wolf by reading *Look to the North: A Wolf Pup Diary* by Jean Craighead George.

TECHNOLOGY LINK

Learn more about animals by visiting the Smithsonian Internet Site.
www.si.edu/harcourt/science

Smithsonian Institution®

LESSON **2**

What Are Mammals and Birds?

In this lesson, you can . . .

 INVESTIGATE how fur helps animals.

 LEARN ABOUT the traits of mammals and birds.

 LINK to math, writing, art, and technology.

◄ **The fur on this deer keeps him warm all winter long.**

Fur Helps Animals

Activity Purpose When it's cold outside, you might put on a jacket or a sweater to keep warm. Animals can't do that. In this investigation you will **use a model** to find out how fur helps keep animals warm.

Materials
- glue
- 2 metal cans
- cotton batting
- hot water
- 2 thermometers
- classroom clock

Activity Procedure

CAUTION

1 Make a chart like the one shown.

2 Spread glue around the outside of one can. Then put a thick layer of cotton around the can. Wait for the glue to dry. Then use your fingers to fluff the cotton. (Picture A)

Time	Water Temperature in Can with Cotton	Water Temperature in Can Without Cotton
Start		
10 min		
20 min		
30 min		

3 **CAUTION** **Be careful with the hot water. It can burn you.** Your teacher will fill both cans with hot water.

4 Place a thermometer in each can, and **record** the temperature of the water. (Picture B)

5 Check the temperature of the water in each can every 10 minutes for a period of 30 minutes. **Record** the temperatures on the chart.

Picture A

Draw Conclusions

1. In which can did the water stay hot longer? Why?

2. How is having fur like wearing a jacket?

3. **Scientists at Work** Scientists often **use a model** to study things they can't observe easily. In this investigation, you made a model of an animal with fur. Why was using a model easier than observing an animal?

Picture B

Investigate Further How do you think your results would be different if you used ice-cold water instead of hot water? Make this change, and do the investigation again.

Process Skill Tip

It would be hard to measure the temperature of a real animal to find out how fur helps it stay warm. **Using a model** helps you learn about animal fur.

A41

Mammals and Birds

FIND OUT

- **four traits of mammals**
- **five traits of birds**

VOCABULARY

mammal
bird

Mammals

In the investigation you learned that fur can help an animal stay warm. Animals that have fur or hair are called **mammals** (MAM•uhlz). Horses, cows, and dogs are all mammals.

Mammals use lungs to breathe. Mammals that live in water, such as whales, also breathe with lungs. But these mammals must come to the surface of the water to breathe the air they need.

Most mammals give birth to live young. A cat gives birth to many kittens at one time. Before the kittens

THE INSIDE STORY

Keeping Warm

A polar bear's fur looks white, but it is really clear. The fur looks white because it reflects sunlight.

hair

fat

The skin of a polar bear is black. The black skin takes in the heat from the sun. Polar bears have a thick layer of fat under their skin. This fat helps keep a polar bear warm.

are born, the mother cat carries them inside her. After the kittens are born, they feed on milk made by their mother's body. Feeding their young with milk from the mother's body is another trait of all mammals.

When a mammal is born, it cannot care for itself. It must be sheltered and fed by its mother. The milk gives them what they need to grow and stay healthy.

Most mammals learn from their parents how to care for themselves. The parents often teach their young how to find food. In time a young mammal learns what it needs to know to live on its own.

✔ **What are four traits mammals inherit from their parents?**

▲ These puppies drink milk from their mother to get the food they need.

◀ Gorillas often live in large families. All the adults help care for the young.

Types of Mammals

There are many types of mammals. Most of them have the four traits you read about. Some also have other traits, such as trunks, pouches, or wings. Mammals are often placed into groups based on traits they share. Some of these groups and their traits are shown on this page.

✔ **Name three traits used to place mammals in groups.**

▲ Bats are the only mammals that fly.

A koala is one of a few mammals that carry their young in a pouch. ▼

▲ This spiny echidna (ee•KID•nuh), an anteater, has fur and lungs. It is a mammal, but it does not give birth to live young. It lays eggs.

This orangutan (oh•RANG•oo•tan) is a primate. Primates are mammals that can use their hands to grasp objects. ▼

Whales are mammals that live in water. They have very little hair. This helps them glide easily through the water. ▶

Birds

Birds are animals that have feathers, two legs, and wings. Most birds use their wings for flying. Some birds, such as penguins, cannot fly. But like other birds, they still have feathers and wings.

Like mammals, birds have lungs for breathing air. Many birds also care for their young for a while after the young are born. Unlike most young mammals, young birds hatch from eggs.

Feathers cover most of a bird's body. But not all feathers are the same. Some feathers help keep a bird warm. Other feathers help birds fly. For example, the wing feathers of many birds have a shape that helps them fly.

✔ **What are five traits of birds?**

▲ **A weaverbird uses leaves to make a hanging nest. The mother bird lays her eggs on soft grass placed inside the nest.**

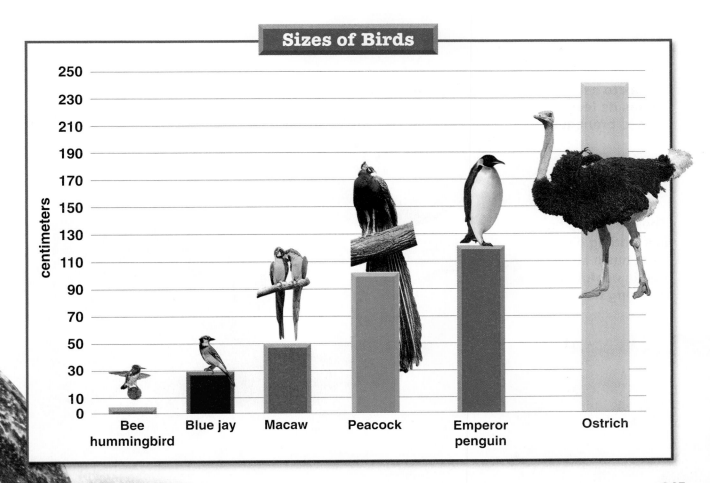

Sizes of Birds

centimeters: 250, 230, 210, 190, 170, 150, 130, 110, 90, 70, 50, 30, 10, 0

Bee hummingbird | Blue jay | Macaw | Peacock | Emperor penguin | Ostrich

Types of Birds

There are many types of birds. Like mammals, birds are grouped together because of traits they share. The most common traits used for grouping birds are beak shape and foot shape.

Beak shape can be used to tell what kind of food a bird eats. For example, wading birds have long beaks that help them catch fish and dig small animals from the mud.

Foot shape can be used to tell where a bird lives. For example, wading birds have long toes that keep them from sinking into the mud. For some birds foot shape is also important in getting food.

✔ **What can you tell about a bird from the shape of its beak or feet?**

▲ A barn owl catches other animals for food. The feet of a barn owl are useful for catching animals such as mice.

A cardinal uses its beak to eat seeds. It uses its feet to hold on to branches. ▶

The purple gallinule (GAL·ih·nool) lives in marshes and swamps. It has long, thin toes that help it walk on lily pads and other plants in the water. ▼

The great blue heron is a wading bird. Its beak has a shape that is useful for catching fish. ▶

Summary

Mammals are animals that have fur or hair and breathe with lungs. Most mammals also give birth to live young and feed their young with milk from the mother's body. Birds are animals that have feathers, two legs, and wings. Like mammals, birds breathe with lungs. Unlike most mammals, birds lay eggs from which their young are hatched.

Review

1. Name a mammal that lives in the water. How does it breathe?
2. How does the spiny echidna differ from most other mammals?
3. What two features of birds are most often used to classify them? Why?
4. **Critical Thinking** A bat can fly, but a bat is a mammal. What traits do you think bats have that make them mammals instead of birds?
5. **Test Prep** Which trait is shared by birds and mammals?
   A have feathers
   B have fur
   C breathe with lungs
   D give birth to live young

LINKS

MATH LINK

Interpret Graphs Look at the graph on page A45. Which birds have the longest tails? If the length of the tails were added to the length of the bodies in the graph, which bird would be the longest?

WRITING LINK

Informative Writing—Classification Go bird-watching in your schoolyard, a park, or in your back yard. If possible, use binoculars. Write a description of each bird to share with your classmates. Identify as many birds as you can.

ART LINK

Animal Tracks You can identify many animals by the tracks they make with their feet. Make a collage of tracks. Label each track with the animal's name.

TECHNOLOGY LINK

Learn more about mammals and birds by investigating *Whose Tracks Are These?* on **Harcourt Science Explorations CD-ROM.**

3

What Are Amphibians, Fish, and Reptiles?

In this lesson, you can . . .

 INVESTIGATE how frogs change as they grow.

 LEARN ABOUT amphibians, fish, and reptiles.

 LINK to math, writing, technology, and other areas.

 **INVESTIGATE**

From Egg to Frog

Activity Purpose Frogs lay eggs in the water. When a young frog hatches, it can live only in water. But as the young frog grows, its body changes. The changes get it ready to live on land. In this investigation you will **observe** these changes in real frogs.

Materials

- gravel
- aquarium
- water
- ruler
- water plants
- rock
- tadpoles
- dried fish food

◀ These frog eggs were laid underwater. They will hatch into tadpoles.

◀ Unlike frogs you may know about, this red-eyed tree frog makes its home in trees.

Activity Procedure

Picture A

1. Put a layer of gravel on the bottom of the aquarium. Add 12 cm to 15 cm of water.

2. Float some water plants on top of the water, and stick others into the gravel. Add the rock. It should be big enough so that frogs can sit on it later and be out of the water. (Picture A)

3. Put two or three tadpoles, or young frogs, in the water. Put the aquarium where there is some light but no direct sunlight.

4. Feed the tadpoles a small amount of dried fish food once a day. Add fresh water to the aquarium once a week.

5. **Observe** the tadpoles every day. Once a week, make a drawing of what they look like.

Draw Conclusions

1. What changes did you see as the tadpoles grew?

2. When the tadpoles began to climb out of the water, what did their bodies look like?

3. **Scientists at Work** Scientists **record** what they **observe.** How did recording your observations help you learn about the growing tadpoles?

Investigate Further How important were the water plants to the growth of the tadpoles? Plan an investigation to answer this question.

Process Skill Tip

When you **observe,** you use your senses of sight, hearing, smell, and touch. Then you **record,** or write down, your observations.

Amphibians, Fish, and Reptiles

Amphibians

FIND OUT

- four traits of amphibians
- four traits of fish
- three traits of reptiles

VOCABULARY

amphibian
gills
fish
scales
reptile

In the investigation, you observed that a tadpole lives in water. But as the tadpole grows into a frog, it spends more time out of the water. Frogs are amphibians. **Amphibians** (am•FIB•ee•uhnz) are animals that begin life in the water and move onto land as adults.

Amphibians lay eggs in the water. The eggs stay there until they hatch. Young amphibians live in the water, just as tadpoles do. Most adult amphibians live on land.

Amphibians have moist skin. But most amphibians still stay close to water.

✔ **Name three traits of an amphibian.**

◀ A salamander moves its body from side to side to help its legs move forward.

Newts live in water for part of the year. Then they live on land. ▼

▲ Toads live most of their adult lives on land. Unlike some other amphibians, toads have rough, bumpy skin.

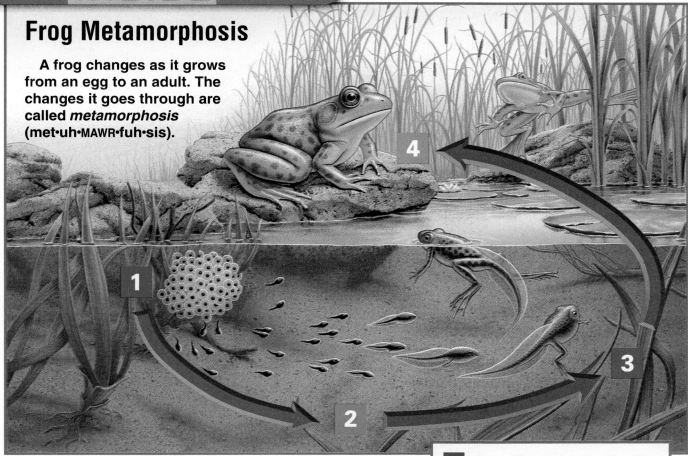

Frog Metamorphosis

A frog changes as it grows from an egg to an adult. The changes it goes through are called *metamorphosis* (met·uh·MAWR·fuh·sis).

1 A frog lays many eggs at one time. The eggs are covered by a jellylike coating.

2 Newborn tadpoles have gills for breathing in water. They also have a tail but no legs.

3 As a tadpole grows, lungs begin to form. Back and front legs begin to grow. These parts allow an adult frog to live on land.

4 Once the lungs work, the gills and the tail disappear. The adult frog is now ready to live on land.

Frogs Grow and Change

As you saw in the investigation, young frogs look very different from adult frogs. Young frogs hatch from eggs and begin life in the water. They breathe with gills. **Gills** are body parts that take in oxygen from the water.

As they grow, young frogs change. In time, they form lungs. Once they have lungs, their gills begin to disappear. Then they develop other body parts that help them live on land. Adult frogs spend most of the year on land near water.

✓ **What body parts do young frogs have that adult frogs do not have?**

A51

Fish

Fish are animals that live their whole lives in water. Like young amphibians, fish have gills. The gills are on the sides of a fish's head. The gills take in oxygen as water moves over them.

Most fish are covered with scales. **Scales** are small, thin, flat plates that help protect the fish.

Different fish have many different shapes and sizes. Like other animals, some fish eat plants and others eat animals. Most fish lay eggs, but some fish give birth to live young.

✔ **What are two traits of fish?**

▲ This Guadeloupe bass has a skeleton made of bone.

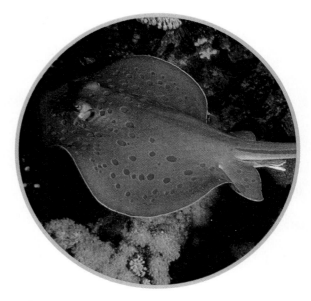

▲ This ray has a cartilage skeleton just like a shark, but its body is flat.

Sharks do not have bones. Instead, their skeletons are made of a softer material called cartilage (KAR•tuh•lij). ▼

The Bodies of Fish

A fish's body is just right for its life in water. Most fish have body shapes that allow them to move easily in water. The smooth scales that cover fish also help them glide through water.

Fish have fins. They use their fins to move forward and backward. The tail fin moves from side to side and helps a fish move forward. Other fins help the fish turn in different directions.

✓ **What are three ways a fish's body is just right for life in water?**

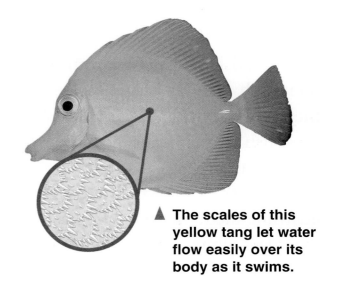

▲ **The scales of this yellow tang let water flow easily over its body as it swims.**

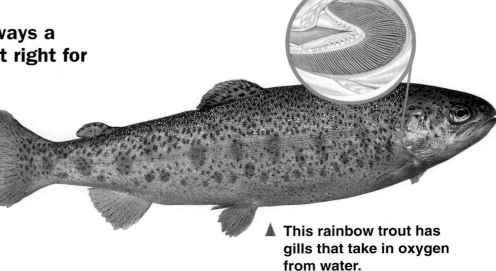

▲ **This rainbow trout has gills that take in oxygen from water.**

▲ **The fins on this goldfish help it swim and turn its body through the water.**

Fish Young

Young fish are hatched from eggs. Some fish carry their eggs inside their bodies until the eggs hatch. But most fish lay their eggs in water. They lay many eggs at a time.

Some fish care for their eggs by guarding them. But most fish leave their eggs alone after they are laid. Other animals eat many of the eggs. The young fish that do hatch are very small. But they must find food and avoid enemies without help from their parents.

✔ **What are two ways fish produce young?**

▲ **This stickleback fish builds a nest to lay its eggs in.**

This cardinal fish carries its eggs in its mouth until they are ready to be hatched. ▼

Reptiles

Reptiles (REP•tylz) are land animals that have dry skin covered by scales. Because they live mostly on land, reptiles use lungs to breathe air. Reptiles that spend a lot of time in water must come to the surface to breathe air. A crocodile, for instance, often stays in water. But it stays near the surface so its nose and eyes are above the water. This allows the crocodile to breathe and see.

Many reptiles hatch from eggs laid on land. The eggs have a tough, leathery shell. Other reptiles are born live. Either way, most of the young are able to meet their needs as soon as they are born.

Reptiles are found almost everywhere on Earth except for the coldest places. Many live in warm, wet tropical rain forests or in hot, dry deserts.

✔ **What are three traits of reptiles?**

▲ The Eastern box turtle hatches from eggs laid on land.

The turtle has a hard shell that protects most of its body. The turtle has scales on its legs and tail. ▼

Types of Reptiles

There are three main groups of reptiles. Lizards and snakes are in one group. Their bodies have rows of scales that overlap. Most lizards live in very warm places. They have four legs and long tails. Snakes don't have legs. They move by pushing their bodies against the ground.

Alligators and crocodiles are another reptile group. They live in water a lot of the time. They come out of the water to sun themselves.

Tortoises and turtles make up the third group of reptiles. They are the only reptiles that have shells. Tortoises live on land. Turtles live in water.

✔ **What are the three groups of reptiles?**

▲ The boa is a large snake. Like other snakes, it sheds its scaly skin and grows new skin.

▲ The Australian frilled lizard uses a fan-shaped body part to scare away enemies.

This is an American crocodile. A crocodile can lie very still in the water, with only its eyes and nose above the water. This helps the crocodile catch animals that can't see it. ▼

▲ This is a Galápagos tortoise. Like turtles, tortoises have hard shells that protect them from enemies.

Summary

Amphibians are animals that begin life in water, change in form, and then live on land. Fish live in the water, use gills for breathing, and have body parts that help them swim. Reptiles are animals that are covered with scales.

Review

1. What happens during the metamorphosis of a frog?
2. List three features that help fish live and move in water.
3. What do gills do?
4. **Critical Thinking** Why do many amphibians stay near the water for their whole lives?
5. **Test Prep** Which trait is shared by most fish, amphibians, and reptiles?

   A fins   C eggs
   B scales   D legs

LINKS

MATH LINK

Using Graphs Take a survey of the kinds of amphibians, fish, and reptiles that people keep as pets. Use a computer graphing program such as *Graph Links* to make a bar graph to show your results.

WRITING LINK

Narrative Writing—Story What if you were a frog? Write a story for a younger child telling how you change from an egg into an adult.

LITERATURE LINK

Verdi To learn more about a snake called a python, read *Verdi* by Janell Cannon.

ART LINK

Collage Make a collage that shows adult animals with their young.

TECHNOLOGY LINK

Learn about endangered reptiles by watching *Endangered Animals* on the **Harcourt Science Newsroom Video.**

CNN
Turner
Le@rning

DISCOVERING Animals

No one knows how many kinds of animals there are. New kinds are found every year. There are more than one and one-half million kinds of animals! More than one million kinds of animals are insects. Some scientists think there could be as many as 50 million kinds of animals!

Grouping Animals

People have been observing animals for centuries. New animals are discovered as scientists and explorers go to new places. One of the first people to observe animals and to write about them was Aristotle. He lived about 350 B.C. He divided animals into two groups. One was made up of animals with backbones and red blood. This group

The History of Animal Discovery

350 B.C.
Aristotle develops a classification system for animals.

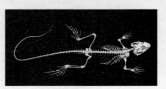

1600s
John Ray discovers that whales are mammals.

350 B.C. — 1400 — 1500 — 1600

1400–1600
Age of exploration—many animals are discovered.

1590
The microscope is invented.

included horses, cats, dogs, and oxen. The other group did not have backbones or red blood.

Since then, scientists have discovered that most animals do not have backbones. Clams, spiders, ants, sponges, worms, jellyfish, and squids are all part of this group.

Your senses can mislead you when you study animals. A whale looks like a fish, and it lives in the water. Not until the 1600s did an English scientist, John Ray, observe whales closely. He learned that they are mammals, just as humans are.

Discovering New Animals

The microscope was invented during the late 1500s. Using this tool, scientists began to discover living things made up of only one cell. In 1665 Robert Hooke published a book of drawings of biological specimens viewed through a microscope. Scientists today use microscopes to study all kinds of cells. These studies help scientists understand how animals are related to one another.

When explorers during the 1500s and 1600s traveled to new places, they returned home with animals that had never been seen before. They brought parrots and other brightly colored birds from tropical areas such as South America. They also brought many different kinds of monkeys from those areas. A giraffe from East Africa was sent to China. All of these animals were studied carefully by scientists.

People continue to find and study new animals. Modern explorers search the oceans for unknown species. We still know very little about animals living at the bottom of the ocean. Thermal vents are places where heat comes from the ocean floor. Many strange creatures live near these thermal vents.

Scientists will continue to explore unfamiliar places, such as rain forests, ocean floors, and volcanoes. Each new place will probably have animals we have never seen before.

1665
Robert Hooke publishes a collection of his drawings.

1700   1900   2000

1977
Animals are discovered living near thermal vents deep in the ocean.

Think About It

- How have microscopes helped scientists learn about animals?

Rodolfo Dirzo
TROPICAL ECOLOGIST

"I am interested in . . . the loss of animals in tropical ecosystems."

Growing up in Mexico, Rodolfo Dirzo used to watch bugs. That early interest led him to study snails and slugs far away in Wales. After completing his education, he returned to Mexico. He has taught for many years at the Organization for Tropical Studies. He does research on tropical forests. Teaching is one of Dirzo's main interests. He especially wants to interest Latin American students in ecology.

Besides teaching, Dirzo studies two different forests in Mexico. In one, the forest has not been disturbed. There are many kinds of plants and animals. In the other, some of the forest has been cut down. As a result, many of the animals that would be expected to live there are no longer there. Dirzo compares the two places. He uses his imagination and his training in science to describe what happens to a habitat that has changed. Without animals to help spread seeds and to trample down the vegetation, the forest plants may change. Dirzo expects that there will be fewer kinds of trees without the animals to help provide places for many different plants to grow.

Think About It

1. What might cause animals to leave a forest?
2. How does comparing the two forests help Dirzo analyze his data?

Rain forest

Shell Study

Why is a spiral shell larger at one end?

Materials

- safety goggles
- gloves
- spiral shell from an animal such as a whelk, conch, or sea snail
- coarse sandpaper
- hand lens

Procedure

1. **CAUTION** **Put on the safety goggles and gloves.** Observe the outside of the shell. Rub the tip of the shell with sandpaper until you have a hole about 5 millimeters (about $\frac{1}{4}$ in.) wide.

2. Use the hand lens to observe the inside of the shell. What do you see?

Draw Conclusions

Animals that live in spiral shells usually keep their shells for their whole lives. When they begin their lives, they are very small. Their shells are very small too.

Think about the shell you observed. Why do you think the spiral is small at one end and gets bigger at the other end?

Feather Study

What are the parts of feathers?

Materials

- 1 or 2 types of feathers from a bird
- hand lens

Procedure

1. Study the feathers. Use the hand lens to look at their parts. Record what you observe.

2. Touch the feathers as you look at them. Record what you feel.

Draw Conclusions

Discuss what you know about birds. Think of ways the feathers help birds fly.

Chapter ② Review and Test Preparation

Vocabulary Review

Use the terms below to complete the sentences 1 through 9. The page numbers in ( ) tell you where to look in the chapter if you need help.

inherit (A38) **gills** (A51)
traits (A38) **fish** (A52)
mammals (A42) **scales** (A52)
birds (A45) **reptiles** (A55)
amphibians (A50)

1. One trait of ___ is a body covering called fur.

2. The features a young animal gets from its parents are called ___.

3. Animals ___ their traits from their parents.

4. Animals that begin life in water and later live on land are ___.

5. ___ have bodies covered with feathers.

Mark each statement *True* or *False.* If a statement is false, change the underlined term to make the statement true.

6. Reptiles and fish have <u>scales</u>.

7. Scales make it easy for <u>mammals</u> to glide through the water.

8. Young amphibians and fish use <u>lungs</u> to take in oxygen from water.

9. <u>Amphibians</u> have dry, scaly skin.

Connect Concepts

Write the terms that belong in the concept map.

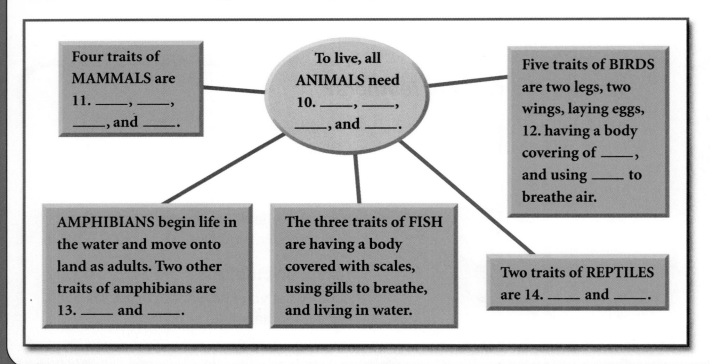

Four traits of MAMMALS are 11. ___, ___, ___, and ___.

To live, all ANIMALS need 10. ___, ___, ___, and ___.

Five traits of BIRDS are two legs, two wings, laying eggs, 12. having a body covering of ___, and using ___ to breathe air.

AMPHIBIANS begin life in the water and move onto land as adults. Two other traits of amphibians are 13. ___ and ___.

The three traits of FISH are having a body covered with scales, using gills to breathe, and living in water.

Two traits of REPTILES are 14. ___ and ___.

Check Understanding

Write the letter of the best choice.

15. What are two things animals use to get the air they need?

    A eyes and ears

    B scales and feathers

    C skin and fur

    D gills and lungs

16. What kind of shelter do beavers build?

    F dam   H den

    G lodge   J nest

17. Which kind of animal feeds its young with milk from its body?

    A fish   C amphibian

    B mammal   D bird

18. Young reptiles —

    F can meet their needs as soon as they are born

    G can swim

    H are carried in a pouch

    J begin life in the water

19. Which kind of animal is a salamander?

    A reptile   C fish

    B mammal   D amphibian

Critical Thinking

20. Describe how the body parts of a shark help it survive.

21. How are polar bears and bats alike?

Process Skills Review

22. Use what you have learned about animals to **classify** these animals into groups: snake, robin, dog, lizard, cow, goose, whale. Explain why you grouped the animals as you did.

23. Explain how making and **using a model** of a bird's nest can help you learn about birds.

24. How can you use your senses to **observe** birds?

Performance Assessment

Grouping Animals

Use the animal cards from the Investigate in Lesson 1. Group them by using what you have learned about animals. Are there any animals that don't belong in a group? What traits did these animals have?

Unit Project Wrap Up

Here are some ideas for ways to wrap up your unit project.

Take Photographs

Use a camera to take photographs to illustrate your handbook. Label each photograph with the time and date it was taken, and identify the subject.

Draw a Map

Draw a map of the area in which you made your observations. Show features like streams and forests. Draw on the map the plants and animals you found in the places you found them. See what conclusions you can draw about the needs of plants and animals based on where they live.

Make a Graph

Find a way to sort the living and nonliving things you found. Then make a bar graph to organize your data. You may want to use a computer graphing program.

Investigate Further

How could you make your project better? What other questions do you have about plants and animals? Plan ways to find answers to your questions. Use the Science Handbook on pages R2-R9 for help.

Plants and Animals Interact

UNIT B

LIFE SCIENCE

Plants and Animals Interact

Unit Project ## Ecosystem Mobile

Collect nonliving objects from an ecosystem. Do not take any item that you can see is being used by an animal or plant. Use an index card to catalog each item you collect. Sketch and describe the item on the card. Display the objects on a mobile. Use the mobile and cards to tell about interactions within the ecosystem.

Where Living Things Are Found

Living things are all around us—in the air, on the land, and in the water. In this chapter you'll explore where living things are found and how their bodies and behaviors help them live in their environments.

Vocabulary Preview

environment	deciduous forest
ecosystem	tropical rain forest
population	coastal forest
community	coniferous forest
habitat	desert
forest	fresh water
salt water	

FAST FACT

One of the most unusual wildflowers of the southwest United States is the ground cone. It looks like a pine cone sitting on the ground. Since most animals don't eat pine cones, this is a great way of hiding!

FAST FACT

There are about 2,500 black rhinoceroses left in the wild. Because of their small numbers, they are endangered.

Endangered Animals

Animal	Number Alive
Giant Pandas	1,000
Manatees	1,900
Black Rhinoceroses	2,500
Cheetahs	11,000

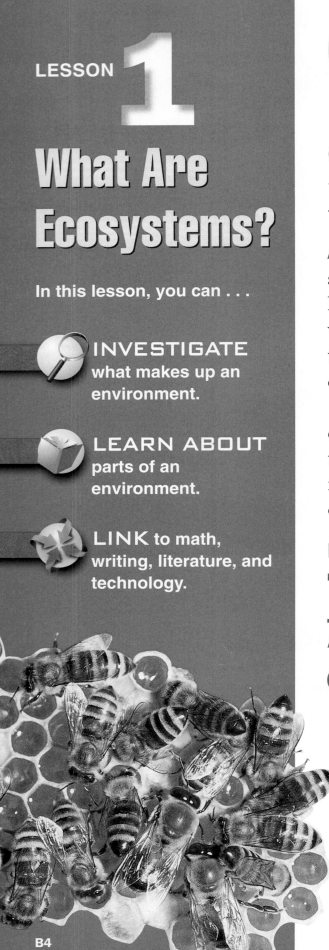

LESSON 1

What Are Ecosystems?

In this lesson, you can . . .

INVESTIGATE what makes up an environment.

LEARN ABOUT parts of an environment.

LINK to math, writing, literature, and technology.

◄ These bees live and raise their young in the hive. They make honey to feed the young.

INVESTIGATE

Observing an Environment

Activity Purpose You may have seen trees, insects, and mammals near your home. You may also have seen grass, flowers, worms, and birds. All these things get what they need to live from their *environment,* or everything around them.

In this investigation you will **observe** an environment to find out what kinds of things live there. You will also observe the nonliving things that are part of the environment.

Materials

■ wire clothes hanger

Activity Procedure

1 Bend your hanger to make a square. Go outside and place the hanger on the ground. Inside this square is the environment you will **observe.** (Picture A)

2 Make a list of all the things you **observe**. Next to each thing on your list, **record** whether it is living or nonliving. Write *L* for living and *N* for nonliving.

3 Ask a classmate to share his or her list with you. **Compare** the environments each of you observed.

4 Choose a living thing you **observed** in your hanger environment. Talk with a classmate about which things in the environment help the living thing survive.

Picture A

Draw Conclusions

1. Describe the environment you **observed**.

2. How can you use **observation** to find out how an animal lives?

3. **Scientists at Work** Scientists learn by **observing** and by **gathering data.** They also learn from the data gathered by others. What did you learn about an environment from your classmate's data?

Investigate Further **Observe** a sample of soil in which an earthworm lives. Describe the environment.

Process Skill Tip

When you **observe** living things in their environments, you can **gather data** about the organisms and the environment. The data can help you learn about the environment and about the things that live there.

Living Things and Their Environments

Where Things Live

Think about where different kinds of plants and animals live. Some kinds of plants and animals live in hot, dry places. Others live in cool, shady forests. Fish live in water. Some insects live in the ground. Others live on plants. In the investigation you observed an environment. An **environment** (en•VY•ruhn•muhnt) is everything around a living thing.

Living things get what they need to live from their environments. They need things such as air, water, food, and shelter. When many kinds of living things share an environment, they must also share the things they need. For example, the plants and animals in a pond all use the air, water, and food from that pond.

✓ **What do living things get from an environment?**

FIND OUT

- how an environment affects a living thing
- what makes up an ecosystem

VOCABULARY

environment
ecosystem
population
community
habitat

A raccoon in a city may find food in trash cans. Many animals can live in more than one environment. ▼

A raccoon in a forest may catch fish to eat. ▶

The Parts of an Ecosystem

In an environment the living and nonliving things that affect each other, or interact, form an **ecosystem** (EK•oh•sis•tuhm). An ecosystem, such as the pond shown on this page, has many parts.

Frogs live in the pond. All of the frogs, as a group, are called a population. A **population** (pahp•yoo•LAY•shuhn) is a group of the same kind of living things that live in the same place at the same time.

Populations of insects, waterlilies, and cattails live in the pond, too. Together these populations form a community. A **community** (kuh•MYOO•nuh•tee) is all the populations that live in an ecosystem.

Within the pond ecosystem, each population lives in a **habitat** (HAB•ih•tat). A habitat provides a population with all its needs and includes nonliving things and living things. There are many habitats in an ecosystem. For example, the cattails live on the edge of the pond. That is their habitat.

✔ **What makes up an ecosystem?**

The frog population, the cattail population, and all the other populations in this pond form a community.

The pond is the habitat, or home, of all the living things that make up the community.

Nonliving things, such as air, sunlight, water, rocks, and soil, are also part of an ecosystem. The community of living things needs the nonliving things to survive.

The ecosystem of this pond is made up of all the living and nonliving things that interact in and around the pond.

Fires in 1988 destroyed the large trees of this ecosystem. Before 1988 these large trees in Yellowstone National Park were the habitat of many living things.

▲ Ten years after the fire, these wildflowers show that life has returned to Yellowstone.

How Ecosystems Change

Ecosystems can change. Some changes to ecosystems are caused by nature. For example, floods or fires can kill many living things and destroy habitats. But some living things survive when an ecosystem is damaged. A fire doesn't destroy all the seeds in the ground. The seeds that survive grow into new plants. As the plants grow, animals that feed on them return to the area.

A flood can also harm an ecosystem. But a flood brings a new layer of rich soil to a riverbank. New plants grow in the soil.

Ecosystems are also changed by living things. Some changes help the living things meet their needs. For example, people cut down trees and use the wood to build homes and make other products. Beavers cut down trees to build dams and lodges in streams. The other animals that lived in the trees must find new homes.

Many spiders spin webs to use as homes and to help capture food. ▼

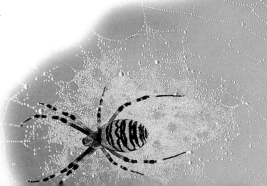

When an ecosystem changes, the animals in it sometimes move to a nearby part of the ecosystem. But sometimes the ecosystem is changed so much that the plants and animals can no longer live there.

✔ **Why do ecosystems change?**

Summary

An environment is everything that surrounds a living thing. The living and nonliving things that interact in an environment make up an ecosystem. An ecosystem is made up of smaller parts that include populations, communities, and habitats, as well as nonliving things, such as air, sunlight, and soil. Nature and living things can change ecosystems.

Review

1. What is an environment?
2. What nonliving things are found in an ecosystem?
3. What is a population?
4. **Critical Thinking** How can building a new road change an ecosystem?
5. **Test Prep** A pond that contains waterlilies, frogs, fish, insects, and cattails is an example of —

   A a population   **C** a habitat
   B an ecosystem   **D** a community

LINKS

MATH LINK

Summing Populations
Suppose an ecosystem has 54 squirrels, 12 rabbits, 15 trees, and 100 grasshoppers. How many animals are in the community? How many populations are there?

WRITING LINK

Informative Writing—Report
What if a flood destroyed part of an ecosystem near your home? Write a newspaper report for your class telling what happened to an animal because of the flood.

LITERATURE LINK

Read About Fire To learn more about how fire can affect an ecosystem, read *Wildfires* by Ann Armbruster.

TECHNOLOGY LINK

Learn more about how changes in an ecosystem can affect the living things there by watching *Tainted Water* on the **Harcourt Science Newsroom Video.**

CNN Turner Le@rning

What Are Forest Ecosystems?

In this lesson, you can . . .

 INVESTIGATE trees in forests.

 LEARN ABOUT different types of forests.

 LINK to math, writing, art, and technology.

 **INVESTIGATE**

Variety in Forests

Activity Purpose Forests have trees. But did you know that there are several types of forests? In this investigation you will **use numbers** to **interpret data** about trees in two kinds of forests.

Materials
- tray of beans, labeled *Tray 1*
- tray of beans, labeled *Tray 2*
- 2 paper cups

Activity Procedure

1 Make a data table like the one shown. Tray 1 stands for the trees in a tropical rain forest. Tray 2 stands for the trees in a deciduous forest. Each kind of bean stands for a different kind of tree.

2 Scoop a cupful of beans from each tray. Carefully pour each cup of beans into its own pile.

◄ **Moose like this one live in coniferous forests.**

Tropical Rain Forest (Tray 1)		Deciduous Forest (Tray 2)	
Kind of Bean	Number of Beans	Kind of Bean	Number of Beans

3 Work with a partner. One partner should work with the beans from Tray 1. The other partner should work with the beans from Tray 2. (Picture A)

4 Sort the beans into groups so that each group contains only one kind of bean.

5 **Record** a description of each type of bean in the data table. Count the number of beans in each small pile. Record these numbers in the data table.

Picture A

Draw Conclusions

1. How many kinds of "trees" were in each "forest"?

2. Which forest had the most trees of one kind? Why do you think this was so?

3. **Scientists at Work** Scientists learn by **gathering, recording,** and **interpreting data.** What did you learn from your data about variety in forests?

Investigate Further Suppose you want to find out what kinds of trees are most common in your community. Explain how you could **use numbers** to find out.

Forest Ecosystems

FIND OUT

- about four kinds of forests
- about living things in different kinds of forests

VOCABULARY

forest
deciduous forest
tropical rain forest
coastal forest
coniferous forest

Types of Forests

You probably know that a **forest** is an area in which the main plants are trees. But many other kinds of plants and animals also live in forests.

Forests grow in many parts of the world. Some forests are named for the types of trees that grow in them. Other forests are named for the area in which they grow.

Each type of forest needs a certain amount of rainfall and sunshine. Each also has certain temperatures that let it grow best. If any of these things change, the kinds of plants that grow in the forest may also change.

✔ **What is a forest?**

This graph shows how much rain falls each year in each kind of forest. ▼

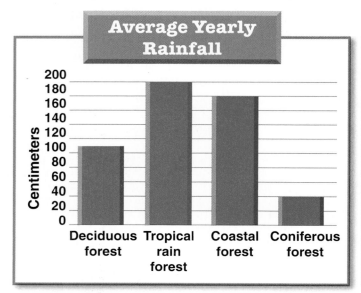

This graph shows the average yearly temperature in each kind of forest. ▼

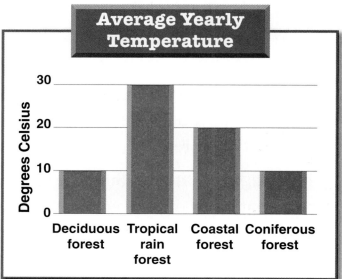

Deciduous Forests

Some trees, such as maples and oaks, have large, flat leaves that drop off each fall. New leaves grow back in the spring. Trees that lose and regrow their leaves each year are called deciduous (dee•SIJ•oo•uhs) trees. Forests made up mostly of these trees are **deciduous forests**. They grow in places that have warm, wet summers and cold winters.

Deciduous leaves change color before they drop in the fall. When a deciduous tree drops its leaves, it needs less water. This helps the tree live through the winter, when water may be frozen.

The deciduous forest is a habitat for many kinds of living things, such as ferns, shrubs, and mosses. Animals such as insects, spiders, snakes, frogs, birds, rabbits, deer, and bears also live here.

✔ **Where do deciduous forests grow?**

The leaves of deciduous trees change color just before they drop from the trees in the fall. ▼

▲ During the winter deciduous trees have no leaves.

Deciduous trees grow new leaves in the spring. ▼

In the summer a deciduous forest looks healthy and green. ▼

Tropical Rain Forests

Tropical rain forests grow in places such as Hawai'i and Costa Rica. These places are hot and wet all year. The trees grow very tall, and their leaves stay green all year.

More types of living things live in rain forests than anywhere else on Earth. Plants and animals make their homes in all the layers of the forest, from the tops of the trees to the ground.

✔ **Where do tropical rain forests grow?**

◄ This moth lives in the tropical rain forest. It feeds on the plants that grow beneath the trees.

THE INSIDE STORY

Layers of the Rain Forest

A tropical rain forest has three main layers. The top layer is called the *canopy.* It is formed by the branches and leaves of the tallest trees. Below the canopy is the *understory.* The understory is formed by plants that don't grow as tall as trees. The *forest floor* is the lowest layer. Many kinds of plants and animals make their homes in each layer of a tropical rain forest.

Coastal Forests

Coastal forests grow where there is a lot of rain. Unlike a tropical rain forest, a coastal forest grows where it does not get too warm or too cold. But like tropical rain forests, coastal forests are thick with many kinds of tall trees. Coastal forests have the same kinds of layers as tropical rain forests.

✔ **Describe a coastal forest environment.**

▲ **The northern spotted owl thrives in the moist, cool environment of the coastal forest.**

Canopy

Understory

Forest Floor

1 The leaves of the canopy get lots of water and sunlight. Many animals drink water that collects on the leaves.

2 Plants of the understory get less sunlight and water than those in the canopy. Orchids, mosses, and ferns grow on the trunks of the tall trees.

3 Little sunlight reaches the rain-forest floor, and few nutrients are found in the soil. Plants that grow here must find other ways to get nutrients.

Coniferous Forests

What kind of trees would you find where there are very cold winters and cool summers? Mostly, you would find *conifers* (KAHN•uh•ferz)—trees that form seeds in cones. Conifers have needle-like leaves. Pines, spruces, and firs are common conifers. Conifers don't lose their needles in the fall. They stay green all year. This is why conifers are often called *evergreens.* Forests that contain mostly these kinds of trees are **coniferous** (koh•NIF•er•uhs) **forests.**

Conifers grow in areas that get less rain than other types of forests. The needle-shaped leaves of these trees help keep the trees from losing too much water.

Many conifers are shaped like triangles. This shape helps keep heavy snow from piling up on a tree's larger branches in winter, which might cause them to break.

Coniferous forests often have many lakes and streams. The trees, lakes, and streams provide habitats for many animals. Squirrels, moose, and wolves are common. Insects such as mosquitoes and flies also live in coniferous forests.

✔ **What kinds of trees grow in a coniferous forest?**

Coniferous forests are homes for animals such as moose, bears, and wolves. ▼

Summary

There are different types of forest ecosystems. The main types of forests are deciduous forests, tropical rain forests, coastal forests, and coniferous forests. These forests provide habitats for many kinds of plants and animals.

Review

1. What is a forest?
2. Which kind of forest has trees that lose their leaves in the fall?
3. What are the layers of a tropical rain forest?
4. **Critical Thinking** What is the main difference between a tropical rain forest and a coastal forest?
5. **Test Prep** A deciduous forest has —
   - **A** cool summers and warm winters
   - **B** warm, wet summers and dry winters
   - **C** warm, wet summers and cold winters
   - **D** warm, dry summers and dry winters

LINKS

MATH LINK

Interpret a Graph Look back at the first graph on page B12. What is the difference in yearly rainfall between the tropical rain forest and the deciduous forest? Which gets more rain each year?

WRITING LINK

Expressive Writing—Friendly Letter Pick a forest from this lesson. Imagine that you live there. Write a letter to a classmate telling what you like most about your forest.

ART LINK

Leaf Prints Gather leaves from the trees that grow in your area. Dip the leaves into paint, and make leaf prints on paper. Label each print.

TECHNOLOGY LINK

Explore forests as you complete the activity *Backpacking Through Forests* on **Harcourt Science Explorations CD-ROM.**

B17

LESSON 3

What Is a Desert Ecosystem?

In this lesson, you can . . .

 INVESTIGATE a desert ecosystem.

 LEARN ABOUT desert ecosystems.

 LINK to math, writing, health, and technology.

 **INVESTIGATE**

Make a Desert Ecosystem

Activity Purpose   A desert is a very dry place. But this ecosystem is home to many kinds of living things. In this investigation you will **make a model** of a desert ecosystem.

Materials

- shoe box
- plastic wrap
- sandy soil
- 2 or 3 desert plants
- small rocks

Activity Procedure

1   **Make a model** of a desert ecosystem. Start by lining the shoe box with plastic wrap. Place sandy soil in the shoe box. Make sure the soil is deep enough for the plants.

2   Place the plants in the soil, and place the rocks around them. Lightly sprinkle the soil with water. (Picture A)

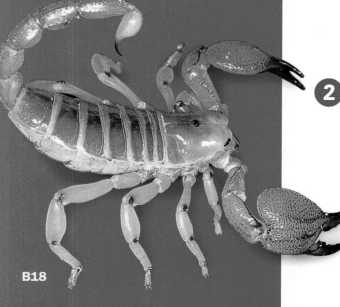

◄ **This scorpion is one type of animal that lives in the desert.**

3 Place your desert ecosystem in a sunny location. (Picture B)

4 Every two or three days, use your finger to **observe** how dry the soil is. If the soil is *very* dry, add a small amount of water. If the soil is damp, do not add water. Be careful not to water the plants too much.

5 Continue to **observe** and care for your desert ecosystem. **Record** what you observe.

Picture A

Draw Conclusions

1. What kind of environment does your desert ecosystem model?

2. How does **making a model** help you learn about a desert?

3. **Scientists at Work** Scientists often learn by **making models**. What other types of ecosystems can you make models of?

Picture B

Investigate Further How would getting rain every day change a desert ecosystem? **Plan an experiment** in which you could **use a model** to find out.

Process Skill Tip

Observing a desert would be difficult to do in the classroom. To learn more about the real thing, you can **make a model** of a desert.

Desert Ecosystems

FIND OUT

- about two kinds of deserts
- how plants and animals get what they need in a desert ecosystem

VOCABULARY

desert

Types of Deserts

A **desert** is an ecosystem found where there is very little rainfall. Most deserts get less than 25 centimeters (about 10 in.) of rain each year. Desert plants and animals need very little water to live.

In the investigation you made a model of a hot desert. In summer, hot deserts can have temperatures over 43°C (about 110°F) during the day. At night, the temperatures drop to around 7°C (about 45°F). Most hot deserts have mild winters in which the temperature usually stays above freezing.

Besides the hot deserts you probably know about, there are cold deserts. These deserts have freezing temperatures and blizzards in the winter. But in the hottest months, they are as hot as hot deserts.

✔ **What are the two kinds of deserts?**

The Taklimakan Desert is a cold desert located in western China. ▼

This hot desert is located in the southwestern part of the United States. ▼

CALIFORNIA

Anza-Borrego Desert State Park

Parts of a Cactus

The parts of the barrel cactus allow it to live in hot deserts. These parts are common to many other desert plants.

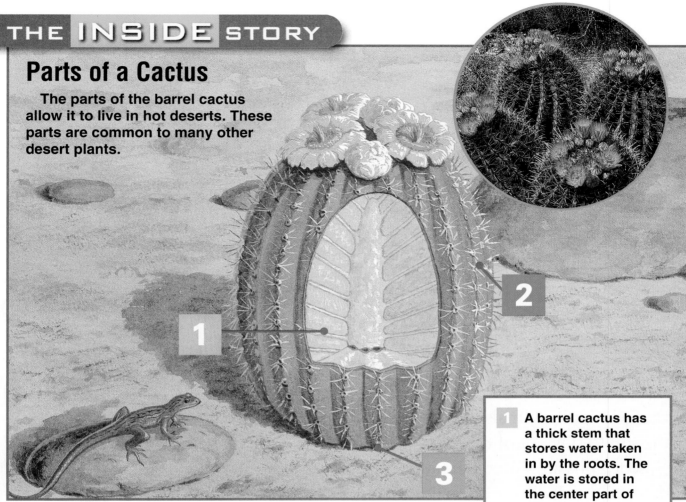

1. A barrel cactus has a thick stem that stores water taken in by the roots. The water is stored in the center part of the stem.

2. Like most cacti, the barrel cactus has a thick skin that is covered with spines. The skin and spines help keep the plant from losing water. The spines also protect the plant from being eaten by animals.

3. The barrel cactus has shallow roots that spread out near the soil's surface. When it rains, these roots quickly soak up the water.

Desert Plants

Deserts are dry places. Plants that grow in deserts have parts that help them save water. Many desert plants grow low to the ground, where it is coolest. Most desert plants have long, shallow roots that spread out near the top of the soil. Here the roots can easily soak up water when it does rain.

Many desert plants have thick stems that store water. Some animals eat these stems to get the water they need to live.

Some desert plants, such as the barrel cactus, have spiny leaves. Spiny leaves help keep the plant from losing water.

✔ **How do desert plants get water?**

Desert Animals

Many animals live in the desert. Desert animals get most of their water by eating plants that store water or by eating other animals.

Reptiles such as snakes and lizards live well in the desert. They stay in the shade during the hot days. During the cold nights they keep warm near rocks, which the sun made hot during the day.

Small mammals such as bats, rabbits, and squirrels also live in deserts. These animals are active at night, when it is cooler. During the day they sleep in their shelters, which shade them from the sun. Some animals burrow into the soil to stay out of the sun.

Scorpions and insects are other desert animals. These animals have hard body coverings that keep them from losing much water.

✔ **How do desert animals get water?**

This sidewinder has dry, scaly skin that helps keep water inside its body. ▼

The shape of this bird's beak helps it get water from the stems of the saguaro cactus. It also uses the saguaro as a home. ▼

◀ Saguaro cactus

Summary

A desert ecosystem has a dry environment. Some deserts are hot, while other deserts are cold. Plants and animals that live in deserts have parts that help them get what they need to live.

Review

1. What is a desert?
2. Where do plants of the hot desert store water?
3. Other than by eating plants, how do desert animals get water?
4. **Critical Thinking** More kinds of animals and plants live in hot deserts than in cold deserts. Why do you think this is so?
5. **Test Prep** The average amount of rain a desert gets in one year is about —
   - **A** 25 mm
   - **B** 25 cm
   - **C** 250 cm
   - **D** 25 m

The large ears of this jackrabbit help it hear enemies. The jackrabbit also gets rid of extra heat from its body through the thin skin on its ears. ▶

LINKS

MATH LINK

Water from Plants Desert plants store water. To get an idea of how much water a plant can store, squeeze a piece of fruit over a bowl. Measure the amount of juice that comes out.

WRITING LINK

Informative Writing— Compare and Contrast Find out about one desert plant. Write a paragraph for your teacher to compare it to a plant that grows in another ecosystem.

HEALTH LINK

Water and Health Your body needs plenty of water when it is hot outside. With a partner, make a list of 10 things you can do to increase the amount of water you give your body on a hot day.

TECHNOLOGY LINK

Learn more about desert plants and animals by visiting this Internet Site.
www.scilinks.org/harcourt

SCI LINKS
THE WORLD'S A CLICK AWAY

B23

LESSON

What Are Water Ecosystems?

In this lesson, you can . . .

 INVESTIGATE freshwater ecosystems.

 LEARN ABOUT two types of water ecosystems.

 LINK to math, writing, social studies, and technology.

INVESTIGATE

Make a Freshwater Ecosystem

Activity Purpose If you have ever visited a lake, you may know that many kinds of plants and animals live there. Lakes and ponds are freshwater ecosystems. In this investigation you will **make a model** of a freshwater ecosystem.

Materials

- aquarium or other large, clear plastic container
- gravel
- sand
- sheet of paper
- fresh water
- freshwater plants
- rocks
- fish and snails

Activity Procedure

1 Put a layer of gravel at the bottom of the tank. Add a layer of sand on top of the gravel.

◀ Dolphins live, swim, and play in saltwater ecosystems.

2 Set the aquarium in a place where it isn't too sunny. Place a sheet of paper over the sand. Slowly add the water to the tank. Make sure you pour the water onto the paper so the sand will stay in place. (Picture A)

3 Remove the paper, and put the plants and rocks into the tank. Let the tank sit for about one week. After one week, add the fish and snails. (Picture B)

4 **Observe** and care for your freshwater ecosystem.

Picture A

Picture B

Draw Conclusions

1. What are some things you **observed** in your freshwater ecosystem?

2. Why do you think you waited to add the fish to the tank?

3. **Scientists at Work** Scientists often **make a model** of an ecosystem so they can **observe** it in a laboratory. How did making a model help you observe a freshwater ecosystem? How is your model different from a real pond?

Investigate Further What other kinds of plants and animals might live in a freshwater ecosystem? To find out, visit a pet shop that sells fish. Make a list of the freshwater plants and animals you find there.

Process Skill Tip

It can be difficult to **observe** all the living things in a freshwater pond or lake. You can learn about the real thing by **making a model** of a freshwater ecosystem.

Water Ecosystems

FIND OUT

- about freshwater and saltwater ecosystems
- what plants and animals live in water ecosystems

VOCABULARY

salt water
fresh water

The blue parts of this map show the major water ecosystems of the world. ▼

Types of Water Ecosystems

Water covers more than 70 percent of Earth's surface. When you look at a globe, you can see that most of this water is in oceans and seas. Oceans and seas contain **salt water**, or water that has a lot of salt in it. Marshes and a few lakes also have salt water in them. These ecosystems are called *saltwater ecosystems*.

In the investigation you made a model of a freshwater ecosystem. **Fresh water** is water that has very little salt in it. Lakes, rivers, ponds, streams, and some marshes are *freshwater ecosystems*.

✔ **What are two types of water ecosystems?**

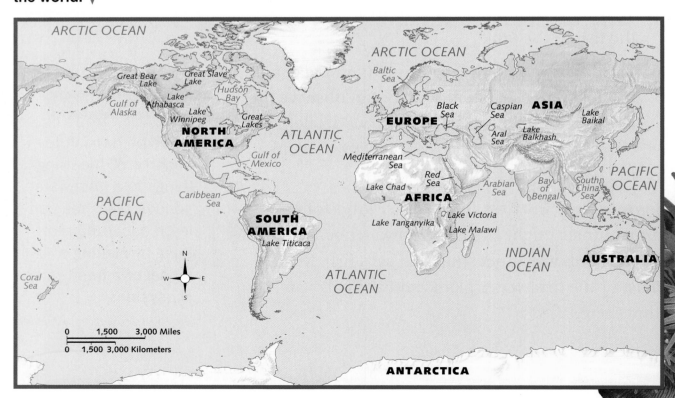

Saltwater Ecosystems

There are many different saltwater ecosystems because salt water is not the same everywhere. The amount of salt in ocean water is different in different places. Near the surface, rain can make the water less salty. Water is also less salty near shores where fresh water from rivers and streams flows into oceans. But no matter where you are in the ocean, the water has more salt in it than fresh water has.

Ocean water that is near shore or at the surface is often warmer than water deep in the ocean. This is because the sun warms the water in these areas. At the shoreline, salt water may collect in tide pools. Many plants and animals live in this warm, shallow water.

✔ **Why might salt water be less salty near shore?**

Barnacles (BAR•nuh•kulz) are small animals that live out their lives stuck to rocks and other objects. ▼

A tide pool is a saltwater ecosystem that forms at a shoreline. ▼

◄ Some anemones (uh•NEM•uh•neez) live in the warm, shallow waters of tide pools.

Ocean Ecosystems

The oceans are Earth's largest ecosystems. Because they are so large, many kinds of plants and animals live in them. All these living things are suited to life in salt water.

Not all parts of the ocean are the same. The saltiness of the water can be different. Water is deeper in some places than in others. The water temperature also changes from place to place. All these differences, along with how deep into the water the sunlight can reach, affect the kinds of living things that are found in different parts of the ocean.

✔ **What do all ocean plants and animals have in common?**

Ocean Zones

The ocean can be divided into zones. Each zone is defined by how much sunlight it gets. Areas that get the most sunlight usually have the warmest temperatures and more plant and animal life. Areas that receive little sunlight are dark and have few animals and very few plants. They also have very cold water.

This underwater kelp forest grows in shallow water. It provides food and shelter for many different fish and other ocean animals.

◄ **These tropical fish live in areas of warm water.**

Where water is shallow, sunlight reaches the ocean bottom. The sunlight allows many plants to grow in this zone. Animals that feed on these plants also live here.

Farther from shore, sunlight cannot reach the ocean bottom. Plants in this part of the ocean float near the surface, where they can get sunlight. Many swimming animals come to the surface to feed. Others feed on the animals that eat the plants.

This angler fish lives in the deep part of the ocean. ▼

Sunlight cannot reach the floor of the deep ocean. This part of the ocean has almost no plants. Water is very cold here. Because there are very few plants (if there are any at all), the deep ocean also has the fewest animals.

Freshwater Ecosystems

Not all freshwater ecosystems are the same. The main kinds of freshwater ecosystems include rivers, streams, lakes, and ponds.

Many plants and animals live in or around rivers and streams. Rivers and streams have moving fresh water. The water may move quickly or slowly. How fast the water moves helps determine what living things can survive in the water.

The water in lakes and ponds is still. Lakes are usually larger and have deeper water than ponds. Water temperature depends on where the lake or pond is and how deep the water is.

As in an ocean, most plants and animals in a lake or pond live in the shallow water. The fewest plants and animals live where the water is too deep for sunlight to reach the bottom.

▲ This cooter turtle is a common shore animal of ponds, rivers, marshes, and lakes in Florida.

✔ **What are two kinds of freshwater ecosystems?**

The American egret is a wading bird that lives near freshwater ecosystems such as lakes. ▼

A young mayfly can stick to a rock or a plant so fast-moving water won't wash it away. ▼

The bullhead catfish makes its home in a lake. ▼

Summary

Water ecosystems may have salt water or fresh water. An ocean is a saltwater ecosystem. Rivers, streams, lakes, and ponds are freshwater ecosystems. Different kinds of plants and animals live in and around these water ecosystems.

Review

1. What are the two kinds of water ecosystems? Name two ways they are different.

2. In a pond, where do most of the animals live?

3. Which zone of the ocean gets the least amount of sunlight?

4. **Critical Thinking** What would happen to the animals and plants in a saltwater ecosystem if it were flooded by fresh water? Explain your answer.

5. **Test Prep** Which is **NOT** a freshwater ecosystem?

   A river   **C** pond

   B lake   **D** tide pool

LINKS

MATH LINK

Using Graphs Use a computer graphing program such as **Graph Links** to make a bar graph of the following water depths: river, 1 meter; lake, 6 meters; ocean, 122 meters. How much deeper is the ocean than the lake?

WRITING LINK

Informative Writing— Narration Suppose you are a tour guide on a submarine in the deep ocean. Write a narration that describes to your passengers the kinds of plants and animals you would expect to find living there.

SOCIAL STUDIES LINK

Mapping Water Ecosystems Make an outline map of your state. Draw the major bodies of water. Label them as fresh or salt water.

TECHNOLOGY LINK

Visit the Harcourt Learning Site for related links, activities, and resources.

WELCOME TO THE LEARNING SITE

www.harcourtschool.com

USING COMPUTERS TO DESCRIBE THE ENVIRONMENT

Do you know what kind of environment you live in? Students all over the world are using computers to help them learn more about the plants, the animals, and other things in their environments.

Ecosystem Movies

Students at Gilliland Elementary School in Blue Mound, Texas, have been using computers to create a multimedia field guide for their hometown. They take careful notes during field trips into the Blackland Prairie near their school. They take photographs and make audio and video recordings. Afterward, the students combine everything on a computer to make the field guide.

The GLOBE Program

-60 -40 -20 0 20 40 60
Maximum Temperature (C)

March 27, 1995
24 Hour Average Forecast
National Meteorological Center

People who use the field guide can see photographs of the wildflowers in the area. They can also watch videos of the class and hear students talk about the history of the prairie.

A World of Information

Students at many schools belong to a program called GLOBE, or Global Learning and Observations to Benefit the Environment. The GLOBE program includes students, teachers, and scientists from all over the world.

First, GLOBE scientists teach teachers how to take samples and make measurements. Then the teachers teach their students how to do it. The teachers and students regularly collect data from their own environments. They measure and record information about soil, water, air, and plants in their area. They enter all their data onto the main GLOBE Web site.

Mapmaking on the Internet

The scientists at GLOBE put together the data from all of the schools. They use the data to learn about specific areas and about patterns occurring all over the world. Because so many schools are sending in data, the scientists can learn much more than they would if they were working on their own. One of the things they do with the data is make environmental maps of the world. Students and teachers can log onto the GLOBE Web site to see these maps.

Think About It

1. What would you include in a field guide for your environment?

2. What kinds of maps could GLOBE scientists make from students' information?

WEB LINK:
For Science and Technology updates, visit the Harcourt Internet site.
www.harcourtschool.com

Careers   Teacher

What They Do
Teachers work with children or adults to help them learn. They often use computers and other tools to make learning new ideas fun.

Education and Training Almost all teachers have college degrees. Most colleges offer courses that help students learn how to teach. Teachers specialize in the subject or the grade level they want to teach.

Margaret Morse Nice

ORNITHOLOGIST

"It was an unknown world and each day I made fresh discoveries."

Ornithologists are people who study birds. Perhaps, like Margaret Morse Nice, you have watched birds in your back yard. By the age of 12, she was recording her observations about birds. What began as fun became her lifework.

After college, Morse married Leonard Nice, whom she had met there. Each time the family moved, Margaret Nice studied the birds around her home.

Nice was one of the first to use colored bands to identify birds. To follow birds over time, she would first capture a bird. Then she would place a colored band of plastic on the bird's leg and let the bird go. In this

way, Nice studied how birds mated, built nests, and raised their young.

Nice and her husband wrote a book together on the birds of Oklahoma. Nice later published a two-part study of song sparrows. She wrote more than 250 articles for magazines during her lifetime. She also translated into English many of the articles that people from other countries had written about birds.

Think About It

1. Why is it helpful to have someone translate articles written by scientists in other countries?

2. What birds can you observe from your home?

Earthworm Habitat

What is the habitat of an earthworm?

Materials

- clear plastic container
- garden soil (not potting soil)
- 2 to 3 earthworms
- small rocks, sticks, and leaves
- wax paper
- water

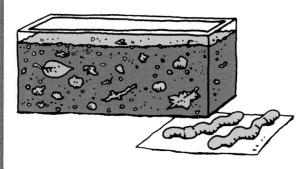

Procedure

① Loosely spread the soil on the wax paper. Add the rocks, sticks, and leaves. Add a small amount of water so the soil is moist but not wet. Mix these materials together.

② Add the soil mixture to the plastic container. Carefully add the earthworms to the loose soil. Place your earthworm habitat in a warm, dark place. Keep the soil moist.

Draw Conclusions

After observing your earthworm habitat for a week, make a list of the things you think the habitat you provided gave your earthworms that they needed to live.

Salt Water and Fresh Water

How are salt water and fresh water different?

Materials

- small jar
- water
- egg in the shell
- small spoon
- salt

Procedure

① Half fill the jar with water. Put the egg in the jar. Record what happens to the egg.

② Remove the egg, and stir a spoonful of salt into the water. Put the egg back into the water, and record what happens to the egg.

③ Continue adding salt to the water until you observe a change.

Draw Conclusions

How do you think salt in the water affects the animals living in the ocean?

Chapter 1 Review and Test Preparation

Vocabulary Review

Use the terms below to complete the sentences 1 through 12. The page numbers in ( ) tell you where to look in the chapter if you need help.

environment (B6)
ecosystem (B7)
population (B7)
community (B7)
habitat (B7)
forest (B12)
deciduous forest (B13)
tropical rain forest (B14)
coastal forest (B15)
coniferous forest (B16)
desert (B20)
salt water (B26)
fresh water (B26)

1. An area where the main plants are trees is called a ＿＿.

2. All the living things of the same kind that live in the same area at the same time make up a ＿＿.

3. The populations that live together in the same place make up a ＿＿.

4. An ecosystem that is very dry is a ＿＿.

5. The interactions between the living and nonliving parts of the environment make up an ＿＿.

6. To a population of frogs living near a pond, the pond is its ＿＿.

7. Rivers and most lakes are ＿＿ ecosystems.

8. A ＿＿ has warm summers and cool winters. The trees drop their leaves in the fall.

9. Two types of forests that get a lot of rain are a ＿＿ and a ＿＿.

10. An ＿＿ is everything that surrounds a living thing.

11. The winters are cold in a ＿＿, and the trees have needle-shaped leaves.

12. The water in the ocean is ＿＿.

Connect Concepts

Write the terms from the Word Bank where they belong in the concept map.

tropical rain   **coastal**   **forests**
coniferous   **deciduous**

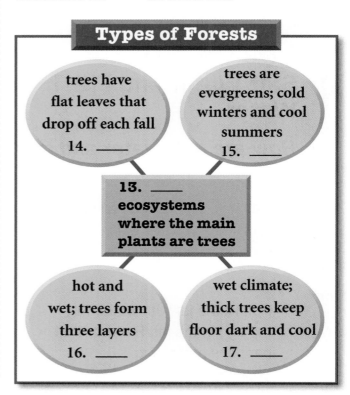

Types of Forests

trees have flat leaves that drop off each fall
14. ＿＿

trees are evergreens; cold winters and cool summers
15. ＿＿

13. ＿＿ ecosystems where the main plants are trees

hot and wet; trees form three layers
16. ＿＿

wet climate; thick trees keep floor dark and cool
17. ＿＿

Check Understanding

Write the letter of the best choice.

18. What might happen to a forest that is damaged by fire?
    A It will grow back.
    B It is destroyed forever.
    C It will stay the same.
    D It will fill up with water and become a marsh.

19. Which characteristic of conifers helps keep them from losing water?
    F broad, flat leaves
    G thick, fleshy leaves
    H triangular shape
    J needle-shaped leaves

20. What are the two types of desert?
    A dry and wet
    B hot and cold
    C fresh and salt
    D tropical and coastal

21. What are the two types of water ecosystems?
    F fresh and salt
    G hot and cold
    H hot and dry
    J deciduous and coniferous

Critical Thinking

22. Why might a raccoon hunt for food in a trash can instead of in a forest?

23. How can the building of new homes and roads by humans affect the plants and animals in an area?

Process Skills Review

24. In Lesson 1 you used your **observations** to **gather data** about organisms in their environment. What are some of the ways that you gathered data?

25. Find three examples in the chapter where you could **use numbers** to **record data**. Why is this a good way to **interpret data**?

26. In Lessons 3 and 4 you **made a model** of two ecosystems—a desert and a pond. How did either model help you learn about the features of these ecosystems?

Performance Assessment

Diagram a Rain Forest

Work with two or three other students. On a large sheet of paper, draw a rain-forest ecosystem. Show the three layers, and label each. Then draw or describe two or more animals that live in each layer.

Vocabulary Preview

interact
producer
consumer
decomposer
food chain
energy pyramid
food web
predator
prey

Living Things Depend on One Another

Like all living things, you depend on plants and animals around you to meet your needs. You eat plants and animal products. You may live in a building made from wood. You wear clothes made from plants fibers. Plants and animals depend on one another to help them meet their needs.

FAST FACT

Some areas of the world have more living things than others. If you want to get an idea of how productive an area is, you can compare how many plants live there with how many live in other areas.

Plant Material in Different Environments	
Area	**Plant matter per square meter**
Tropical Rain Forest	2000 g
Grassland	800 g
Arctic Tundra	140 g
Desert	80 g

Tropical rain forest

FAST FACT

Hippopotamuses live in the rivers of central Africa. They eat grasses and other plants that grow in the water. The wastes they produce are rich in nutrients, and they help the plants to grow.

How Do Animals Get Food?

In this lesson, you can . . .

INVESTIGATE how animals use their teeth to help them get food.

LEARN ABOUT how living things get food.

LINK to math, writing, health, and technology.

INVESTIGATE

Animal Teeth

Activity Purpose Bite into an apple. Which teeth do you use? Which teeth do you use to chew the apple? In this investigation you will **observe** the shapes of teeth of different animals.

Materials
- blank index cards
- books about animals

Activity Procedure

1 **Observe** the pictures of the animals. Look closely at the shape of each animal's teeth.

2 Use one index card for each animal. **Record** the animal's name, and draw the shape of its teeth.

◄ Animals that are pets get their food from people. But animals that are wild must find their own food.

Shark ▼

Bobcat ▼

3 With a partner, make a list of words that describe the teeth. **Record** these words next to the drawings on the index cards. (Picture A)

4 Think about the things each animal eats. Use books about animals if you need help. On the back of each index card, make a list of the things the animal eats.

Picture A

Draw Conclusions

1. Which animals might use their teeth to catch other animals? Which animals might use their teeth to eat plants? Explain.

2. Some animals use their teeth to help them do other things, too. **Observe** the beaver's teeth. How do its teeth help it cut down trees?

3. **Scientists at Work** Scientists learn by **observing**. Scientists can learn how animals use their teeth by watching how and what the animals eat. From what you observed in this investigation, what can you **infer** about the shapes of animals' teeth?

Process Skill Tip

Observing and inferring are not the same. When you **observe**, you use your senses. When you **infer**, you form an opinion using your observations.

Wolf ▼

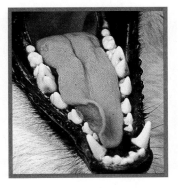

Horse ▼

Beaver ▼

B41

Living Things and Food

Making and Getting Food

FIND OUT

- how plants and animals interact with the environment
- how living things get food

VOCABULARY

interact
producer
consumer
decomposer

All living things need food. In the investigation you saw that an animal's teeth match the food it eats. But not all living things have teeth. Some living things get their food in other ways. For example, a bird uses its beak to get food. Plants make their own food.

Plants and animals work together, or **interact** (in•ter•AKT), with the environment to get what they need. Plants interact with sunlight, air, and water to make food. Animals interact with plants or other animals to get their food. Animals also interact with nonliving things in their environment, such as water, sunlight, soil, and rocks. For example, a snake lies in the sun for warmth and drinks water. The same snake may make its home in the soil or under a rock.

✔ **Why do plants and animals interact with the environment?**

This strawberry plant uses energy from the sun to make its own food. ▼

This strawberry provides a chipmunk with some of the energy it needs to live. ▼

The chipmunk provides energy for a snake that catches and eats it. ▼

B42

Producers

Plants are producers. A **producer** (proh•DOOS•er) is a living thing that makes its own food. Producers use the food they make to live and to grow.

Plants make more food than they need. This extra food is stored in roots, leaves, seeds, and fruit. People and other animals then eat this stored food as their own food.

✔ **What is a producer?**

Consumers

Animals cannot make their own food. They must eat plants or other animals. An animal is a **consumer** (kuhn•SOOM•er). A consumer is a living thing that eats other living things as food.

Consumers can be grouped by the kinds of food they eat. Some consumers eat only plants. Sheep, like this bighorn sheep, eat the leaves, twigs, fruits, and nuts of many plants.

A few consumers eat only one kind of plant. Giant pandas eat only bamboo. To survive, they must live where bamboo grows.

Animals that eat only plants may have body parts that help them eat. For example, the giant panda has an extra bone in its hand that helps it hold bamboo as it eats.

▲ These foods come from plants. Plants are producers that make their own food. Animals then eat plants as food.

The bighorn sheep is a consumer that eats grass. ▼

B43

Some animals get food by eating other animals. Often they must hunt and kill their food. Animals that get food in this way have body parts that help them catch and eat their food. For example, an owl has strong claws that it uses to catch animals. Its sharp beak helps it tear meat.

Some animals eat both plants and other animals. A box turtle eats both berries and insects. The meats you eat come from animals and the vegetables you eat come from plants.

✔ **What is a consumer?**

Decomposers

A **decomposer** (dee•kuhm•POHZ•er) is a living thing that breaks down dead things for food. Decomposers also break down the wastes of living things. As decomposers feed, they help clean the environment. Two decomposers you may know of are fungi, such as mushrooms, and earthworms.

✔ **What is a decomposer?**

This owl catches small animals for its food. ▼

▲ Many bacteria are decomposers.

The fungi growing on this log are decomposers. The fungi are using the dead log as food. ▼

Summary

Plants and animals interact. They depend on their environments and on one another to get the food they need. Plants are producers. Animals are consumers. Decomposers get food by breaking down wastes or dead things.

Review

1. How do producers get their food?
2. How do consumers get their food?
3. What are the three groups of consumers?
4. **Critical Thinking** How do decomposers help keep the environment clean?
5. **Test Prep** Which of the following is **NOT** a consumer?

   A bird   **C** squirrel

   B tree   **D** human

LINKS

MATH LINK

Consumers on an Island
Scientists studied 60 moose on an island. They found that during the summer, each moose eats the fruit of 25 blackberry bushes. What is the minimum number of blackberry bushes on the island?

WRITING LINK

Informative Writing— Explanation Suppose that the bushes on the island in the Math Link all die. Write a paragraph for your teacher explaining what you think might happen to the moose population.

HEALTH LINK

Teeth Think about how you use your teeth to eat. Which teeth do the cutting? The chewing? How are the teeth different?

TECHNOLOGY LINK

Learn how scientists help injured animals get food by visiting the Smithsonian Institution Internet Site.
www.si.edu/harcourt/science

 Smithsonian Institution®

What Are Food Chains?

In this lesson, you can . . .

INVESTIGATE a food-chain model.

LEARN ABOUT food chains and energy pyramids.

LINK to math, writing, literature, and technology.

INVESTIGATE

Make a Food-Chain Model

Activity Purpose You get energy from the food you eat. All living things get energy from the food they eat. In this investigation you will **make a model** to show how living things interact to get their energy from food.

Materials
- index cards
- marker
- 4 pieces of yarn or string
- tape

Activity Procedure

1 In the bottom right-hand corners, number the index cards 1 through 5.

2 On Card 1, draw and label grass. On Card 2, draw and label a cricket. On Card 3, draw and label a frog. On Card 4, draw and label a snake. On Card 5, draw and label a hawk. (Picture A)

◄ **A puffin eats different kinds of sea animals. It can catch as many as ten small fish at one time in its beak.**

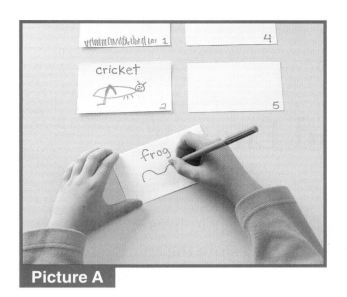

Picture A

Picture B

3 Order the cards in a line with Card 1 first and Card 5 last. Use yarn and tape to connect the cards. (Picture B)

4 Stretch the connected cards out on a table. The cards form a model called a food chain.

5 Discuss with a classmate how each living thing in the food chain gets its food. Tell which things in your model show producers. Tell which things show consumers.

Draw Conclusions

1. In your model, which living thing is last in the food chain? Why do you think it is in this place?

2. In which part of the food chain is the producer found? Why do you think it is there?

3. **Scientists at Work** Scientists **use models** to help them study things in nature. How does using a model of a food chain help you understand living things and the food they eat?

Process Skill Tip

It is hard to **observe** a real-life food chain. **Using a model** of a food chain helps you learn about the real thing.

Food and Energy

FIND OUT

- how living things get energy
- how energy moves through a food chain

VOCABULARY

food chain
energy pyramid

Food Chains

All living things need energy to live. Producers get energy from sunlight. They store the energy in the food they make. Consumers can't make their own food. They get their food by eating other living things. In this way, the consumers get the energy they need.

In the investigation you saw that the path of food from one living thing to another forms a **food chain**. A food chain also shows how energy moves through the environment. For example, grass uses the energy in sunlight to make its food. A cricket that eats the grass gets the energy stored in the grass. If a frog eats the cricket, it gets energy that is stored in the cricket. In this way, the energy that started with the sun is passed from the grass to the cricket to the frog.

✔ **What is a food chain?**

This turtle eats slugs that eat leaves. ▶

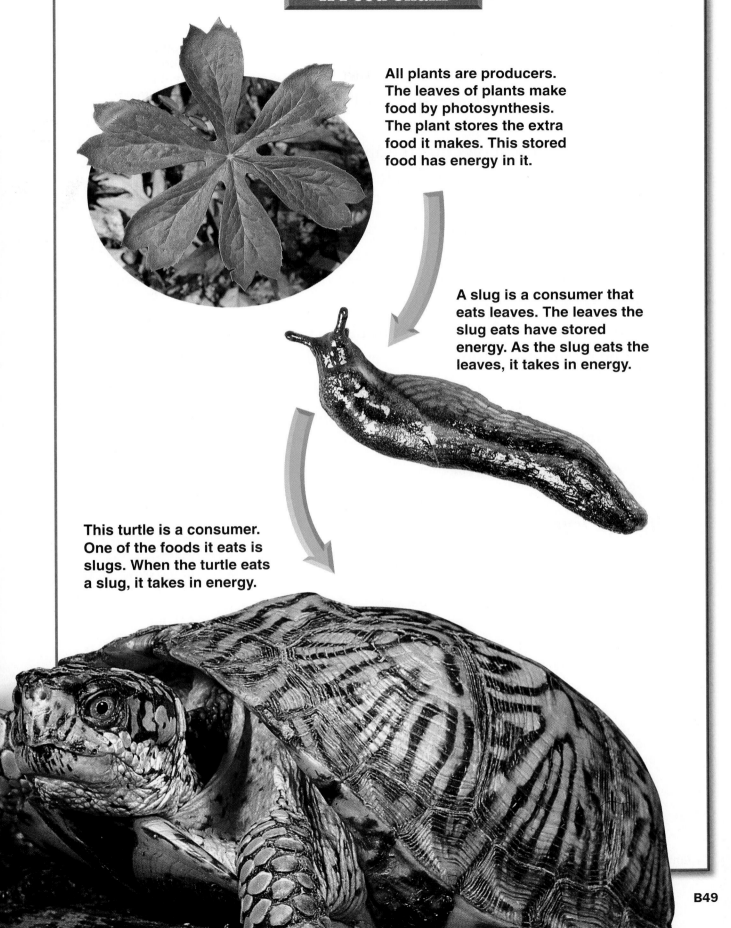

All plants are producers. The leaves of plants make food by photosynthesis. The plant stores the extra food it makes. This stored food has energy in it.

A slug is a consumer that eats leaves. The leaves the slug eats have stored energy. As the slug eats the leaves, it takes in energy.

This turtle is a consumer. One of the foods it eats is slugs. When the turtle eats a slug, it takes in energy.

Energy from Food

Every living thing uses energy to live and to grow. The energy that a living thing uses cannot be passed along through the food chain. Because of this, the higher on the food chain a living thing is, the less energy there is.

An **energy pyramid** shows that the amount of useable energy in an ecosystem is less for each higher animal in the food chain.

In an energy pyramid, there are more producers than any other kind of living thing. Most of the energy in an ecosystem is found in plants. Animals that eat plants make up the next level. The upper parts of the pyramid are made up of animals that eat other animals. The higher in the pyramid an animal is, the fewer of that animal there are. This is because there is less energy available to them.

✔ **What is an energy pyramid?**

1 Energy from the sun is taken in by plants and other producers. This energy is used by plants for growth and to make fruits and seeds. Energy that is not used by the plant is stored.

2 Animals that eat plants are called first-level consumers. These animals must eat many plants to get the energy they need. Energy not used by the animal is stored in its body.

3 Animals that eat other animals are called second-level consumers. There are fewer of these animals. Some of the energy that is stored in first-level consumers can be passed on to these animals.

4 There are very few animals at the top of the pyramid. The energy these top-level consumers get has been passed through all the other parts of the food chain.

THE INSIDE STORY

An Energy Pyramid

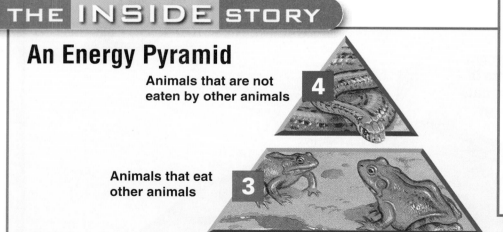

4 Animals that are not eaten by other animals

3 Animals that eat other animals

2 Plant-eating animals

1 Plants

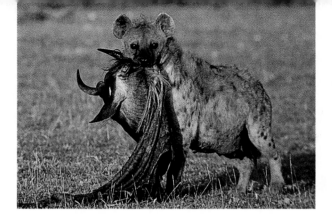

▲ A hyena is a *scavenger,* an animal that feeds on dead animals.

Summary

Living things get their energy from food. Animals cannot make their own food, so they eat other living things to get energy. A food chain is the flow of food in an ecosystem from one living thing to another. An energy pyramid shows that the amount of useable energy in an ecosystem is less for each higher animal in the food chain.

Review

1. How does energy get from a producer to a meat-eating consumer?
2. What kind of living thing is at the top of a food chain?
3. Where is the most food energy in an energy pyramid found?
4. **Critical Thinking** What is the source of all the energy on Earth?
5. **Test Prep** Which is passed in a food chain from one living thing to another?

   A producers   C sunlight
   B animals   D energy

LINKS

MATH LINK

Animals in the Food Chain
One food chain is made up of a producer, a consumer that eats plants, a consumer that eats both plants and animals, and a consumer that eats only animals. What fraction of living things in this food chain eats plants?

WRITING LINK

Expressive Writing—Poem
You are part of many food chains. Pick your favorite dinner. Write a poem for your family about how the different foods fit into food chains.

LITERATURE LINK

Underwater Food Chains
Plants and animals that live in water are parts of food chains, too. In the book *Mangrove Wilderness,* Bianca Lavies tells about food chains in an estuary.

TECHNOLOGY LINK

To learn more about food chains, watch the video *Poisoned Eagles* on the **Harcourt Science Newsroom Video.**

What Are Food Webs?

In this lesson, you can . . .

 INVESTIGATE food webs.

 LEARN ABOUT how food chains overlap to form food webs.

 LINK to math, writing, literature, and technology.

INVESTIGATE

Make a Food Web

Activity Purpose Most animals eat more than one kind of food. Because of this, one living thing can be a part of more than one food chain. Food chains in an ecosystem overlap to form *food webs.* In this investigation you will **make a model** of a food web.

Materials
- index cards, cut into fourths
- poster board
- tape or glue
- crayons

Activity Procedure

1 Write the name of each living thing from the chart on its own card.

2 Glue the cards onto a sheet of poster board so they form a circle. Leave room for writing. (Picture A)

◄ A sea otter is part of an ocean food web. It feeds on abalone and other shellfish. As the otter floats on its back, it cracks open the shellfish by banging it against a rock it carries on its chest.

Living Thing	What It Eats
clover	uses the sun to make its own food
grasshopper	clover
frog	grasshopper
snake	frog, mouse
owl	snake, mouse
mouse	clover

Picture A

3 Look at the chart again. List two different food chains you could make.

4 Draw arrows between the parts of each food chain. Use a different color for each food chain. You have now made a food web. (Picture B)

5 **Observe** your model to see how the food chains overlap. What other living things could you add to your food web?

Picture B

Draw Conclusions

1. What is the producer in this food web?

2. What does your food web tell you about producers and consumers?

3. **Scientists at Work** Scientists sometimes **make models** to help them learn about things. How did drawing a food web help you learn about animals in a real ecosystem?

Investigate Further Cut out magazine pictures of different plants and animals. Work with a partner to make a food web that includes these plants and animals.

Process Skill Tip

It is hard to observe a real-life food web. **Using a model** of a food web helps you learn about the real thing.

Food Webs

FIND OUT

- about food webs
- how living things interact in food webs

VOCABULARY

food web
predator
prey

Predator and Prey

There are many food chains in an ecosystem. Sometimes these food chains overlap. A model that shows how food chains overlap is called a **food web**. A food web contains producers and consumers that are used as food by more than one living thing.

Food webs contain animals that eat other animals. An animal that hunts another animal for food is called a **predator** (PRED•uh•ter). The animal that is hunted is called **prey** (PRAY). Some animals can be both predator and prey. For example, when a snake eats a mole, the snake is the predator. The mole is the prey. If the snake is eaten by a hawk, the snake becomes the prey. The hawk is the predator.

✔ **What is a food web?**

This marsh ecosystem has many kinds of animals. These animals may be predators, prey, or both. ▼

Many overlapping food chains make up the food web for this marsh ecosystem.

1 The plants in the marsh use the energy of the sun to make food.

2 Insects eat the plants that grow in the marsh.

3 Fish eat the insects. Some fish also eat the plants. Smaller fish are eaten by larger fish.

4 Birds eat the fish in the marsh. Some birds also eat the insects and the plants that grow in the marsh.

5 Alligators eat both fish and birds. Alligators are top-level consumers. They are not eaten by other animals in the marsh.

What other food chains can you identify in this food web?

An Ocean Food Web

The living things in the ocean also interact to form food webs. Plants and other producers that grow in ocean waters are food for some ocean animals.

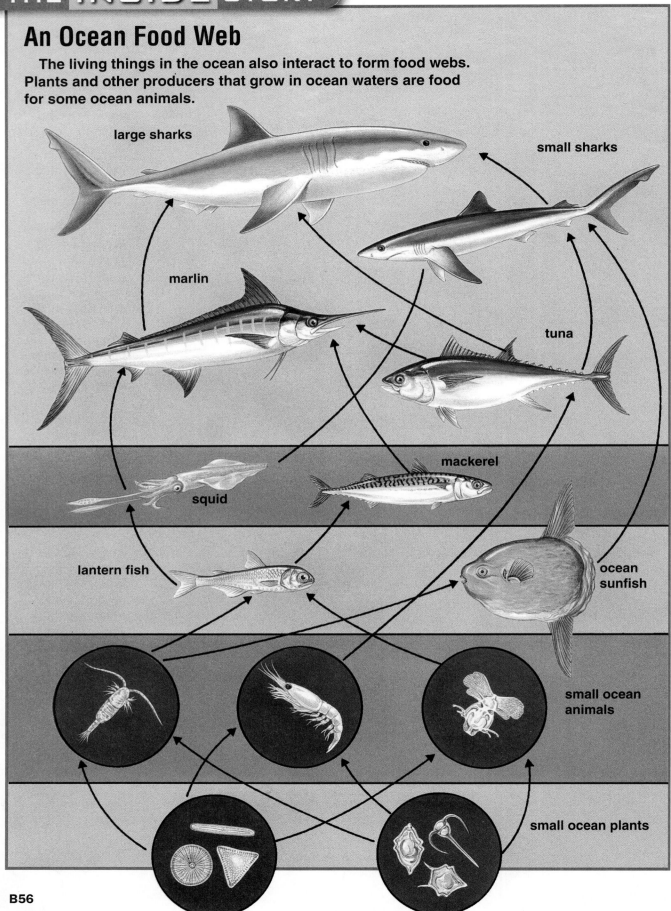

large sharks

small sharks

marlin

tuna

squid

mackerel

lantern fish

ocean sunfish

small ocean animals

small ocean plants

Summary

Most ecosystems have many food chains. These food chains overlap and link together to make food webs. An animal in a food web may be a predator, prey, or both.

Review

1. How are food webs and food chains alike? How are they different?
2. How can an animal be both predator and prey?
3. How does an alligator get energy?
4. **Critical Thinking** In the following food chain, name the predators and the prey.

   insect → frog → snake
5. **Test Prep** Which of the following is a producer in an ocean ecosystem?

   A shark   **C** starfish

   B seaweed   **D** fish

Other animals prey on these shrimp. Just like animals that live on land, many ocean predators have body parts that help them catch and eat their prey. ▼

LINKS

MATH LINK

Recording Food Web Data
Choose a food web from this lesson. Count the different food chains in that web. How many animals in the web are predators, and how many are prey? Record your findings in a table.

WRITING LINK

Informative Writing— Explanation Study the ocean food web on page B56. Pick one of the animals and write a paragraph for your classmates that explains how the animal fits into a food chain and a food web.

LITERATURE LINK

Read About Predators Learn about some amazing predators, such as a fishing spider or a vampire bat. Read *Extremely Weird Hunters* by Sarah Lovett.

TECHNOLOGY LINK

Visit the Harcourt Learning Site for related links, activities, and resources.
www.harcourtschool.com

WELCOME TO
THE
LEARNING
SITE

People and Animals —A Long Relationship

Animals and humans have had a long relationship. People learned many thousands of years ago to domesticate, or tame, animals. Animals have also been hunted for food and clothing for thousands of years.

Uses of Animals

Animals are part of the web of life. They are consumers, living off plants and smaller animals. But people use animals and animal products as food. Some people choose not to eat animals. Many of those people do eat products that come from animals, such as milk, eggs, or honey. All of us depend on animals to pollinate the flowers of many fruits and vegetables.

Animal fur or skins may be used for clothing. Perhaps some of the clothing you are wearing today came

The History of People and Animals

15,000 B.C.
Horses are drawn in cave paintings in France.

| 15,000 B.C. | 7500 B.C. | B.C./A.D. | 1500 | 1600 | 1700 |

8000 B.C.
People begin to tame animals.

1400 B.C.
Hittites who live in Turkey train horses.

1519
Spanish explorers bring horses to North America.

from an animal. We get wool from sheep. Silkworms make silk.

Over the centuries, people have used animals to work. Large animals like oxen can be used to plow fields. Horses, camels, and elephants are good for carrying people and goods. Some dogs can guard, rescue, hunt, herd, or guide. Cats catch mice.

For some of us, domestic animals are best friends. You may have a cat or a dog as a family pet. Some people have more unusual pets, such as small reptiles or birds from foreign countries.

The Camel—A Very Useful Animal

The camel is one animal that is very useful to humans. Most camels now live in the deserts of Asia and Africa. But scientists have evidence that camels lived in North America before the Ice Age. They died out

before Europeans came to the continent. But the U.S. Army brought camels back to North America to carry cargo from Texas to California during the mid-1800s. The railroad was faster than camels, though. After the railroad across the country was finished, most camels went to live in zoos and circuses.

People in Asia still use camels to carry heavy loads, especially in desert areas. One camel can carry more than 136 kilograms (300 lb). A working camel travels about 40 kilometers (25 mi) a day at about 5 kilometers per hour (3 mph). Also, camels can go for a long time without water.

Camels provide meat and milk. People make cheese and butter from their milk. Camel hair makes warm blankets, clothes, and tents.

As you can see, the relationship of animals and humans is complicated. Think of all the types of animals you have studied—fish, reptiles, birds, amphibians, and mammals. Then look around at home and at school. What should you thank an animal for today?

Think About It
- Why do you think people train animals to do specific jobs?

1850
Camels arrive in the United States.

1800   1900   2000

1973
The United States passes the Endangered Species Act to protect animals.

Akira Akubo

OCEANOGRAPHER

Growing up in Japan, a country surrounded by water, Akira Akubo became interested in the ocean. His interest led him to study oceanography.

Questions Akubo has studied include why and how fish live in schools. Fish gather in schools for protection. A school may break up at night to feed, but the fish gather again the next morning. A school may have as few as two dozen fish or as many as several million. All the fish in a school are about the same size. Adult fish and young fish are never in the same school. Some fish form schools when they are young and stay together all their lives. Other species of fish form schools for only a few weeks after hatching.

Akubo has also studied plankton—tiny animal-like and plantlike living things that float near the water's surface. Most plankton are so small that they can be seen only with a microscope. Plankton is food for many other living things in the sea. Animal-like plankton eat the plantlike plankton. A lot of plankton is eaten by fish. Some whales eat nothing but tons of plankton!

Akubo is interested in land animals, too. He believes that studying land animals can help him learn more about animals in the water. He hopes that comparing ocean animals with land animals will help him predict animal behavior.

Think About It

1. Why is plankton important?
2. What is the advantage for fish of traveling in schools?

Food Chains

How do animals get their food?

Materials
- name tags
- colored game markers
- small plastic bags

Procedure
Play this game with ten or more people.

1. Have each player wear a tag that names him or her as a grasshopper, a snake, or a hawk. Scatter the game markers over a large area. The game markers are food.

2. Each round of the game is 30 seconds. In the first round, only grasshoppers play. They collect as many markers as they can and put them in their bags.

3. In the next round, only snakes play.

4. In the final round, only hawks play.

Draw Conclusions
Which animals had the most food after three rounds? Talk about your answer.

Energy Flow

How does energy flow through a food chain?

Materials
- index cards
- crayons
- pushpins
- yarn

Procedure
1. Divide the class into five groups: producers, plant eaters, plant and animal eaters, animal eaters, and decomposers.

2. Have each person in your group draw on an index card and label a kind of plant or animal that is from your group.

3. Form teams made up of one member from each group. Each team should make a food chain with the pictures. Use yarn to connect the parts on a bulletin board.

Draw Conclusions
How does energy flow through the food chain?

Vocabulary Review

Use the terms below to complete the sentences 1 through 9. The page numbers in ( ) tell you where to look in the chapter if you need help.

interact (B42)

producer (B43)

consumer (B43)

decomposer (B44)

food chain (B48)

energy

pyramid (B50)

food web (B54)

predator (B54)

prey (B54)

1. A ____ feeds on the wastes of other living things.

2. A fish that is hunted and eaten by another consumer is called ____.

3. The path of food in an ecosystem from one living thing to another can be shown as a ____.

4. A ____ makes its own food.

5. A living thing that eats other living things is called a ____.

6. The living things in a community ____ with each other and with nonliving things.

7. Several linked food chains make up a ____.

8. A shark is a ____ because it hunts its food.

9. A model of how energy moves through a food web is called an ____.

Connect Concepts

Use the words listed below to complete the concept map.

consumer   horse

decomposer   mushroom

grass   producer

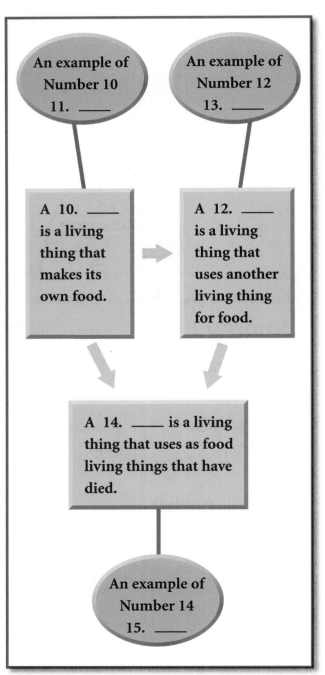

An example of Number 10

11. ____

An example of Number 12

13. ____

A 10. ____ is a living thing that makes its own food.

A 12. ____ is a living thing that uses another living thing for food.

A 14. ____ is a living thing that uses as food living things that have died.

An example of Number 14

15. ____

Check Understanding

Write the letter of the best choice.

16. Which is **NOT** a producer?

    A tree   C grass
    B flower   D bird

17. A model that shows how energy moves through a food chain is —

    F a decomposer
    G an ecosystem
    H an energy pyramid
    J a food web

18. A spider hunts and kills other animals for food. It is —

    A prey
    B a decomposer
    C a predator
    D a producer

19. Producers get their energy from —

    F other living things
    G the soil
    H an energy pyramid
    J the sun

Critical Thinking

20. A bear lives in the woods near a river. How might the bear interact with its environment to get food?

21. Where do you fit into a food chain? Draw a food chain that includes a plant or animal you ate for lunch.

Process Skills Review

22. How can you use **observation** to find out what a goat eats? How might you **infer** what the goat eats?

23. Use what you know about **models** to draw a food web that includes a bear, a water plant, berries, a big fish, a small fish, and a mouse.

Performance Assessment

Diagram a Food Web

Work with a partner. Choose an animal with which you are familiar. Draw a food web that includes the animal. Identify the producers and the consumers in each food chain. Identify predators and prey in as many food chains as you can.

Unit Project Wrap Up

Here are some ideas for ways to wrap up your unit project.

Display at a Science Fair

Display your mobile and cards in a school science fair. You may want to include books or other resources that tell about your ecosystem.

Draw a Mural

Show your ecosystem in a mural. Include all the living and nonliving things you saw. Label each one.

Make a Terrarium

Find samples from your ecosystem to make a terrarium. Write about how the terrarium is a model ecosystem and how the living and nonliving things in the ecosystem interact.

Investigate Further

How could you make your project better? What other questions do you have about ecosystems? Plan ways to find answers to your questions. Use the Science Handbook on pages R2-R9 for help.

Earth's Land

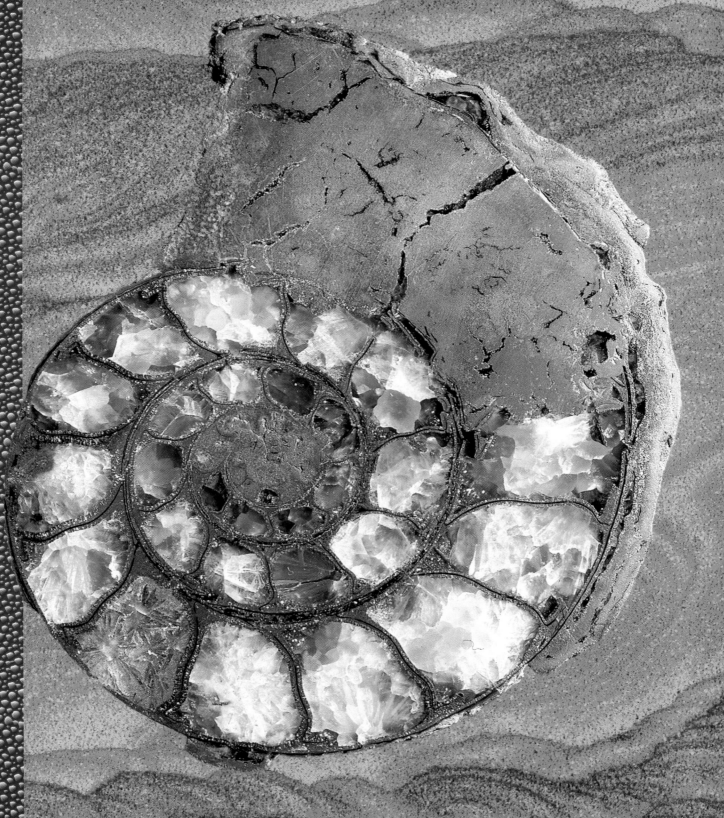

UNIT C

EARTH SCIENCE

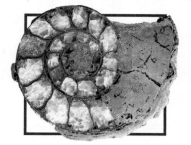

Earth's Land

Unit Project

Earth Museum

Collect specimens of rocks, minerals, fossils, and soils and display them as exhibits in an Earth museum. Identify and label your exhibits. Plan ways to guide others through your museum.

Chapter 1

Vocabulary Preview

mineral
rock
crust
mantle
core
igneous rock
sedimentary rock
metamorphic rock
rock cycle
fossil

Rocks, Minerals, and Fossils

Take a look around at rocks. Some may be on the ground. Others may have been used to build homes and office buildings. Some rocks are shiny. Others may have different-colored pieces in them. You may even be able to see traces of once-living animals or plants in some rocks.

FAST FACT

If lightning strikes the beach, a new kind of rock may form. The heat from the lightning melts sand to make a glassy rock called fulgurite (FUHL·gyuh·ryt).

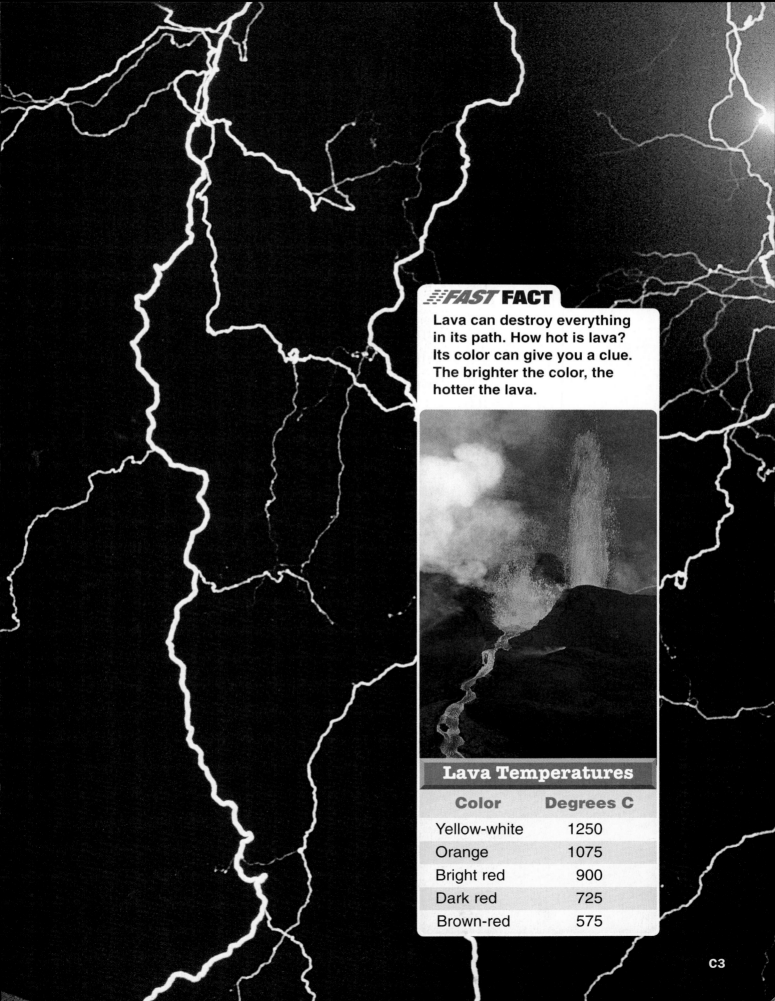

FAST FACT

Lava can destroy everything in its path. How hot is lava? Its color can give you a clue. The brighter the color, the hotter the lava.

Lava Temperatures

Color	Degrees C
Yellow-white	1250
Orange	1075
Bright red	900
Dark red	725
Brown-red	575

What Are Minerals and Rocks?

In this lesson, you can . . .

INVESTIGATE the hardness of minerals.

LEARN ABOUT how people identify and use minerals and rocks.

LINK to math, writing, literature, and technology.

◄ A geode is a hollow rounded rock with mineral crystals inside.

INVESTIGATE

Testing Minerals

Activity Purpose How do scientists tell minerals apart? They test them for specific properties. A property is a feature that identifies something. In this investigation you will test seven minerals for the property of hardness. Then you will **order** the minerals from softest to hardest.

Materials
- minerals labeled *A* through *G*

Activity Procedure

1 Make a chart like the one shown.

2 A harder mineral scratches a softer mineral. Try to scratch each of the other minerals with Sample A. **Record** which minerals Sample A scratches. (Picture A)

3 A softer mineral is scratched by a harder mineral. Try to scratch Sample A with each of the other minerals. **Record** which minerals scratch Sample A.

Mineral to Test	Minerals It Scratches	Minerals That Scratch It
Sample A		
Sample B		
Sample C		
Sample D		
Sample E		
Sample F		
Sample G		

4 Repeat Steps 2 and 3 for each mineral.

5 Using the information in your chart, **order** the minerals from softest to hardest. Give each mineral a number, starting with 1 for the softest mineral.

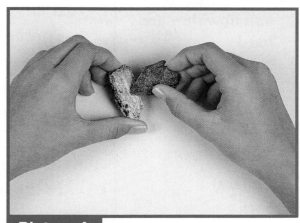

Picture A

Draw Conclusions

1. Which mineral was the hardest? Which was the softest? How do you know?

2. How did you decide the **order** of the minerals?

3. **Scientists at Work** Scientists often put objects in **order.** By doing this, they can show that different objects have different properties. How can putting objects in order of hardness help you identify them?

Investigate Further To test for hardness, scientists sometimes scratch an unknown mineral with common objects. That's because they don't always have other minerals with them. But to use common objects, scientists need to know how hard the objects are. Using the minerals from this investigation, find out the hardness of glass, a copper penny, and your fingernail.

Process Skill Tip

In a scratch test, you **observe** the results and **record** them on a chart. You use the chart to put the objects in **order.**

Minerals and Rocks

FIND OUT

- what minerals are and how they are used

- what is under the surface of the Earth

VOCABULARY

mineral
rock
crust
mantle
core

What Minerals Are

If an object is a solid, was formed in nature, and has never been alive, it's likely to be a **mineral** (MIN•er•uhl). There are many kinds of minerals. No two are exactly alike. For example, gold is metallic and shiny. Graphite is dark and dull. Diamonds are hard enough to cut steel. Chalk is so soft that you can write with it.

In the investigation you saw that hardness is one property of minerals. Other properties of minerals are color and shape. Every mineral can be identified by its properties.

✔ **Name three properties of minerals.**

▲ Diamond is the hardest mineral.

▲ This sapphire has a beautiful deep blue color.

▲ Corundum, the second hardest mineral, may be many colors. The ruby shown here is a red corundum.

▲ Quartz is a common mineral. It is almost as hard as diamond.

▲ An emerald is among the most valuable minerals. It is very rare and very hard.

How Minerals Are Used

You use a mineral whenever you pick up a glass or put salt on your food. You use a mineral when you write with a pencil. The "lead" in the pencil is the mineral graphite.

Your body needs small amounts of minerals such as iron and zinc to stay healthy. You get these minerals from the foods you eat.

Minerals are in many of the things around you. For example, iron comes from the mineral hematite. Iron is used to make steel for airplanes, buildings, and washing machines.

Minerals such as gold and diamond are used to make jewelry. The pennies in your pocket contain copper. That's a mineral, too.

✔ **Name three ways that minerals are used.**

▲ **Aluminum comes from the mineral bauxite. Aluminum is molded into many products, such as baseball bats, cooking pots, and airplanes.**

Gold is a soft mineral. It can be pressed into very thin sheets called gold leaf. The top of this building is covered with gold leaf. ▼

▲ **The mineral quartz is used to make glass. These sand grains are tiny pieces of quartz.**

What Rocks Are

The Earth is made mostly of rocks. A **rock** is made of minerals. Some rocks are made of just one. Other rocks are made of many minerals.

If you could cut the Earth open, you would see three different layers of rocks. At the surface of the Earth is the solid outside layer, called the **crust**. The crust is probably the only part of the Earth you have seen.

The crust sits on the **mantle**, the middle layer. The mantle is so hot that some of the rocks have nearly melted. They are soft like taffy.

Below the mantle, at the center of the Earth, is the **core**. It is even hotter than the mantle. The rocks in the outer part of the core are so hot that they are liquid. The liquid rock is called *magma*. The inner part of the core is much hotter than the mantle, but it is solid. Because the weight of the whole planet presses in on the core, the inner part stays solid.

✔ **Name the three layers of the Earth.**

Biotite

Feldspar

Quartz

Muscovite

THE INSIDE STORY

Layers of Earth

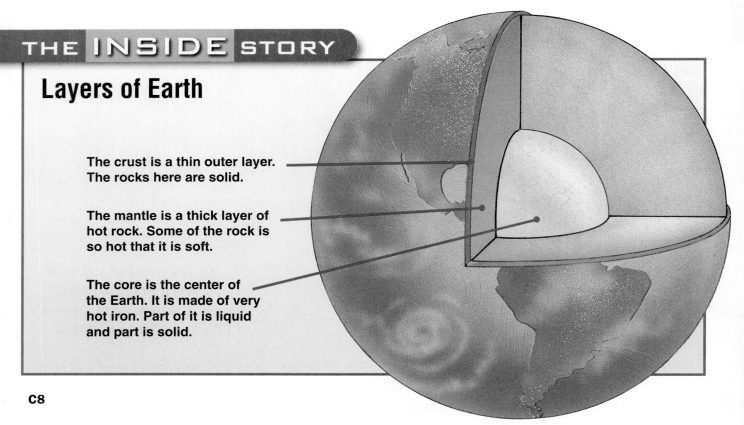

The crust is a thin outer layer. The rocks here are solid.

The mantle is a thick layer of hot rock. Some of the rock is so hot that it is soft.

The core is the center of the Earth. It is made of very hot iron. Part of it is liquid and part is solid.

◄ Granite is a rock that is made of the minerals shown here.

Summary

A mineral is a solid natural material that has never been alive. Rocks are made of minerals. The Earth is a ball of rock with three layers.

Review

1. What is a mineral? List three uses of minerals.
2. What is a rock?
3. Describe the layers of the Earth.
4. **Critical Thinking** How is the mantle of the Earth different from the crust? How are the mantle and crust alike?
5. **Test Prep** Which of these minerals is the hardest?
   A quartz
   B diamond
   C hematite
   D corundum

LINKS

MATH LINK

Crystal Shapes The particles in minerals form patterns called crystals. There are seven types of crystal shapes. Gather information on crystal shapes. How are they alike, and how are they different?

WRITING LINK

Informative Writing— Description Look for rocks where you live. Choose one that looks interesting. For a family member, make a list of words that describe it.

LITERATURE LINK

Magic School Bus Take a ride on the Magic School Bus to explore the center of the Earth. Read *Inside the Earth* by Joanna Cole. List three new things you learn about the Earth's layers.

TECHNOLOGY LINK

Learn more about rocks by visiting the Smithsonian Institution Internet Site.
www.si.edu/harcourt/science

 Smithsonian Institution®

How Do Rocks Form?

In this lesson, you can . . .

INVESTIGATE
different types of rock.

LEARN ABOUT
how rocks form.

LINK to math, writing, literature, and technology.

INVESTIGATE

Types of Rocks

Activity Purpose In this investigation you will **observe** six different rocks and **compare** their properties. Then you will use your observations to group the rocks.

Materials
- 3 rocks labeled *I*, *S*, and *M*
- hand lens
- 3 unknown rocks labeled *1*, *2*, and *3*

Activity Procedure

1 Make a chart like the one shown.

2 Rocks *I*, *S*, and *M* are three different types of rocks. Look at them with and without the hand lens. **Record** your observations in the chart.

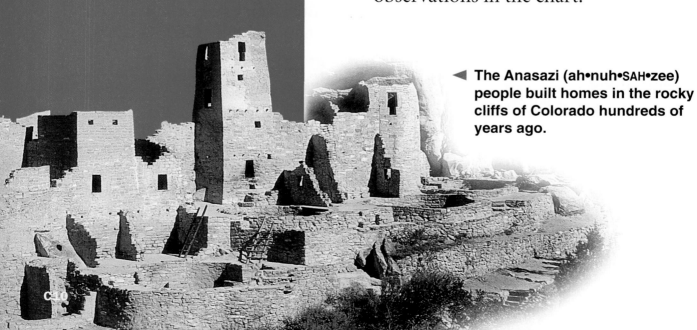

◀ The Anasazi (ah•nuh•SAH•zee) people built homes in the rocky cliffs of Colorado hundreds of years ago.

Rock	Observations
I	
S	
M	
1	
2	
3	

Picture A

3 Look at each of the numbered rocks with and without the hand lens. **Record** your observations in the chart. (Picture A)

4 **Compare** the properties of the lettered rocks with the properties of the numbered rocks. Think about how the rocks are alike and how they are different.

Draw Conclusions

1. What properties did you use to **compare** the rocks?

2. Which numbered rock is most like Rock *I*? Which numbered rock is most like Rock *S*? Which numbered rock is most like Rock *M*? Explain your answers.

3. **Scientists at Work** Scientists learn about new objects when they **compare** them with objects they have already studied. What did you learn about the rocks when you compared them?

Investigate Further Look near your school or home for small rocks. **Compare** them with Rocks *I*, *S*, and *M*. Try to **classify** the rocks as *I*, *S*, or *M*.

Process Skill Tip

When you **compare** objects, you **observe** their properties to find out how the objects are alike and how they are different. Comparing can help you put things into groups.

How Rocks Form

FIND OUT

- **how rocks form**
- **ways people use rocks to make things**

VOCABULARY

igneous rock
sedimentary rock
metamorphic rock
rock cycle

Three Types of Rocks

Exploding volcanoes, flowing water, and heat and pressure inside the Earth all form rocks. Rocks are grouped by how they form. There are three groups of rocks.

Igneous rock (IG•nee•uhs RAHK) is rock that was once melted but has cooled and hardened.

Sedimentary rock (sed•uh•MEN•ter•ee RAHK) forms from material that has settled into layers. The layers are squeezed together until they harden into rock.

Metamorphic rock (met•uh•MAWR•fik RAHK) is igneous or sedimentary rock that has been changed by heat and pressure.

✔ **What did the *I*, *S*, and *M* stand for in the investigation?**

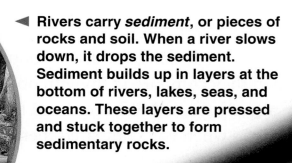

◄ Rivers carry *sediment*, or pieces of rocks and soil. When a river slows down, it drops the sediment. Sediment builds up in layers at the bottom of rivers, lakes, seas, and oceans. These layers are pressed and stuck together to form sedimentary rocks.

Igneous rocks form from melted rock that has cooled and hardened. Some igneous rocks come from volcanoes. ▼

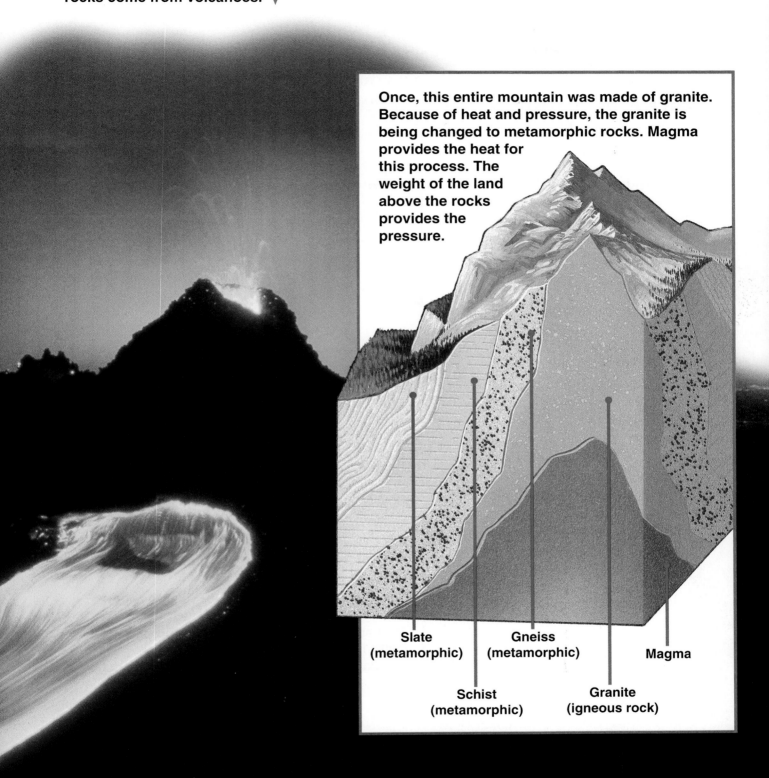

Once, this entire mountain was made of granite. Because of heat and pressure, the granite is being changed to metamorphic rocks. Magma provides the heat for this process. The weight of the land above the rocks provides the pressure.

Slate (metamorphic)

Schist (metamorphic)

Gneiss (metamorphic)

Granite (igneous rock)

Magma

How Rocks Form and Change

You know that there are three types of rocks—igneous, metamorphic, and sedimentary. But did you know that each type can be changed into the other types? This process of changing is called the **rock cycle** (RAHK SY•kuhl).

The diagram shows how rocks can change. The arrows show what is happening to make the rocks change. They tell about heat and pressure being applied to rocks. They also show how rocks break apart to form sediments. Use your finger to trace the changes that can happen to each type of rock.

✔ **What is the rock cycle?**

Metamorphic

Quartzite

Marble

Slate

Heat and pressure can change metamorphic rocks into other metamorphic rocks.

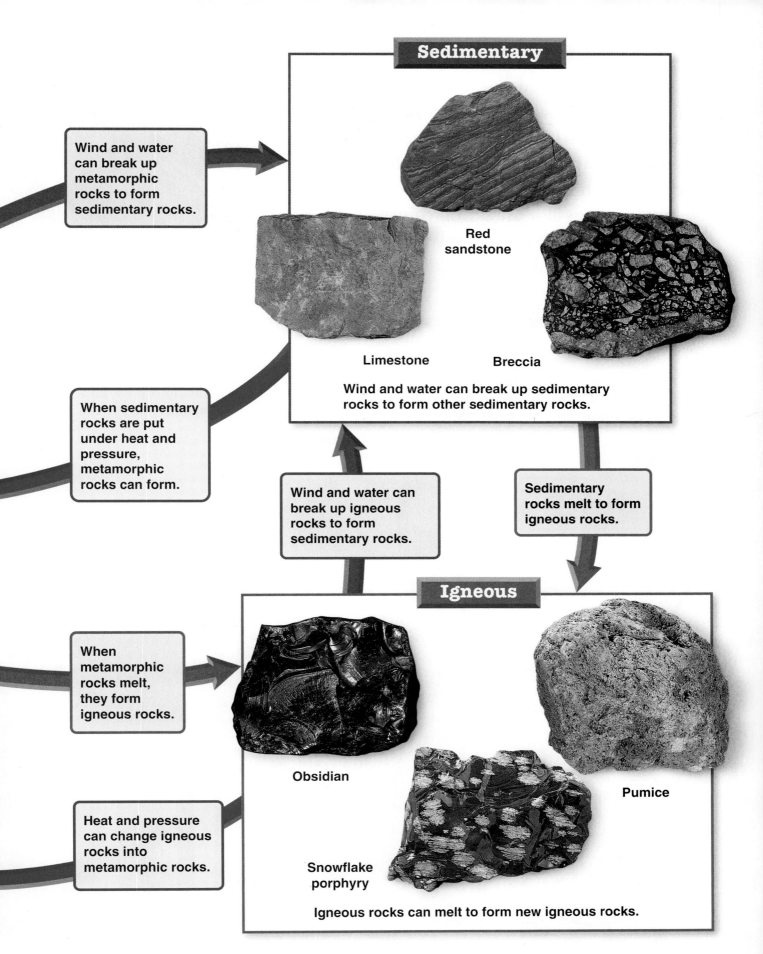

Sedimentary

Red sandstone

Limestone

Breccia

Wind and water can break up sedimentary rocks to form other sedimentary rocks.

Wind and water can break up metamorphic rocks to form sedimentary rocks.

When sedimentary rocks are put under heat and pressure, metamorphic rocks can form.

Wind and water can break up igneous rocks to form sedimentary rocks.

Sedimentary rocks melt to form igneous rocks.

Igneous

When metamorphic rocks melt, they form igneous rocks.

Obsidian

Snowflake porphyry

Pumice

Heat and pressure can change igneous rocks into metamorphic rocks.

Igneous rocks can melt to form new igneous rocks.

How People Use Rocks

Rocks are all around you. You see them all the time. But rocks are also in places you might not think of. Did you know that rocks help you play video games? The games use silicon chips, and silicon comes from rocks. Computers, satellites, and microwave ovens also use silicon chips.

Colorful rocks are worn as jewelry. Roads are paved with rocks, and many buildings and statues are made of rocks.

✔ **What are two uses of rocks?**

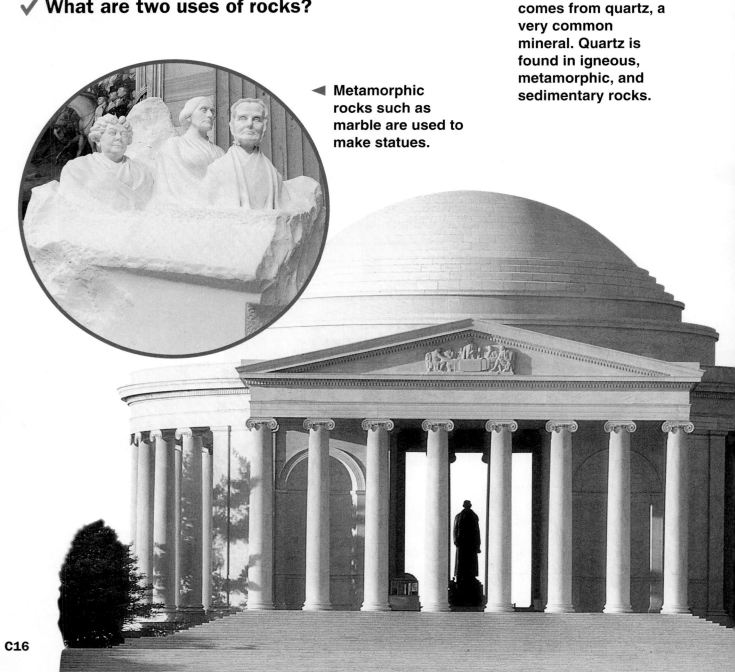

▲ The chips that run computers are made of silicon. Silicon comes from quartz, a very common mineral. Quartz is found in igneous, metamorphic, and sedimentary rocks.

◄ Metamorphic rocks such as marble are used to make statues.

Summary

There are three types of rocks. Igneous rocks form from melted rock that has cooled and hardened. Sedimentary rocks form from layers of sediment. Metamorphic rocks have been changed by heat and pressure. The rock cycle shows how one type of rock can be changed into another type of rock.

Review

1. Where do igneous rocks come from?
2. How can igneous rocks become sedimentary rocks?
3. How can metamorphic rocks become igneous rocks?
4. **Critical Thinking** Choose a rock, and tell about some things that are made from it.
5. **Test Prep** Which type of rock forms in layers?
   - **A** igneous
   - **B** metamorphic
   - **C** sedimentary
   - **D** All rocks form in layers.

◀ The Jefferson Memorial in Washington, D.C., is made of marble, a metamorphic rock.

LINKS

MATH LINK

Rock Model Suppose you were asked to make a model of the rock cycle. You were told to include 3 types of each kind of rock in your model. How many rocks are in the model?

WRITING LINK

Informative Writing—Report Interview someone who works with minerals and rocks. Find out how he or she uses them at work. Write a report for your teacher about what you learn. Share it with your class.

LITERATURE LINK

Rock On Want to find out more about rocks? Read *The Rock* by Peter Parnall. Tell how the rock changed over time.

TECHNOLOGY LINK

Learn more about the rock cycle by observing rocks as they change. Try *Rock Processor* on **Harcourt Science Explorations CD-ROM**.

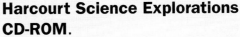

What Are Fossils?

In this lesson, you can . . .

INVESTIGATE how fossils form.

LEARN ABOUT different types of fossils.

LINK to math, writing, literature, and technology.

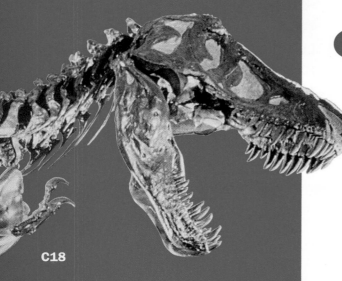

◀ **Fossil bones show how dinosaurs looked. This fossil is of a Tyrannosaurus rex.**

INVESTIGATE

Fossil Layers

Activity Purpose You have never seen a live dinosaur. But you may know a lot about dinosaurs because of fossils (FAHS•uhlz). A *fossil* is what's left of a plant or animal that lived long ago. In this investigation you will **make a model** of rock layers and fossils.

Materials
- 5 colors of modeling clay
- 5 sheets of wax paper
- 5 different seashells labeled *A* through *E*

Activity Procedure

1 Make a chart like the one shown.

2 Use clay of one color to make a layer about the size and shape of a hamburger. Put the layer of clay on a sheet of wax paper.

3 Press a shell into the clay to make a print. Remove the shell. **Record** the clay color and the shell letter in your chart. (Picture A)

Rock Layer	Clay Color	Shell Letter
1 (bottom layer)		
2		
3		
4		
5 (top layer)		

4 Place a sheet of wax paper over the clay layer.

5 Repeat Steps 2, 3, and 4 until you have made new layers with each color of clay and each shell.

6 Trade your group's clay layers and shells with another group's. Make a second chart. Remove each layer of clay, and **observe** it. Do not change the order of the layers. Match each shell to its print. Fill in the second chart. Check your answers with the group that made the model.

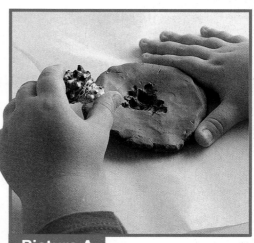

Picture A

Draw Conclusions

1. How did you know the correct layer for each shell?

2. Pretend the shell prints are fossils and the clay is sedimentary rock. List the shell letters from the oldest to the newest. Do this by using what you know about sedimentary rock layers.

3. **Scientists at Work** Scientists **use models** to understand how things happen. How did **using a model** help you understand how fossils are left in layers in time order?

Process Skill Tip

In class you can't see how real rock layers and fossils form. So **using a model** is helpful. It shows what the layers can tell you about the order in which the fossils were formed.

What Fossils Are

FIND OUT

- **how fossils form**
- **how fossils show that life on Earth has changed**

VOCABULARY

fossil

How Fossils Form

Some places are better for fossil hunting than others. Sedimentary rocks usually have more fossils than other kinds of rocks. That's because what's left of a plant or animal is sometimes trapped in the sediments that form the layers of the rock. The heat and pressure that form metamorphic and igneous rocks often destroy fossils.

Every **fossil** is something that has lasted from a living thing that died long ago. But there are different types of fossils. Some are body parts, such as bones or teeth, that have turned into stone. Other fossils are only marks, such as animal tracks.

The fossils of the shells in the picture on C21 show two ways fossils can form. The fossil shell on the top is a mold. You made a mold in the investigation.

Fossils often form in sedimentary rocks, such as limestone and shale.

1 The soft parts of an animal rot away.

2 Bones are slowly buried under layers of sediment.

A *mold* is the shape of a plant or animal left in sediments when the rock formed. The shell that made the mold in the picture dissolved.

The other fossil shell is a cast. A *cast* forms when mud or minerals fill a mold. The cast has the exact shape of the animal that made the mold.

Look at the fossil fern leaf. Fossil *imprints* are molds of leaves or other thin objects. Some imprints are of animal parts such as wings or feathers. The leaves or animal parts rotted away long ago.

✔ **What are fossils?**

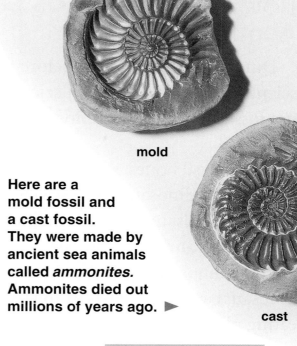

mold

Here are a mold fossil and a cast fossil. They were made by ancient sea animals called *ammonites.* Ammonites died out millions of years ago. ▶

cast

▲ This is a fossil imprint of a dragonfly.

Plant fossils are much less common than animal fossils. This is because plant parts are more easily destroyed as rocks form. ▶

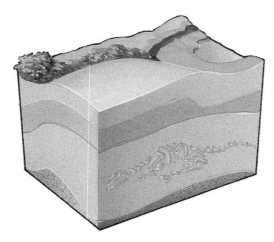

3 Over a long time, the sediment turns into rock.

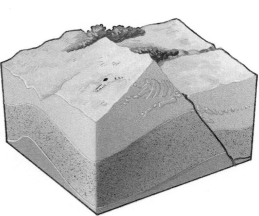

4 Movement of the Earth's crust brings the rock and fossils closer to the surface. Wind and rain wear away the rock on top of the fossils.

How Fossils Help Us Learn About Dinosaurs

Dinosaurs died out long before there were any scientists to study them. But scientists today can use fossils to learn how dinosaurs looked and how they lived.

Using fossil bones, scientists can put together skeletons of dinosaurs. The skeletons show how large the dinosaur was and whether it walked on two legs or four.

Fossil dinosaur teeth show the kinds of foods dinosaurs ate. The shapes of the teeth are suited to eating plants or other animals. Some dinosaurs ate other dinosaurs. How do we know that?

▲ This dinosaur fossil was recently discovered. Look at its teeth and you will see that it ate other animals.

This paleontologist (a scientist who studies fossils) is digging up fossil dinosaur bones. ▼

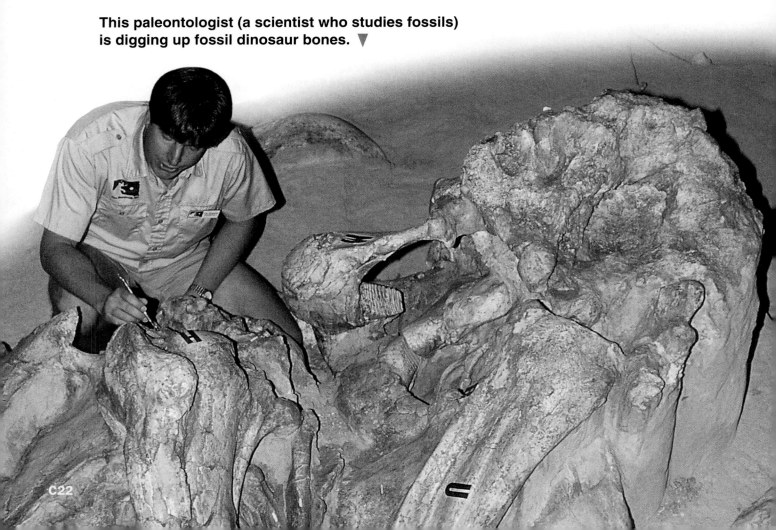

Scientists have found fossil dinosaur bones with the teeth of other dinosaurs broken off in them!

New dinosaur fossils are being discovered all the time. Each new discovery increases what we know about dinosaurs.

✓ **How do scientists learn about dinosaurs?**

Summary

A fossil is something that has lasted from a living thing that died long ago. Fossils are found mostly in sedimentary rocks. Scientists can use fossils to understand how dinosaurs looked and lived.

Review

1. Why are most fossils found in sedimentary rocks?
2. Name two types of fossils, and tell how they formed.
3. What dinosaur fossils have scientists used to learn how dinosaurs looked?
4. **Critical Thinking** Would you find fossils in igneous rock? Why?
5. **Test Prep** Which of the following rocks would be most likely to have a fossil in it?

   A granite
   B limestone
   C marble
   D quartz

LINKS

MATH LINK

How Big? Find the sizes of the largest and smallest dinosaurs. Make a model to show the difference in their sizes. Subtract to find the difference in their sizes.

WRITING LINK

Write to Describe Choose a type of dinosaur, and make a card that describes it. At the top of the card, draw the dinosaur. Then write information about it under your drawing. Share your card with your classmates.

LITERATURE LINK

Would you like to know more about fossils? Read *Dinosaurs Walked Here* by Patricia Lauber. Choose a fossil described in the book. Then make a model showing how the fossil formed.

TECHNOLOGY LINK

Learn more about finding dinosaur fossils by watching *Dinosaur Discovery* on the **Harcourt Science Newsroom Video.**

DISCOVERING Dinosaurs

As early as the third century, people in China wrote about dragon teeth and dragon bones. But what those people described weren't dragons. They were dinosaurs.

Dinosaur Discoveries

No one knew what dinosaur fossils were before the 1800s. One early scientist thought the giant thighbone he had found was from a giant human. In 1824 William Buckland gave the name Megalosaurus ("great lizard") to the animal whose jaw and teeth he had been studying. The next year, Mary Ann Mantell found a large tooth partly buried in a rock in England. She didn't know what it was. Her husband, Gideon Mantell, was a doctor who collected fossils. He thought the tooth came from a large reptile like an iguana. So he called it Iguanodon, which means "iguana tooth."

During the next few years, many remains were found. In 1842 Richard Owen, an English scientist, gave the name Dinosauria to the whole group of fossil remains. Dinosaur means "terrible lizard."

The first dinosaur craze was in the 1850s in England. There was an exhibit at the Crystal Palace in

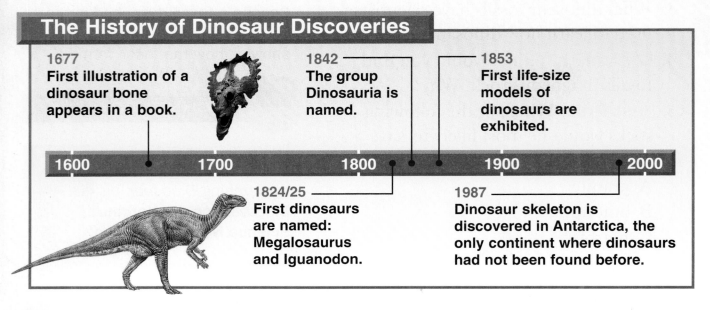

The History of Dinosaur Discoveries

1677
First illustration of a dinosaur bone appears in a book.

1842
The group Dinosauria is named.

1853
First life-size models of dinosaurs are exhibited.

1600   1700   1800   1900   2000

1824/25
First dinosaurs are named: Megalosaurus and Iguanodon.

1987
Dinosaur skeleton is discovered in Antarctica, the only continent where dinosaurs had not been found before.

London in 1853. Sir Richard Owen and Waterhouse Hawkins, an artist, made some life-size dinosaur models. The models have errors, but they are still on view at the Crystal Palace Park.

Studying Dinosaur Fossils

Dinosaur fossils have been found on every continent. The largest numbers of sites are in the United States and Europe. At a fossil site, or dig, scientists use chisels to carefully free the fossils from the surrounding rock. Each fossil is cleaned and carefully packed in a plaster or foam jacket. Detailed notes are taken about where the bones were found.

The bones are then taken to a laboratory to be analyzed. Scientists try to determine how the bones may have fit together. This job is easier if the muscles have left marks, called muscle scars, where they were attached to the bones. A scientific artist sketches the bones and muscles, and adds skin. Drawing the skin is mostly guesswork. No one knows for sure whether dinosaurs had stripes or spots, or what color their skin was.

Interesting Dinosaurs

Dinosaurs began to appear in books during the mid 1800s. Today, some museums feature exhibits of dinosaurs. Dinosaur robots that move and make noises are made of steel and latex. They are shown throughout the world at theme parks and museums.

Think About It

- Why do you think people in China thought dinosaur bones were from dragons?

Dinosaur Model

Charles Langmuir

PETROLOGIST, GEOCHEMIST

"I had no idea of the excitement of sea-going science."

Charles Langmuir says that when he was a boy, his father played at science with him. They made musical instruments together and changed the tone of a flute by blowing carbon dioxide through it instead of air. They made a model of a diver in a bottle. They watched dry ice evaporate and grew crystals. All this play taught Langmuir that science was a combination of fun, amazement, and careful observation. Although his mother didn't play at science with him, Langmuir says she taught him other things. She taught him that exploration never stops, that limits don't matter, and that a sense of humor is important.

These lessons led Langmuir to the study of geology and petrology, the study of rocks. Langmuir began studying ocean rocks while in graduate school. Most of the rocks he studies are basalts, a type of igneous rock. Studying the ocean leads to greater knowledge about Earth's land. Learning about Earth's land gives more information about the ocean.

Langmuir thinks of the ocean floor as a wonderful frontier. He finds it exciting to be working with the two-thirds of Earth's surface that is underwater.

Think About It

1. What kinds of things would you expect to find on the ocean floor?
2. What school subjects do you "play at" outside school?

Atlantic Coast

Mid-Atlantic Ridge

Growing Crystals

How do salt crystals grow?

Materials
- salt
- hand lens
- hot tap water
- small jar
- plastic spoon
- small nail
- cotton string
- pencil

Procedure

1. Observe the salt with the hand lens. Record what you see.

2. **CAUTION** Be careful with hot water. Fill your jar with hot water. Add salt one spoonful at a time. Stir. Keep adding salt until no more will dissolve.

3. Set up the jar as shown. The nail should not touch the jar.

4. Leave the jar for five days. Then describe what you see on the nail and string.

Draw Conclusions

Observe this material with the hand lens. Compare it with the salt crystals you examined in Step 1.

Minerals in Sand

What minerals are found in sand?

Materials
- sand
- sheet of paper
- hand lens
- toothpick
- mineral descriptions

Procedure

1. Spread the sand on a sheet of paper.

2. Observe the colors and shapes of the sand grains with the hand lens. Each type of mineral grain has a different color and shape.

3. Use the toothpick to move the grains of each mineral into a separate pile.

Draw Conclusions

Identify the minerals. Use the descriptions your teacher gives you. Which mineral is the most common?

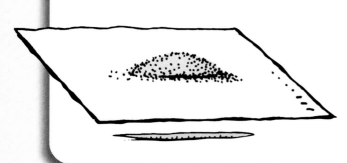

Chapter 1 Review and Test Preparation

Vocabulary Review

Use the terms below to complete the sentences 1 through 10. The page numbers in ( ) tell you where to look in the chapter if you need help.

mineral (C6)

rock (C8)

crust (C8)

mantle (C8)

core (C8)

igneous rock (C12)

sedimentary rock (C12)

metamorphic rock (C12)

rock cycle (C14)

fossil (C20)

1. A ____ is something that has lasted from a living thing that died long ago.

2. Rock that has been changed by heat and pressure in the Earth is ____.

3. The ____ is the rock layer at the center of the Earth.

4. A solid material made of minerals is a ____.

5. A ____ is a solid natural material found in the Earth.

6. Rock that forms from layers of sediment is ____.

7. The ____ is Earth's middle layer of soft rock.

8. One type of rock turns into another type as rocks move through the ____.

9. The ____ is Earth's outer layer.

10. Melted rock that has cooled is ____.

Connect Concepts

Write the terms where they belong in the concept map.

minerals   **sedimentary**

igneous   **metamorphic**

melted rock that cools and hardens

layers of sediment and plant and animal remains

rock that has been changed by heat and pressure inside the Earth

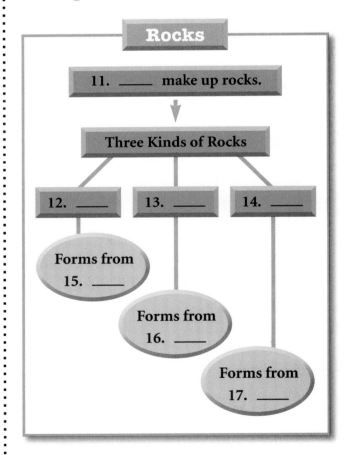

Rocks

11. ____ make up rocks.

Three Kinds of Rocks

12. ____   13. ____   14. ____

Forms from 15. ____

Forms from 16. ____

Forms from 17. ____

Check Understanding

Write the letter of the best choice.

18. A rock is made of —
    A only living things
    B one or more minerals
    C only two minerals
    D minerals that are hard

19. Heat helps form —
    F igneous and metamorphic rocks
    G sedimentary and metamorphic rocks
    H only igneous rocks
    J only metamorphic rocks

20. Fossils often last in sedimentary rocks because the rocks —
    A are very hot
    B are often near animals
    C have layers that save animal and plant shapes
    D don't ever change

21. A _____ mineral will scratch a _____ mineral.
    F rare, common   H hard, soft
    G soft, hard   J small, big

22. As you go deeper into Earth, —
    A the pressure increases and it gets hotter
    B the rocks get smaller
    C it gets cold
    D the pressure decreases and the rocks get smaller

Critical Thinking

23. Why are fossils not often found in igneous rocks?

24. You find a mineral sample. You think it may be calcite or quartz. How could you decide which mineral your sample is?

Process Skills Review

25. What tools are useful in putting minerals in **order** by hardness?

26. You want to **compare** three unknown rocks with three known rocks. What properties would you use?

27. How can you **make a model** of the way sedimentary rocks form?

Performance Assessment

Changing Rocks

Choose a type of rock. Tell how it could move through the rock cycle by changing into different types of rocks. Draw a picture showing the stages your rock could go through.

Chapter

2

Forces That Shape the Land

Over millions of years, a river wears away layer after layer of rock to form a canyon. Wind picks up sand and drops it in another place, forming a dune. Fast or slow, the land is always changing.

Vocabulary Preview

mountain	weathering
landform	erosion
valley	glacier
canyon	earthquake
plain	volcano
plateau	flood
barrier island	

FAST FACT

There are many reasons why desert people move from place to place. One is that the sand surface they live on changes. As the wind blows the sand, dunes can move forward between 10 and 50 meters (33 to 164 ft) a year. Sand dunes have even been known to cover small villages.

Death Valley, California

The West Chop Lighthouse on Martha's Vineyard has had to be moved three times since 1817 to keep it from falling off the cliff! Every year the water wears away more of the rocky cliff it stands on.

Earthquakes can be destructive, but they can also make new landforms. In 1811 and 1822, three earthquakes centered in Missouri destroyed the town of New Madrid. But they also formed Lake Saint Francis in Arkansas.

Midwest Earthquakes

Damage to Homes	About How Often It Happens
Few repairs	every year
Many repairs	every 11 years
Heavy structural damage	every 80 years
Most buildings heavily damaged	every 377 years
Total destruction of buildings	every 875 years

LESSON 1

What Are Landforms?

In this lesson, you can . . .

INVESTIGATE how mountains form.

LEARN ABOUT landforms.

LINK to math, writing, physical education, and technology.

Folds in Earth's Crust

Activity Purpose Scientists know that some mountains are formed by folds in Earth's surface. But how can the surface of Earth fold? In this investigation you will **use a model** to find out.

Materials
- 4 paper towels
- plastic cup
- water

Activity Procedure

1 Stack the four paper towels on a table. Fold the stack in half.

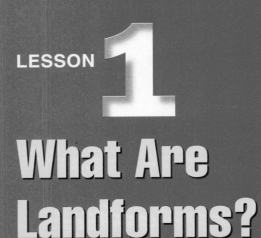

◀ **This rock, called Devil's Tower, was once lava inside a volcano. Wind and rain have worn away the volcano that was around it.**

2 Sprinkle water on the towels. They should be damp but not very wet.

3 Place your hands on the edges of the damp towels.

4 Push the edges slowly toward the center. (Picture A)

Picture A

Draw Conclusions

1. What happened as you pushed the edges of the towels together?

2. How did the height of the towels change as you pushed them?

3. **Scientists at Work** Scientists **use models** to understand how things happen. How did this model help you understand how mountains form?

Investigate Further Some mountains, such as the Rocky Mountains shown below, form when two separate pieces of Earth's crust push together. How would you **make a model** to show this process?

Process Skill Tip

You cannot see real mountains form. The process takes thousands of years. But you can **use a model** to find out about something that happens very slowly.

Earth's Surface

FIND OUT

- what forces change Earth's surface
- the way some landforms look

VOCABULARY

landform
mountain
valley
canyon
plain
plateau
barrier island

The Shape of the Surface

Earth's surface has many natural shapes, or features, called **landforms**. The landforms you've seen or know about are on dry land. But there are also interesting landforms under the oceans!

Look at the diagrams below. You can see that the crust is thicker under the dry land than it is under the oceans. You can also see places where the crust rises above the water to form land.

✔ **What are landforms?**

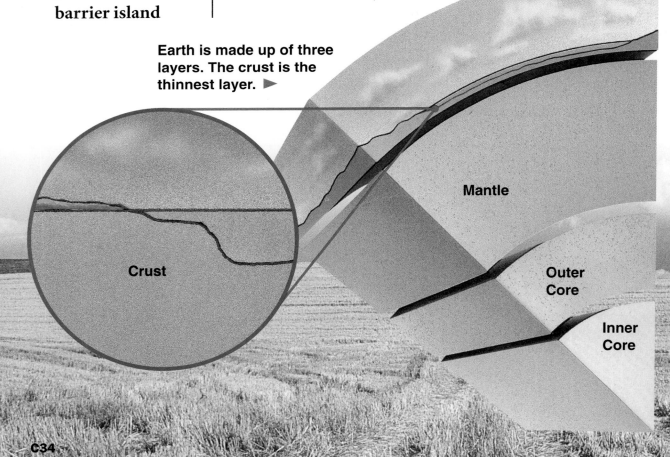

Earth is made up of three layers. The crust is the thinnest layer. ▶

Crust

Mantle

Outer Core

Inner Core

Types of Landforms

In the investigation you saw how Earth's crust can fold to form mountains. A **mountain** is a place on Earth's surface that is much higher than the land around it.

Some parts of Earth's surface are low areas. A **valley** is a lowland area between higher lands such as mountains. A **canyon** is a deep valley with very steep sides.

A **plain** is a flat area on Earth's surface. The middle of the United States is a large plain. A **plateau** (pla•TOH) is a flat area higher than the land around it. In some places plateaus have steep sides. They look like tables made of rock.

You might see another kind of landform at the seashore. A **barrier island** (BAIR•ee•er EYE•luhnd) is a thin island near a coast. Barrier islands have wide, sandy beaches.

✔ **List and describe three landforms.**

▲ A valley is a lowland between higher areas. Rivers can wear away rock to form valleys.

▲ A mountain is at least 600 meters (about 2,000 ft) higher than the land around it. Some mountains are tall and rocky. Others are rounded and covered with trees.

A plain is a flat area on Earth's surface. The soil of some plains is good for growing crops. ▼

▲ Barrier islands can form when sand in moving water is dropped near the shore.

◀ The east coast of the United States has the longest chain of barrier islands in the world. They go from New York to Florida. In North Carolina, shown here, the islands (red) are called the Outer Banks.

A canyon can form where a river cuts a path through a plateau. The Grand Canyon is 1.6 kilometers (1 mi) deep. It took the Colorado River millions of years to cut the canyon in the Colorado Plateau. ▶

Summary

Landforms are the shapes, or features, found on Earth's surface. Landforms include mountains, valleys, canyons, plains, plateaus, and barrier islands.

Review

1. What is a landform?
2. What is a mountain?
3. How are plateaus and plains different?
4. **Critical Thinking** Compare a valley with a canyon. How could a valley become a canyon?
5. **Test Prep** Which landform is higher than the land around it?
   - **A** valley
   - **B** plateau
   - **C** plain
   - **D** canyon

 LINKS

 MATH LINK

Earth's Layers Earth's core is 3,486 kilometers from its center to its edge. The mantle is 2,885 kilometers thick. The crust is 30 to 40 kilometers thick in some areas. List the layers in order from thinnest to thickest.

 WRITING LINK

Informative Writing— Description What is the most unusual landform you've ever seen? What is special about it? Write a paragraph about the landform for your teacher. Explain what it looks like. Describe the land around it. Tell what you like best about it.

 PHYSICAL EDUCATION LINK

Climbing Mountains Mountain climbing is a popular sport. It can be fun, but it can be dangerous. Find out what equipment people need to climb a mountain safely.

 TECHNOLOGY LINK

Learn more about landforms by visiting this Internet Site.
www.scilinks.org/harcourt

 SCLINKS™
THE WORLD'S A CLICK AWAY

What Are Slow Landform Changes?

In this lesson, you can . . .

INVESTIGATE how sand wears away rock.

LEARN ABOUT weathering and erosion.

LINK to math, writing, literature, and technology.

◄ Wind has worn away parts of this rock. Now it looks like an elephant. As more rock wears away, the elephant will lose its "trunk."

INVESTIGATE

Sand at Work

Activity Purpose Wind picks up sand and blows it against rocks. This wears away the rock and changes its shape. In this investigation you will **interpret data** to learn how sand wears away rock.

Materials
- balance
- extra masses for the balance
- sandstone rocks
- sand
- glass jar with lid

Activity Procedure

1 Copy the table on page C39.

2 **Measure** the mass of all the rocks. **Record** your results in the table. (Picture A)

3 Fill the jar one-fourth full with sand. **Measure** the mass of the jar with the sand in it. **Record** your results. Add to get the total.

	Mass of Rocks	Mass of Jar and Sand	Total Mass of Rocks, Jar, and Sand
Before			
After			

4 Put the rocks into the jar. Put the lid on. Shake the jar for 30 minutes. Then put the jar aside. Shake the jar for 30 minutes every day for one week.

5 After one week, **measure** the mass of the jar and its contents. Then remove the rocks from the jar. **Measure** their mass. **Record** your results. Subtract to find the mass of the jar with the sand inside.

Picture A

Draw Conclusions

1. What did the sandstone look like before the shaking? What did the sand look like? Did they look different after the shaking? How?

2. **Compare** the masses before and after the shaking. How did the mass of the rocks change?

3. **Scientists at Work** Scientists **interpret data** to understand how things work. Use the data from this investigation to tell what happened to the sand and the rock. How is what happened like wind wearing away rock?

Process Skill Tip

When you **interpret data,** you look for patterns in recorded information. Then you use the patterns to **draw conclusions** about what happened.

Slow Changes to the Land

FIND OUT

- why landforms are always changing

- how wind, water, and ice change Earth's surface

VOCABULARY

weathering
erosion
glacier

How Rocks Are Broken Down

In the investigation you saw how sand smashes against rock, wears it down, and breaks it apart. This process is called weathering. **Weathering** (WETH•er•ing) is the way rocks are broken down into smaller pieces. Weathering is always changing the surface of Earth.

You have learned that Earth's crust is rock. But most of the land around you is covered with soil, sand, or pebbles. That's because of weathering. Very slowly, weathering acts on rocks. Bit by bit the rocks are worn away. After thousands of years, the solid rocks are broken down into soil.

◄ "Mushroom Rock" has this shape because the wind blows sand and soil around the bottom of the rock.

◄ This rock has not been weathered. You can tell because it has sharp edges.

Weathering is caused by more than the wind. Water also causes weathering. Even plants help break apart rocks on the surface of the Earth.

Water causes weathering when it freezes. Most things take up less space when they freeze. But frozen water takes up more space. Water flows into cracks and holes in rock. As the temperature drops, the water freezes. Since the ice takes up more space, it pushes against the rock around it. The force of the ice widens the cracks and breaks the rock into pieces.

Water also causes weathering when it is not frozen. The movement of water wears rock away. Also, rivers pick up rocks and bounce them around. This wears the rocks down.

Plants cause weathering, too. Roots grow into cracks in rock. As the roots get bigger, they split the rock.

✓ **What is weathering?**

▲ **Tree roots grow into cracks in rocks to reach minerals and water. As the roots grow, they split the rocks.**

▲ **Water breaks rock when it freezes in cracks. Water and ice are important causes of weathering.**

◄ **After weathering by water, a rock has rounded edges. These rocks tumbled in a river and smashed against other rocks. Their sharp edges were worn away.**

How Rock Pieces Move

After weathering breaks up rocks, erosion moves the pieces around. **Erosion** (ee•ROH•zhuhn) is the movement of weathered rock and soil. Sometimes erosion happens very fast. The waves of a big storm can tear the sand away from a beach in just a few hours. A big dust storm can quickly blow away tons of soil. But most erosion happens very slowly.

Creep is a type of slow erosion. *Creep* is the movement of soil down steep hills. Creep happens so slowly that you don't notice it. But you can see what creep does. Sometimes a fence that was straight becomes crooked over a long time. The crooked fence shows that there was creep.

Erosion can be caused by water. Rain washes soil from hills and fields. The soil flows with the rainwater into rivers. The flowing water in rivers

▲ Creep moves trees and bends fences and walls. It can also push roads out of line.

Satellite view of the Mississippi Delta ▼

carries soil downstream. The soil is dropped whenever the rivers slow down. Sometimes the soil is dropped along the banks. But soil can also be dropped at the mouth of a river to form a delta. A delta is a piece of land that forms at the mouth of a river. Deltas are often shaped like triangles.

Just like water, wind carries loose pieces of rock and sand from one place to another. The faster the wind blows, the more rock and sand it can carry. When wind slows down, it drops some of the sand it carries.

✔ What is erosion?

▲ Wind blows sand into large piles called dunes. Dunes form in deserts and along sandy coasts. The dunes in this picture are on the shore of Lake Michigan.

Erosion sometimes makes a delta by moving soil to the mouth of a river. The Mississippi River has one of the world's biggest deltas. It is larger than the states of New Jersey and Rhode Island combined. ▼

How Glaciers Change the Land

Erosion can also be caused by moving ice. **Glaciers** (GLAY•sherz) are huge sheets of ice. They form in places where it's so cold all year that the snow doesn't melt. Glaciers move downhill, but they move very slowly. Glaciers travel less than 30 centimeters (about 1 ft) each day.

Glaciers change the land as they slide over it. They scrape up rocks and soil and pile them up into hills. They scoop out rocks and soil to form huge holes. Sometimes these holes fill with water to become lakes.

Valley glaciers form near mountain peaks. They move slowly downhill like rivers of ice. As they move, they scoop out deep valleys.

Continental glaciers are sheets of ice that are much bigger than valley glaciers. They build up at the center of a continent.

✔ **What is a glacier?**

Glaciers (white) cover one-tenth of Earth's land surface. Most glaciers are valley glaciers. Continental glaciers, which are bigger, cover most of Greenland and Antarctica. ▼

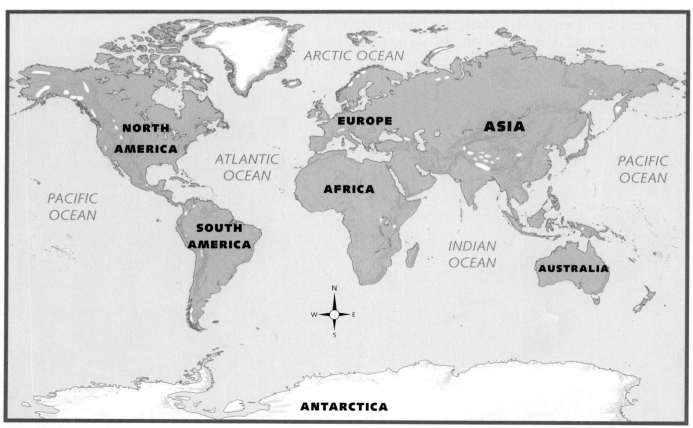

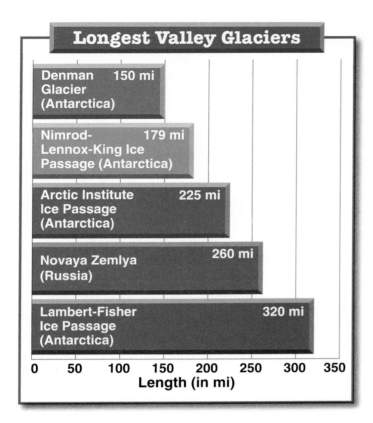

Longest Valley Glaciers

Glacier	Length (in mi)
Denman Glacier (Antarctica)	150 mi
Nimrod-Lennox-King Ice Passage (Antarctica)	179 mi
Arctic Institute Ice Passage (Antarctica)	225 mi
Novaya Zemlya (Russia)	260 mi
Lambert-Fisher Ice Passage (Antarctica)	320 mi

Length (in mi)

Summary

Weathering breaks the rock of Earth's crust into pieces. Erosion moves the broken rock and soil on Earth's surface. Wind, water, and glaciers shape the land by moving rock and soil.

Review

1. How can ice cause weathering?
2. How do plant roots break rock?
3. How do glaciers change Earth's surface?
4. **Critical Thinking** Why must weathering happen before erosion?
5. **Test Prep** Which causes erosion?

   A sand   **C** weathering

   B wind   **D** plant roots

 LINKS

 MATH LINK

Creep There is a straight fence on a steep hill. Creep moves the middle of the fence 5 centimeters per year. What will the fence look like in 1 year? In 10 years? How far will it have moved?

 WRITING LINK

Narrative Writing—Personal Story Thousands of years ago, a huge glacier covered most of the northern United States. Ice and snow always covered the ground. Suppose that you lived at that time. Write a story for your family that describes a day in your life.

 LITERATURE LINK

Find Out About Landslides Read about what causes erosion in *Landslides, Slumps, & Creep* by Peter H. Goodwin.

 TECHNOLOGY LINK

Visit the Harcourt Learning Site for related links, activities, and resources.
www.harcourtschool.com

What Are Rapid Landform Changes?

In this lesson, you can . . .

INVESTIGATE how volcanoes change the land around them.

LEARN ABOUT rapid changes in the land.

LINK to math, writing, social studies, and technology.

INVESTIGATE

A Model Volcano

Activity Purpose An erupting volcano sends out hot liquid rock and ash. An eruption quickly changes the look and shape of the land around the volcano. In this investigation you will **make a model** to see how a volcano can change the land around it.

Materials

- large tray
- wax paper
- tall, thin plastic jar
- safety goggles
- lab apron
- measuring spoons
- flour
- baking soda
- measuring cup
- red, green, and blue food coloring
- soil
- water
- white vinegar

Activity Procedure

CAUTION

1. Cover the tray with wax paper. Place the jar in the middle of the tray.

2. **CAUTION** **Put on safety goggles and a lab apron.** Mix $\frac{1}{2}$ teaspoon flour and 1 teaspoon baking soda in a measuring cup. Put this mixture into the jar. Add 10 drops of red food coloring.

◀ Red-hot lava escapes from deep in the Earth through volcanoes.

3 Moisten the soil slightly. Put the soil around the jar. Then mold the soil into the shape of a volcano. The top of the jar must be even with the top of the soil. (Picture A)

4 Slowly pour $\frac{1}{4}$ cup white vinegar into the jar. (Picture B)

5 **Observe** what happens. Remove the jar and throw away the contents. Replace the jar. Then wait 15 minutes for the "lava" to dry.

6 Repeat steps 2, 4, and 5 with the green food coloring and then with the blue food coloring.

Picture A

Picture B

Draw Conclusions

1. What happened when you poured the vinegar into the mixture in the jar?

2. What did the material that came out of your volcano stand for?

3. **Scientists at Work** Scientists **make a model** to understand how things happen in nature that are difficult to **observe** in person. How did your model help you understand the way an erupting volcano changes the land around it?

Investigate Further Different kinds of volcanoes have different kinds of eruptions. How could you find out what these eruptions are like? Choose one type of eruption, and **plan and conduct an investigation** to model it.

Process Skill Tip

An erupting volcano is dangerous. When you **make a model** of an eruption, you can **observe** the process without taking a risk.

Rapid Changes to the Land

FIND OUT

- how earthquakes and volcanoes change the land
- how floods change the land

VOCABULARY

earthquake
volcano
flood

Earthquakes

Earth's crust and mantle are made up of many pieces that fit together like pieces of a puzzle. These pieces move around in different ways. They push into each other. They pull away from each other. They slide past each other. Sometimes their movements cause earthquakes. An **earthquake** is the shaking of Earth's surface caused by movement of the crust and mantle.

Most earthquakes are too small to feel. But each year about 200 earthquakes cause great damage. Very big earthquakes can leave cracks and uneven areas in Earth's surface. They can destroy cities and move rivers. Earthquakes under the sea can cause huge waves that flood coastlines.

✔ What is an earthquake?

The San Andreas fault (left) is a crack in Earth's crust in California. A *fault* is a place where two pieces of Earth's crust are slowly sliding past each other. Sometimes the pieces of crust get stuck. Then they suddenly break free and move again. That's when the ground around the fault shakes. Earthquakes can destroy buildings and roads.

C48

Volcanoes

A **volcano** is an opening in Earth's surface from which lava flows. Lava and ash build up around the opening to form a mountain.

You saw in the investigation that an erupting volcano can quickly change the land around it. The eruption can blow off mountaintops. It can cover the land with ash and liquid rock called *lava*. It can also send out hot clouds of ash, rock, and gases. The heat can burn nearby forests and buildings.

✔ **What is a volcano?**

▲ A volcano erupted on Montserrat in 1997. It destroyed Plymouth, the island's capital city. It set trees on fire and left ash on most of the island. Thousands of people had to leave their homes.

Floods

You have already read that water can cause slow changes on Earth's surface. Sometimes water can change Earth's surface quickly. Big storms dump heavy rain on the land. Then the rainwater runs into rivers. If the rivers can't hold all the water, they overflow their banks and cause a flood. A **flood** is a large amount of water that covers normally dry land.

Flood water flows into cities, towns, and farms near the rivers. Floods damage buildings, roads, and soil.

When flood water goes down, it leaves soil and sand behind. Buildings that have been flooded are left full of mud. But the flood also leaves rich soil on fields. This soil is good for growing crops.

✔ **What can cause a flood?**

▲ Mudslides begin when heavy rains fill soil with too much water. Soil turns to mud and slides downhill. The mud can take houses and trees with it as it moves.

THE INSIDE STORY

How Floods Affect the Land

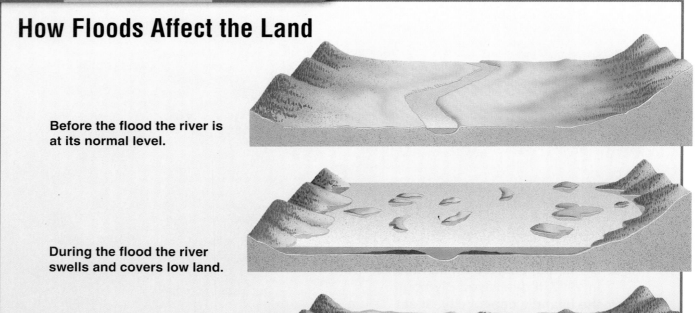

Before the flood the river is at its normal level.

During the flood the river swells and covers low land.

After the flood the river returns to its banks. It leaves behind much of the soil it was carrying.

Summary

Several kinds of events can change Earth's surface quickly. Earthquakes shake Earth's surface and destroy buildings. Erupting volcanoes spread lava, ash, or rock in large areas around them. Floods wash away soil and buildings and can cause mudslides. But flood water leaves a new layer of soil on the land.

Review

1. What causes earthquakes?
2. What is lava?
3. What damage can be caused by a flood?
4. **Critical Thinking** Can people protect the land from floods? Explain your answer.
5. **Test Prep** Which can cause rapid changes to the land?
   - **A** volcano
   - **B** glacier
   - **C** wind
   - **D** weathering

LINKS

MATH LINK

Largest Earthquakes Look up earthquakes in an encyclopedia or almanac. Make a list of earthquakes that have happened during the past 40 years in the United States. Make a bar graph that shows the four strongest.

WRITING LINK

Informative Writing—Narration What would it be like to live in an area where there could be an earthquake? Write a story for your classmates that describes what you might see, hear, and feel.

SOCIAL STUDIES LINK

Report the News Research the eruption of a famous volcano. Write a news report about the event.

TECHNOLOGY LINK

To learn about how people can make buildings safer during an earthquake, watch the video *Earthquake Springs* on the **Harcourt Science Newsroom Video.**

CNN
Turner
Le@rning

Earthquake-Proof Buildings

Transamerica Building

Earthquakes are hard to predict. People now know where they are likely to happen, but they still don't know when. In fact, only two major earthquakes have ever been correctly predicted.

Technology Helps

Most damage, deaths, and injuries from earthquakes happen when buildings fall down. Scientists and engineers are working together to learn how to build buildings that won't fall down during earthquakes. In the 1940s researchers began putting recording instruments in buildings. During earthquakes, these instruments record the movement of the buildings they are in. When there is an earthquake, scientists gather information from these instruments. The information helps them design better buildings.

New Designs for Buildings

Using the information from these instruments, engineers began to design buildings that move with the shaking of an earthquake. They designed skyscrapers to sway during a quake. Some of these buildings may crack, but they won't fall apart and crush the people inside.

During an earthquake in California in 1989, the 48-story Transamerica Building in San Francisco shook for more than a minute. It swayed more than a foot from side to side. But the building had been *designed* to move during an earthquake. It didn't fall down.

Engineers are also designing low-rise buildings that sit on rubber pads. Just as your thick-soled sports shoes protect your feet when you jump or run, these rubber pads protect buildings against the shock waves of an earthquake.

Computer Modeling

Scientists also use computers to model what happens to buildings in an earthquake. Using the computer, they can make models of small earthquakes and of big earthquakes. Each time, they watch how the computer earthquakes affect the building. Computer models give scientists information much faster than the instruments placed in buildings waiting for real earthquakes to happen.

Think About It

- Even though scientists have computer models, they still use instruments to measure movement in buildings during real earthquakes. Why do you think they do this?

WEB LINK:
For Science and Technology updates, visit the Harcourt Internet site.
www.harcourtschool.com

| Careers | Construction Worker |

What They Do Construction workers build new buildings or fix older ones. They often work outside in all kinds of weather.

Education and Training Often a construction worker trains with a master craftsperson, such as a carpenter or a plumber. College classes in engineering and mathematics help construction workers understand plans, electrical system drawings, and blueprints.

Scott Rowland

VOLCANOLOGIST

Scott Rowland studies lava flows from volcanoes. He studied and now teaches at the University of Hawai'i. He also travels to such places as Mexico, Guatemala, and the Galápagos Islands to study volcanoes.

People who study volcanoes look at the nature and causes of eruptions. They set up observatories on the rims or slopes of volcanoes to learn more about the volcanoes. Their work can save many lives. When they know a volcano is about to erupt, they can warn people to leave the area.

There are six types of volcanoes. They are classified by the kind of material that comes out of the volcano and by the violence of the eruption. Most eruptions in Hawai'i are not very violent. The lava usually flows quietly out of vents in Earth's surface.

Volcanoes in Hawai'i have a built-in warning system. Many small earthquakes occur as magma collects and rises inside the volcano. As the magma collects, the outside of the volcano expands slightly. This expansion can be detected with sensitive scientific instruments.

Think About It

1. What would cause the outside of a volcano to expand before it erupts?
2. What is the advantage of an early warning that a volcano is about to erupt?

Shake the Earth

What are some effects of earthquakes?

Materials

- baking pan filled with gelatin
- plastic wrap
- large croutons

Procedure

1. Cover the top of the gelatin with plastic wrap.

2. Use croutons to make buildings on top of the gelatin.

3. Move the pan up and down. Then move the pan from side to side. Then tap one end of the pan as you move it. Observe the movement of the gelatin.

Draw Conclusions

Did the movement damage your buildings? **Record** your observations. How is this model like an earthquake?

Weathering

Can chemicals in water wear away rock?

Materials

- 6 small glass jars without labels
- wax pencil
- 3 types of rock chips (limestone, sandstone, quartzite)
- water
- white vinegar

Procedure

1. Label two jars *limestone*. Write *sandstone* on two jars. Write *quartzite* on the last two jars.

2. Put a few rock chips in each jar. Make sure the chips match the jar's label.

3. Fill one jar of each pair with water. Fill the other jar with vinegar.

4. Observe what happens. Wait 30 minutes, and observe again. Let the jars sit overnight. Then, observe them again.

Draw Conclusions

How did the vinegar and the water affect the rocks?

Chapter ② Review and Test Preparation

Vocabulary Review

Use the terms below to complete the sentences 1 through 13. The page numbers in ( ) tell you where to look in the chapter if you need help.

landform (C34)   **weathering** (C40)
mountain (C35)   **erosion** (C42)
valley (C35)   **glacier** (C44)
canyon (C35)   **earthquake** (C48)
plain (C35)   **volcano** (C49)
plateau (C35)   **flood** (C50)
barrier island (C35)

1. A flat area on Earth's surface is a ___.

2. ___ breaks down rock into smaller pieces.

3. A lowland between higher lands such as mountains is a ___.

4. A ___ is a flat area higher than the land around it.

5. A place on Earth's surface that is much higher than the land around it is a ___ .

6. A ___ occurs when water covers an area of land that is normally dry.

7. The movement of weathered rock by wind, water, or ice is called ___.

8. A ___ is an opening in Earth's surface, from which lava may flow.

9. A ___ is any feature on Earth's surface.

10. An ___ is the shaking of Earth's surface, caused by movement in the crust and mantle.

11. A deep valley with steep sides is a ___.

12. A ___ is a large sheet of ice that moves slowly downhill.

13. A ___ is a thin, sandy island that forms near a coast.

Connect Concepts

Write the terms that complete the concept map.

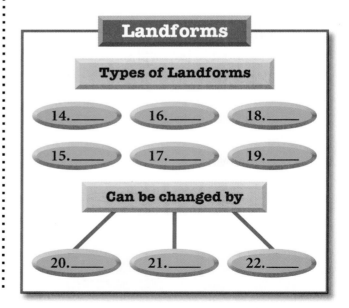

Landforms

Types of Landforms

14. ___   16. ___   18. ___

15. ___   17. ___   19. ___

Can be changed by

20. ___   21. ___   22. ___

Check Understanding

Write the letter of the best choice.

23. Rivers can cut through land to form —

   A canyons   **C** mountains

   B plains   **D** crust

24. An example of erosion is —

   F plant roots growing

   G water freezing in cracks

   H water moving soil

   J ice that does not move

25. Creep causes —

   A dust storms   **C** mudslides

   B bent fences   **D** floods

26. Volcanoes can form —

   F mountains **H** barrier islands

   G plains   **J** canyons

27. Mountains can form —

   A when Earth's crust folds

   B when rivers cut through plateaus

   C when soil is smashed against rock

   D on barrier islands

Critical Thinking

28. Will Earth's landforms look the same 1,000 years from now? Explain your answer.

29. Would Earth's surface be different without weathering and erosion? Explain your answer.

30. How could it help people if we could predict earthquakes?

31. Why do some farmers plant crops next to rivers?

Process Skills Review

32. How could you **make a model** to show erosion caused by a glacier?

33. How could you **interpret data** to find how high the water got during a flood? What data would you need?

Performance Assessment

Changing Landforms

Draw a picture of a landform discussed in the chapter. Under your picture, write sentences about the landform. Tell how it formed and how it might change.

Soils

Soil covers almost all of Earth's land.
We walk on it. We put buildings on it.
We grow plants in it. We couldn't live
without it!

Vocabulary Preview

soil	resource
humus	conservation
topsoil	strip cropping
clay	contour plowing
loam	

FAST FACT

Animals use soil too. Pigs
need soil more than many
animals. Because pigs can't
sweat, they roll around in
mud to keep cool.

You dig a hole. Worms crawl away. Tiny bugs scatter. What else lives in soil? If you could take a cross section of soil and remove 1000 grams of the living things, here's what you'd find:

Mass of Living Things in Soil

Plant Roots 660 g

Bacteria 171 g

Other Stuff 28 g

Fungi 131 g

Insects 3 g

Earthworms 7 g

Earth isn't the only planet with soil. Mars has soil also. The soil is red — that's why Mars looks red when we view it from Earth.

How Do Soils Form?

In this lesson, you can . . .

INVESTIGATE how soils form.

LEARN ABOUT what is in soil.

LINK to math, writing, technology, and other areas.

INVESTIGATE

Enrich the Soil

Activity Purpose There are many kinds of soils. Some are better for growing plants than others. In this investigation you will look at a way of changing soil. Then you will predict how this change will affect plant growth.

Materials

- 1-L wide-mouthed plastic jar
- measuring cup
- 2 cups of soil with humus mixed in
- teaspoon
- water
- apple peels
- banana slices
- $\frac{1}{4}$ cup dry unsweetened cereal
- plastic wrap
- rubber band
- pencil

Activity Procedure

1 Put one cup of soil into the jar. Sprinkle two teaspoons of water on top of the soil.

◀ Compost is a mixture of material from once-living things. People use food scraps and yard clippings to make compost. Then they add it to the soil to make plants grow better.

2 Spread the fruit and cereal on top of the soil. The apple peels and banana slices must touch the sides of the jar. (Picture A)

3 Put another cup of soil on top of the fruit and cereal. You should see pieces of fruit and cereal through the sides of the jar.

Picture A

4 Cover the jar with plastic wrap. Put a rubber band around the jar to hold the plastic wrap. Use a pencil point to make three small holes in the plastic wrap.

5 Leave the jar in a warm place, but do not put it in direct sunlight. Keep the jar there for four weeks.

6 Look at the jar once each week for four weeks. **Record** what you **observe.**

Draw Conclusions

1. What changes did you **observe** in the jar after one week? After four weeks?

2. **Predict** what would happen to the soil after eight weeks. Would the material in the jar look different? Explain.

3. **Scientists at Work** Scientists use their observations to **predict** what will happen in the future. How did you use observations to predict what would happen to the soil?

Investigate Further **Plan and conduct an investigation** to find out if your soil with compost is better than plain soil for growing plants.

Process Skill Tip

When you **predict,** you say what you think will happen in the future. To make a prediction, you use what you know. Some of what you know comes from your observations.

How Soils Form

FIND OUT

- where soil comes from
- why soil is important

VOCABULARY

soil
humus
topsoil

What Soil Is

In the investigation you learned that decayed food scraps can become part of soil. Other things are part of soil, too. **Soil** is the loose material in which plants can grow in the upper layer of Earth.

Soil is a mixture of four different materials. Weathered rock is one part of soil. The bits of weathered rock contain minerals. These minerals make up most of soil. Soil also contains humus. **Humus** (HYOO•muhs) is the part of soil made up of decayed parts of once-living things. The compost and soil you worked with in the investigation could have become humus after more time. Humus is dark and soft. It contains much of what plants need for growth.

Between the bits of rock and humus are spaces. Air and water fill up the spaces. So soil also contains air and water.

Soil takes a long time to form. It takes 500 to 1,000 years to make 2.5 centimeters (1 in.) of soil. Deep soil takes thousands of years to form.

✔ **Name the four parts of soil.**

1 Soil forms in layers. Topsoil is the top layer. It is made up of the smallest grains. It also has the most humus, making it the richest layer of soil.

2 Subsoil is the layer under topsoil. It has larger grains and less humus than topsoil.

3 Bedrock is the solid rock under soil. Weathering breaks down bedrock into soil. Bedrock is made of different minerals in different places. So different soils contain different minerals.

Life in Soil

Moles dig tunnels and make their homes underground. They may build small nests made of grass and twigs in the tunnels. Moles eat tiny worms and insects that live in the soil.

1 Pill bugs live in soil. They can roll into balls to protect themselves.

2 Ants build their homes underground. An anthill you see above the ground is the entrance to the ant nest below.

3 Earthworms need dark, wet places to live. As they make tunnels in the soil, worms use the soil for food.

Importance of Soil

You could not live without air or water. You also would have a hard time living without soil. That's because soil contains the minerals all living things need.

These minerals are found in Earth's crust. But plants and animals can't take minerals from solid rock. First, weathering has to break down Earth's crust into soil. Then, plants can grow in the soil. Through their roots, plants take the minerals from the soil. Plant-eating animals then get the minerals from the plants they eat. You get minerals from the plants and animals you eat, too.

✔ **Where do plants get the minerals they need?**

Summary

Soil is a mixture of weathered rock, humus, air, and water. Soil is important to all living things. It contains minerals and other things that plants and animals need for growth. Soil takes a long time to form, so we must take care of it.

Review

1. What is humus?
2. What is topsoil?
3. How do people get the minerals they need?
4. **Critical Thinking** What would soil be like without weathering?
5. **Test Prep** Which of these is **NOT** part of soil?
   - **A** humus
   - **B** minerals
   - **C** water
   - **D** weathering

LINKS

MATH LINK

Soil Formation How much time does it take to form 5 in. of new soil if it takes 500 years to form 1 in. of soil?

WRITING LINK

Persuasive Writing— Opinion Soil is an important material. Pretend you are selling soil. Write a radio or TV ad for adults that will get them to buy it.

SOCIAL STUDIES LINK

Crops What kinds of crops grow in the soil where you live? Which of the crops do you like to eat?

LITERATURE LINK

Explore Compost Take a close look at a compost pile. What lives there? Read *Compost Critters* by Bianca Lavies to find out.

TECHNOLOGY LINK

Visit the Harcourt Learning Site for related links, activities, and resources.

www.harcourtschool.com

How Do Soils Differ?

In this lesson, you can . . .

INVESTIGATE
different types of soil.

LEARN ABOUT
how soils differ.

LINK to math, writing, physical education, and technology.

INVESTIGATE

Types of Soil

Activity Purpose Soil has minerals, humus, air, and water in it. But different soils have different amounts of these things. In this investigation you will **observe** soils to see how they are different.

Materials

- 2 soil samples
- paper plates
- petri dish
- low-power microscope
- toothpick
- paper towel

Activity Procedure

1. Get two soil samples from your teacher.

2. Place a few grains of one sample in the petri dish. Put the dish under the microscope. (Picture A)

3. **Observe** the soil. Move the soil grains around with the toothpick. What do the grains look like? **Record** what you **observe.** Make a drawing of the grains.

◄ Many living things depend on soil. Without soil, there would be few plants. And without plants, most other living things could not survive.

Picture A

Picture B

4 Pick up some soil from the petri dish. Rub it between your fingers. How does it feel? **Record** what you **observe.** (Picture B)

5 Clean the petri dish with the paper towel. Repeat Steps 2 through 4 with the other soil sample.

Draw Conclusions

1. What senses did you use to **observe** the soil?

2. Describe your observations.

3. **Scientists at Work** Scientists **observe** to see how things are alike and how they are different. How were the soil samples alike? How were they different?

Investigate Further **Investigate** another way soils differ. How much water can different soils hold? Get two different types of soil from your teacher. Put each type into a separate jar. Now get two cups of water from your teacher. Pour one of the cups of water into each jar of soil. Which soil holds more water? How do you know?

Different Types of Soil

FIND OUT

- how soils are different
- what kinds of soils are good for plants

VOCABULARY

clay
loam

A Closer Look at Soil

In the investigation you observed two types of soil. But there are also many other types. They differ in color. They have different grain sizes. They contain different minerals. They hold different amounts of water.

Soil can be black, brown, gray, red, yellow, or white. The color of soil depends on what's in it. For instance, black soils have lots of humus. White soils often form from light rocks, such as limestone.

Clay has small grains. It holds water easily. This makes clay sticky. ▼

In the investigation you rubbed different types of soil between your fingers. You learned that not all soils feel the same. Some types, such as sand, have large grains. These types feel gritty. Other soils have small grains. **Clay** soil, for example, is made up of very small grains. When clay soil dries after a rain, it often forms hard clods. When the clods are broken up, they feel like powder.

Some soils hold water. Some soils do not. This difference is caused by the size of the spaces between the grains in the soil. Water drains out of sandy soils quickly. That's because sandy soils have large spaces between the grains. Clay soils have small spaces between the grains. Water becomes trapped there. This makes the clay soil wet and heavy and difficult for plant roots to grow through.

✔ **What is clay?**

Sand has large grains. It also has large spaces between the grains. This lets water leave it quickly. Sand has less humus than other soils. ▼

Loam has large and small grains. It also has lots of humus, which makes it dark and rich. Loam holds enough water for plants. But it also drains well. ▼

Soils Good for Growing Plants

Soil that is good for growing plants is called topsoil. It is the top layer of soil. It has the most humus. Some topsoil has the things that plants need for growth.

Good topsoils have the right mixture of minerals and humus. **Loam** is one type of topsoil. It is a rich soil with lots of humus. It has a lot of water and air for plants. Most farm soils are loam.

Other topsoils do not have all the things plants need. Dry clays are too hard. Wet clays are too soggy. Sand is too dry and does not have enough nutrients.

Farmers can change the soil to make it better for plants. One way they can do this is to add fertilizers to poor soils. *Fertilizers* are materials that are rich in the things that plants need for growth.

✔ **What is topsoil?**

▲ Potting soil has a lot of humus. Once some sand is added, it is good for growing plants indoors.

The circle graph shows a soil that is good for plants. For every 100 grams of soil, 45 grams are minerals. Humus makes up 5 grams of this soil. There are 25 grams each of water and air. ▶

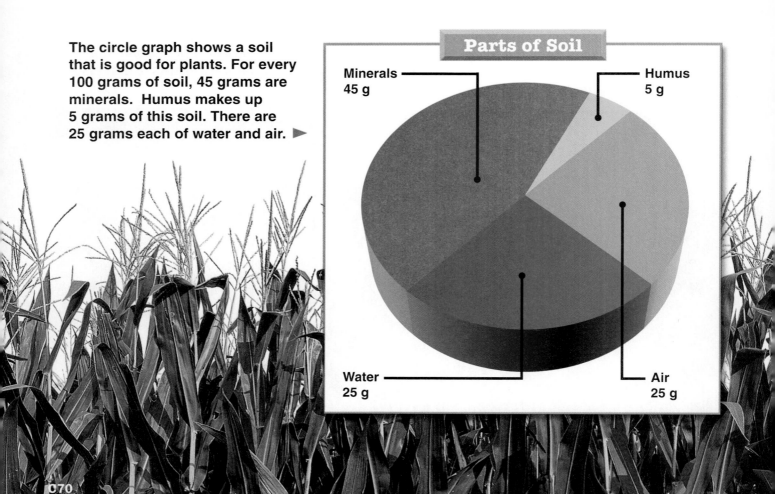

Parts of Soil

Minerals
45 g

Humus
5 g

Water
25 g

Air
25 g

Summary

There are many types of soil. Soils are made from different minerals. They have different colors and different-sized grains. Soils can hold different amounts of water. Soils that are best for plants have the right mixture of minerals and humus.

Review

1. Describe clay soil.
2. Describe loam soil.
3. Why do farmers add fertilizers to soil?
4. **Critical Thinking** Why is sand alone not good for plants?
5. **Test Prep** Which of these is a type of soil?
   A clay
   B limestone
   C fertilizer
   D bedrock

LINKS

 MATH LINK

Using Graphs Dig up a little soil. Observe the soil. Classify what you observe as plants, animals, or other. Use a computer graphing program such as **Graph Links** to make a bar graph that shows the numbers in each group.

 WRITING LINK

Persuasive Writing—Business Letter Write to your state Department of Agriculture. Ask for information, maps, and pictures of the types of soil in your state. Use the information to write a paragraph for your teacher that describes the soils.

 PHYSICAL EDUCATION LINK

Take a Hike Take a walk in your town with an adult family member. Collect soil from three places. Compare the soils.

 TECHNOLOGY LINK

Learn more about soils by visiting the Smithsonian Institution Internet Site.
www.si.edu/harcourt/science

 Smithsonian Institution®

LESSON **3**

How Can People Conserve Soil?

In this lesson, you can . . .

INVESTIGATE how soils can be saved.

LEARN ABOUT how farmers conserve soil.

LINK to math, writing, music, and technology.

Saving Soil

Activity Purpose It takes a very long time for new soil to form. So it is important to save the soil we have. In this investigation you will **observe** soil with and without plants. Then you will **infer** how plants help save soil.

Materials
- 2 baking pans
- soil
- piece of sod
- 2 wooden blocks
- large Styrofoam cup with holes in the bottom
- pitcher
- water

Activity Procedure

1 Put soil in both baking pans. Put sod over the soil in one pan.

◀ Contour plowing stops soil from washing down hills.

2 Set one end of each pan on a wooden block. One end of each pan should be lower than the other.

3 **Predict** what will happen when water is dripped into each pan. **Record** your prediction.

4 **Make a model** of rain over the pan that has just soil. Have one person hold the cup over the upper end of the pan. Have another person pour water from the pitcher into the cup. (Picture A)

Picture A

5 **Observe** what happens in the pan. **Record** what you see.

6 Repeat Steps 4 and 5, using the pan that has sod.

Draw Conclusions

1. What did you **observe** in each pan? **Compare** your observations for the pans.

2. What caused the difference?

3. **Scientists at Work** Scientists use their **observations** to **infer** why things happen. Infer how you might keep soil from washing away in the rain.

Investigate Further **Plan and conduct an investigation** to show how different plants keep soil from eroding when it rains.

Process Skill Tip

When you **observe** something, you use your senses to record what happens. When you **infer,** you use your observations to **draw a conclusion.**

How Soil Can Be Saved

FIND OUT

- what harms soil
- how soil can be saved

VOCABULARY

resource
conservation
strip cropping
contour plowing

How Soil Can Be Harmed

In the investigation you learned that plants help keep soil from eroding. Saving our soil is important because soil is an important resource. A **resource** (REE•sawrs) is a material found in nature that living things use.

Water, air, trees, and minerals are resources. Soil is a resource, too. Soil is used to grow food.

Many things can harm soil. Even farming can do this. It may harm the soil if the same type of crop is planted for many years on the same land. The plants use up the minerals in the soil. Then the soil is too poor for growing more crops.

As you saw in the investigation, plants hold soil in place. Sometimes people cut down too many trees and other plants. Then water and wind carry away the soil.

✓ **What is a resource?**

◀ Wind blows away soil that is bare and dry. It takes thousands of years to replace the soil.

▲ Rain forests have many trees.

▲ Farmers cut them down to grow crops.

▲ But rain forests have thin, poor soil. Crops cannot grow in this soil for long. After the crops are harvested there are no plants to hold the soil in place. Heavy rain washes it away.

This is a pine forest in the western United States. ▼

People cut down pine trees to make paper and furniture. ▼

Then tree farmers plant more trees. A new forest can grow and will replace the trees that were cut down. ▼

Ways to Save the Soil

Farmers need good soil to grow crops. They practice conservation to save the soil. **Conservation** (kahn•ser•VAY•shuhn) is saving resources by using them carefully.

Some farmers use strip cropping to save soil. **Strip cropping** is planting strips of thick grass or clover between strips of crops. The thick mat of plants helps keep water in the soil. It also stops soil from washing away.

Some farmers use contour plowing. **Contour plowing** (KAHN•toor PLOW•ing) is planting rows of crops around the sides of hills instead of up and down. This keeps water from running off in straight lines, so the soil isn't washed away.

There are also other ways to save soil. In the fall after the harvest, many farmers turn over the soil in their fields. This is called *tilling.* Tilling leaves the soil loose until spring planting. This can add water and air to the soil. But it can also cause loss of soil. During the winter, wind and water can remove the loose soil. To save their soil, some farmers have stopped tilling.

✔ **What is conservation?**

▲ The farmer has not tilled this field. New crops grow through plants left from the past year.

The farmer used strip cropping on this field. Strip cropping can save soil. ▼

Summary

Growing the same type of crop on the same land for many years removes minerals. When people remove plants and trees, soil may be washed away. Farmers conserve soil by strip cropping, contour plowing, and other methods.

Review

1. How does planting the same crop every year in the same soil harm the soil?

2. How does taking away plants harm soil?

3. How can tilling harm soil?

4. **Critical Thinking** In the United States many pine trees are cut down to make paper. A whole forest could be cut down at once and replanted. Or part of it could be cut down at a time. Which would be better? Explain your answer.

5. **Test Prep** Which of these is a method that farmers can use to save soil?
   - **A** erosion
   - **B** strip cropping
   - **C** strip resourcing
   - **D** clear-cutting

LINKS

MATH LINK

Soil Erosion Suppose you are a farmer. You notice that there is less topsoil on your land every year. The first year you farmed there were 10 in. of topsoil. You are losing $\frac{1}{2}$ in. of topsoil every year. In how many years will no topsoil be left?

WRITING LINK

Narrative Writing—Story Suppose that all the trees and other plants on Earth were cut down. Then all the soil on Earth was worn away. Write a story for your classmates about a day on Earth without soil.

MUSIC LINK

On the Farm Do you know any songs about farms? Share them with the class. Bring a tape or CD, or sing the songs yourself.

TECHNOLOGY LINK

To learn more about farming, watch *Agripost* on the **Harcourt Science Newsroom Video**.

FARMING WITH GPS

Farmers have used strip cropping and contour plowing to conserve soil for many years. Now farmers are using a new technology called GPS to help them protect and conserve soil.

What Is GPS?

GPS stands for Global Positioning System. GPS is a tracking system that uses satellites and radio transmitters and receivers to help guide ships, trains, and soldiers on the ground. Now farmers are using GPS and computers to get more crops from their land and plan for better use of their fields.

How Does GPS Help?

The combine, shown below, is a machine used to harvest crops. This combine has a yield monitor and a radio receiver. As the combine moves through the corn and cuts it, the monitor keeps track of how much corn is collected. The receiver uses

GPS to keep track of the exact location of the combine.

All this information is stored on a data card. At the end of the day, the farmer puts the card into a computer. The computer then makes color-coded maps that show the farmer the crop yield for each area. Then the farmer knows exactly how much corn each part of the field produced.

Farming with Computers

What the farmer learns from these maps is useful in many ways. This information can be used to calculate the right amounts of fertilizer, insecticide, herbicide, and water for each spot. Using the correct amounts will increase the amount of corn produced in the field. The amounts of fertilizer, insecticide, and herbicide used will probably decrease. Environmentalists hope that this new technology will reduce the waste water and chemicals that go into rivers and lakes.

By using GPS and other information systems, farmers can learn immediately where their fields need help. In the past, farmers had to wait 10 to 15 years to see results. They used trial and error to make their fields produce more crops. Now farmers can learn about problems, fix them, and see the results in the next harvest.

Think About It

1. How could GPS and crop monitors help farmers increase crop yields?
2. How could knowledge gained by using GPS change the price of a field?

WEB LINK:
For Science and Technology updates, visit the Harcourt Internet site.
www.harcourtschool.com

Careers Farmer

What They Do
Most farmers specialize in raising two or three crops that grow well in their region. The farmers of the United States produce 80 percent of all the food we use in this country.

Education and Training A farmer must have many skills. Many of today's farmers grew up on farms. Some of these farmers also get college degrees in agriculture. Farmers also need to know bookkeeping and the latest computer skills.

Diana Wall

ECOLOGIST

"My major professor . . . let me explore. He had the patience to let me try experiments that didn't work, so I could learn from the process."

While growing up near the Kentucky River, Diana Wall wondered about the effect of water on cliffs. This led her to a career in ecology. Wall studies the soils of many different ecosystems.

Some of her most interesting work has taken place in Antarctica, where she went to study roundworms that live in the soil. Soil roundworms are common garden pests. In warm climates there may be 60 or 70 kinds of roundworms in just a handful of soil. But there are only 6 kinds of roundworms in all of Antarctica. The roundworms of Antarctica survive the

harsh climate by freezing and thawing. No one knows how old any of the worms are, since they do not follow the life cycle of roundworms found in warmer climates. By studying the roundworms that live in the cold, Wall is helping solve the mysteries of their lives. She hopes that by understanding the roundworms of Antarctica, she can better understand what roundworms do in all ecosystems.

Think About It

1. How can doing experiments that don't work help a scientist get new information?
2. Why don't people know how old the roundworms in Antarctica are?

Soil and Plants

How does soil help plants grow?

Materials

- 4 plants of the same kind
- potting soil
- sand
- water
- measuring cup
- ruler

Procedure

1. Take the plants from their store pots. Dump out the soil. Rinse the roots.

2. Put each plant back into its empty pot. Put potting soil around two plants. Put sand around the other two plants. Water each plant with the same amount of water.

3. Put the plants in the same sunny place. Use the measuring cup to give the plants the same amount of water each day.

4. Observe the plants for 14 days. Measure their heights. Count the leaves.

Draw Conclusions

Which soil is best for growing the plants?

Food from Soil

Where do the foods you eat come from?

Materials

- outline map of the United States
- an encyclopedia
- crayons or colored pencils

Procedure

1. Get a map of the United States from your teacher.

2. Make a list of some of the foods you like to eat. Find out where these foods are grown. Look up the information in an encyclopedia.

3. Use the map to share your findings. Draw a picture of each food on your list. Glue each picture onto the map to show where the food is grown.

Draw Conclusions

Where do the foods you eat come from?

Chapter 3 Review and Test Preparation

Vocabulary Review

Use the terms below to complete the sentences 1 through 9. The page numbers in ( ) tell you where to look in the chapter if you need help.

soil (C62)	**conservation** (C76)
humus (C62)	**strip**
topsoil (C63)	**cropping** (C76)
clay (C69)	**contour**
loam (C70)	**plowing** (C76)
resource (C74)	

1. Rich soil with lots of humus is ____.

2. ____ is a type of soil with very small grains and small spaces between them.

3. Planting strips of different crops next to each other is ____.

4. A ____ is a material found in nature that living things use.

5. ____ is the layer of bits of rocks and humus found on Earth's crust.

6. ____ means saving resources by using them carefully.

7. The top layer of soil is ____.

8. ____ is planting rows of crops around hills instead of up and down their sides.

9. The decayed remains of dead plants and animals in soil is ____.

Connect Concepts

Write the terms where they belong in the concept map.

minerals	clay	not tilling the soil
bedrock	water	strip cropping
topsoil	sand	contour plowing
loam	air	
humus	subsoil	

Soils			
Parts of Soil	**Layers of Soil**	**Three Types of Soil**	**Three Ways to Save Soil**
10._____	14._____	17._____	20._____
11._____	15._____	18._____	21._____
12._____	16._____	19._____	22._____
13._____			

Check Understanding

Write the letter of the best choice.

23. Plants get ____ from soil.
    - **A** clay
    - **C** loam
    - **B** minerals
    - **D** sand

24. ____ is a feature of loam.
    - **F** Mostly large particles
    - **G** White color
    - **H** Lots of humus
    - **J** A sticky feeling

25. ____ harms soil.
    - **A** Strip cropping
    - **B** Erosion
    - **C** Contour plowing
    - **D** Not tilling

26. The solid rock under soil is called —
    - **F** bedrock
    - **H** subsoil
    - **G** topsoil
    - **J** humus

Critical Thinking

27. Why is water an important part of soil?

28. Would loam or sand need fertilizer more?

Process Skills Review

29. **Predict** what might happen if plants and animals did not decay in soil.

30. Suppose someone gave you a soil sample and asked you to describe it. What features would you **observe**?

31. Suppose heavy rain falls. You **observe** soil washing down a bare hill. There are two other hills like the ones shown below. **Infer** which hill will lose more soil.

Performance Assessment

Identifying Soil

Identify three soil samples by observing them.

Vocabulary Preview

resource
renewable
    resource
inexhaustible
    resource
nonrenewable
    resource
recycle

Earth's Resources

Every day you use Earth's resources. The paper you use is made from trees. Your soda can is made of metal that was dug out of the Earth. Plastic bottles are made from oil pumped out of the Earth. You can't live a single day without using hundreds of Earth's resources.

FAST FACT

The deepest lake on Earth is Lake Baikal in Russia. This giant lake, which is 1620 meters (5,300 ft) deep, holds one-fifth of Earth's liquid fresh water!

Air is one of Earth's resources. So are water and food. How much of these important resources do we use?

The Needs of an Average Adult

Resource	Daily Use
Air	30 pounds
Food	2 to 3 pounds
Water	4 to 5 pounds

What Are Resources?

In this lesson, you can . . .

INVESTIGATE
how resources are mined.

LEARN ABOUT
resources people use.

LINK to math, writing, literature, and technology.

Mining Resources

Activity Purpose

We use many materials from Earth's crust to make things. These materials are called *resources*. Some resources, such as oil, are pumped out of Earth's crust. Other resources, such as diamonds, must be dug out, or mined. In this investigation you will "mine" raisins from a cookie.

Materials

- oatmeal-raisin cookie
- paper plate
- dropper
- water
- toothpick

Activity Procedure

1 **Observe** your cookie. How many raisins do you see?

2 Fill the dropper with water. Put a few drops of water around each raisin. The cookie should be moist but not wet. (Picture A)

◀ This pump brings oil to Earth's surface. Gasoline and plastics are just two of the things made from oil.

Picture A

Picture B

3 Use the toothpick to "mine" all the raisins from the cookie. If the raisins are hard to get out, put a few more drops of water around them. Put the removed raisins on the plate. (Picture B)

4 **Observe** the cookie again. Were there any raisins you didn't see in the cookie the first time? Why didn't you see them?

Draw Conclusions

1. What did you "mine" from the cookie?

2. How did the water help you?

3. How is mining raisins from a cookie like mining materials from the Earth?

4. **Scientists at Work** Scientists **observe** things to see how they work. They use their observations to **infer** how similar things work. Use your observations to infer how mining could affect the land around the mine.

Resources People Use

FIND OUT

• what resources are

• how we use resources

VOCABULARY

resource

Where Resources Are Found

A **resource** is a material that is found in nature and that is used by living things. Think about the resources you use each day. You breathe air. You drink water. You ride in cars, trains, and buses. When you eat dinner, you use a metal fork. When you use a computer, you push plastic buttons that are made from oil. Air, water, gasoline, metals, coal, and oil are resources.

All living things need water. You need to drink 2 liters (about 2 qt) of water each day to stay healthy. ▼

People need to take in oxygen. We get it from the air. The air also contains gases that plants need for making their own food and staying healthy. ▶

In the investigation you learned that some resources are found below Earth's surface. Some examples are oil, coal, and diamonds.

Some resources are on Earth's surface. Water and soil are important resources on Earth's surface. Without water and soil, there would be no life on Earth.

Air is a resource that is above Earth's surface. Air has many gases that living things need. One of these is oxygen, a gas you take in when you breathe.

✔ **Where do resources come from?**

Forests cover one-third of the land on Earth. People get wood, paper, food, and other resources from the plants and animals in these forests. ▼

Resources Under Earth's Surface

Resources that are under Earth's surface are mined in different ways. Diamonds and emeralds are mined by people who dig tunnels deep under the ground. Some coal is mined in deep tunnels, too.

To mine other resources, big machines scrape away soil and rock. Then the machines take the materials from the holes that are left. This is known as strip mining. Some coal is strip-mined. The picture on page C91 shows copper being mined this way.

Still other resources, such as oil and water, can be pumped from Earth's crust. People dig wells in the ground to reach these materials.

✔ **List three ways resources are taken from under Earth's surface.**

Oil is an important resource. Oil derricks hold equipment used to drill for oil. People use oil to make many things. ▶

▲ **Gasoline is a fuel that comes from oil. Most cars use gasoline.**

Some power plants burn oil to produce electricity. ▼

◀ **Plastic is made from some of the things that are found in oil.**

▲ People mine copper from Earth's crust. This mine in Montana is one of the largest copper mines in the world.

Summary

A resource is a material that living things use. Resources include air, water, soil, trees, and minerals. We need resources such as air and water to live. We use other resources, such as minerals, to make things we need.

Review

1. List two products that come from trees.

2. Name two resources that people need to live.

3. List two ways people use oil.

4. **Critical Thinking** Is it harder to get resources from under Earth's surface or on it? Explain your answer.

5. **Test Prep** Which resource is found below Earth's surface?
   A trees C air
   B oil   D soil

 # LINKS

 MATH LINK

How Much? Water is an important resource. How much of Earth's surface is covered by water? Visit the media center to find the answer to this question. Make a display that shows what you learn.

 WRITING LINK

Narrative Writing—Story Suppose you are a magazine writer. Write a story for young children about a resource that is in the news. Tell where it is found and how it is used.

 LITERATURE LINK

Garbage Resources often become garbage after being used. But where does the garbage go? Find out in the book *Where Does Garbage Go?* by Isaac Asimov.

 TECHNOLOGY LINK

Visit the Harcourt Learning Site for related links, activities, and resources.
www.harcourtschool.com

WELCOME TO
THE
LEARNING
SITE

What Are Different Kinds of Resources?

In this lesson, you can . . .

INVESTIGATE
resources and the products made from them.

LEARN ABOUT
how resources are classified.

LINK to math,
writing, social studies, and technology.

INVESTIGATE

Resource Use

Activity Purpose Every product around you is made from a resource. There are many kinds of resources. In this investigation you will **compare** pictures of resources with pictures of products. You will **classify** the products by the resources they are made from.

Materials
- resource picture cards
- product picture cards

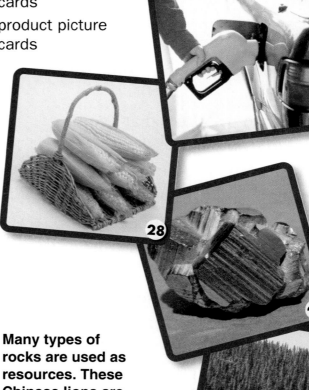

◄ **Many types of rocks are used as resources. These Chinese lions are made of marble.**

Activity Procedure

1. Look closely at all the cards. Sort the cards into two groups— resources and products.

2. **Classify** the products. To do this, match each product with the resource from which it comes. (Picture A)

3. Make a drawing to show how you sorted your cards.

Picture A

Draw Conclusions

1. How did you **classify** the products?

2. Does a product always look like the resource it was made from? Explain.

3. **Scientists at Work** Scientists **compare** objects to see how they are alike and how they are different. How did comparing the products to the resources help you **classify** the products?

Investigate Further Identify five or more products in your home. **Classify** the products by the resources they came from.

Process Skill Tip

When you **compare** things, you think about how they are alike and how they are different. When you **classify** things, you group things that are alike.

Kinds of Resources

FIND OUT

- which resources will never run out
- which resources could be used up one day

VOCABULARY

renewable
   resource
inexhaustible
   resource
nonrenewable
   resource

Resources That Can Last Forever

Some resources can last forever. Some of these resources, called **renewable resources**, can be replaced in a human lifetime. Trees are renewable resources. When people cut down trees, they can plant new trees to replace the cut trees.

Other resources will never run out. **Inexhaustible resources** are used over and over and can't be used up. Water and air are inexhaustible resources. Even polluted water and air can be used again if they are cleaned. Earth's processes help clean water and air. The sun is an inexhaustible resource, too. It gives us light and heat all the time.

✔ **How are renewable and inexhaustible resources different?**

Wood for houses, furniture, pencils, and paper comes from trees. Trees also provide places for animals to live. When trees are replanted, this resource is renewed for the future. ▼

▲ The air is always there for you to breathe. Sometimes, cars, trucks, and factories pollute the air. Wind and rain can clean the pollution out of the air. People can work to reduce pollution so the air will stay clean.

The sun never stops shining. It warms Earth's land and oceans. Plants use the sun's energy to make food. People use the sun's energy to heat water and to meet other needs. All living things on Earth use energy from this inexhaustible resource to live. ▼

◄ People need water every day for drinking, cooking, and bathing. Factories and farms use water to make products people use. Water is inexhaustible, but dirty water must be cleaned before it can be used again.

C95

Resources That Won't Last Forever

Some resources will not last forever. A **nonrenewable resource** is a resource that will be used up someday. It might surprise you just how many resources are nonrenewable. Coal, oil, iron, and copper are only a few of them.

Soil is a nonrenewable resource. You know that new soil can be formed, but it takes thousands of years for rocks to break down and become soil. That's why soil is called nonrenewable.

Trees are renewable resources. But some kinds of forests are nonrenewable. Old-growth forests have never been cut down. When people cut down an old-growth forest, they may plant new trees. But the new forest has fewer types of plants and animals than the old forest had. It takes hundreds of years for another old-growth forest to grow.

✔ **What is a nonrenewable resource?**

▲ *Old-growth forests* have trees that are 200 years old or older. When people cut old-growth forests, the forests will never grow back the way they were.

The United States mines a lot of coal. Coal is burned to produce electricity. When all the coal is burned, another fuel will have to be used. ▼

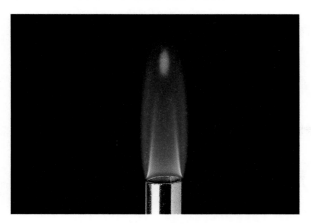

▲ Natural gas is an important fuel. Many people use it for heating their homes and cooking their food. When all the natural gas has been burned, there will be no more for people to use.

Summary

Renewable resources, such as trees, can be replaced. Inexhaustible resources, such as air, water, and the sun, are used over and over again and do not run out. Nonrenewable resources can be used up. Oil, soil, minerals, and old-growth forests are nonrenewable resources.

Review

1. What are renewable resources?
2. Why is water an inexhaustible resource?
3. Why is an old-growth forest nonrenewable?
4. **Critical Thinking** Why should nonrenewable resources be used wisely?
5. **Test Prep** Choose the resource that is nonrenewable.

   A iron   C water

   B air   D the sun

 LINKS

 MATH LINK

Using Up Resources Suppose your community has enough coal to produce energy for 20 years. Your community uses 5 tons of coal a year. But what if it used only 4 tons each year? How long would the coal last?

 WRITING LINK

Informative Writing— Explanation Make a list of the nonrenewable resources you used today. Choose one, and write a story for your teacher explaining how your life would be different without this resource.

 SOCIAL STUDIES LINK

Old Growth Where in the United States are old-growth forests found? Make a map that shows where they are. Are there any in your state?

 TECHNOLOGY LINK

Learn more about resources by visiting this Internet Site.

www.scilinks.org/harcourt

How Can We Conserve Earth's Resources?

In this lesson, you can . . .

INVESTIGATE items that can be recycled.

LEARN ABOUT how recycling conserves resources.

LINK to math, writing, music, and technology.

INVESTIGATE

Recycling

Activity Purpose Every day people use more and more of Earth's resources. Many of these resources end up as trash. Trash is taken away and put into landfills. In this investigation you will **record** one type of resource your family uses. Using data from all the members of your class, you will **use numbers** to find out how much landfill space your class could save by recycling aluminum cans.

Materials

- aluminum cans your family uses in one week
- large plastic trash bag
- bathroom scale

Activity Procedure

1. Get permission from a parent to participate in this activity. Save all of the aluminum cans your family uses for one week. Rinse them in the sink. Put the cans in the trash bag. (Picture A)

◀ Recycling saves resources and reduces pollution.

2 Weigh the cans. If your cans are too light to weigh, you can find their weight by multiplying the number of cans you have collected by 1.5 oz. **Record** the weight.

3 Bring your results to class. Use your data to draw a bar on the class graph. The graph will show the weight of each family's cans.

Picture A

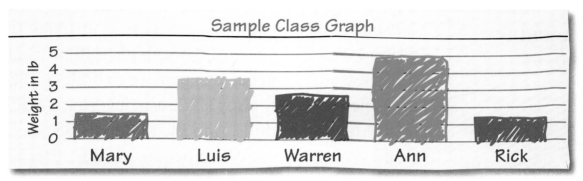

Sample Class Graph

4 Add up all the weights shown on the graph. The sum tells you how much aluminum all the families used in one week.

Draw Conclusions

1. Suppose that 1 lb of cans takes up 2 ft of space. How much landfill space would your class save by recycling all the cans?

2. What other resources might be saved if your cans were recycled instead of thrown away?

3. **Scientists at Work** There are many ways you could tell someone how much aluminum was used in one week. In this investigation you **used numbers** to describe the weight of aluminum used. How does using numbers help you tell people what you found out?

Process Skill Tip

Using numbers helps you tell others exactly what data you have collected. Scientists use numbers to explain things such as how big or small things are, how hot or cold things are, and how fast things go.

Conserving Resources

FIND OUT

• what recycling is

• how recycling saves resources

VOCABULARY

recycle

Recycling

People use a lot of resources. They also throw a lot of resources away. Think about how much trash you have seen people throw away in one week. This trash is usually taken to landfills, where it is buried in the ground. Landfills take up space that could be used in other ways. They are also expensive to build and keep up. If people threw away less trash, less space would be needed for landfills. And the materials people save could be used again. When people **recycle**, they reuse a resource to make something new.

Recycling makes resources last longer. If aluminum is recycled, less aluminum ore, called *bauxite,* needs to be mined. If plastic is recycled, less oil is needed to make new plastic.

Many of the things people throw away can be recycled. Recycling saves resources. Every ton of recycled paper saves 17 trees. ▼

What People Throw Away

Percent of Total Trash

40, 36, 32, 28, 24, 20, 16, 12, 8, 4, 0

Paper Plants Metal Glass Food Dairy Furniture Liquid

Materials

Recycling renewable resources is helpful, too. When paper is recycled, fewer trees must be cut down.

Recycling helps save energy. Reusing resources saves the energy needed to find, mine, or harvest more of the resource. It also saves the energy needed to move it from place to place.

Recycling helps reduce pollution. Making paper from trees pollutes both air and water. So does making new plastic from oil. Making products from recycled paper and plastic causes less pollution.

Many towns have recycling programs. Families save paper, aluminum, glass, and plastic. Trucks take the materials to recycling centers. These centers send the materials to factories. There the recycled materials are made into new products.

✔ **What does it mean to recycle?**

▲ **Plastic can be recycled. But fewer plastic containers are recycled than aluminum or glass containers.**

Each person in the United States throws away about 2 kilograms (about $4\frac{1}{2}$ lb) of trash every day. But we recycle more now than we did ten years ago. ▼

Most trash is buried in landfills. Recycling aluminum means using less space in landfills. ▼

C101

Recycling Aluminum

Many things we use are made of aluminum. These include food cans and cooking pots. Aluminum is used to make foil and electrical equipment, too. Most aluminum objects are thrown away after being used once. But this is not true for aluminum cans. Out of every 100 aluminum cans used in the United States, almost 67 are recycled!

Billions of aluminum cans are made each year. Half the aluminum in most aluminum cans has been recycled. Recycling aluminum saves resources. Using one ton of recycled aluminum saves four tons of bauxite from being mined.

Recycling aluminum also saves electricity. It takes a lot of electric power to produce new aluminum from bauxite. Making products from recycled aluminum uses less electricity. Electric power plants burn nonrenewable fuels such as coal and oil. So recycling aluminum saves fuel. It also reduces pollution.

✔ **How does recycling aluminum help save resources?**

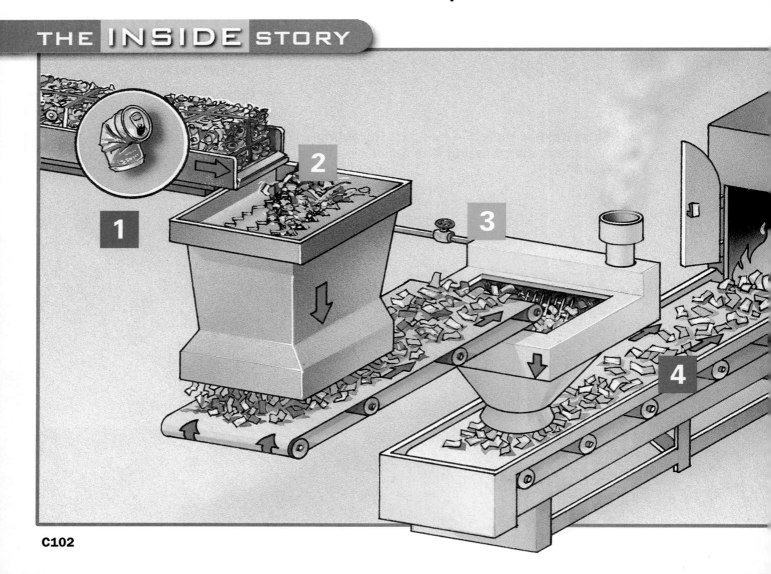

▲ Most bauxite is mined from open pits. This type of mining, also called strip mining, destroys soil and plants. Recycling aluminum means mining less bauxite.

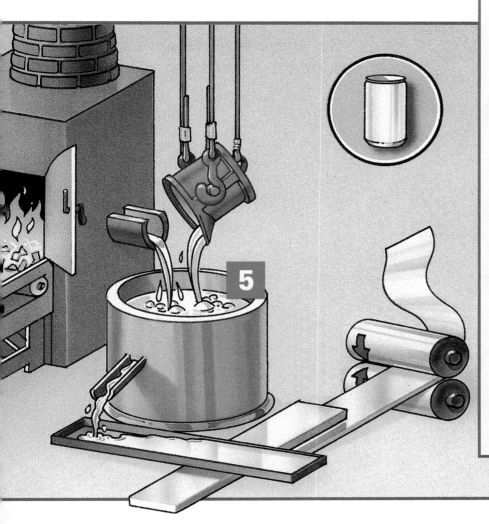

1 Recycling starts with the cans you use. You finish your apple juice. Then you put the can into the recycling bin. Someone collects the bin of aluminum cans. A truck takes the aluminum to a recycling center.

2 People unload the cans at the recycling center. They put the cans on a moving belt. The belt takes the cans to a chopper. The chopper cuts the cans into many pieces.

3 The next job is removing paint from the pieces of can. The pieces go into a machine full of very hot air. The air has a temperature of 482° Celsius (900°F). The hot air melts the paint from the can pieces. But the hot air doesn't melt the aluminum. Clean pieces of aluminum come out of the machine.

4 The clean aluminum pieces then go to a furnace. The furnace is even hotter than the hot-air machine. It has a temperature of 660°Celsius (1,220°F). That's hot enough to melt aluminum. The furnace turns the aluminum into a hot silvery liquid.

5 The melted aluminum is poured out of the furnace. It flows into molds. The molds shape the hot metal into big blocks. The blocks cool. People use the blocks to make new cans and other products. Aluminum from the can you recycle today could be back in the store in eight weeks.

Conserving Resources

Some resources can't be recycled. People can't recycle the gasoline, oil, or coal that are used as fuels because they are burned up. But people can conserve them. When people *conserve*, they use less of a resource at one time. Conserving resources makes them last longer.

Coal and oil can be saved when people use less electricity. People can turn off lights when not using them. A house can be kept warmer in summer to use less air conditioning. It can be kept cooler in winter to use less heat.

Sometimes people must conserve water when there has been no rain. There may not be enough water for everyone in a community to use. If your community has a water shortage, here are some things you can do. Take short showers. Don't run the water while you brush your teeth. Make sure the dishwasher is full when you use it. Fix leaky faucets. Leaks waste lots of water.

Preventing pollution is a way to conserve resources. Earth's supply of air and water will never be used up. But air and water can become dirty. If they become too dirty, they are unhealthful to use. It's important for everyone to help keep Earth's air and water clean. You can help protect Earth's resources.

✔ **List three ways to save water during a water shortage.**

Summary

Recycling is using old or used materials. When we recycle, we need fewer new resources to make new products. This makes the resources last longer. People can conserve, or use less of a resource, when they can't recycle.

Review

1. What resources are saved when you recycle aluminum?
2. List the steps in recycling aluminum.
3. Name two ways to save water.
4. **Critical Thinking** Suppose the population of a city is growing. But the amount of water the city can use stays the same. Why is it important for people in the city to conserve water?
5. **Test Prep** Choose the resource that you can conserve by recycling paper.
   - **A** aluminum
   - **B** coal
   - **C** gasoline
   - **D** trees

LINKS

MATH LINK

Order It Make a table that lists the kinds of materials people recycle. Include paper, glass, aluminum, and plastic. Find out how much of each material is recycled in the United States. List the materials in order from the highest recycling rate to the lowest rate.

WRITING LINK

Informative Writing—How to Write a set of recycling directions for your class. What materials should students collect? When can the recyclables be picked up?

MUSIC LINK

Recycling Tune Write the words to a song that tells people why it's good to recycle. Use a tune you already know. Sing your song in class.

TECHNOLOGY LINK

To learn more about wise use of resources, watch *Graffiti Plastics* on the **Harcourt Science Newsroom Video**.

CNN Turner Le@rning

Recycling Plastics to Make Clothing

Putting a plastic bottle in a recycling bin is the first step in recycling. Next, the bottle must be made into something new that can be used again.

What Do They Do with Those Plastic Bottles?

Recycling plastic is not as easy as recycling glass, aluminum, or paper. There are seven kinds of

▲ Flake

plastic. Each kind needs to be treated in a different way. The easiest way to recycle plastic bottles and jars is to melt them all together. Then you can make big, solid objects from them, such as picnic tables and park benches.

Today machines are used to sort plastic bottles. Bottles that have a number 1 stamped on them can be used in a new, exciting way, so they are separated from the rest. Their labels and caps are removed. Then the bottles are crushed and chopped into tiny pieces called flake. The flake is melted and pulled into long, thin threads. The threads are stretched and kinked. After that, they look like threads of cotton. In the last step, the threads are gathered up into big square bunches called bales.

What Happens to the Baled Threads?

The bales of thread are sent to factories. At the factories, the threads are pulled from the bales and twirled together to make yarn. The yarn is called EcoSpun™. EcoSpun can be knitted or woven to make almost anything that can be made from wool or cotton or other types of cloth. EcoSpun is used to make carpets, backpacks, blankets, T-shirts, soft suitcases, socks, and many other things.

How Does This Help the Environment?

When people know their recycled plastic is actually being used, they are more likely to recycle. And that's good for the environment. About two and one-half billion recycled plastic bottles are used every year to make EcoSpun. Instead of becoming trash, the bottles are becoming clothing. Instead of filling up the landfills, two and one-half billion bottles are being used again.

Think About It

• Can the products made from recycled plastic be used to help the environment even more? Explain.

WEB LINK:
For Science and Technology updates, visit the Harcourt Internet site.
www.harcourtschool.com

▼ **EcoSpun blankets**

Careers — Recycling Plant Worker

What They Do
Workers in a recycling plant sort the items that have been collected in the recycle bins. They operate the machines

that crush glass or shred paper. Then they make sure the recycled materials get to the factories that can use them.

Education and Training A recycling plant worker needs a high school diploma. Workers who already know how to do their jobs show new workers what to do.

Marisa Quinones
GEOLOGIST

When you think of a geologist, you may think only of rocks. But geologists do many things. They study the history of Earth, find water in dry climates, and search for precious rocks and minerals, such as gold and diamonds. For Marisa Quinones, geology involves looking for oil underground. Oil companies look for oil by setting off an explosion in the ground or by firing an air gun into the ocean floor. The rocks underground respond to the sound waves that result. Their responses are recorded on a computer. Quinones studies the patterns of rock responses. By studying them, she can decide whether oil is likely to be found in a certain spot.

Once drilling begins, Quinones looks at the cuttings, or rock chips, from the hole. The cuttings help her predict whether there could be any danger as the drilling is being done. They also let her know when the area that holds the oil has been reached.

Quinones also supervises the lowering of scientific instruments into the hole that has been drilled. These instruments keep a record of what happens in the well. The record provides information about the underground rocks and areas that hold oil. These findings tell Quinones whether to continue drilling.

Think About It

1. What dangers might occur when drilling for oil?
2. Why do you think oil companies are searching for oil under the sea?

How Much Waste?

How much waste does your class throw away each day?

Materials

- paper
- pencil

What We Threw Away Today	
Newspaper and Magazines	
Cardboard and Other Paper	
Glass Containers	
Plastic Containers	
Plastic Wrapping and Bags	
Other	

Procedure

1. Copy one chart for the class. Put the chart and a pencil next to the trash can.

2. All students in your class should record what they throw away. If a paper is thrown away, then a *1* is written in the Paper row. If 3 plastic bottles are thrown away, then *3 bottles* is written in the Plastic Containers row.

Draw Conclusions

After gathering data for one day, total all the things that were thrown away. How could your class recycle more?

Reuse It!

How can some classroom materials be reused?

Materials

- large cardboard or plastic boxes
- black marking pen
- tape

Procedure

1. Use the chart from "How Much Waste?" As a class, decide which materials could be reused instead of being thrown away. Work with your teacher to find a place in the room to store materials that can be reused.

2. Find cardboard boxes or plastic bins for keeping the materials. Label each box with the material it will hold. Be sure that items that had food in them, such as plastic containers, are rinsed before being put in the boxes.

Draw Conclusions

After you have started your REUSE IT! center, check your trash again. How does the amount of trash compare with the amount of trash before the REUSE IT! center was started?

Chapter ④ Review and Test Preparation

Vocabulary Review

Use the terms below to complete the sentences 1 through 5. The page numbers in ( ) tell you where to look in the chapter if you need help.

resource (C88)

renewable resource (C94)

inexhaustible resource (C94)

nonrenewable resource (C96)

recycle (C100)

1. A resource that can be replaced after it is used is called a ____.

2. When you ____, you reuse a resource to make something new. Then the resource can be used again and again.

3. An ____ is a resource that will never run out.

4. A material found in nature that living things use is a ____.

5. A ____ is a resource that could be used up one day.

Connect Concepts

Write the terms where they belong in the concept map.

coal   renewable   water   inexhaustible
oil   aluminum   air   old-growth forests
soil   natural gas

Kinds of Resources		
6. _____	Nonrenewable	13. _____
trees	7. _____	the sun
	8. _____	14. _____
	9. _____	15. _____
	10. _____	
	11. _____	
	12. _____	

Check Understanding

Write the letter of the best choice.

16. Most mineral resources are found ___ Earth's surface.
    A above   C alongside
    B under   D on

17. Oil is used to make —
    F paper   H plastic
    G glass   J aluminum

18. Trees are used to make —
    A paper   C plastic
    B glass   D aluminum

19. Which resource can get dirty but can never run out?
    F trees   H coal
    G water   J aluminum

20. Which resource can be renewed?
    A soil   C the sun
    B water   D trees

Critical Thinking

21. How would life be different without resources taken from under Earth's surface?

22. How can pollution stop people from using inexhaustible resources?

Process Skills Review

23. List the resources that you can **observe** on your way to school. Be sure to include at least one of each type of resource.

24. Suppose people are mining a mineral from Earth's crust. What can you **infer** about the kind of resource it is? Explain your answer.

25. **Compare** renewable and inexhaustible resources.

Performance Assessment

Classify Resources

Observe a group of objects. Classify each object as a renewable, an inexhaustible, or a nonrenewable resource.

Unit Project Wrap Up

Here are some ideas for ways to wrap up your unit project.

Publish a Museum Guide

Use a computer to publish a guide that gives information about the exhibits in your museum. Include a map that shows where each exhibit is located.

Compare Rocks

Compare two or more rocks. Make a chart or Venn diagram that shows how they are alike and how they are different.

Make a Diorama

Use a shoebox to make a diorama showing earth's resources. Write a report about how people can conserve these resources.

Investigate Further

How could you make your project better? What other questions do you have about rocks, minerals, soil, and fossils? Plan ways to find answers to your questions. Use the Science Handbook on pages R2-R9 for help.

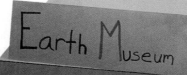

Cycles on Earth and in Space

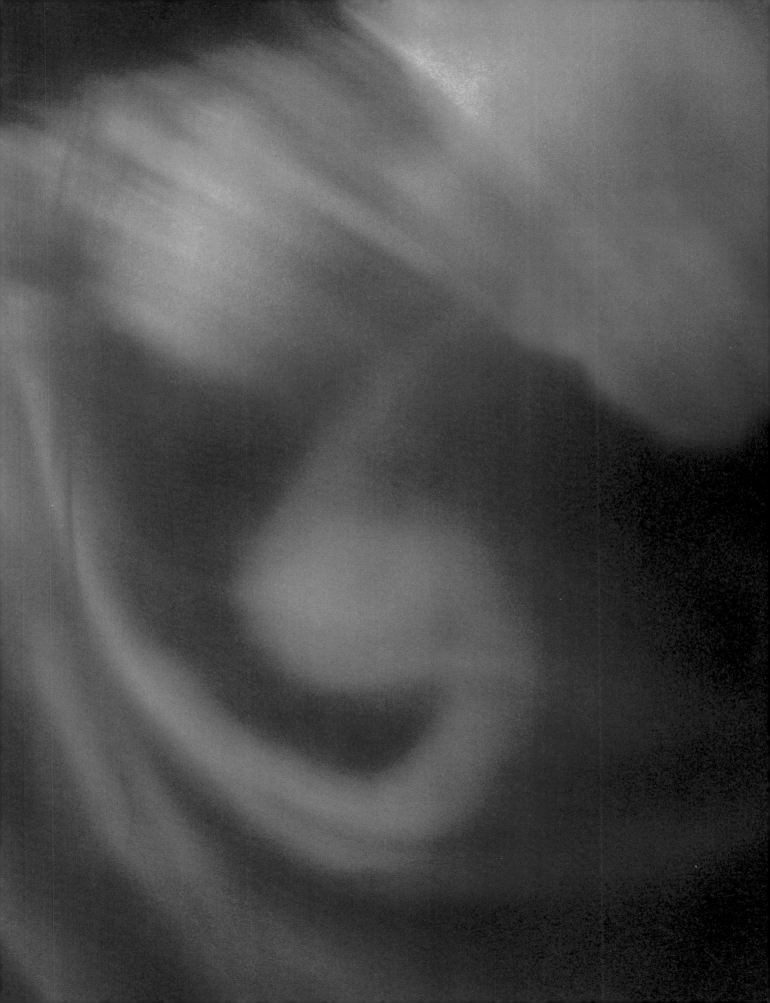

EARTH SCIENCE

Cycles on Earth and in Space

Unit Project ## Sky Observations

Plan a schedule for recording sky observations for one month. Make daily notes about the weather including temperature, precipitation, and cloud formations. If you like, add a weekly weather map. Sketch the appearance of the moon each night. At the end of the month, review your notes and describe the cycles you see.

Chapter 1

The Water Cycle

There's plenty of water on Earth. In fact, Earth is nearly covered with it. Most of the water on Earth is frozen or salty. And even though water seems to be everywhere, in some places on Earth there is almost no water at all.

Vocabulary Preview

groundwater
estuary
evaporation
condensation
precipitation
water cycle

⚡FAST FACT

A leaky faucet wastes about 76 liters (20 gal) of water a day. If you wait a week to fix the leak, the faucet will drip 800,000 drops!

Each person in the United States uses about 380 liters (100 gal) of water every day. That's enough to fill an average bathtub about 5 times!

How Much Water

Activity	Liters
Brushing teeth for two minutes	23
Running a dishwasher	45
Shower	95
Washing a load of laundry	190

FAST FACT

It takes 159,000 liters (42,000 gal) of water to grow and prepare the food for a Thanksgiving dinner for eight people. That's enough water to fill a swimming pool!

Where Is Water Found on Earth?

In this lesson, you can . . .

INVESTIGATE how much water covers Earth's surface.

LEARN ABOUT why water is important to living things.

LINK to math, writing, art, and technology.

If you live in a cold place, you may see water in the form of snow.

INVESTIGATE

Land or Water

Activity Purpose Does Earth's surface have more land or more water? In this investigation you will play a game to **collect data** about Earth's surface. Then you will **use numbers** to estimate the amount of water on Earth's surface.

Materials
- plastic inflatable globe

Activity Procedure

1 Work in groups of five. Choose one person to be the recorder. The other four people will toss the ball.

2 Have the four ball tossers stand in a circle. The recorder hands the ball to the first person, who gently tosses the ball to another person in the circle. (Picture A)

3 The catcher should catch the ball with open hands. Check to see if the tip of the catcher's right index finger is on land or water. The recorder should **record** this data.

4 Continue tossing and recording until the ball has been tossed 20 times.

Picture A

5 Repeat Steps 3 and 4 two more times.

Draw Conclusions

1. Total your counts. How many times did the catcher's right index finger touch water? Touch land?

2. Where did the catchers' fingers land more often? Why do you think so?

3. **Scientists at Work** Scientists **use numbers** to **collect data.** Using your data, estimate how much of Earth's surface is covered by water.

Investigate Further You did this investigation 3 times. The more data you collect, the better your data becomes. How would doing the investigation 10 times change your data? Try it to find out.

Process Skill Tip

Collecting data by **using numbers** can help you answer questions. By doing the activity several times, you increase the amount of data you collect. Then you can **interpret the data** to find an answer to your question.

This view of Earth from space makes it easy to see why Earth is sometimes called the water planet. ▶

Water on Earth

FIND OUT

- why water is important
- where water is found on Earth

VOCABULARY

groundwater
estuary

The Importance of Water

From space, Earth looks like a blue marble. The water that covers most of the planet makes it look blue. Earth's lands are really small islands in the middle of huge oceans and seas.

Without water there could be no life on Earth. Plants and animals need water to live. So do people. Two-thirds of your body is water. People must have at least 2 liters (about 2 qt) of water each day to survive. Even the foods you eat are full of water. Chicken is three-fourths water. A potato is four-fifths water.

Water is important to Earth's environment. Without water there could be no rain or snow. Water helps make winds and storms. Water even changes the shape of Earth's surface.

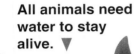

All animals need water to stay alive. ▼

▲ Industry uses about half of our fresh water. Water is used to wash things, to cool things down, and to make products.

Look at a map of Earth. You can see that most water on Earth is found in the oceans. This water is salt water. Many plants and animals live in the ocean. But salt water isn't good for the plants and animals that live on land or in fresh water.

Living things on land need fresh water. Only a little of Earth's water is fresh water. But not all the fresh water can be used. Most fresh water is frozen as ice in glaciers or in icecaps near the poles. Only a small amount of Earth's fresh water can be used to meet the needs of living things.

✔ **What are the two types of water on Earth?**

▲ Irrigation is the moving of water to dry places. Irrigation helps plants grow in dry areas. Almost two-fifths of Earth's liquid fresh water is used for irrigation.

Water on Earth

 Fresh Water

Ice

If you could put all the water on Earth into 100 buckets, 97 buckets would hold the salt water of the oceans and seas, and 2 buckets would hold the frozen fresh water of glaciers and icecaps. Only 1 bucket would hold liquid fresh water.

Salt Water

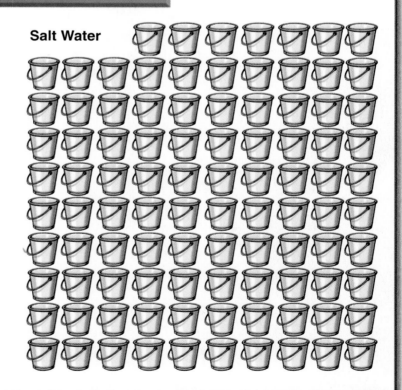

Fresh Water

Nearly every person in the United States uses more than 380 liters (about 100 gal) of fresh water every day. You use fresh water when you take a drink. You take baths in fresh water. You water your plants with fresh water. You cook with fresh water. Farmers grow your food with fresh water. Factories use fresh water to make everything from bread to steel. People find the fresh water they need in many places. The rain or snow that falls to Earth is fresh water. This water flows over the ground and into rivers and streams. Ponds and most lakes also hold fresh water.

There is also fresh water under Earth's surface. This water is called **groundwater**. Groundwater begins as rain soaking into the soil. The water moves down through the soil and broken rocks under the soil until it reaches solid rock. Much of Earth's fresh water is stored underground as groundwater.

Fresh water is not found evenly on Earth's surface. Some places have a great deal of fresh water. Other places have very little. In those places there may not be enough water to meet the needs of the people who live there. In some places pollution makes the water dirty. Polluted water cannot be used by people.

◄ **Most of Earth's fresh water is frozen. Glaciers and icecaps cover one-tenth of Earth's land surface. This iceberg has broken away from a glacier and is floating in the ocean.**

To make sure there is enough clean, fresh water for everyone, it is important to conserve, or save, water when you can. Take short showers. Turn off the water when you brush your teeth. And don't pour paints, oils, or other harmful liquids down the drain. These liquids can get into the water people drink and make it unhealthful.

✔ **Where is fresh water found on Earth?**

THE INSIDE STORY

Water on Earth

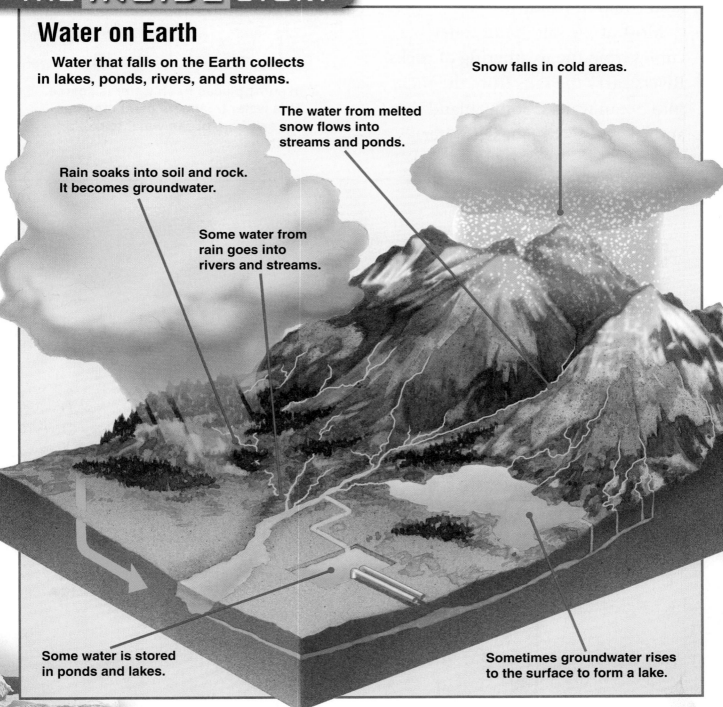

Water that falls on the Earth collects in lakes, ponds, rivers, and streams.

Snow falls in cold areas.

The water from melted snow flows into streams and ponds.

Rain soaks into soil and rock. It becomes groundwater.

Some water from rain goes into rivers and streams.

Some water is stored in ponds and lakes.

Sometimes groundwater rises to the surface to form a lake.

Salt Water

Earth is a watery planet. Much of that water is salt water. The salt water of Earth's oceans covers more than two-thirds of our planet's surface. The Pacific Ocean is Earth's largest ocean. It is so big that all of Earth's land could fit inside it.

Most of the salt in salt water comes from the weathering of rocks. Rivers carry the salts from the rocks into ocean waters. Some inland seas and lakes also contain salt water.

▲ In some places fresh water is scarce. This water treatment plant removes the salt from ocean water to make fresh water.

The continents are really islands of land surrounded by Earth's large oceans. ▶

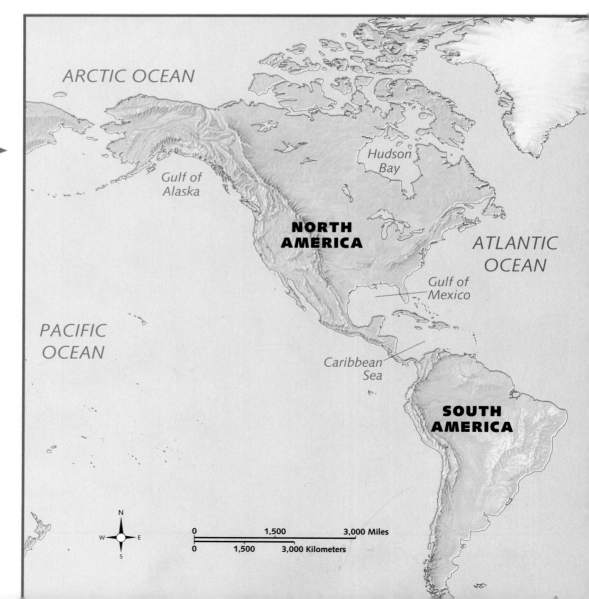

ARCTIC OCEAN

Hudson Bay

Gulf of Alaska

NORTH AMERICA

ATLANTIC OCEAN

Gulf of Mexico

PACIFIC OCEAN

Caribbean Sea

SOUTH AMERICA

N
W   E
S

| 0 | 1,500 | 3,000 Miles |
| 0 | 1,500 | 3,000 Kilometers |

The Great Salt Lake in Utah is one of the world's saltiest bodies of water.

You may think that ocean water isn't important because you don't drink it. But ocean water helps keep the planet from being very cold in some places and very hot in others. The sun warms ocean water near the equator. This warm water moves through the ocean, warming the cooler water around it as it moves.

The warm water helps keep the air above it warm, too.

The resources of the ocean are important. Fish and other ocean animals and plants are food for millions of people. Many useful products come from the ocean. For example, people pump oil from wells deep under the ocean. About one-fourth of our oil comes from wells under the sea.

✔ **Where is salt water found on Earth?**

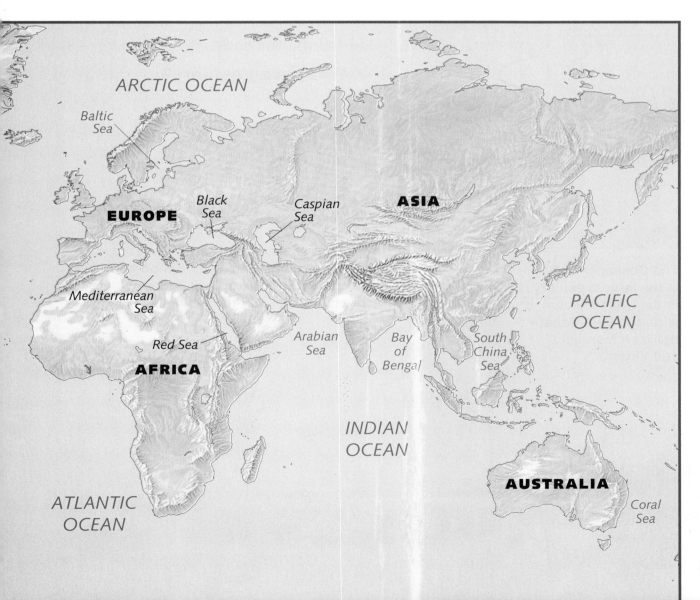

Where Fresh Water and Salt Water Meet

Suppose you could walk along the whole coast of the United States. As you walked, you would find places where rivers bring fresh water to the ocean. These places are estuaries. An **estuary** (ES•tyoo•air•ee) is a place where fresh water from a river mixes with salt water from the ocean.

Estuaries are unusual ecosystems. The plants and animals there must be able to live in both fresh water and salt water.

PENNSYLVANIA NEW JERSEY

DELAWARE

MARYLAND

VIRGINIA

Chesapeake Bay

▲ The Chesapeake Bay is the largest estuary in the United States. It is on the East Coast between Maryland and Virginia.

Many kinds of animals live in or near estuaries. Birds build their nests in the plants on the edges of estuaries. Young fish, crabs, clams, shrimp, and oysters live and grow in the shallow waters of an estuary. Many people make their living by catching these animals, which are then sold as food.

Estuaries are important for other reasons, too. The roots of the many plants that live there slow down the water that enters the estuary. The roots also trap the soil that the slow water carries. This helps build up the land along the coast.

✔ **What is an estuary?**

Tall grasses grow around the edges of estuaries. Many birds and other animals find food and shelter there. The roots trap soil and provide a home for small fish and other animals. ▼

▲ Mangrove trees grow in estuaries that are warm all year long. Because of the way their roots grow, mangroves provide a home for small fish and other animals.

Summary

More than two-thirds of Earth's surface is covered by water. Most of this water is the salt water of oceans and seas. Fresh water is found in lakes, ponds, rivers, and streams. Nothing could live on Earth without water.

Review

1. List three ways fresh water is used.
2. How does water get underground?
3. Where do the salts in Earth's oceans come from?
4. **Critical Thinking** Why don't estuaries hold only salt water?
5. **Test Prep** Which of the following is true of all ocean water?
   A It is warm.
   B It is salt water.
   C It is fresh water.
   D It is frozen.

LINKS

MATH LINK

Graph It Use a computer graphing program such as **Graph Links** to make a bar graph that shows the part of Earth's water that is salty and the part that is fresh.

WRITING LINK

Persuasive Writing—Opinion Is it fun to visit the water? Write a paragraph describing a trip you have taken on a boat. Or describe a trip to a beach, lake, or river. What was it like? What did you do? What was the water like? Persuade others that it would be a good place to visit.

ART LINK

Mobile Find out about the kinds of animals that live in an estuary. Then make a mobile that shows some of these animals.

TECHNOLOGY LINK

Learn more about the water on Earth by visiting the National Air and Space Museum Internet Site. **www.si.edu/harcourt/science**

 Smithsonian Institution®

What Is the Water Cycle?

In this lesson, you can . . .

INVESTIGATE
how fresh water and salt water evaporate.

LEARN ABOUT
the movement of water on Earth and in the air.

LINK to math, writing, health, and technology.

◀ **Water on these berries turned to ice in the cold night air. The sun's heat will melt the ice.**

INVESTIGATE

Evaporation

Activity Purpose During a storm, rain forms puddles. After the rain stops, the puddles disappear. This process is called *evaporation*. In this investigation you will **control variables** to find out if some kinds of water evaporate faster than others.

Materials
- masking tape
- 4 identical jars
- measuring cup
- water
- salt
- spoon
- 2 jar lids
- ruler

Activity Procedure

1 Put a strip of masking tape down the side of each jar. (Picture A)

2 Using the measuring cup, pour $\frac{1}{2}$ cup water into each jar. Stir a spoonful of salt into 2 of the jars. Mark these jars with an *S*. Mark the other 2 jars with an *F*.

3 Make a mark on the tape on each jar to show how high the water is. Then put the lids on one *S* jar and one *F* jar. (Picture B)

4 **Predict** which jar the water will evaporate from first. **Record** your prediction.

5 Place the jars in a sunny place.

6 **Observe** the jars every day for a week. Each day, mark how high the water in each jar is.

Picture A

Picture B

Draw Conclusions

1. Did all the water evaporate from any of the jars? If so, which one?

2. **Compare** your prediction with your results. How did you make your prediction? Was your prediction correct?

3. **Scientists at Work** To find the answers to some questions, scientists test things that will change. These things are called *variables*. Then they add something to the experiment that they know won't change. This is called a *control*. What were the controls in this investigation?

Investigate Further Infer what would happen if you repeated the activity but used different amounts of salt. How would the results change? Try the activity to see if your inference was correct. Don't forget to use controls.

Process Skill Tip

A control shows what would happen if no variable were being tested. **Controlling variables** is one way scientists make sure that their experiments are fair tests.

The Water Cycle

FIND OUT

- how water changes form
- how water moves from place to place

VOCABULARY

evaporation
condensation
precipitation
water cycle

How Water Changes

Water is the only material on Earth that has three forms in nature. You can find liquid water in lakes and rivers. You can find ice on a freezing winter day. Water is in the air around you in the form of a gas you can't see. It is called water vapor.

The form that water takes depends on the amount of heat, or *thermal energy,* in it. Adding heat or taking away heat changes the form of water.

Water changes form as temperatures change. The warm rays of the sun melt ice. Cold temperatures turn liquid water back into ice again. The sun warms a rain puddle, and the water becomes invisible water vapor.

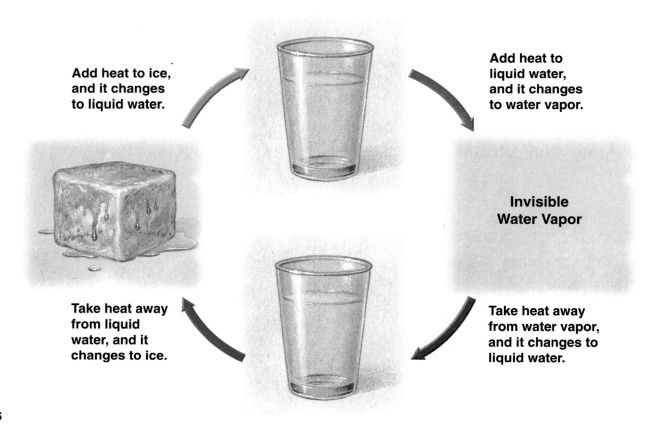

Add heat to ice, and it changes to liquid water.

Add heat to liquid water, and it changes to water vapor.

Invisible Water Vapor

Take heat away from liquid water, and it changes to ice.

Take heat away from water vapor, and it changes to liquid water.

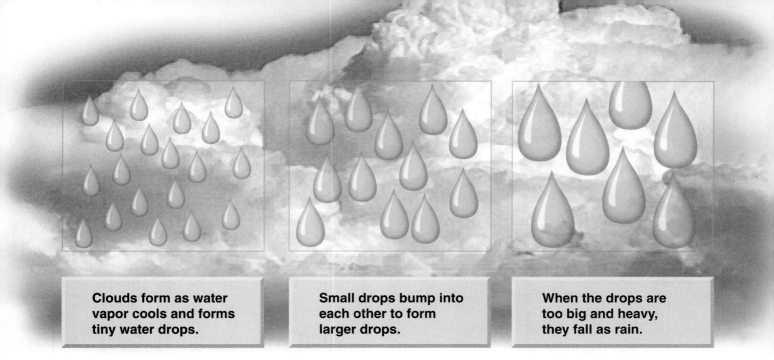

Clouds form as water vapor cools and forms tiny water drops.

Small drops bump into each other to form larger drops.

When the drops are too big and heavy, they fall as rain.

In the investigation you used the sun to heat water. The heat changed the liquid water in the open jars into a gas that spread out in the air. **Evaporation** is the changing of a liquid into a gas. Heat must be added to a liquid to make it evaporate. Evaporation changes liquid water into invisible gas—water vapor.

Water vapor in the air can condense to form dew. You can see dew on spider webs and on leaves on cool mornings. ▼

When you see rain falling, you are seeing what happens because of cooling. **Condensation** is the changing of a gas into a liquid. Taking heat away from a gas, or cooling it, changes the gas into a liquid. When water vapor cools, the water changes form. It becomes liquid water.

✔ **What three forms can water take?**

Water vapor in the air can also freeze as it condenses, to form frost. Air must be cold for frost to form. ▼

Water Changes and Moves

Water evaporates all the time from Earth's surface. So why hasn't all the water on Earth turned into water vapor? After water becomes vapor, it cools to form water again. The water returns to Earth as precipitation. **Precipitation** is water that falls to Earth as rain, snow, sleet, or hail.

Earth uses the same water over and over again. The water you use to brush your teeth is billions of years old. This recycling of water over and over again is called the water cycle. The **water cycle** is the movement of water from Earth's surface into the air and back to the surface again. This cycle is powered by heat from the sun. The picture below shows how the water cycle works.

✔ **What is the water cycle?**

The Water Cycle The sun's rays warm the land and water on Earth's surface. This causes water to evaporate and form water vapor. Warm air carries water vapor upward.

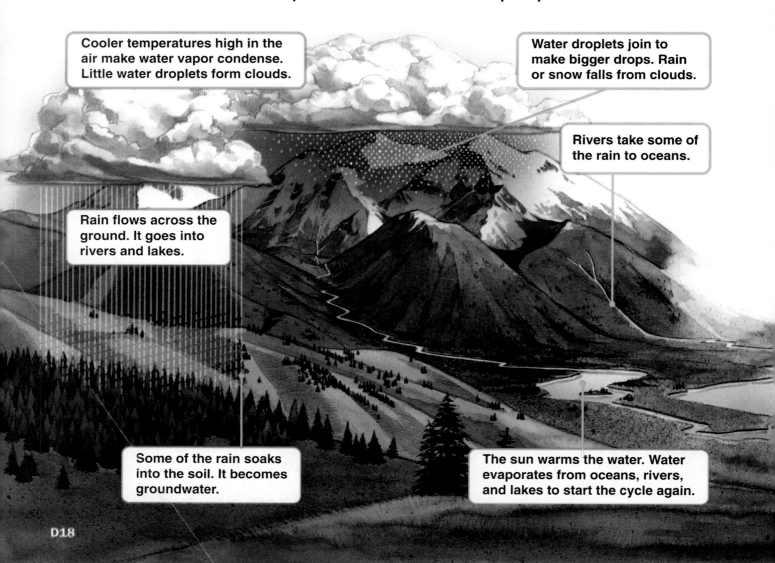

Cooler temperatures high in the air make water vapor condense. Little water droplets form clouds.

Water droplets join to make bigger drops. Rain or snow falls from clouds.

Rivers take some of the rain to oceans.

Rain flows across the ground. It goes into rivers and lakes.

Some of the rain soaks into the soil. It becomes groundwater.

The sun warms the water. Water evaporates from oceans, rivers, and lakes to start the cycle again.

Summary

Evaporation changes water from a liquid into a gas. Condensation changes water from a gas back into a liquid. The water cycle is the movement of water from Earth's surface into the air and back to the surface again. The water moves by evaporation and condensation.

Review

1. What is evaporation?
2. What is condensation?
3. What is the water cycle?
4. **Critical Thinking** What would happen if water could evaporate but could not condense?
5. **Test Prep** How does water on land return to Earth's oceans in the water cycle?

   A by evaporating
   B by turning to ice
   C by the flow of rivers
   D by entering plants

LINKS

MATH LINK

How Much Water? Suppose that 100 liters of water evaporate from a lake; 50 liters fall back on the lake as rain; 10 liters turn to ice on a mountain. The rest of the water flows back to the lake from a river. How much of the 100 liters does the river carry?

WRITING LINK

Informative Writing—Description Find pictures in magazines that show the parts of the water cycle. For each picture, write a sentence that tells what is happening. Share your work with a family member.

HEALTH LINK

Keeping Cool Evaporation helps keep your body cool on a hot day. Look up *perspiration* in a health book to find out how.

TECHNOLOGY LINK

Learn more about how people use technology to control water by watching *Inflatable Dams* on the **Harcourt Science Newsroom Video.**

A Filter for Clean WATER

Scientists developed a filter to clean water in the space shuttle. Now they are using what they learned to clean water on Earth.

Why Clean Water?

In the United States, most people use water that has been cleaned at a water treatment plant or pumped from the ground. You get water from the faucet, knowing it is safe to drink. Some places in the world, however, don't have clean water. The people in those places often drink unsafe water. The World Health Organization estimates that one

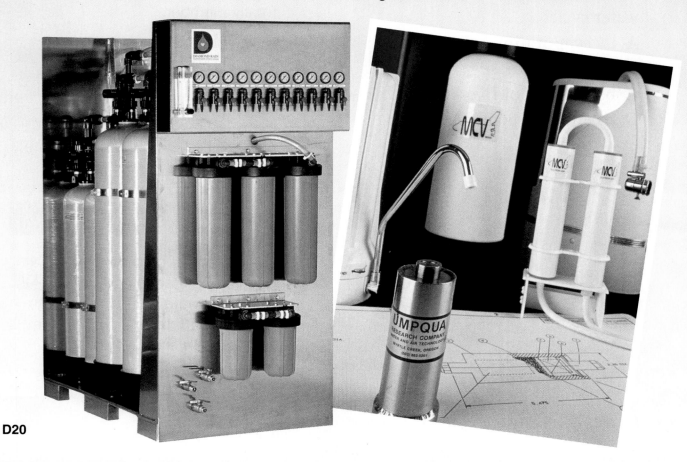

billion people are not able to get clean, safe drinking water every day.

Water in Space

Astronauts taking long space flights need lots of water. But water is heavy and takes up a lot of room. The space shuttle can't carry all the clean water that astronauts need. So scientists at NASA and at the Umpqua Research Company developed a filter to clean the used water on the space shuttle. Astronauts take only a little water on each mission, and they use the filter to clean the water after they use it.

The Umpqua Filter

After its success in space, scientists decided to use the filter on Earth. Communities suffering from natural disasters like floods and hurricanes need to clean their water. So do communities that don't already have water treatment systems.

The Umpqua filter doesn't remove dirt and chemicals from the water. It only kills bacteria. So water is first passed through another filter that removes dirt and chemicals. Then it goes through the Umpqua filter.

Several companies are now making small water-cleaning systems that use the Umpqua filter to kill bacteria in water. These filters last a long time. And it costs less than one cent per gallon to clean water by using these systems.

Think About It

1. Why is cleaning water at a disaster site better than shipping in bottled water?
2. Why is it important for people to have clean water to drink?

WEB LINK:
For Science and Technology updates, visit the Harcourt Internet site.
www.harcourtschool.com

Careers	Environmental Technician

What They Do Environmental technicians look for sources of pollution in the environment, especially in water. They also look for  ways to control that pollution.

Education and Training An environmental technician needs to study environmental science and math. It is also important for a technician to learn to write and speak well.

Lisa Rossbacher

GEOLOGIST

When you think of the National Aeronautics and Space Administration (NASA), you may not think of rocks and minerals. But some people who work at NASA study rocks and minerals. Learning about rocks and landforms on Earth helps us understand more about other planets.

Lisa Rossbacher has helped NASA study erosion on the planet Mars. She uses maps and photographs taken by space probes. She compares the patterns of erosion she sees on Mars with those she has studied on Earth. From her observations she makes inferences about how the landforms on Mars may have been shaped. She has inferred that water once moved over the surface of Mars, just as it does on Earth. Other geologists agree with her.

Rossbacher applies what she learns from her studies to help people. Geologists such as Rossbacher can help people by telling them where floods, landslides, earthquakes, or sinkholes are likely to occur. Once a community knows about the danger, it can make plans to use the land wisely. For example, people who live in areas that may flood might build dams to control the flow of water. In areas where earthquakes are likely, builders try to make buildings safer in case of an earthquake.

Think About It

1. What kinds of science skills does Rossbacher use in her work?
2. How might you use photographs of Mars to study erosion there?

Cloud in a Jar

How do raindrops form?

Materials

- metal pie pan
- freezer
- glass jar without lid
- hot water
- ice cubes

Procedure

1. Put the pan in the freezer for an hour.

2. Just before you take the pan out, have your teacher fill the jar half way with hot water.

3. Remove the pan from the freezer, and fill it with ice cubes. Place the pan on top of the jar. Leave it there for a few minutes.

Draw Conclusions

Observe what happens inside the jar. How is this like part of the water cycle?

Making Raindrops

Why do raindrops fall?

Materials

- dropper
- water
- clear plastic coffee-can lid
- pencil

Procedure

1. Fill the dropper with water.

2. Turn the lid so the top of the lid rests flat on the table. Drop small drops of water onto the lid. Put as many drops as you can on the lid without having the drops touch.

3. Quickly turn the lid over.

4. Holding the lid upside down, move drops together with the pencil point. What happens?

Draw Conclusions

How is this similar to what happens in clouds?

Chapter 1 Review and Test Preparation

Vocabulary Review

Use the terms below to complete the sentences 1 through 6. The page numbers in ( ) tell you where to look in the chapter if you need help.

groundwater (D8)

estuary (D12)

evaporation (D17)

condensation (D17)

precipitation (D18)

water cycle (D18)

1. Water that falls to Earth as rain, snow, sleet, or hail is ____.

2. The process that changes a liquid into a gas is ____.

3. An ____ is a place where fresh water from a river mixes with salt water from the ocean.

4. The process that changes a gas into a liquid is ____.

5. The ____ is the movement of water from Earth's surface into the air and back to the surface again.

6. Fresh water found under Earth's surface is ____.

Connect Concepts

Write the terms where they belong in the concept map. Use the terms in the Word Bank. One term will be used twice.

water vapor　　　**liquid water**　　　**ice**

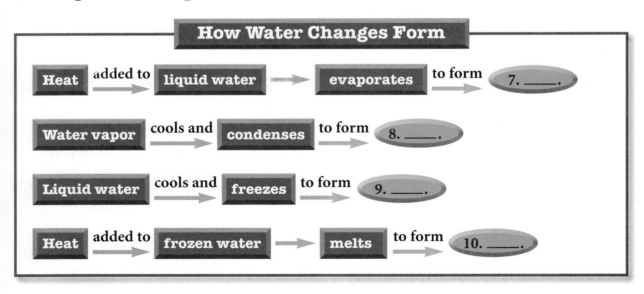

How Water Changes Form

| Heat | added to | liquid water | → | evaporates | to form | 7. ____. |

| Water vapor | cools and | condenses | to form | 8. ____. |

| Liquid water | cools and | freezes | to form | 9. ____. |

| Heat | added to | frozen water | → | melts | to form | 10. ____. |

Check Understanding

Write the letter of the best choice.

11. Which is mostly water?
    A rocks   C shells
    B plants   D soil

12. The oceans help control —
    F types of soil
    G temperature
    H groundwater
    J sunlight

13. Where does the energy for the water cycle come from?
    A the sun   C the soil
    B the wind   D the ocean

14. Fresh water is **NOT** found —
    F under Earth's surface
    G in lakes
    H in oceans
    J in rivers

15. Rain and snow are forms of —
    A precipitation
    B transpiration
    C condensation
    D evaporation

Critical Thinking

16. Some people think Earth's glaciers are important resources. Why might they think so?

17. Why is it important to not pour paint, oil, and other harmful liquids down a drain?

18. Why is an estuary an important environment?

19. Explain why the sun is important to the water cycle.

Process Skills Review

20. Suppose you are asked to keep track of the water used by your class. Tell how **using numbers** could make it easier to organize this data.

21. You see drops of rain falling. How could you **make a model** to find out what happens to the rain? Tell how you could **control variables** to find out.

Performance Assessment

Diagram the Water Cycle

Work with a partner. Together, draw a simple picture of the water cycle. Label the changes in the water. Tell whether water has been warmed or cooled to make each change.

Chapter 2

Observing Weather

No matter where you go, it seems someone is talking about the weather. That's because the weather affects what people do every day. Should you wear a coat? Will it rain during your picnic? Many of life's decisions depend on the weather.

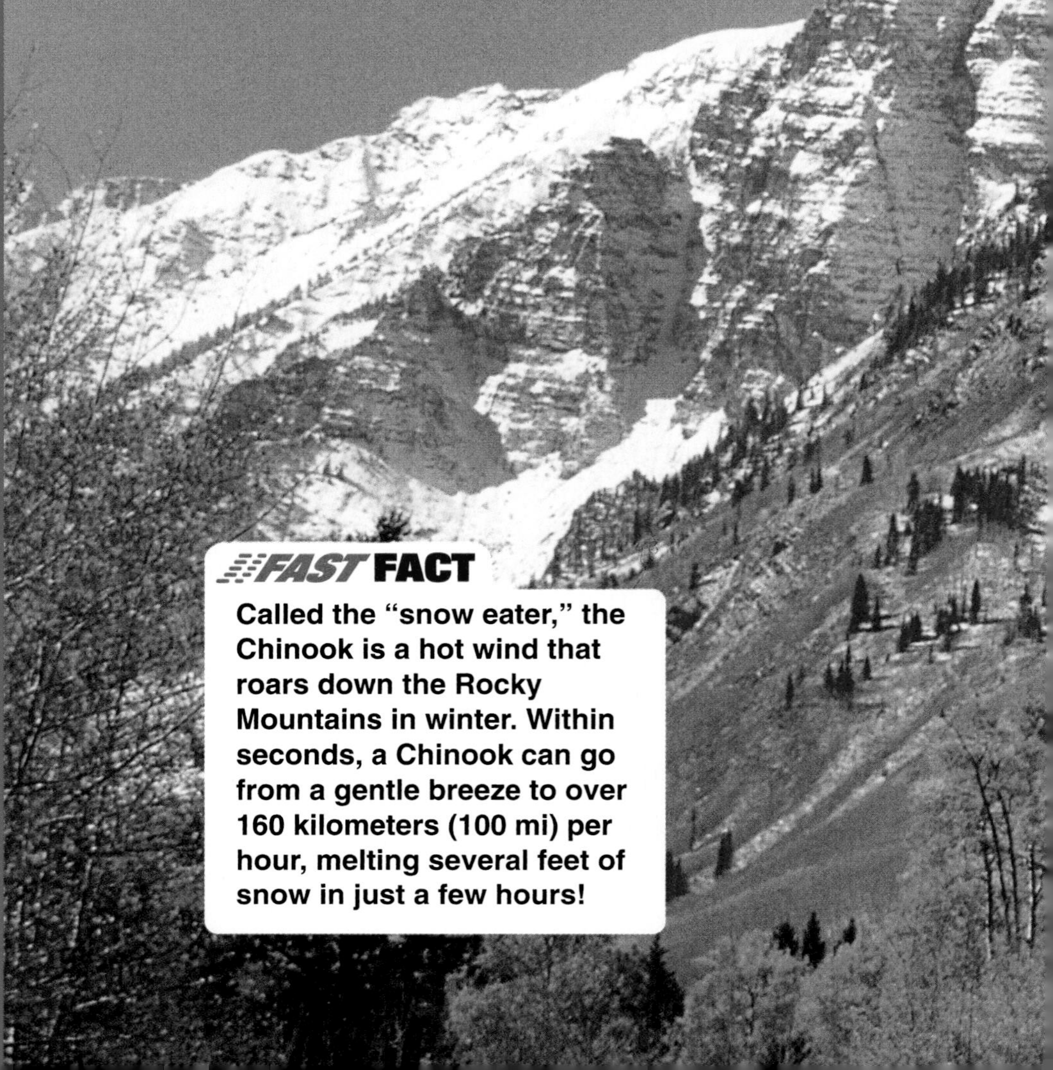

FAST FACT

Called the "snow eater," the Chinook is a hot wind that roars down the Rocky Mountains in winter. Within seconds, a Chinook can go from a gentle breeze to over 160 kilometers (100 mi) per hour, melting several feet of snow in just a few hours!

Vocabulary Preview

- atmosphere
- weather
- temperature
- front
- wind
- anemometer
- weather map

≡FAST FACT

The biggest storms on Earth are hurricanes. If the energy in one average hurricane could be captured, it would supply the United States with electricity for six months!

Record Hurricanes

Record Type	Where	When	Name
Deadliest 6000 killed	Galveston, Texas	1900	unnamed
Strongest 322 kph (200 mph) winds	Florida Keys	1935	"Labor Day"
Costliest $25 billion	Louisiana and South Florida	1992	Andrew

What Is Weather?

In this lesson, you can . . .

INVESTIGATE the properties of air.

LEARN ABOUT what weather is.

LINK to math, writing, social studies, and technology.

INVESTIGATE

Properties of Air

Activity Purpose Air is all around you. You can't see it, but you can **observe** its properties. In this investigation you will make observations. Then you will use them to **infer** some of the properties of air.

Materials
- plastic container
- water
- paper towel
- plastic cup
- index card

Activity Procedure

Part A

1. Half-fill the plastic container with water.

2. Crumple the paper towel. Push it to the bottom of the plastic cup.

◄ Water in the air can form clouds. These tall storm clouds are called thunderheads.

3 Turn the cup upside down. Push the cup to the bottom of the plastic container. Do not tilt the cup as you are pushing it downward. Then pull the cup straight up and out of the water. **Observe** the paper towel. **Record** your observations. (Picture A)

Part B

4 Remove the paper towel from the cup. Half-fill the cup with water. Put the index card over the cup opening.

5 Hold the cup over the plastic container. Use your right hand to hold the cup and your left hand to hold the index card in place. Quickly turn the cup over. Take your left hand off the index card. **Record** your observations. (Picture B)

Picture A

Picture B

Draw Conclusions

1. What did you **observe** in Part A?

2. What did you **observe** in Part B?

3. **Scientists at Work** Scientists **observe** things that happen all around them. They use their observations to **infer** why those things happen. Use your observations to infer one property of air for each part of this investigation.

Investigate Further Suppose you repeat Part B with a cup that is almost filled with water. **Predict** what will happen. Then try it.

Process Skill Tip

When you **observe**, you use your senses to examine things. Then you can **record** what you observe. When you **infer**, you use your observations to explain why something happens.

Where Weather Happens

FIND OUT

- about the layers of the atmosphere
- what weather is

VOCABULARY

atmosphere
weather

The Air Around You

It's easy to observe the air around you. But how do you study the air high above the planet? Long before the airplane was invented, scientists had wanted to study air high above the Earth. Some scientists put weather instruments on kites that they sent into the atmosphere. The **atmosphere** (AT•muhs•feer) is the air that surrounds Earth.

Today we know a lot about the atmosphere. We know that it has layers. We also know that the air in the atmosphere has certain properties. Air takes up space. That's why the paper towel in the cup stayed dry. Air also has weight and presses on things. In the investigation air pushed up on the index card, holding it in place. This pressing by the air is called *air pressure.*

The atmosphere acts like a blanket for Earth. The sun shines on Earth's surface and warms it. The surface gives off heat. Earth's atmosphere holds in the heat. Without the atmosphere, most of the energy that keeps Earth warm would escape into space.

✔ **What is the atmosphere?**

◀ **A person flew in a hot-air balloon for the first time in 1783. After that, scientists flew in balloons to study the atmosphere.**

The Atmosphere

The atmosphere has layers. You can't see where the layers begin and end. But the air in each layer is different.

1 thermosphere

2 mesosphere

3 stratosphere

4 troposphere

1 Temperatures in the *thermosphere* (THER·muhs·feer) can be higher than 2,000°C (3,632°F). Air particles can be miles apart in this part of the atmosphere. Some parts of this layer glow as the sun's rays hit them. Those parts form the northern and southern lights.

2 Temperatures are lower in the *mesosphere* (MES·uhs·feer) and can go below ⁻120°C (⁻184°F).

3 The *stratosphere* (STRAT·uhs·feer) contains the atmosphere's ozone. Ozone is a type of oxygen. It absorbs harmful rays from the sun. Because ozone absorbs some of the sun's energy, temperatures increase as you go higher in the stratosphere. Even so, the temperatures are usually below freezing. Long-distance jets sometimes fly low in the stratosphere.

4 The *troposphere* (TROH·puhs·feer) is the layer of the atmosphere where you live. Air particles in this layer are close enough for you to breathe easily. All our weather takes place in the troposphere. Near the surface, temperatures are warm. But the higher you go in the troposphere, the cooler the air temperature gets. At the top of the troposphere, the temperature drops to ⁻80°C (⁻112°F).

Weather

Earth's atmosphere is more than 160 kilometers (100 mi) thick. But weather takes place only in the 10 kilometers (6 mi) of air directly above Earth's surface.

Everybody talks about the weather, but what is it? **Weather** is what is happening in the atmosphere at a certain place. Temperature, wind, and precipitation are all parts of weather. There would be no weather without the sun. The sun's heat causes clouds, winds, and precipitation to form.

Meteorologists are scientists who study weather and the atmosphere. They measure and record changes in air. These changes help them know if the weather will be sunny or stormy.

✔ **What is weather?**

▲ Blizzards are large snowstorms. They have low temperatures and strong winds of 50 kilometers per hour (about 31 mph) or more. These winds blow the snow so that it is almost impossible to see.

▲ Hurricanes are strong, dangerous storms that form over warm ocean waters. Hurricanes have winds of 120 kilometers per hour (about 75 mph) or more.

Rain can come as gentle showers or pouring storms. ▼

▲ Tornadoes are violent windstorms. The winds are so strong that they can destroy homes and lift trains from their tracks. More tornadoes occur in the United States than anywhere else on Earth.

Summary

The atmosphere has layers. Weather takes place in the lowest layer of the atmosphere. Weather is what is happening in the atmosphere at a certain place. Temperature, wind, and precipitation are all parts of weather.

Review

1. List three properties of air.
2. What does ozone do?
3. List three things that are parts of the weather.
4. **Critical Thinking** What might Earth be like without the atmosphere?
5. **Test Prep** Where does weather happen?
   A in the layer of the atmosphere next to Earth's surface
   B in the coldest layer of the atmosphere
   C where air particles are far apart
   D in the ozone layer

LINKS

MATH LINK

Wind Speed How windy has it been lately? Look on the weather page in a newspaper to find out. Record the wind speed for seven days. Write the speeds in order from most windy to least windy.

WRITING LINK

Expressive Writing—Poem
Pick a type of weather, and write the letters of the name down the side of a page. For each letter, think of words that describe the weather. Use your words to make a poem for a younger child.

SOCIAL STUDIES LINK

Bad Weather Report on the worst weather disaster that has happened where you live. Interview someone who was there. Record the interview on tape, and share it with others.

TECHNOLOGY LINK

Learn more about weather by visiting the National Air and Space Museum Internet Site.
www.si.edu/harcourt/science

 Smithsonian Institution®

LESSON 2

How Are Weather Conditions Measured?

In this lesson, you can . . .

INVESTIGATE how a thermometer works.

LEARN ABOUT how weather is measured.

LINK to math, writing, physical education, and technology.

Measuring Temperature

Activity Purpose Temperatures change from place to place. In this investigation you will **use numbers** and a simple thermometer to **compare** temperatures.

Materials

- water
- 1-L plastic bottle
- red food coloring
- clear drinking straw
- clay
- clear plastic cup
- dropper
- metric ruler

Activity Procedure

1. Put water in the bottle until it is almost full. Add ten drops of food coloring.

2. Put the straw in the bottle. Three-fourths of the straw should stick out of the bottle. Seal the opening around the straw with clay. (Picture A)

◀ Weather vanes show wind direction. The head of the lobster points toward the direction the wind is blowing.

3 Half-fill the cup with water. Add three drops of food coloring.

4 Use the dropper to put water from the cup into the straw. Add water until you can see the water in the straw above the clay stopper.

Picture A

Picture B

5 Make a mark at the water level in the straw. You have made a thermometer. The higher the level of liquid in the straw, the higher the temperature.

6 Take the thermometer to five different places at school. Leave it at each place for 15 minutes. Use a ruler to **measure** the water level in the straw from the mark to the top of the water level. Do not squeeze the bottle while you measure. **Record** the measurement and the location. (Picture B)

Draw Conclusions

1. What happened to the water levels in the straw in the different locations?

2. What information could you learn by using your thermometer? What information is impossible to learn by using your thermometer?

3. **Scientists at Work** Scientists sometimes **use numbers** to put things in order. Look at the numbers you recorded. Use the numbers to order the locations from warmest to coolest.

Process Skill Tip

You can **use numbers** to do many things. You can count, put things in order, and **compare** one set of things to another.

How Weather Is Measured

FIND OUT

- how weather changes
- the ways temperature, precipitation, and wind are measured

VOCABULARY

temperature
front
wind
anemometer

Measuring Temperature

The highest temperature ever measured on Earth was 58°C (136°F) in northern Africa. The lowest temperature was ⁻89°C (⁻128°F) in Antarctica. **Temperature** is a measure of how hot or cold something is. Temperatures on Earth can feel burning hot or freezing cold. Thermometers are used to measure temperatures.

Air temperature is always changing. You've probably noticed changes in temperature from day to night. Air is warmer in the sun. It is cooler after the sun sets. During the day the sun warms the ground more in some places than in others. It warms land faster than water.

Usually, air over land is warm and dry. Air over water is cool and damp. A large body of air with the same temperature and moisture is called an *air mass*. An air mass can be hundreds of kilometers wide. It can cover many states or a whole ocean. A moving air mass causes many weather changes.

✔ **What is temperature?**

Temperature	
40°C/104°F	Heat wave
30°C/86°F	Good day for a swim
20°C/68°F	Perfect day!
10°C/50°F	A bit chilly—wear a light jacket!
0°C/32°F	Time for a coat (water freezes)
⁻10°C/14°F	Bundle up! It's cold outside!
⁻20°C/⁻4°F	There's ice on the windows!
⁻40°C/⁻40°F	Brrrrr! Stay inside!

°C   °F
50 — 120
40 — 100
30 — 80
20 — 60
10 — 40
0 — 20
10 — 0
20 — 20
30 — 20
40 — 40

MADE IN U.S.A.

Air masses are always moving. A front is a place where two air masses of different temperatures meet. Most weather changes happen at fronts.

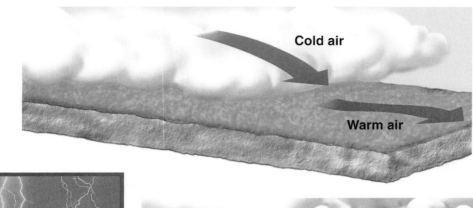

Cold air

Warm air

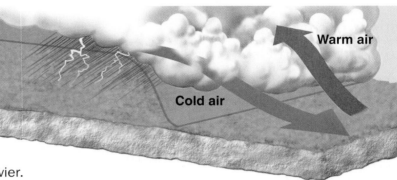

Warm air

Cold air

At a cold front, cold air bumps into warmer air. The cold air is heavier. It pushes the warm air up quickly. This forms tall clouds and thunderstorms. Wind and heavy rain often occur. Cold fronts move fast, so the rain doesn't last long. Cold air replaces the warm air at the surface. This makes the temperature drop after the rain.

Warm air

Cold air

At a warm front, warm air bumps into colder air. The warm air is pushed up gently by the cold air. It forms a long line of clouds. Warm fronts bring long periods of gentle rain, gray skies, and light winds. Warm air replaces the cold air at the surface. This makes the temperature rise after the rain.

Measuring Precipitation

Many people live near rivers. Rivers are usually good neighbors, helping people move goods, supplying sources of power, and providing places to fish and swim. But when there are heavy rains, rivers can rise and spill over their banks. Flood waters can cover fields and towns, causing much damage.

People need to know when a flood might occur. That's why it's important to measure precipitation. Precipitation is any kind of water that falls from the sky. It might be rain, snow, sleet, or hail.

Meteorologists measure rain by using rain gauges. A rain gauge looks like a cup or a glass. It collects precipitation as it falls.

Meteorologists measure snow by using snow boards. Snow boards are like long rulers. People stick them into snow to see how high it is. During storms, people measure snow levels every six hours. It takes 10 inches of snow to equal the amount of water in 1 inch of rain.

✔ **How is precipitation measured?**

Rain gauges, like this one, are used to measure precipitation. ▶

The ways clouds look often give us clues about the coming weather. Stratus clouds are low gray clouds. They usually show that rain is on the way. ▼

Cumulus clouds are puffy and white. Small cumulus clouds appear in clear, sunny weather. If the clouds gather and grow tall, a storm is coming. ▼

Inside a Thunderhead

Thunderheads are giant clouds that form along cold fronts.

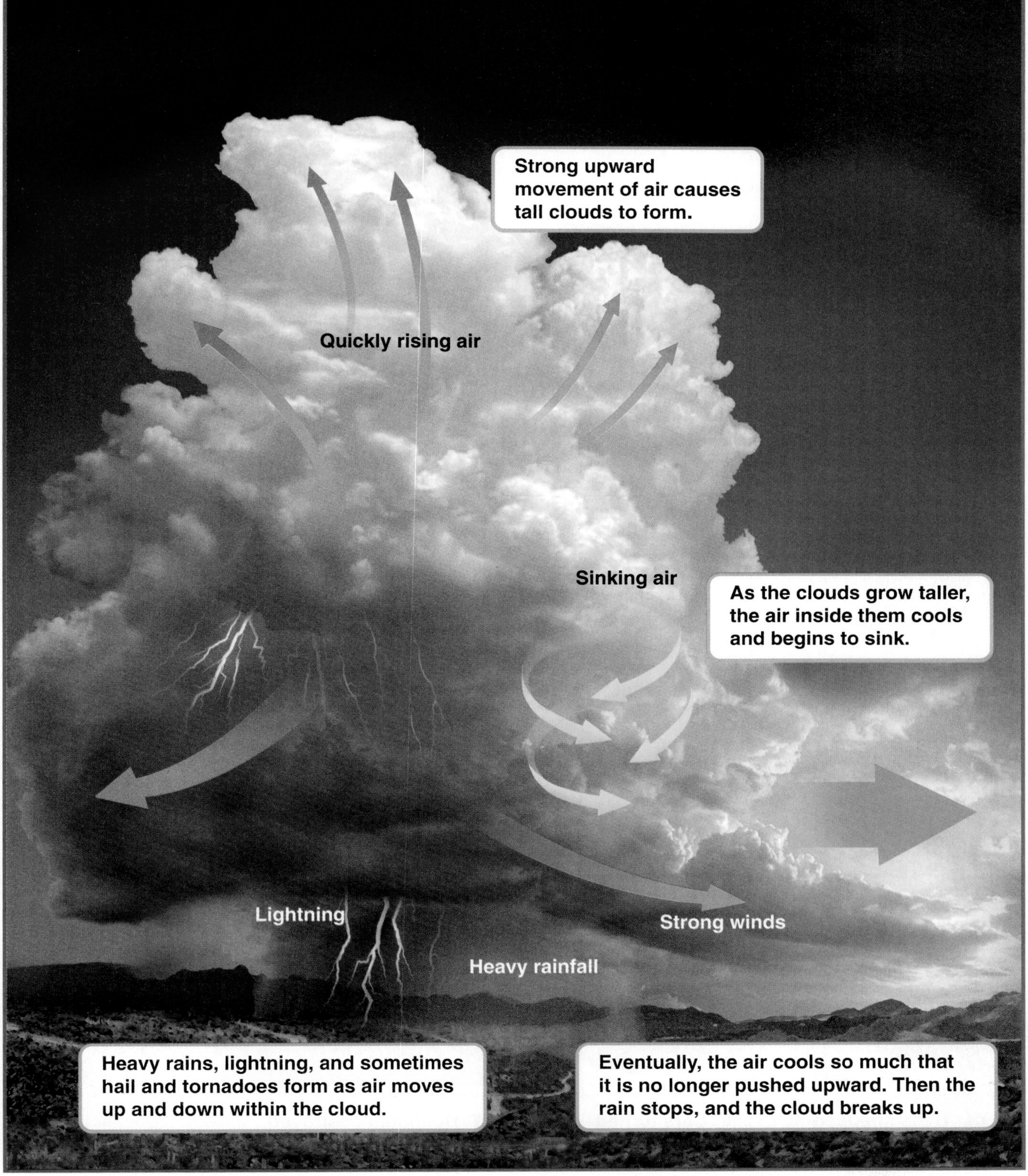

Strong upward movement of air causes tall clouds to form.

Quickly rising air

Sinking air

As the clouds grow taller, the air inside them cools and begins to sink.

Lightning

Strong winds

Heavy rainfall

Heavy rains, lightning, and sometimes hail and tornadoes form as air moves up and down within the cloud.

Eventually, the air cools so much that it is no longer pushed upward. Then the rain stops, and the cloud breaks up.

Measuring Wind

Winds can be helpful. They cool us on a hot day. They clear pollution from the air. But winds also can do damage. They can blow down buildings or tear up trees.

Wind is the movement of air. Wind happens because air pressure is different in different places. Air, in the form of wind, moves from areas of high pressure to areas of low pressure—like water flowing downhill.

The direction the wind comes from can be recorded, and its speed can be measured. A weather vane shows wind direction. An **anemometer** (an•uh•MAHM•uht•er) measures wind speed.

Beaufort Wind Scale

One way to estimate the speed of the wind is to look at the movements of objects around you. The pictures show one way to estimate the speed of the wind. This wind scale is called the Beaufort (BO•furt) Wind Scale.

0 Air is still; smoke rises straight up.

1 Smoke drifts; flags hang still.

2 Smoke drifts with wind.

3 Flags and leaves move gently.

4 Loose paper blows.

5 Small waves on water.

6 Umbrellas blow inside out.

7 Hard to walk into wind.

8 Branches ripped off trees.

9 Roofs and chimneys damaged.

10 Trees snapped in half.

11 Cars turned over.

12 Buildings destroyed.

The strongest winds occur in storms. Hurricanes are the biggest storms on Earth. They can be 650 kilometers (400 mi) across. The slowest hurricane winds are 120 kilometers per hour (75 mph).

Tornadoes are shaped like spinning funnels. They are much smaller than hurricanes, but they have stronger winds. The wind at the center of a tornado can be more than 480 kilometers per hour (300 mph).

✓ **What is wind?**

Summary

Many weather changes happen at fronts. People use tools to measure changes in weather. Thermometers measure temperature. Rain gauges measure rainfall. Anemometers measure wind speed.

Review

1. What is an air mass?
2. What is a front?
3. What makes the wind blow?
4. **Critical Thinking** What changes happen when a front passes through an area?
5. **Test Prep** An anemometer measures wind —

   A direction   **C** sounds
   B destruction   **D** speed

LINKS

MATH LINK

Temperature Table Make a table showing each day's high and low temperature for 1 week. Which day had the greatest difference in temperature? What was the difference?

WRITING LINK

Informative Writing— Description Write a paragraph to describe today's weather. How does the weather make you feel? Read your description in class. Compare your description with those of your classmates.

PHYSICAL EDUCATION LINK

Fly a Kite Find directions for making a kite. Look in books with projects on wind, weather, air, and Earth science. Fly your kite on different days when the wind is blowing at different speeds. When does your kite fly best?

TECHNOLOGY LINK

To learn more about measuring weather, watch *Phoenix Monsoon* on the **Harcourt Science Newsroom Video.**

CNN Turner Le@rning

INVESTIGATE

LESSON **3**

What Is a Weather Map?

In this lesson, you can . . .

 INVESTIGATE how to read a weather map.

 LEARN ABOUT the way people predict weather.

 LINK to math, writing, social studies, and technology.

Reading Weather Maps

Activity Purpose Maps show a lot of data. Often the data is shown as symbols. In this investigation you will **interpret data** on a weather map. Then you will answer questions about the weather.

Materials
■ weather map

Activity Procedure

1 Study the weather map and the key to the symbols that it uses.

2 Use the map to answer the questions.

◀ These red and black flags tell people that a hurricane is coming.

D42

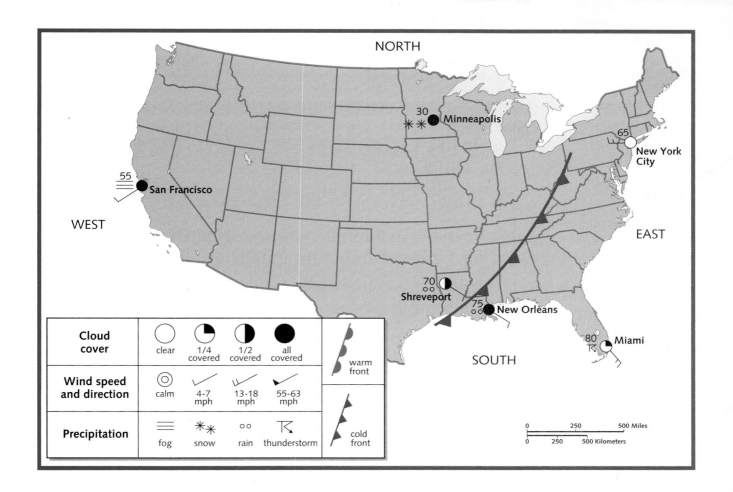

Draw Conclusions

1. Where is there a thunderstorm?

2. Find the cold front. What can you tell about the weather along the cold front?

3. **Scientists at Work** Scientists **interpret data** on weather maps to learn about the weather in different places. Interpret data on this map to describe the weather in Minneapolis, Minnesota.

Investigate Further The weather in the United States generally moves from west to east. Imagine that you are in New York City. Use the data on the map to **predict** what your weather may be like about one week from now.

Process Skill Tip

When you **interpret data**, you must first **observe** it and try to understand it. Then you use the data to answer questions, to make predictions, or to make inferences.

Forecasting Weather

FIND OUT

- how people forecast the weather

- how to read a weather map

VOCABULARY

weather map

Gathering Weather Data

You turn on the TV. Joyce Bishop, the weather forecaster, stands in front of a big map. She points to it and says there will be rain tomorrow. So you know you should take an umbrella to school.

You depend on the TV weather forecaster. But she doesn't predict the weather by herself. She has help.

Information about the weather comes from thousands of weather stations all over the world. At each station, data about temperature, precipitation, air pressure, wind, and clouds are recorded.

◀ Thousands of stations collect weather data each day. The government runs some of the stations like this one. Some people have instruments at their homes to collect data.

▲ Weather satellites circle Earth many times each day. Satellite data can show cloud patterns over large areas.

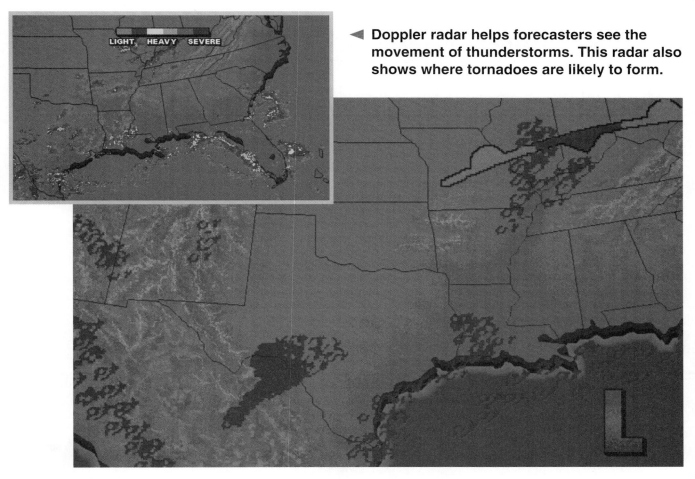

◄ Doppler radar helps forecasters see the movement of thunderstorms. This radar also shows where tornadoes are likely to form.

LIGHT HEAVY SEVERE

▲ TV weather forecasters get data and forecasts from the National Weather Service. Sometimes they use the data to make their own forecasts for a local area.

Weather planes gather data about storms. Meteorologists on these planes try to find out how strong the winds are and what direction a storm is likely to move.

Data also comes from weather balloons. Meteorologists send up weather balloons every 12 hours. Instruments carried by the balloons take readings of temperature, precipitation, and wind. They record data on weather high in the atmosphere.

Satellites in space send weather data back to Earth. Satellites also take pictures that show clouds and storms as they move across the country.

Each day the National Weather Service collects all these pieces of data. The data goes into computers that organize the information into maps. Computers also help meteorologists make predictions. They send all this information to the weather forecasters you see on TV.

✔ **Name three sources of weather data.**

Weather Maps

Meteorologists use the data from the National Weather Service to make forecasts. They also use the data to make weather maps. A **weather map** is a map that shows weather data for a large area. The maps show temperatures and precipitation. They show warm fronts and cold fronts. They show areas of high air pressure and low air pressure.

Some weather maps use station-model symbols. You saw some of these symbols in the investigation. A station model is shown on the next page. Meteorologists often use these symbols instead of the symbols used in many newspapers. These symbols give more exact data about the weather in a certain place.

✔ **What is a weather map?**

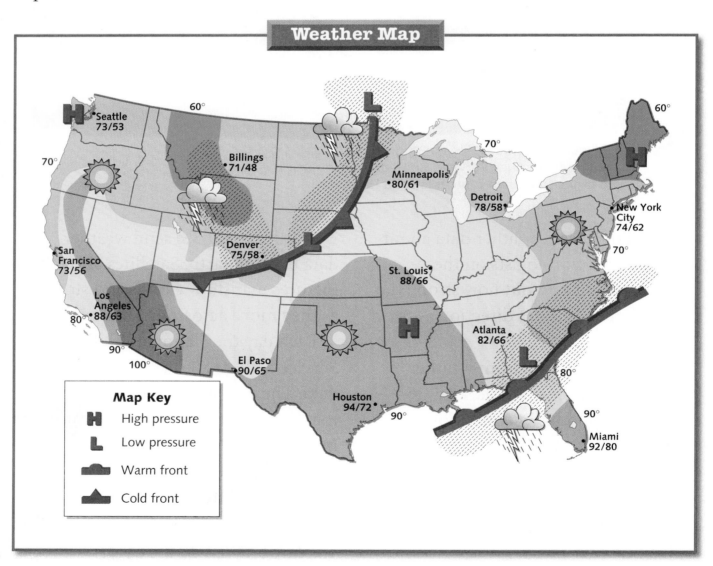

Weather Map

Seattle 73/53
Billings 71/48
Minneapolis 80/61
Detroit 78/58
New York City 74/62
San Francisco 73/56
Denver 75/58
St. Louis 88/66
Los Angeles 88/63
El Paso 90/65
Atlanta 82/66
Houston 94/72
Miami 92/80

Map Key

H — High pressure
L — Low pressure
▬ — Warm front
▲ — Cold front

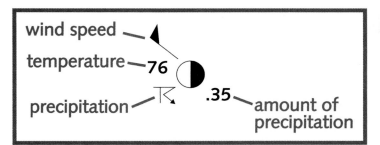

wind speed

temperature — 76

precipitation

.35 — amount of precipitation

▲ **A station model shows the weather at one place. The weather at this station is cloudy with winds out of the northwest at about 55–63 miles per hour. The temperature is 76°F, and there are thunderstorms.**

Summary

Meteorologists use data from surface stations, airplanes, weather balloons, and satellites. Weather maps use symbols to show weather conditions over large areas.

Review

1. What kinds of weather data do we get from airplanes?
2. How do satellites help meteorologists predict the weather?
3. What is a station model?
4. **Critical Thinking** Why do meteorologists collect data many times each day?
5. **Test Prep** A weather map does **NOT** show —
   A temperature
   B precipitation
   C seasons
   D wind speed

LINKS

MATH LINK

Forecast Fractions Keep track of the TV weather forecast for five days. Each day check to see if the forecast was right or wrong. Write a fraction to compare how many forecasts were right (top number) with the total number of forecasts (bottom number).

WRITING LINK

Informative Writing— Explanation Suppose a meteorologist comes to your class. Write one question about weather. With your classmates, find the answers to the questions. Publish your findings.

SOCIAL STUDIES LINK

Types of Maps A weather map is only one kind of map. Find another kind of map in a book or a magazine. Explain to the class what the map shows.

TECHNOLOGY LINK

Learn more about weather maps by visiting this Internet Site.

www.scilinks.org/harcourt

*SCi**LINKS***
THE WORLD'S A CLICK AWAY

Controlling Lightning Strikes

The clouds are black. The sky is dark. You know there's going to be a thunderstorm. Then you see the lightning. It flashes down from the sky in giant forks. You know you will be safe if you stay inside a building or a car. But what about all the power lines and other structures that attract lightning? How safe are they?

Lightning Damage

Each year $138 million worth of damage is caused by lightning strikes in the United States. These strikes are especially harmful to energy plants, airports, and military bases. When lightning struck an energy company in Japan, the company was unable to provide power for a week. That's hard on families, but it's even worse for hospitals and fire departments. Researchers around the world have been studying lightning, hoping to find a better way to protect buildings.

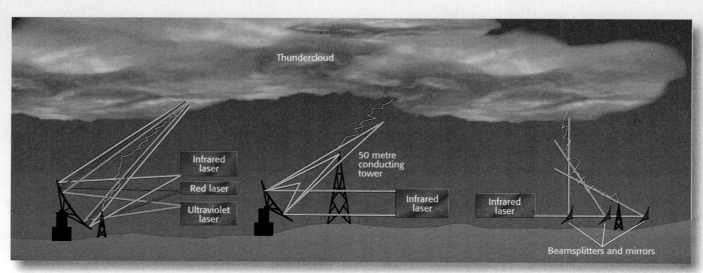

Thundercloud

Infrared laser

Red laser

Ultraviolet laser

50 metre conducting tower

Infrared laser

Infrared laser

Beamsplitters and mirrors

▲ Some plans for attracting lightning

Lightning Rods

The idea of protecting people and property from lightning is not new. The original idea of lightning rods began with Benjamin Franklin in 1752. A lightning rod is a metal rod that is placed on top of the highest point on a building. Because the lightning rod is the highest thing around, lightning will strike it instead of the building. When lightning strikes the rod, the electricity passes through the rod, along a cable, and harmlessly into the ground.

Using Lasers to Attract Lightning

Lightning rods wait to be hit by lightning. Now scientists are working out a way to use lasers to pull lightning out of the sky and conduct it into the ground. That way they can make lightning strike where and when they want.

Researchers began experimenting with lasers and lightning in the early 1990s. They fire ultraviolet (UV) lasers into the sky. The laser beams make a path through the air. Lightning bolts follow this path back to the laser like water flowing through a pipe. A metal plate in front of the laser protects it from the lightning. As lightning follows the laser beam, its power is turned aside harmlessly. If all goes as planned, portable lasers could be used to draw lightning away from power lines, airplanes, and important buildings.

Think About It

- Why would it be useful for lightning lasers to be portable?

WEB LINK: For Science and Technology updates, visit the Harcourt Internet site. www.harcourtschool.com

Careers | Weather Researcher

What They Do Weather researchers are people who work behind the scenes of the weather reports you watch on TV. Some researchers record the weather where they live. Others collect data to make charts and maps for weather prediction.

Education and Training A weather researcher needs a college degree in meteorology, math, or physics. Weather researchers also need writing skills because they often publish the results of their work.

June Bacon-Bercey

METEOROLOGIST

"I was discouraged [from becoming a meteorologist] and other women were discouraged. If they feel they've got some money behind them, it might be better."

The words above explain why June Bacon-Bercey decided to set up a scholarship fund for women who want to be meteorologists. Meteorologists are people who study weather. They observe weather and map weather conditions. They use information from computers to predict the weather.

Bacon-Bercey has been interested in the weather since she was a young girl. She has worked on television as a meteorologist. She has also worked for the National Weather Service. In 1979 she became chief administrator of television activities for the National Oceanic and Atmospheric Administration. She coordinates the agency's services to schools, the government, and the general public.

Bacon-Bercey has seen a lot of changes in the ways weather data is gathered and shared with people. Years ago people who gave TV weather reports just read information a weather service gave them. Now many TV stations hire their own meteorologists.

Think About It

1. What might a person who studies the weather talk about if he or she came to your school?
2. If you were setting up a scholarship fund, what groups of people would you most like to help?

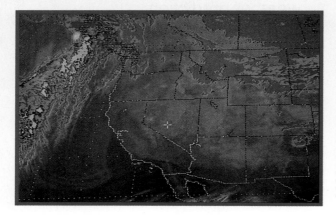

Measure Precipitation

How can you find out how much rain falls?

Materials
- masking tape
- ruler
- clear plastic 1-L bottle with top cut off

Procedure
1. Tape the ruler to the outside of the bottle. The 1-in. mark should be at the bottom of the bottle.

2. Put your rain gauge outside before it rains. Do not place it under a tree or under an object that might block the rain.

3. Check the amount of water in the bottle after the rain stops.

Draw Conclusions
Look on the weather page of the newspaper. How much rain fell the day you used your gauge? Was your measurement correct? How close was your measurement?

Measure the Wind

How fast does the wind blow?

Materials
- 2 cardboard strips
- scissors
- stapler
- wire
- cap of a ballpoint pen
- 4 small paper cups (3 white, 1 red)
- watch with second hand

Procedure
1. Make an X with the cardboard strips. Staple the strips together.

2. Use the scissors to make a hole in the middle of the X. Push the pen cap into the hole as shown

3. Cut a slit in the opposite sides of each cup. Attach the cups as shown.

4. Push the piece of wire deep into the ground outside. Balance the pen cap on the wire.

5. Count the times the red cup spins by in 1 minute. Divide this number by 10. The answer tells how many miles per hour the wind is blowing.

Draw Conclusions
Measure the speed of the wind over the next several days. How does the speed change?

Chapter **2** Review and Test Preparation

Vocabulary Review

Use the terms below to complete the sentences 1 through 8. The page numbers in ( ) tell you where to look in the chapter if you need help.

atmosphere (D30)

weather (D32)

temperature (D36)

front (D37)

wind (D40)

anemometer (D40)

weather map (D46)

1. What is happening in the atmosphere at a certain place is ___.

2. A tool that measures wind speed is an ___.

3. A ___ shows the weather over a large area.

4. The air that surrounds Earth is the ___.

5. The ___ is the measure of how hot or cold something is.

6. The movement of air is ___.

7. A ___ is a place where two air masses meet.

8. Weather occurs in the lowest layer of the ___.

Connect Concepts

Write the terms where they belong in the concept map.

anemometer   **temperature**

precipitation   **wind vane**

rain gauge

Weather Measuring Tools	
Weather Condition	**Tools That Measure It**
9. _____	thermometer
wind	11. _____
	12. _____
10. _____	13. _____
	snow board

Check Understanding

Write the letter of the best choice.

14. The atmosphere is important to our weather because —
    A it is clear
    B it holds in Earth's heat
    C winds are light
    D it has ten layers

15. At a cold front, —
    F warm air replaces cold air
    G there is gentle rain
    H winds are light
    J there can be thunderstorms

16. A ___ collects weather data on the ground.
    A satellite   C weather station
    B airplane   D weather balloon

Critical Thinking

Use the diagram below to answer the questions.

17. What type of front is shown?

18. What will the weather be like along the front?

19. How will the weather change as the front moves on?

Process Skills Review

20. Observe the table below, which shows the high temperature in one place for five days in a row. **Interpret the data.** What can you **infer** about the weather during the week?

Day	High Temperature (°F)
Monday	20°
Tuesday	19°
Wednesday	21°
Thursday	45°
Friday	47°

21. How would you **use numbers** to find out how much rain is equal to 10 in. of snow?

Performance Assessment

Reading Weather Maps

Use the weather map to tell what the weather is like in Charlotte, North Carolina. Next, use the data from the map to forecast how Charlotte's weather will change. Then, draw a new station model for Charlotte showing what the weather will be like after the change.

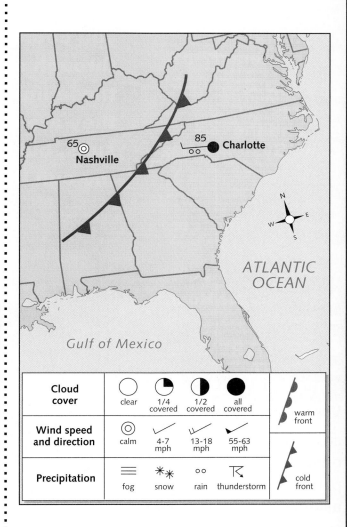

Vocabulary Preview

solar system	revolution
orbit	phases
planet	lunar eclipse
asteroid	solar eclipse
comet	star
rotation	constellation
axis	telescope

Earth and Its Place in the Solar System

Looking up at a clear night sky, you will see tiny points of light. If you could leave Earth and travel through space to get closer to those lights, you would see that they are other worlds and other suns, but not like the Earth and the sun that we know.

FAST FACT

If you want to find the coldest place in the solar system, go to Triton, Neptune's largest moon. Temperatures there average ⁻235 degrees C. It's so cold on Triton that volcanoes erupt with ice instead of lava!

The sun is big enough to hold over 1 million Earths. Even so, the sun is an average-sized star! Here's how the sun compares with some of the biggest stars that you can see in the night sky.

Star Sizes

Star	Miles Across
Sun	870,000
Mu Cephi	2,000,000,000
VV Cephi	2,000,000,000
Epsilon Auriga	46,000,000,000

This drawing shows how scientists think the surface of Triton looks.

What Is the Solar System?

In this lesson, you can . . .

INVESTIGATE the planets.

LEARN ABOUT objects in the solar system.

LINK to math, writing, health, and technology.

INVESTIGATE

The Planets

Activity Purpose Nine planets circle the sun. They are not all alike. In this investigation you will use some of the planets' properties to **order** them. Then you will **classify** the planets by using the data you have organized.

Materials
- pencil
- paper

Activity Procedure

1 Copy the Ordering Planet Data chart.

2 **Use numbers** from the data table to find each planet's distance from the sun. **Record** in your table the names of the planets, beginning with the one closest to the sun.

3 **Use numbers** from the data table to find the distance across each planet. The planet with the shortest distance across is the smallest planet. Use numbers to **order** the planets by size. **Record** the names of the planets in order, beginning with the smallest planet.

◄ Telescopes help us see things that are far away.

Ordering Planet Data

Closest to the Sun to Farthest from the Sun	Smallest to Largest	Shortest Year to Longest Year

Planet Data

Planet	Distance from Sun (in millions of kilometers)	Distance Across (in kilometers)	Length of Year (y=Earth year d=Earth day)
Earth	150	12,750	365 d
Jupiter	778	143,000	12 y
Mars	228	6,800	2 y
Mercury	58	4,900	88 d
Neptune	4,505	49,000	165 y
Pluto	5,890	2,300	248 y
Saturn	1,427	120,000	29 y
Uranus	2,869	51,000	84 y
Venus	108	12,000	225 d

Draw Conclusions

1. Which planet is closest to the sun? Farthest from the sun?

2. Which is the largest planet? The smallest?

3. **Scientists at Work** Scientists sometimes **use numbers** to put things in **order**. Scientists have studied the same data you used in this investigation. How did using numbers help you realize the **space relationships** between the planets?

The Solar System

FIND OUT

- the names of the planets
- about other bodies in the solar system

VOCABULARY

solar system
orbit
planet
asteroid
comet

The Structure of the Solar System

The **solar system** is the sun and the objects that orbit around it. An **orbit** is the path an object takes as it moves around another object in space. All the planets you studied in the investigation, including Earth, orbit the sun.

You learned about some parts of the solar system in the investigation. The solar system has nine planets, including Earth. A **planet** is a large body of rock or gas that orbits the sun. The solar system also has many moons. Moons are large, rocky objects that orbit planets. Earth has one moon. Other planets have no moons or many moons. Comets and asteroids are also parts of the solar system.

✔ **What is the solar system?**

THE INSIDE STORY

The Solar System

All of the planets are much smaller than the sun. The distances tell how far from the sun each planet really is.

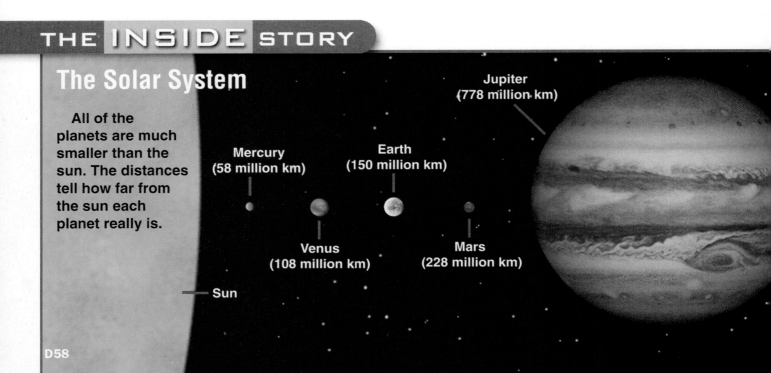

Jupiter
(778 million km)

Mercury
(58 million km)

Earth
(150 million km)

Venus
(108 million km)

Mars
(228 million km)

Sun

The Sun

The sun is the center of the solar system. It is a *star*—a hot ball of glowing gases. It looks different to us from other stars because it is closer to us than other stars are.

The sun is very hot and bright. The sun is also big. All of the planets and moons of the solar system could fit inside it.

Gravity on the sun is very strong. That's because of its great size. *Gravity* is the force of one object's pull on another. The sun's gravity helps hold the objects in the solar system in orbit.

✔ **What is the sun?**

The sun is 1.35 million kilometers (about 838,900 mi) across. The Earth is tiny compared with the sun. The sun could hold more than one million Earths inside it. ▶

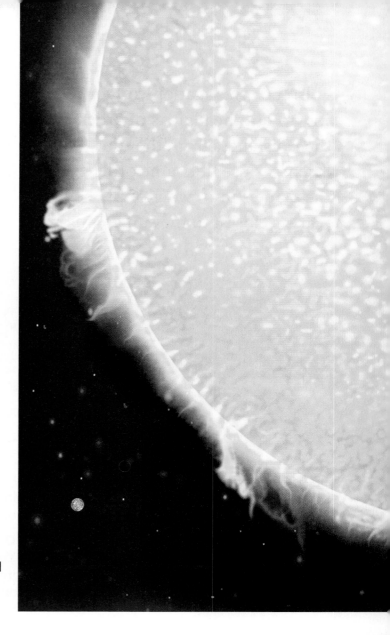

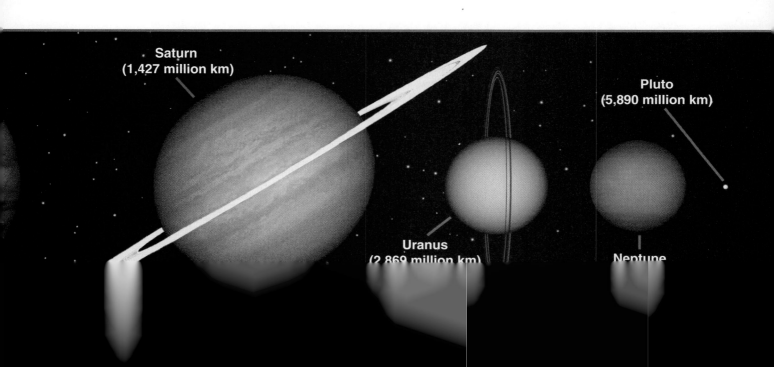

Saturn
(1,427 million km)

Uranus
(2,869 million km)

Pluto
(5,890 million km)

Neptune

The Inner Planets

In the investigation you found a way to put the planets in order by their distances from the sun. Scientists use this same order to put the planets into two groups. The four planets closest to the sun are in one group. They are called the *inner planets*. The five other planets are the *outer planets*.

The inner planets are Mercury, Venus, Earth, and Mars. They are alike in many ways. They all have rocky surfaces. Because they are

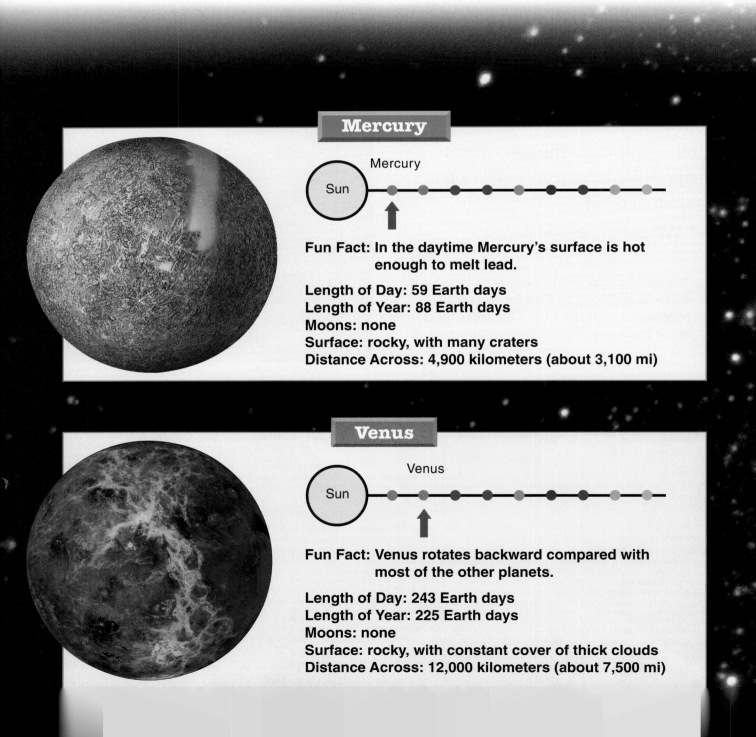

Mercury

Fun Fact: In the daytime Mercury's surface is hot enough to melt lead.

Length of Day: 59 Earth days
Length of Year: 88 Earth days
Moons: none
Surface: rocky, with many craters
Distance Across: 4,900 kilometers (about 3,100 mi)

Venus

Fun Fact: Venus rotates backward compared with most of the other planets.

Length of Day: 243 Earth days
Length of Year: 225 Earth days
Moons: none
Surface: rocky, with constant cover of thick clouds
Distance Across: 12,000 kilometers (about 7,500 mi)

closer to the sun, they are warmer than the outer planets. The inner planets are also smaller than most of the outer planets. None of them has more than two moons.

Earth is different from the other inner planets. It has a watery surface. It is the only planet with a lot of oxygen in its atmosphere. Earth also has plant life and animal life.

✔ **List the inner planets in order from the sun.**

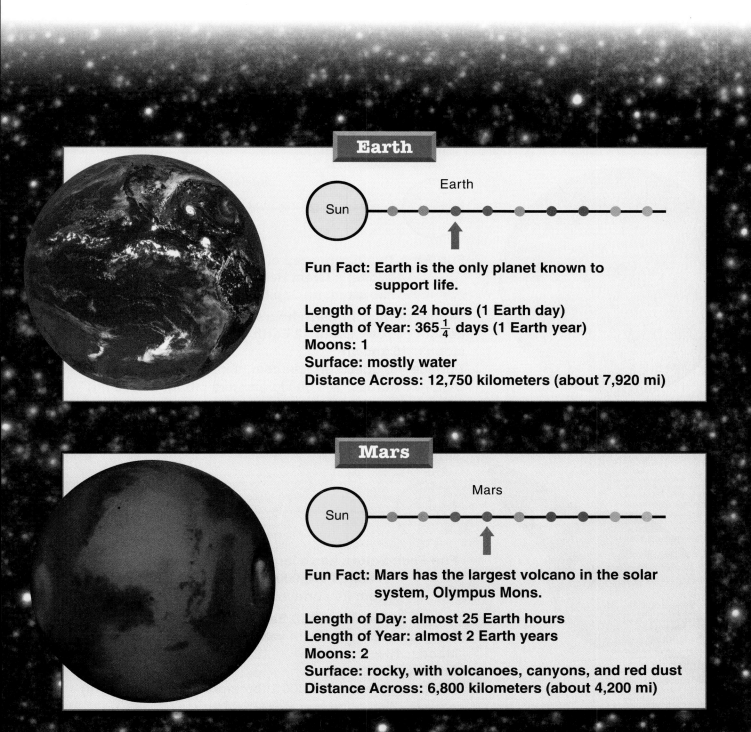

Earth

Fun Fact: Earth is the only planet known to support life.

Length of Day: 24 hours (1 Earth day)
Length of Year: $365\frac{1}{4}$ days (1 Earth year)
Moons: 1
Surface: mostly water
Distance Across: 12,750 kilometers (about 7,920 mi)

Mars

Fun Fact: Mars has the largest volcano in the solar system, Olympus Mons.

Length of Day: almost 25 Earth hours
Length of Year: almost 2 Earth years
Moons: 2
Surface: rocky, with volcanoes, canyons, and red dust
Distance Across: 6,800 kilometers (about 4,200 mi)

The Outer Planets

The five planets farthest from the sun are called the outer planets. The outer planets are Jupiter, Saturn, Uranus, Neptune, and Pluto.

The outer planets are alike in many ways. They are made mostly of frozen gases. They are very far from the sun, so their surfaces are much colder than the inner planets. All but Pluto are much larger than the inner planets. Jupiter is the solar system's largest planet. It is more than 1,000 times larger than Earth. Most of the outer planets have many moons. Many also have rings of dust and ice around them.

Pluto is different from the other outer planets. It is the smallest planet in the solar system. It is smaller than Earth's moon.

✔ **List the outer planets in order from the sun.**

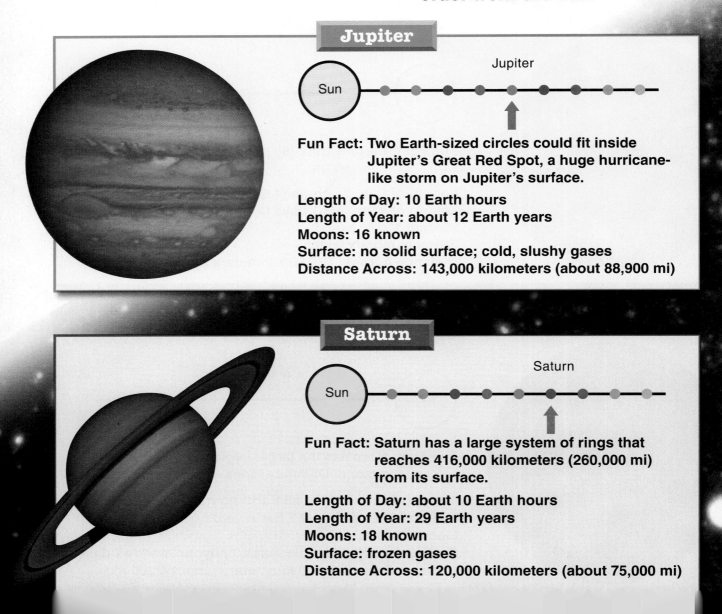

Jupiter

Fun Fact: Two Earth-sized circles could fit inside Jupiter's Great Red Spot, a huge hurricane-like storm on Jupiter's surface.

Length of Day: 10 Earth hours
Length of Year: about 12 Earth years
Moons: 16 known
Surface: no solid surface; cold, slushy gases
Distance Across: 143,000 kilometers (about 88,900 mi)

Saturn

Fun Fact: Saturn has a large system of rings that reaches 416,000 kilometers (260,000 mi) from its surface.

Length of Day: about 10 Earth hours
Length of Year: 29 Earth years
Moons: 18 known
Surface: frozen gases
Distance Across: 120,000 kilometers (about 75,000 mi)

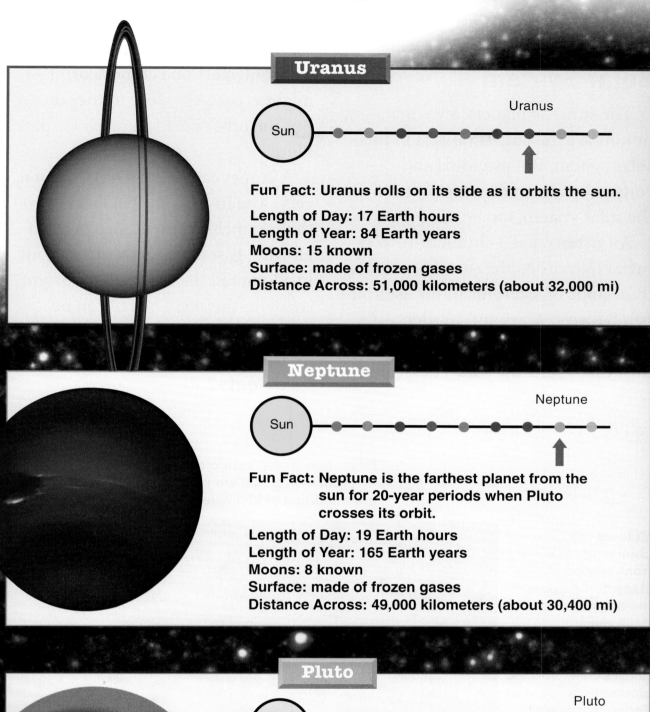

Uranus

Uranus

Fun Fact: Uranus rolls on its side as it orbits the sun.

Length of Day: 17 Earth hours
Length of Year: 84 Earth years
Moons: 15 known
Surface: made of frozen gases
Distance Across: 51,000 kilometers (about 32,000 mi)

Neptune

Neptune

Fun Fact: Neptune is the farthest planet from the sun for 20-year periods when Pluto crosses its orbit.

Length of Day: 19 Earth hours
Length of Year: 165 Earth years
Moons: 8 known
Surface: made of frozen gases
Distance Across: 49,000 kilometers (about 30,400 mi)

Pluto

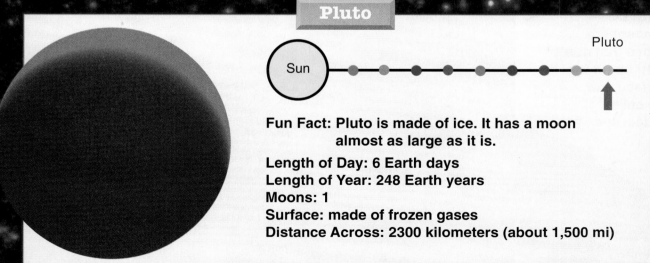

Pluto

Fun Fact: Pluto is made of ice. It has a moon almost as large as it is.

Length of Day: 6 Earth days
Length of Year: 248 Earth years
Moons: 1
Surface: made of frozen gases
Distance Across: 2300 kilometers (about 1,500 mi)

Other Bodies in the Solar System

The sun, the planets, and their moons are the largest objects in the solar system. But asteroids and comets, while smaller, are parts of the solar system, too.

An **asteroid** is a chunk of rock or metal that orbits the sun. There are thousands of asteroids in the asteroid belt between Mars and Jupiter.

A **comet** is a large ball of ice and dust that orbits the sun. The orbit of a comet is shaped like a large, flat oval. One part of a comet's orbit might come very close to the sun. But the other part can reach far past Pluto.

A comet can be seen only when it gets close to the sun. The heat from the sun melts a comet's ice to form glowing gases. The gases stream out in a long tail that looks like a bright streak in the sky. The tail can be millions of kilometers long.

✔ **What are asteroids and comets?**

More than 20,000 asteroids are in the asteroid belt. Some are small. Others are hundreds of kilometers wide. ▼

Meteors are chunks of rock from space. Many come from the asteroid belt. Each day, hundreds of meteors enter Earth's atmosphere. Those that don't burn up hit the surface and are called meteorites. ▼

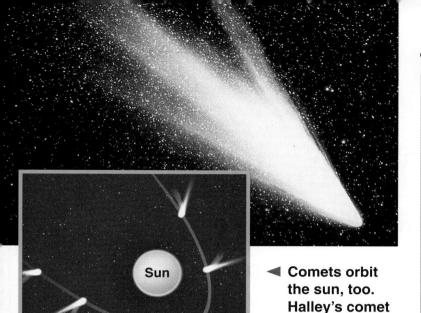

◀ Comets orbit the sun, too. Halley's comet can be seen from Earth every 76 years.

Summary

The solar system has nine planets that orbit the sun. Earth is one of those planets. Asteroids and comets are also parts of the solar system.

Review

1. What is a planet?
2. List three ways the inner planets are alike.
3. List three ways the outer planets are alike.
4. **Critical Thinking** How are asteroids and meteorites alike? How are they different?
5. **Test Prep** A comet is visible in the sky only when it is close to —
   A the sun
   B Earth
   C Mars
   D Pluto

LINKS

MATH LINK

How Many Moons? Make a bar graph showing the number of moons each planet has. How does the number of Earth's moons compare with the number of moons of other planets?

WRITING LINK

Narrative Writing—Story Pick a planet. Write a story for your teacher that tells what life would be like on that planet. Describe what it might be like to visit there. Share your story with your classmates.

HEALTH LINK

Sun Safety The sun's rays can harm the skin. That's why people use sunscreen. Sunscreens have an SPF number. Find out what *SPF* means. What SPF number sunscreen should you wear every day to protect you from the sun?

TECHNOLOGY LINK

Learn more about Mars by viewing *Mars Pathfinder Discovery* on the **Harcourt Science Newsroom Video**.

CNN Turner Le@rning

What Causes Earth's Seasons?

In this lesson, you can . . .

 INVESTIGATE how Earth's tilt causes seasons.

 LEARN ABOUT the seasons.

 LINK to math, writing, art, and technology.

 **INVESTIGATE**

How the Sun Strikes Earth

Activity Purpose Many places on Earth are hot in summer and cold in winter. In this investigation you will find out why. You will **compare** the way light rays strike a surface. Then you will **infer** how this affects Earth's temperatures.

Materials

- clear tape
- graph paper
- large book
- flashlight

- meterstick
- black marker
- wooden block
- red marker

Activity Procedure

1. Tape the graph paper to the book.

2. Hold the flashlight about 50 cm above the book. Shine the light straight down. The beam will make a circle on the paper. If the circle is bigger than the paper, bring the light closer.

◀ **The leaves of some trees turn red, orange, and gold in the fall.**

3 Have a partner use the black marker to draw around the light beam on the paper. (Picture A)

4 **Observe** the brightness of the light on the squares. **Record** your observations.

5 Keep the flashlight in the same position. Have a partner put the block under one end of the book and use the red marker to draw around the light on the paper. (Picture B)

6 **Observe** the brightness on the squares again. **Record** your observations.

Picture A

Draw Conclusions

1. How many squares are inside the black line? How many squares are inside the red line?

2. Inside which line was the light brighter?

3. **Scientists at Work** Scientists **compare** things to find out how they are the same and how they are different. Compare the results of Steps 3 and 5 of the investigation. Do straight light rays or tilted light rays give stronger light? Suppose the paper is Earth's surface. The light is the sun. Which area would have warmer weather? Explain.

Investigate Further **Predict** what will happen if the book is tilted even more. Test your prediction.

Picture B

Process Skill Tip

When you **compare**, you **observe** the properties of two or more things to see how they are alike and how they are different.

The Seasons

FIND OUT

- why there are seasons
- what causes day and night

VOCABULARY

rotation
axis
revolution

How Earth Moves in Space

You are sitting reading this book. It seems like you are still. But you're not. Earth is traveling through space at almost 107,800 kilometers (67,000 mi) per hour. You are moving with Earth. You are also flying around the solar system as Earth orbits the sun.

Earth moves in two ways. First, Earth spins like a top. This is called rotation. **Rotation** (roh•TAY•shuhn) is the spinning of an object on its axis. Earth's **axis** (AK•sis) is an imaginary line that goes through the North Pole and the South Pole. Earth rotates on its axis once every 24 hours. One rotation takes one day.

Earth also circles the sun. This is called revolution. A **revolution** (rev•uh•LOO•shuhn) is the movement of one object around another object. Earth makes one revolution around the sun every $365\frac{1}{4}$ days. One revolution takes one year.

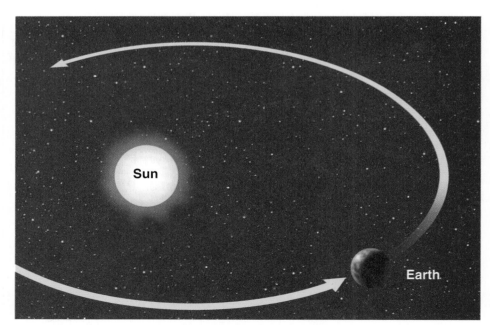

Earth rotates on its axis as it revolves around the sun. ▶

Sun

Earth

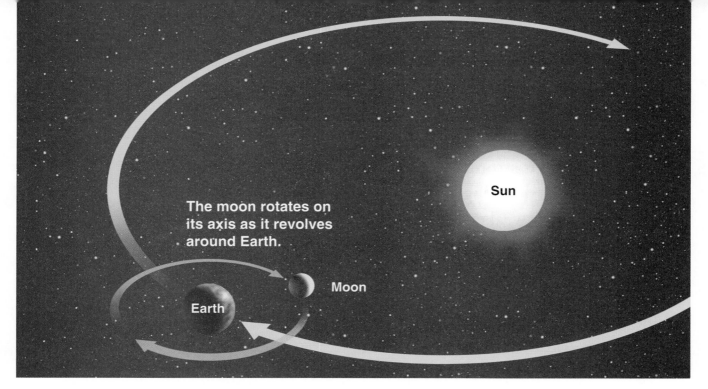

The moon rotates on its axis as it revolves around Earth.

Sun

Moon

Earth

▲ Both Earth and the moon rotate. The Earth rotates once a day. The moon rotates about once a month.

The moon also rotates and revolves. It rotates on its axis. It revolves around Earth. A day on the moon, or one rotation, is about 29 Earth days long. The moon takes this same amount of time to revolve around Earth.

Objects on Earth cast shadows. Shadows can help us observe Earth's rotation. As Earth rotates, the sun's position seems to change in the sky. But it is really the Earth that is moving.

In the morning the sun seems low in the sky. Objects cast long shadows. As the Earth rotates, the sun seems to move higher in the sky. Shadows get shorter. At noon, the sun is overhead. Objects cast short shadows—or no shadows at all. As Earth continues to rotate, the sun looks lower in the sky again. Shadows get longer until the sun sets.

✔ **What is rotation?**

Shadows are short at noon. They're longer at 2:00 P.M. because the sun is lower in the sky. ▼

What Causes Seasons

In most places on Earth, summer and winter are different. Summer is hot. There are many hours of daylight. Sunlight is strong. Winter is cold. The hours of daylight are shorter. Sunlight is weaker. Summer and winter are two seasons.

Earth has seasons because its axis is tilted. This means Earth is tipped to one side, like the book in the investigation was tilted. The tilt changes the way sunlight hits Earth at different times of the year. Sometimes the sun's rays are almost straight when they hit Earth's surface. At other times the sun's rays are slanted. This changes the amount of light and heat the surface gets.

Earth's axis is always pointing the same way in space. But because Earth is moving, the axis changes position compared with the position of the sun.

For part of the year the top of the axis (the North Pole) points in the direction of the sun. When Earth is in this position, it is summer in the northern half. During that time the bottom of the axis (the South Pole) points away from the sun. When Earth is in this position, it is winter in the southern half.

Earth has a curved surface. Some sunlight hits the surface straight on. Some sunlight hits the surface on a slant. ▼

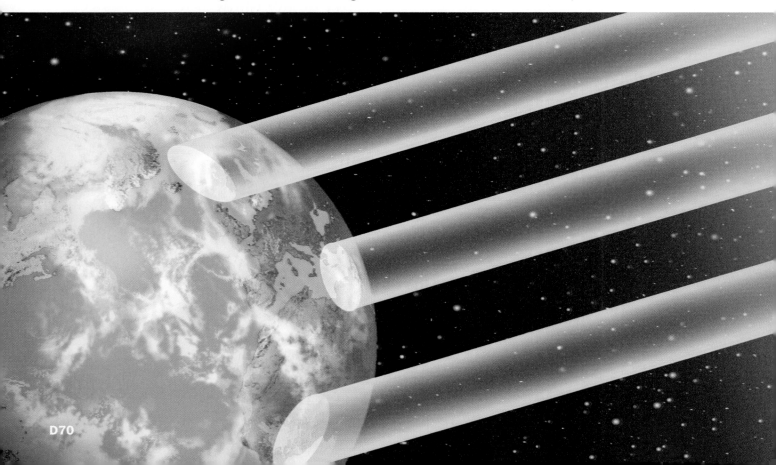

Seasons on Earth's Northern Half

Spring

Summer

Winter

Fall

Whichever end of Earth's axis points in the direction of the sun, the sun shines more directly on that part of Earth. This direct sunlight heats the ground and the air. It is summer.

Earth is always moving around the sun. Three months after summer starts, the top of the axis is not pointing in the direction of the sun anymore. Neither is the bottom of the axis. Days and nights are of equal length. Both the top half and the bottom half of the Earth get the same amount of light. Temperatures are cooler than in summer and warmer than in winter. It is fall in the northern half.

Three months later the northern half of the Earth points away from the sun. The sun shines less directly on its surface. Rays are slanted. Slanted rays cover a larger area, so the ground and the air are heated less. This makes the northern half of the Earth colder. It is winter.

Another three months pass. Again neither axis points in the direction of the sun. Days and nights are almost equal in length. Now it is spring. A full year has passed. Then the cycle starts again with summer.

Seasons in the northern and southern halves of Earth are reversed. When the northern half of Earth has spring, the southern half has fall. When the northern half has winter, the southern half has summer. Australia is on the southern half of Earth. So in Australia December is in the middle of summer. July is in the middle of winter.

✔ **Why are there seasons?**

What Causes Day and Night

It's 4:00 P.M. Your family decides to call a friend in Asia. When your dad makes the call, he wakes up your Asian friend. He was sleeping. It's the middle of the night there.

As you move from place to place on Earth, time changes. When you are eating dinner, people on the other side of the world might be having breakfast.

▲ When it is day in Chicago, Illinois, . . .

. . . it is night in Hong Kong, China. Hong Kong is on the other side of Earth from Chicago. ▼

Sunlight always shines on half of Earth. The other half is in darkness. ▼

Sun

Earth's rotation causes this difference in time. At any one time, half of Earth is in sunlight. The other half is in darkness. The half in sunlight has day. The half in darkness has night.

✔ **How much of Earth's surface is in sunlight at one time?**

Summary

Earth rotates on its axis and revolves around the sun. Earth has seasons because its axis is tilted. The sun heats Earth's surface differently at different times of the year. Night and day happen as Earth rotates. Places on Earth's surface move from sunlight into darkness and back.

Review

1. What is a revolution?
2. When it is winter in the northern half of Earth, what season is it in the southern half?
3. Why are many places warmer in summer than in winter?
4. **Critical Thinking** How would day and night be different if Earth did not rotate?
5. **Test Prep** The tilt of Earth's axis causes —

   A rotation
   B day and night
   C seasons
   D sunlight

LINKS

MATH LINK

Measuring Shadows Put a stick in the ground. Measure the length of its shadow each hour. How does the shadow change? How could you use this shadow as a clock?

WRITING LINK

Persuasive Writing—Opinion Which is your favorite season? Write a paragraph for your family about why you like that season. Try to persuade them to agree with you.

ART LINK

Season Mobile Make a mobile about your favorite season. Include pictures or objects to show both things you see and activities you enjoy during that season.

TECHNOLOGY LINK

Learn more about seasons and other chapter topics by visiting this Internet Site.
www.scilinks.org/harcourt

SCI LINKS
THE WORLD'S A CLICK AWAY

How Do the Moon and Earth Interact?

In this lesson, you can . . .

INVESTIGATE the phases of the moon.

LEARN ABOUT why the moon seems to change.

LINK to math, writing, literature, and technology.

INVESTIGATE

The Moon's Phases

Activity Purpose If you look at the moon each night, you will see that its shape seems to change. These shapes are called *phases*. In this investigation you will **observe** how a light shining on a ball looks different as you move around the ball.

Materials
- lamp with no shade
- softball

Activity Procedure

1 Work with a partner. Turn on the lamp. Your teacher will darken the room.

2 Have Person 1 hold the ball and stand with his or her back to the lighted bulb. Hold the ball as shown. Continue holding the ball this way until the end of the procedure. (Picture A)

◀ You see the moon rise from Earth. But if you were on the moon, you would see Earth rise!

3 Have Person 2 stand in position 1 in Picture A. **Observe** the ball. Make a drawing of the ball's lighted side.

4 Person 2 now moves to position 2. Turn toward the ball. Make a drawing of the lighted part of the ball.

5 Have Person 2 move to position 3. Make a drawing of the lighted part of the ball.

6 Person 2 again moves. This time to position 4. Turn toward the ball. Make a drawing of the lighted part of the ball.

7 Switch roles and repeat the procedure so Person 1 can observe the patterns of light on the ball.

Picture A

Draw Conclusions

1. What part of the ball was lighted at each position?

2. The ball represents the moon. What does the light bulb represent? What represents a person viewing the moon from Earth?

3. **Scientists at Work** Scientists **use models** to make **inferences** to explain how things work. If the ball represents the moon, what can you infer that the different parts of the lighted ball represent?

Process Skill Tip

When you **observe** something, you use your senses to get information about it. When you **infer**, you use your observations to form an opinion.

How the Moon and Earth Interact

FIND OUT

- what the moon's phases are
- what causes eclipses

VOCABULARY

phase
lunar eclipse
solar eclipse

The Phases of the Moon

If you watch the moon for a month, its shape seems to change. Sometimes it looks like a big round ball. At other times you see a thin sliver. Why do these changes happen?

The half of the moon that faces the sun is always lighted. As the moon moves around Earth, different amounts of its lighted and dark sides face Earth. The moon's phase depends on the part of the lighted half you can see. **Phases** are the different shapes the moon seems to have in the sky.

It takes about one month for the moon to revolve around Earth. It takes the same amount of time for the moon to rotate. This causes the same side of the moon to always face Earth. ▶

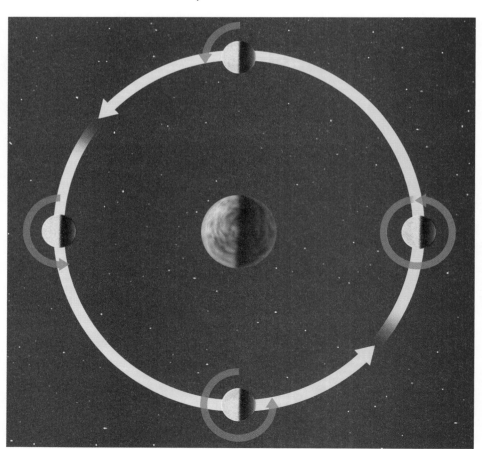

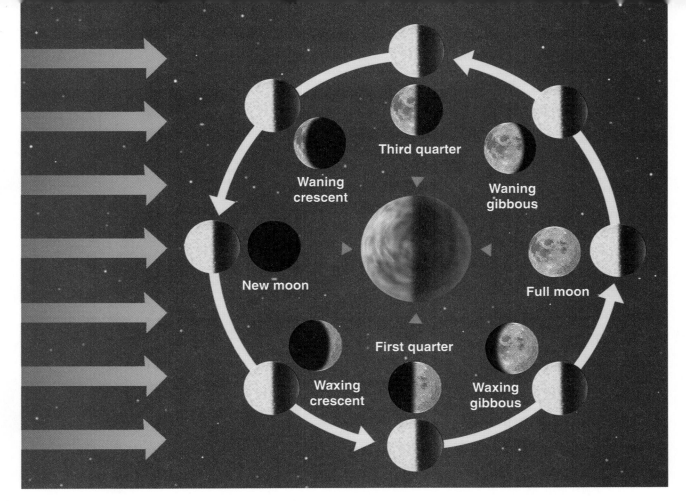

▲ The photographs show what the moon looks like from Earth. The drawings show what the moon would look like from space.

The moon goes through all of its phases every $29\frac{1}{2}$ days. During the phase called the new moon, the lighted half faces away from Earth. You can't see the moon at all. After the new moon, the moon seems to get bigger.

As the moon continues in its orbit around Earth, one lighted edge comes into view. This is a crescent moon. About one week after the new moon, half of the moon's lighted face can be seen. This is the first quarter. The next phase is the gibbous moon.

It shows a little less than $\frac{3}{4}$ of the moon's lighted side.

About two weeks after the new moon, you see the full moon. At full moon you can see the whole face of the moon. The moon has completed half of its orbit around Earth.

After the full moon, the phases reverse. The lighted part you see gets smaller. First you see the gibbous moon again. Then you see the third quarter. The last phase is another crescent moon.

✔ **What are the moon's phases?**

Eclipses of the Moon

Everything the sun shines on casts a shadow. Earth and the moon cast shadows, too. Most of the time these shadows fall on empty space. But sometimes these shadows can be seen from Earth's surface.

You know the moon revolves around Earth. At times the Earth is between the sun and moon. If the sun, Earth, and moon are in a straight line, Earth blocks some of the sun's light from falling on the moon. Although you should see a full moon, the moon gets dark for a time. This is called a lunar eclipse. A **lunar eclipse** happens when Earth's shadow falls on the moon.

✔ **What causes a lunar eclipse?**

When the sun shines on you, you cast a shadow. ▶

Sun

A total lunar eclipse causes all of the moon's face to look dark red. Total lunar eclipses do not happen as often as partial eclipses. This is because the sun, the Earth, and the moon need to be in a straight line for Earth's shadow to completely cover the moon.

A partial lunar eclipse blocks only part of the sun's light. Watching partial eclipses helped early scientists figure out that Earth is round. Why would eclipses help them see that Earth is round? ▼

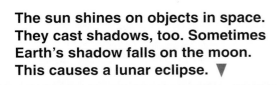

The sun shines on objects in space. They cast shadows, too. Sometimes Earth's shadow falls on the moon. This causes a lunar eclipse. ▼

Earth

Moon

Eclipses of the Sun

A shadow slowly covers the sun. The whole sky turns dark in the middle of the day. Ancient peoples thought this was the end of the world. Today we know it's a solar eclipse. A **solar eclipse** happens when the moon's shadow falls on Earth. This happens when the moon moves between the Earth and the sun.

During a total solar eclipse, the moon blocks out the sun. Only a halo of sunlight remains around the moon. The areas where a total eclipse can be seen is small. Outside this area only part of the sun is covered.

✔ **What causes a solar eclipse?**

A total solar eclipse happens when the moon moves between Earth and the sun. These photos show what the sun looks like as a total solar eclipse takes place. Total solar eclipses are rare. ▶

People in the small shadow area see the total eclipse. Those outside the shadow see a partial eclipse. ▼

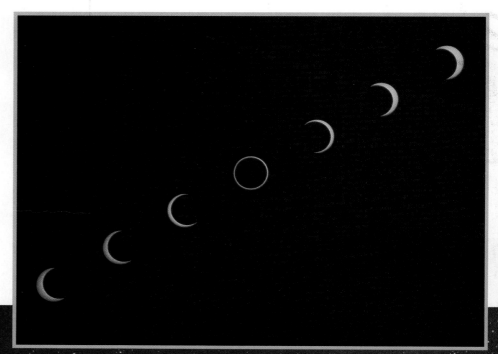

Sun

Summary

Phases are the different shapes the moon seems to have in the sky. The moon goes through its phases every $29\frac{1}{2}$ days. Eclipses happen when one object in space moves into the shadow of another. There are lunar eclipses and solar eclipses.

Review

1. Describe a new moon.
2. Compare and contrast a lunar and a solar eclipse.
3. What do you see from Earth during a total solar eclipse?
4. **Critical Thinking** Tell what phase the moon is in during a lunar eclipse. Explain your answer.
5. **Test Prep** Which of these is **NOT** a phase of the moon?

   A new   **C** crescent
   B full   **D** eclipse

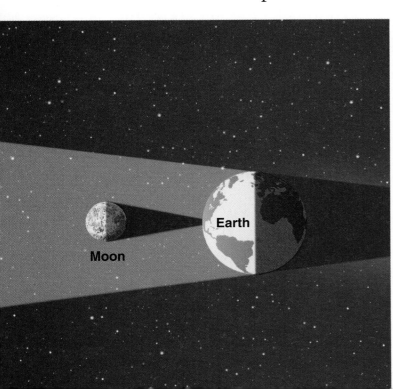

LINKS

MATH LINK

Sketch It Sketch the shape of the moon each night for one month. Start with the new moon. How much time does it take for all eight phases to take place? Predict the date of the next new moon.

WRITING LINK

Narrative Writing—Personal Story When the sun got dark in ancient times, people thought the sun was gone. Suppose that you lived then. You are seeing a solar eclipse. Write a story for a younger child to explain what you think is happening.

LITERATURE LINK

Find Out More Find out more about the sun, the moon, or eclipses by reading *The Sun and the Moon* by Patrick Moore.

TECHNOLOGY LINK

Learn more about interactions in space by investigating *Blast Off into Orbit* on **Harcourt Science Explorations CD-ROM.**

What Is Beyond the Solar System?

In this lesson, you can . . .

INVESTIGATE star patterns.

LEARN ABOUT the stars we see in the sky.

LINK to math, writing, literature, and technology.

INVESTIGATE

Star Patterns

Activity Purpose Can you see patterns in the stars? People saw star patterns in ancient times. They saw horses, bears, and dragons in the sky. In this investigation you will make your own star pattern. Then you will **compare** the pattern to objects you know about.

Materials

- gummed stars
- black construction paper
- white crayon or chalk

Activity Procedure

1 Take the stars in your hand. Hold your hand about a half meter above the paper. Drop the stars onto the black paper. Glue the stars where they fall on the paper. (Picture A)

◀ Telescopes were invented many years ago. This telescope was used by scientists around the year 1620.

2 **Observe** the stars. Look for a picture that the stars make. Use the white crayon to connect the stars to show the picture or pattern. You can connect all of the stars or just some of them.

3 Trade star patterns with other people in your class. See if they can tell what your star pattern is.

Draw Conclusions

1. People have looked at the stars for thousands of years. Different people have seen different pictures in the stars. Why do you think this is so?

2. Some people look at a star pattern and see different things. A star pattern that looks like a water dipper to one person might look like part of a bear to another person. Look again at the stars on your paper. What other patterns can you find in them?

3. **Scientists at Work** Scientists **compare** things to see how they are alike. In the investigation you compared your star pattern to objects you know about. What person, animal, or object does your star pattern look like?

Investigate Further **Observe** real star patterns. Choose a star pattern, and draw it as you see it with the unaided eye. Look at the star pattern again using binoculars or a telescope. Use another color to add anything to the pattern that you didn't see before. **Compare** what you saw in your two observations.

Process Skill Tip

When you **compare** things, you look for properties that are the same.

The Way We See Stars

FIND OUT

- what constellations are
- how telescopes help us see stars

VOCABULARY

star

constellation

telescope

Star Patterns

A **star** is a hot ball of glowing gases—like our sun. The stars you see at night are much like the sun, but they are farther away. This makes the stars look very small. It also makes the stars look like they are all the same distance from Earth. But they are not. Some stars are not too far from the solar system. Some are very, very far away.

Ursa Major Native Americans named the constellation shown here the Great Bear (Ursa Major). The seven stars highlighted inside the bear make up the Big Dipper. The people of ancient China thought the stars of the Big Dipper looked like a chariot. The chariot carried the king of the sky. ▼

Just as you did in the investigation, ancient people looked for patterns in the stars. Then they made up stories to explain the patterns. A group of stars that forms a pattern is a **constellation**. People all over the world looked at the same stars and saw different patterns.

✔ **What is a constellation?**

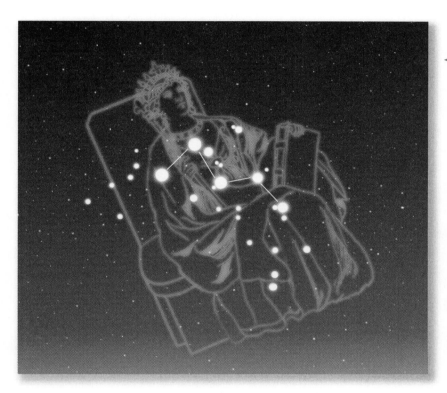

◀ **Cassiopeia** The people of ancient Greece called this constellation Cassiopeia. In the story they made up, Cassiopeia was the queen of part of Africa. She said that her daughter was more beautiful than anyone. Her bragging made one of the Greek gods angry. So he tried to take away Cassiopeia's daughter. A hero named Perseus saved the girl. But the angry god punished Cassiopeia. He turned her into a constellation.

◀ **Tayamni** This constellation was named by the Native American people called the Lakota. Tayamni means "the animal." The ancient Greeks had a different name for Tayamni. They called part of the same pattern Orion, the hunter. The three bright stars in the middle of Tayamni form the animal's back. The same stars form the belt of Orion.

Stars Seem to Move

Pick a constellation. Find it at the start of the evening and again later that night. You will see that it has moved. Stars don't really move around us. But they seem to move because Earth rotates. The spot where you are moves as Earth spins, so the stars above you change. Since Earth turns toward the east, the stars rise above the horizon in the east. As Earth keeps turning, the stars keep moving across the sky. When they finally get to the horizon in the west, they go below the horizon. They seem to disappear.

Stars and Seasons

This is the Big Dipper, part of the constellation Ursa Major. If you watch carefully, you can see how this constellation seems to move from place to place as the seasons change.

▲ In the spring, the Big Dipper is high in the sky. It looks upside down.

▲ In the summer, the Big Dipper has moved down in the sky. Its handle is pointing up.

You see different constellations at different times of the year. This is because Earth revolves around the sun. As Earth circles the sun, you see stars in different parts of space.

Polaris, or the North Star, is the only star that seems to stand still. The North Star is above Earth's axis.

The constellations near the North Star don't move across the sky. They just circle around the North Star. The Big Dipper is a constellation that circles the North Star.

✔ **Why do stars seem to move across the sky?**

▲ **In the fall, the Big Dipper is low in the sky. It looks as if it could hold water.**

▲ **In the winter, the Big Dipper has moved up in the sky. Its handle is pointing down.**

Observing Stars

People have looked at the stars for thousands of years. But many stars were not bright enough for people to see until the invention of the telescope. A **telescope** makes things that are far away look clearer and bigger. Many more stars can be seen with the telescope than with the unaided eye.

The astronomer Galileo used one of the first telescopes. He saw Saturn's rings through it in the early 1600s. Galileo's telescope made things look about 30 times as close as they are. Now telescopes can make things look thousands of times as close.

✔ **What does a telescope do?**

To see stars, you look through the eyepiece.

This piece helps you point the telescope to the right spot.

Light from the stars goes through this tube to the eyepiece.

Light enters the telescope here. It goes through a lens. The bigger this lens is, the larger the stars look.

The telescope stands on three legs. The legs are called a tripod. The tripod holds the telescope still while you use it.

LINKS

▲ Some binoculars are made to look at the stars. Like telescopes, they make faraway things look bigger. Most of them aren't as powerful as telescopes, but they are easier to use and carry.

Summary

Constellations are groups of stars that form patterns. A telescope is a tool that makes faraway things look clearer and bigger. More stars can be seen with a telescope than without one.

Review

1. What is a star?
2. In which direction do most constellations move in the sky?
3. How do the number of stars you can see without a telescope compare to the number you can see with a telescope?
4. **Critical Thinking** Why might different people see different patterns in the same stars?
5. **Test Prep** Stars seem to move across the sky each night because —
   A they orbit Earth
   B they are bright
   C Earth rotates
   D Earth is tilted

MATH LINK

Star Track Pick a constellation. Find it in the night sky. Draw its position each week on a sheet of paper. After three months, look at your results. Use arrows to show the constellation's movement. How did it move?

WRITING LINK

Expressive Writing—Poem
Write a poem about the night sky. What does it look like? How does it make you feel? Share your poem with classmates.

LITERATURE LINK

Studying Stars What are stars like? How did they form? How do they change? Find out in *The Stars: Light in the Night Sky* by Jeanne Bendick.

TECHNOLOGY LINK

Visit the Harcourt Learning Site for related links, activities, and resources.
www.harcourtschool.com

WELCOME TO THE LEARNING SITE

Sky Watchers

For centuries people around the world observed the night sky by using only their eyes. These sky watchers made detailed observations and charted what they saw. They used the information they gathered to decide when to plant their crops or to take journeys.

Early Observatories

The Anasazi of North America were one of the cultures that made early observatories. An Anasazi observatory has been found in New Mexico.

In England there is a group of huge stones called Stonehenge. The stones are set in a circle in a way that would allow risings and settings of the sun and the moon to be tracked. Scientists and historians hypothesize that Stonehenge is a giant calendar made of rocks.

The First Telescopes

With the use of lenses to make telescopes, people learned much more about the night sky. Galileo, a scientist in Italy, read about the telescope and made his own. It could magnify objects 20 or 30 times. From his observations, Galileo made inferences about the objects in the

The History of Astronomy

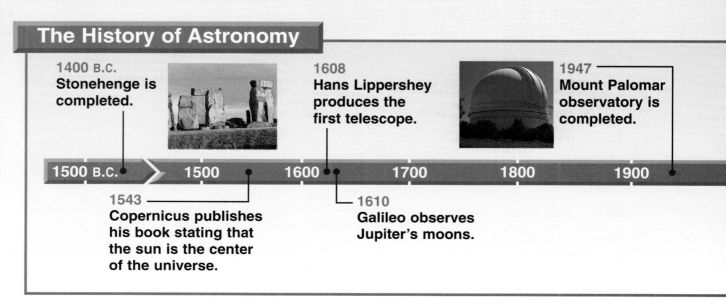

1400 B.C.
Stonehenge is completed.

1608
Hans Lippershey produces the first telescope.

1947
Mount Palomar observatory is completed.

1500 B.C.   1500   1600   1700   1800   1900

1543
Copernicus publishes his book stating that the sun is the center of the universe.

1610
Galileo observes Jupiter's moons.

sky. He even saw moons orbiting Jupiter.

Modern Telescopes

During the twentieth century, bigger and bigger telescopes were designed. These telescopes use mirrors instead of lenses. The larger the mirror, the more detail in the image it produces. One of the newest of these telescopes is at the Keck Observatory at the top of Mauna Kea, Hawai'i. At 10 meters (400 in.) across, the two Keck telescopes have the largest mirrors of any telescopes in the world.

Radio telescopes have made it possible to explore space day or night, rain or shine. That's because these telescopes pick up radio waves instead of light. The largest radio telescope is near Arecibo in Puerto Rico. In New Mexico, the Very Large Array is made up of 27 radio telescope antennas, each one measuring 25 meters (82 ft) across.

Scientists are always trying to find better ways of observing the night sky. They've even put a telescope in space. The Hubble Space Telescope orbits high above the atmosphere of Earth. Without the atmosphere to look through, it can make clearer pictures than ground-based telescopes.

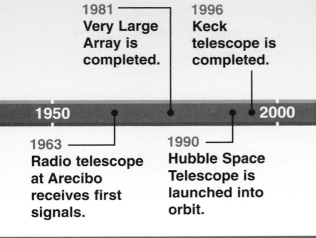

1981
Very Large Array is completed.

1996
Keck telescope is completed.

1950   2000

1963
Radio telescope at Arecibo receives first signals.

1990
Hubble Space Telescope is launched into orbit.

Think About It

1. Why would people in ancient civilizations be interested in the stars and planets?

2. Why does the Hubble Space Telescope take clearer pictures than telescopes on Earth?

Mae Jemison

ASTRONAUT, PHYSICIAN, BIOMEDICAL ENGINEER

"I want to make sure we use all our talent, not just 25 percent."

Mae Jemison was the first African-American woman in space. She was a mission specialist on the 1992 *Endeavour* space shuttle flight. Before the flight, she helped check the shuttle, its computer software, and the tiles that protect the ship from burning up when returning to Earth.

For Jemison, becoming an astronaut was a childhood dream come true. She began her career by going to medical school. While a student, she traveled to Thailand, Cuba, and Kenya to offer medical help. She joined the Peace Corps after graduating from medical school. She spent two years in West Africa.

Jemison returned to the United States and became a doctor in Los Angeles. She applied to the National Aeronautics and Space Administration (NASA) to be an astronaut. She was not accepted the first time she applied. She applied again and was accepted. After five years of training and working at NASA, she was selected for the *Endeavour* mission. All her hard work had paid off!

Think About It

1. How could living in a foreign country help a person get ready for a trip in outer space?

2. How can studying in school help a person make his or her dreams come true?

Earth Model

Why do we have seasons?

Materials
- Styrofoam ball
- flashlight
- two pencils

Procedure

1 Stick a pencil through the middle of the ball. This represents Earth's axis.

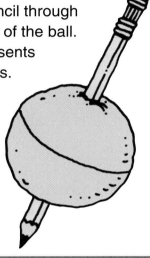

2 With the other pencil, draw a line around the middle of the ball. This is the equator. Put the Earth on a table. The axis should lean to the right.

3 Shine the flashlight on the left side of the Earth. The light represents the sun. Place the light about 13 cm away. Observe where the light rays hit the ball.

4 Shine the light on the right side of the Earth. Where do the light rays hit the ball? Compare how the light hits the ball each time.

Draw Conclusions

How does this explain seasons in the northern half of the Earth?

A Look at Rotation

How does day become night?

Materials
- a small self-stick note
- spinning Earth globe
- flashlight

Procedure

1 Write where you live on the self-stick note. Place the note on your state on the globe.

2 Shine the flashlight on the globe. Your teacher will then turn off the lights.

3 Slowly spin the globe counterclockwise.

Draw Conclusions

What happens to the place where you put your note? What does this represent?

Chapter ③ Review and Test Preparation

Vocabulary Review

Use the terms below to complete the sentences 1 through 14. The page numbers in ( ) tell you where to look in the chapter if you need help.

solar system (D58)   **revolution** (D68)
orbit (D58)   **phases** (D76)
planet (D58)   **lunar eclipse** (D78)
asteroid (D64)   **solar eclipse** (D80)
comet (D64)   **star** (D84)
rotation (D68)   **constellation** (D85)
axis (D68)   **telescope** (D88)

1. A large body of rock or gas that orbits the sun is a ___.

2. An ___ is a chunk of rock or metal that orbits the sun.

3. When the moon's shadow falls on Earth we see a ___.

4. A ___ makes faraway things look clearer and bigger.

5. The spinning of an object on its axis is called ___.

6. A ___ is a large ball of ice and dust that orbits the sun.

7. The moon has ___ that make it seem to change shape.

8. A ___ is a group of stars that forms a pattern.

9. Earth has an imaginary line, or ___, that runs through the North Pole and the South Pole.

10. The movement of one object around another object is called ___.

11. The ___ is made up of the sun and all the objects that orbit around it.

12. An ___ is the path of an object as it moves around another object in space.

13. When Earth's shadow falls on the moon, we see a ___.

14. A ___ is a ball of hot, glowing gases.

Connect Concepts

The motions of the Earth and the moon cause certain things to happen. Choose a term below to fill in the chart and complete each sentence.

day and night   **seasons**
lunar eclipses   **solar eclipses**
phases   **years**

Motions of the Earth and the Moon	
Earth's tilt	causes 15. ___.
Earth's rotation	causes 16. ___.
Earth's revolution	causes 17. ___.
Earth's shadow	causes 18. ___.
The moon's shadow	causes 19. ___.
The moon's movement	causes 20. ___.

Check Understanding

Write the letter of the best choice.

21. The outer planets are —
    A like Earth
    B Mars and Jupiter
    C mostly larger than Earth
    D made of rock

22. Two revolutions of Earth take —
    F two days   H two months
    G two weeks   J two years

23. When the moon looks like a lighted circle in the sky, it is in the ___ phase.
    A full moon
    B new moon
    C crescent moon
    D gibbous moon

Critical Thinking

24. In what ways is Pluto like an inner planet?

25. How would Earth be different if its axis were not tilted?

Process Skills Review

26. You can use distance from the sun to classify planets. Some are inner planets. Some are outer planets. **Classify** the inner planets as those *with moons* and those *without moons.*

27. **Compare** the revolutions of the moon and Earth. How are they alike? How are they different?

28. It is always cold at the North Pole. What can you **infer** about the way the sun's rays hit the North Pole?

Performance Assessment

Ordering Planets

Use the table to put the planets in order from largest to smallest based on their mass. Record your results. Then sort the planets into two groups, those with rings and those without rings. Compare your lists. What conclusions can you draw by organizing this data?

Planet	Mass of Planet (The mass of Mercury = 1.)	Planet Has Rings?
Earth	17	no
Jupiter	5300	yes
Mars	2	no
Mercury	1	no
Neptune	288	yes
Pluto	$\frac{1}{5}$	no
Saturn	1587	yes
Uranus	243	yes
Venus	14	no

Unit Project Wrap Up

Here are some ideas for ways to wrap up your unit project.

Display at a Science Fair

Display the results of your project in a school science fair. Prepare a written report describing the procedure you used and your results. Display the data you collected.

Make Weather Predictions

Use the weather information you gather to make predictions about weather. Compare your predictions with the actual weather.

Make a Weather Map

Learn about the symbols shown on weather maps. Then make your own map showing weather patterns in the United States on one day.

Investigate Further

How could you make your project better? What other questions do you have? Plan ways to find answers to your questions. Use the Science Handbook on pages R2-R9 for help.

Investigating Matter

Investigating Matter

Unit Project | ## Soap Tests

Analyze advertisements for soap and record the manufacturer's claims. Choose at least three kinds of soap and plan ways to test them to see if the claims are true. Organize your findings on graphs, tables, or charts. Compare the results of your tests to the advertisements.

Vocabulary Preview

matter
physical property
solid
liquid
gas
atom
evaporation
volume
mass

Properties of Matter

Every day we look at, listen to, feel, smell, and taste different kinds of matter. We even breathe it! Because matter comes in so many shapes and sizes, people have come up with many ways to measure it.

FAST FACT

People use lasers and satellites to measure really big objects. Mt. Everest in the Himalayas is the tallest mountain in the world. At 8848 meters (29,028 ft), it is as tall as a building with 2,950 stories!

Our senses help us observe and describe matter. Dogs are famous for their sense of smell. Bloodhounds can use their sense of smell to follow a trail more than 100 miles long and 100 hours old.

Type of Animal	Best Smeller
Insects	Silkworm moths
Fish	Sharks
Mammals	Elephants
Amphibians	Newts
Birds	Petrels and albatrosses
Reptiles	Snakes and lizards

What Are Physical Properties of Matter?

In this lesson, you can . . .

INVESTIGATE kinds of matter.

LEARN ABOUT the properties of different objects.

LINK to math, writing, art, and technology.

INVESTIGATE

Physical Properties

Activity Purpose Can you pour paper? Can you fold milk? Why not? Different objects have different properties. In this investigation you will **observe** different properties of matter.

Materials

- penny
- nickel
- marble
- key
- cotton balls
- piece of peppermint candy
- index card
- book
- uncooked macaroni
- twist tie
- peppercorns

Activity Procedure

1 Copy the charts shown.

2 Look at the objects you have been given. Notice whether they look shiny or dull. Notice how many colors each one has. **Record** your **observations.**

◀ **This picnic basket is made of straw. The basket can hold many other things that are made of matter.**

E4

How It Looks				How It Feels			
Object	Shiny	Dull	Color	Hard	Soft	Rough	Smooth

How It Smells				How It Sounds			
Object	Sweet	Sharp	No Smell	Loud	Soft	Makes a Ping	No Sound

3 Touch the objects. Feel whether the objects are hard or soft. Feel whether they are rough or smooth. **Record** your **observations.** (Picture A)

4 Next, tap each object lightly with your fingernail. What kind of sound does it make? **Record** your **observations.**

5 Smell each object. **Record** your **observations.**

Picture A

Draw Conclusions

1. Which objects are hard and rough? Which objects are hard and smooth? Which objects are soft and rough? Which objects are soft and smooth?

2. **Compare** your chart with the chart of another group. Are any objects in different columns? Why?

3. **Scientists at Work** Scientists learn about the world by **observing** with their five senses. Which of the five senses did you *not* use in the investigation?

Process Skill Tip

Scientists study the world closely and **record** what they sense. This is called **observing.** Observing is one way scientists answer questions about matter.

Physical Properties of Matter

Matter

FIND OUT

- **how to observe matter**
- **about three states of matter**

VOCABULARY

matter
physical property
solid
liquid
gas

Look around your classroom. You may see desks, books, other students, and the teacher. What else do you see? Everything you see takes up space. Your classroom must have enough space to hold you and all the other things that are in it. Everything in the classroom is matter. **Matter** is anything that takes up space.

Look at your desk. Can you pick it up with one arm? It is probably too heavy. Can you bend it? It is probably too stiff. You can use many different words to describe your desk. Each word you use to describe an object names a physical property of the object. A **physical property** (FIZ•ih•kuhl PRAHP•er•tee) is anything you can observe about an object by using your senses.

✔ **What is matter?**

◀ The girl, the raincoat, and the rain are matter. Even the air is matter. Everything in this picture is matter.

What Matter Looks Like

You can observe some physical properties of matter with your sense of sight. In the investigation you observed some things that are dull and some things that are shiny. You also looked at the colors of the objects.

There are some things, such as most glass windows, that you can see through. Some of these things don't have any color. Then you can see the colors of the things on the other side. But some things you can see through, such as tinted windows, do have color. Then you can't tell the colors of things on the other side.

Another physical property you can see is size. Have you ever seen a group of basketball players? They don't seem tall by themselves. But when a player is standing next to you, you can see that the player is tall. Size is easiest to see when you can compare one object to another.

A property you cannot see is temperature. But you can see the effects of temperature. You can

▲ The glass has no color, so when you look through it, you can see that the liquid in it is pink. You can tell the drink is cold because it has ice in it. The steam rising from the cup of tea lets you infer that it is hot.

infer that something is hot if you see steam coming from it. You can guess that something is cold if you see it with ice or snow.

✔ **What properties of matter can you learn about with your sense of sight?**

One of these horses is much larger than the other one. Size is a physical property of matter. ▶

What Matter Feels Like

Many people wear shirts under wool sweaters because wool sweaters feel scratchy. You can learn about some physical properties of matter by using your sense of touch.

Sandpaper feels rough, but sand feels smooth. The bark on a tree and gravel against bare feet both feel rough. *Smooth* can describe objects as different as a mirror and a book cover.

You can feel some things that you can't see. You can feel the push of the wind. You can also feel whether something is hot or cold.

Different parts of the same object may feel different. A wool jacket feels rough, but the buttons may feel smooth. A cat's fur is soft, but its claws are sharp.

✔ **What are some words you can use to describe how matter feels?**

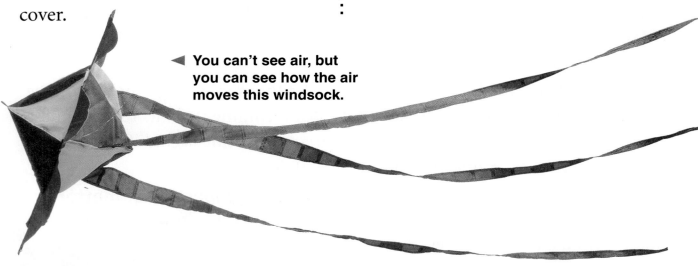

◄ **You can't see air, but you can see how the air moves this windsock.**

◄ **Snow feels cold and wet. Temperature and wetness are both physical properties of matter.**

Different parts of these slippers feel different. The fur is soft, but the soles feel hard and smooth. ▼

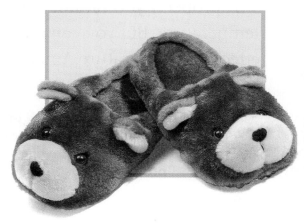

What Matter Tastes and Smells Like

People have to be careful about tasting things. Some things can make you ill, even if you taste just a small piece of them. But if you are careful, you can learn by tasting things. Your tongue can taste things that are sweet, sour, salty, and bitter.

You enjoy your favorite foods partly because of their smell. You may begin to feel hungry when good smells come from the kitchen.

Not all smells are pleasant. But people can get used to smells so they don't notice them anymore. Barnyards have strong smells. A visitor from the city might notice them right away. A farmer who works every day in a barn may not notice the strong smells at all. But smell comes from matter, and it is a physical property of matter.

✔ **What can we learn from our senses of taste and smell?**

▲ **The unpleasant odor of a skunk is a warning to stay away.**

◄ **Roses usually smell nice.**

Humans can taste many foods but don't always like what they eat. ►

Other Properties of Matter

Matter has many other properties that you can see, hear, and feel. Many objects break if you drop them. Others bounce. Rubber bands stretch. Kite string doesn't stretch at all. A paper clip can bend, but a twig will snap in two if you try to bend it. Magnets attract objects that contain iron. You can feel the force it takes to pull the object away from the magnet.

▲ Magnets attract objects that contain iron.

✔ **What are some of the other properties of matter?**

Putty, clay, and this gel are things that can bend. ▼

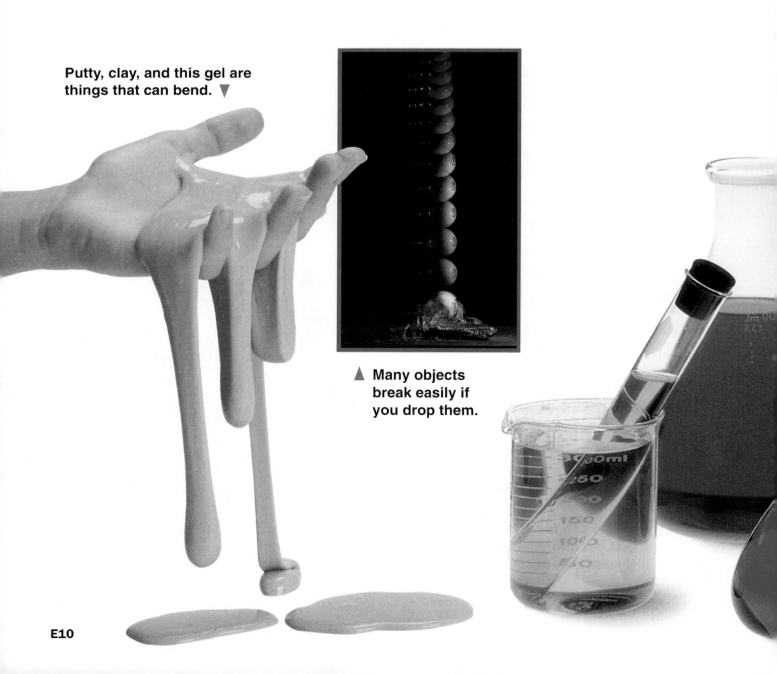

▲ Many objects break easily if you drop them.

Three States of Matter

Matter has different forms, called states. The three states of matter we can observe are solids, liquids, and gases.

Solids A **solid** takes up a specific amount of space and has a definite shape. A solid does not lose its shape. For example, a book keeps its shape when it is on a shelf or in your hands. A solid also has a volume that stays the same. That means a solid object takes up the same amount of space all the time.

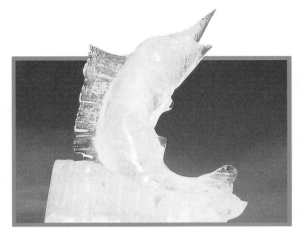

▲ This sculpture of a fish is made of ice. Ice is a solid. As long as the sculpture stays frozen, it will keep its shape. If the ice warms up, it will melt and become a liquid. Then the sculpture will lose its shape.

▲ Solid

Liquid

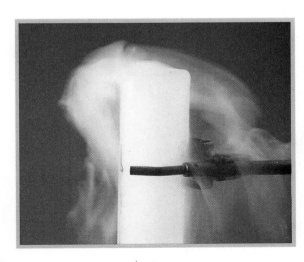

▲ Gas

Liquids A **liquid** has a volume that stays the same, but it can change its shape. A liquid takes the shape of any container it is put into. But one cup of water always takes up one cup of space, in any container.

One cup of water might not look like very much in a short, wide glass. But in a tall, skinny glass, one cup of water can look like a lot. No matter what it looks like, it is the same volume of water in both glasses.

Gases You may know that a gas takes the shape of the container it is in. A **gas** does not have a definite shape or a definite volume. It takes up all the space in its container. The air in your classroom is a gas. It takes the shape of your classroom. It also takes up all the space inside the classroom. If you put the same amount of air into a larger classroom, the air would spread out to take up all the space in that room.

✔ **What are the three states of matter we can observe?**

▲ The shape of the water changes as it falls. When it hits the stream, the banks help it hold a shape.

We breathe a gas. It is called air. ▼

Summary

Matter is anything that takes up space. Matter has many physical properties that you can observe using your five senses. You can feel matter, taste matter, see matter, hear matter, and smell matter. Matter has different states. The three states we can observe are solids, liquids, and gases.

Review

1. What is matter?
2. What is a physical property?
3. How can we learn about matter?
4. **Critical Thinking** Think of last night's dinner. What properties of matter did you observe?
5. **Test Prep** Which set of words all name physical properties of matter?
   - **A** solids, liquids, diamonds
   - **B** ice, water, steam
   - **C** hard, soft, sticky
   - **D** rocks, rubies, emeralds

LINKS

MATH LINK

Cups Per? How many cups of matter does it take to fill a liter container? A gallon container?

WRITING LINK

Narrative Writing—Story
Helium is a gas that is lighter than air. When you fill a balloon with helium, the balloon rises. Write a story for your classmates about the travels of a helium balloon that floats away.

ART LINK

Statues in Stone Sculptors choose their stone carefully. Different kinds of stone have different physical properties that can make it easier or harder to work with. Investigate the stone statues in your city or state. Find out what kind of stone they are made from.

TECHNOLOGY LINK

To learn more about properties of matter, watch *Fun With Matter* on the **Harcourt Science Newsroom Video.**

CNN
Turner
Le@rning

INVESTIGATE

What Are Solids, Liquids, and Gases?

In this lesson, you can . . .

 INVESTIGATE three states of matter.

 LEARN ABOUT the differences between the three states of matter.

 LINK to math, writing, language arts, and technology.

One Way Matter Can Change

Activity Purpose Matter can change from one state to another. Think about what happens when you make ice cubes. You put water in a freezer, and it turns into ice. What might happen to an ice cube that is left out in a warm room? Investigate to see if your idea is correct.

Materials

- clear plastic cup
- paper towel
- 2 ice cubes
- marker

Activity Procedure

1 Place the plastic cup on the paper towel. Put the ice cubes in the cup. (Picture A)

◀ Three states of matter surround us everywhere. Liquid water is in the ocean and in fog. The lighthouse is a solid. We breathe air, which is a gas.

2 **Predict** what the ice cubes will look like after 45 minutes. Use your past observations of ice cubes to predict what will happen this time. **Record** your prediction.

3 **Observe** what's in the cup after 45 minutes. **Record** what you see. Was your prediction correct?

4 Mark the outside of the cup to show how high the water is. **Predict** what you will see inside the cup in the morning if you leave it out all night. Then leave the cup sitting out.

Picture A

5 **Observe** the cup the next morning. **Record** what you see.

Draw Conclusions

1. What do you think caused the ice to change?

2. What do you think happened to the water when you left it out all night?

3. **Scientists at Work** Scientists make **predictions** based on things they have **observed** before. What had you observed before that helped you make your predictions?

Investigate Further Fill half an ice cube tray with water. Fill the other half with orange juice. **Predict** which will freeze first, the water or the orange juice. **Communicate** what you **observe.**

Process Skill Tip

Scientists **observe** things that happen. They use their observations to **predict** what will happen the next time a similar thing happens.

E15

Solids, Liquids, and Gases

FIND OUT

- what matter is made of
- how matter changes

VOCABULARY

atom
evaporation

Atoms

A puzzle has many pieces that fit together to form a picture. If you look closely, you can see each piece. If you look even more closely, you can see the tiny dots of color on each piece. All matter is like the puzzle. The more closely you look, the smaller the pieces you can see.

Some pieces of matter are so small that you can see them only by using special tools. Some pieces are so small that you cannot see them at all. But scientists can observe the effects of what these pieces of matter do. These pieces are called atoms. **Atoms** are the basic building blocks of matter.

✔ **What are atoms?**

◀ From far away, you can see the carved figure of a woman sitting down.

◀ When you move closer, you can see the colors and roughness of the stone.

◀ If you use a microscope, you can see some of the tiny pieces that make up the stone.

How Particles Are Connected

The particles in matter are arranged differently in each state of matter. But in all the ways they are arranged, the particles move.

▲ In a gas, such as this iodine gas, the particles are not connected to each other and are not close to each other. Each particle moves in a straight line until something stops it. Then it bounces. It moves off in another straight line until something else stops it.

▲ In a liquid the particles are more loosely arranged than in a solid. This allows the particles to slide past each other.

▲ A solid is hard because its particles do not move very much.

How Matter Changes States

Adding heat or taking heat away causes matter to change states. This is because adding heat makes the particles in matter move faster. Taking away heat, or cooling, makes the particles slow down.

In the investigation the warm air in the classroom added enough heat to the ice to change it to liquid water. The heat caused the particles in the ice to move faster. As the particles moved faster, the connections between them became looser. In time, the connections got so loose that the particles could slide past each other. At that point, the solid ice became liquid water.

With still more heat, the particles broke apart from each other completely. The liquid became a gas. The process by which a liquid becomes a gas is called **evaporation** (ee•vap•uh•RAY•shuhn).

If you take heat away from liquid water, the opposite happens. The particles slow down and solid ice forms.

✔ **What causes matter to change state?**

Hot lava, or liquid rock, comes from this volcano. When the lava hits water, the heat in the lava causes some of the water to turn to steam. Then the lava cools and changes into solid rock. ▼

Summary

Atoms are small particles that make up matter. In solids atoms fit tightly together and do not move very much. In liquids, they slide past each other. The atoms in gases are far apart and are not connected. They keep moving until something stops them. Adding or taking away heat can cause matter to change states.

Review

1. What are the building blocks of matter?
2. In which state of matter are the particles most tightly connected?
3. Why does gas **NOT** have a definite shape?
4. **Critical Thinking** When you boil water, what makes the liquid water turn into a gas?
5. **Test Prep** Which set of words names three states of matter?
   A solid, gas, water
   B solid, liquid, gas
   C hard, soft, smooth
   D salty, sweet, sour

LINKS

MATH LINK

Measuring Heat People often need to know the temperature of what they cook. Find out the names of two kinds of kitchen thermometers and what each kind is used for.

WRITING LINK

Informative Writing—Description Write a description of a lake or pond for a younger child. Tell what it is like in each season. Be sure to describe what happens to the water in each season.

LANGUAGE ARTS LINK

Parts of Speech Find out what parts of speech the words *solid, liquid,* and *gas* are. Use each word in a sentence.

TECHNOLOGY LINK

Learn more about how matter changes state by investigating *Solids, Liquids, and Gases* on **Harcourt Science Explorations CD-ROM.**

LESSON 3

How Can Matter Be Measured?

In this lesson, you can . . .

INVESTIGATE the mass and volume of objects.

LEARN ABOUT ways to measure mass and volume.

LINK to math, writing, language arts, and technology.

Measuring Mass and Volume

Activity Purpose

If you pick up a C-cell battery and a D-cell battery, which feels heavier? In this investigation you will find out the difference in mass between the two batteries. You will also **measure** the amount of space a liquid takes up.

Materials

- balance
- 3 C-cell batteries
- 3 D-cell batteries
- clear plastic cup
- marker
- water
- masking tape
- 3 clear containers of different sizes

Activity Procedure

Part A

1. Put a C-cell in the pan on the left side of the balance. Put a D-cell in the pan on the right side. **Record** which battery is heavier. (Picture A)

◄ Tools have been invented for measuring all sorts of things. Here an elephant is being weighed.

2 Add C-cells to the left side and D-cells to the right side until the pans are balanced. You may need to use some of the small masses from the balance to make the cells balance perfectly. **Record** the number of C-cells and D-cells you use.

Part B

3 Fill the cup half-full with water. Use a piece of tape to mark how high the water is in the cup. **Predict** how high the water will be in each container if you pour the water into it. Mark each prediction with a piece of tape. Write *P* (for *Prediction*) on the tape.

4 Pour the water into the next container. (Picture B) Mark the height of the water with a piece of tape. Write *A* (for *Actual*) on the tape.

5 Repeat Step 4 for each of the other containers.

Picture A

Picture B

Draw Conclusions

1. **Compare** the numbers of C-cells and D-cells it took to balance the pans. **Draw a conclusion** from these numbers about the masses of the batteries.

2. Describe the height of the water in each container. Why did the same amount of water look different in the different containers?

3. **Scientists at Work** Scientists **measure** matter by using tools that are marked with standard amounts. What was the standard amount you used in this activity to measure the water?

> **Process Skill Tip**
>
> Using tools to **measure** allows scientists to study and **compare** different pieces of matter.

Measuring Matter

Measuring Volume

Suppose you fill a glass all the way to the top with orange juice. Then you try to put ice cubes into it. The orange juice will spill out over the top of the glass. The orange juice takes up space, and the ice cubes take up space. If you want to add ice cubes to the drink, you have to leave enough space for them.

All matter takes up space. The amount of space matter takes up is called its **volume** (VAHL•yoom). Scientists measure volume by using tools. The volume of a liquid can be measured by using a measuring cup.

✔ **What is volume?**

FIND OUT

- how to measure matter
- how to use tools to measure matter

VOCABULARY

volume
mass

The same volume of liquid looks different in different containers. A measuring cup will show the volume in a standard unit you can understand.

Like liquids, solids have volume. Since a solid holds its shape, you cannot measure its volume easily in a measuring cup. A rock or a marble will not take the shape of the cup. ▶

◀ You can measure the volume of a small rock. Pour some water into a measuring device. Record the level of the water. Gently place the rock in the water. Record the new water level. The difference in the water levels equals the volume of the rock.

U.S.A.
20°C
ML

500

450

400

350

300

Measuring Mass

All matter has mass. **Mass** is the amount of matter in an object. You can't tell how much mass an object has if you just look at it. A golf ball and a Ping Pong ball are about the same size. But a golf ball has much more mass than a Ping Pong ball. You have to measure to find out how much mass an object has.

In the investigation you used a pan balance to measure mass. You may have used another kind of balance in the grocery store to measure the

The balloon filled with air has more mass than the empty balloon. This shows that air has mass. ▶

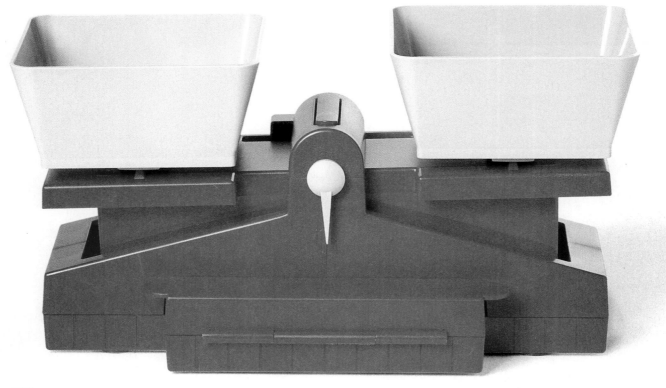

An empty pan balance has the same amount of mass on both sides. ▼

masses of fruits and vegetables. You may use a scale at home to measure your own mass.

You can't see air. In fact, you can't see most gases. But like all matter, gases have mass. Look at the balloons on the previous page. You can see that when you put air into a balloon you add to its mass. If you put too much air into a balloon, the balloon will pop. Then you can feel the mass of air rushing out of the balloon.

✔ **What is mass?**

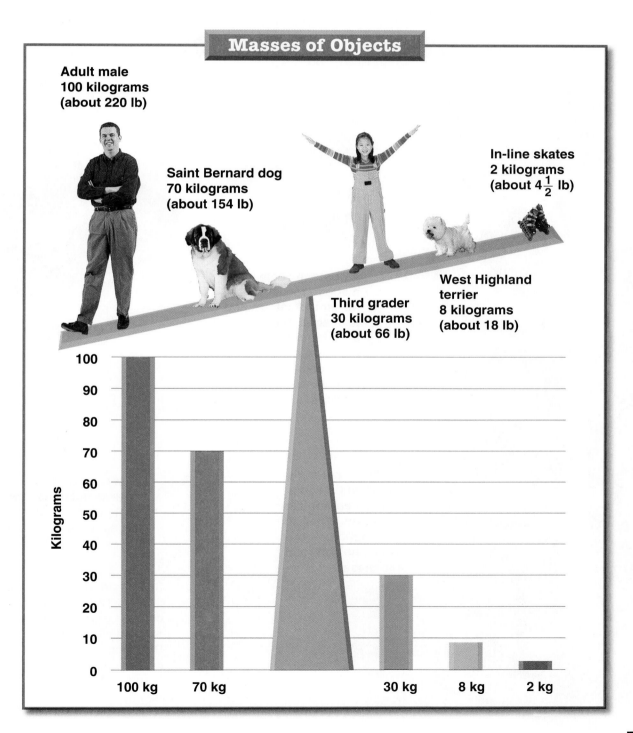

Masses of Objects

Adult male
100 kilograms
(about 220 lb)

Saint Bernard dog
70 kilograms
(about 154 lb)

In-line skates
2 kilograms
(about $4\frac{1}{2}$ lb)

Third grader
30 kilograms
(about 66 lb)

West Highland terrier
8 kilograms
(about 18 lb)

Kilograms: 100, 90, 80, 70, 60, 50, 40, 30, 20, 10, 0

100 kg   70 kg   30 kg   8 kg   2 kg

Tools for Measuring Mass and Volume

Suppose you need 1 teaspoon of salt. You would use a measuring spoon, not a scale. Measuring tools are made for certain tasks. Using the right tool makes measuring easy.

This scale makes measuring fruits and vegetables easy. The large pan can hold big items like bags of apples or bunches of bananas. ▶

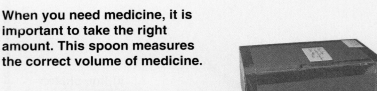

▲ When you need medicine, it is important to take the right amount. This spoon measures the correct volume of medicine.

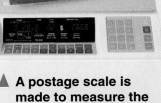

▲ A postage scale is made to measure the masses of letters and packages. A letter has a small mass. To measure its mass, you need a scale that can measure small masses.

◀ To find a person's mass, you need a scale a person can stand on. When the boy stands on this scale, he can read his mass.

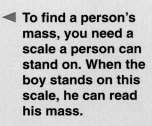

▲ Restaurants make food in large volumes. This measuring tool can hold large amounts of liquid.

◀ Scientists often measure liquids. This container, called a *graduate,* is marked along the side. By using it, a scientist can see exactly what the volume of a liquid is.

Adding Masses

Suppose you draw a picture on a large sheet of paper. Then you cut the paper into pieces to make it into a puzzle. When you put the puzzle back together, it's the same size as the whole sheet of paper. And it still has the same mass.

Suppose you measure the mass of an apple. Then you cut the apple in half and measure the mass of each piece. If you add the masses of the two pieces, you will find that the total is the same as the mass of the whole apple.

When you cut the apple in half, you still have the same amount of apple to eat. In any way matter is arranged, its mass stays the same.

✔ **What happens to the mass of an object when you cut the object into pieces?**

The balance is holding two identical boxes of crayons. Taking the crayons out of the box does not change their mass. The mass is the same when the crayons are in the box and when they are out of the box. ▼

Comparing Mass and Volume

Different kinds of matter can take up the same amount of space but have different masses. A Ping Pong ball takes up about the same amount of space as a golf ball. But the Ping Pong ball has much less mass. A lime has about the same volume as an egg. But the lime has more mass.

✔ **Which do you think has more mass, a cup of water or a cup of air?**

Mass and Volume

All the jars are filled. They all have the same volume of matter in them. But look closely at the matter in each jar. Each kind of matter has a different mass. The jelly beans have more mass than the pasta. The sand has more mass than the marbles.

Summary

Volume is the amount of space an object takes up. Mass is how much matter is in an object. The mass of an object stays the same in any way its matter is arranged. Different objects can have the same volume but different masses.

Review

1. Name one kind of tool for measuring the volume of a liquid.
2. Do objects that are the same size always have the same mass? Explain.
3. Name some tools you could use to measure mass.
4. **Critical Thinking** Name two kinds of fruit. Which do you think has more mass? Explain.
5. **Test Prep** Choose the best definition of *volume*.
   A the amount of air an object holds
   B how much something weighs
   C the amount of matter in an object
   D the amount of space something takes up

LINKS

MATH LINK

Measuring Water Fill a film canister to the top with water, and put the lid on it. Measure the height of the canister. Then freeze it. In two hours, measure the height of the canister again. What happened to the water?

WRITING LINK

Informative Writing— Explanation Think about going shopping for milk. Tell what it would be like if there were no standard volumes of milk sold. Write a story for your teacher that explains what you would have to do.

LANGUAGE ARTS LINK

Many Word Meanings Look up the words volume and mass in a dictionary. Write two sentences for each word. But use meanings that are not from science.

TECHNOLOGY LINK

Learn more about measuring matter by visiting this Internet Site.

www.scilinks.org/harcourt

Classifying Matter

Many centuries ago, Greek thinkers tried to understand what matter was made of. They thought that everything—gold, silver, sulfur, trees, dogs, and horses—was made of different combinations of four different materials. These materials, called elements, were earth, air, fire, and water. Some other Greek thinkers thought matter was made up of small particles. They called these particles atoms. But the element theory was more popular. Nobody thought or wrote about atoms again until the early 1800s.

The Atomic Theory

In 1803 John Dalton published his studies of what he called ultimate particles. He had carried out many experiments with water. Using electricity, he split water into its two elements—hydrogen and oxygen. He found that the two elements had different weights. He found that he could predict the amount of oxygen formed if he knew how much hydrogen was formed. Dalton had read about the old Greek idea of atoms. He thought it explained many of the things he had observed. From

The History of Matter

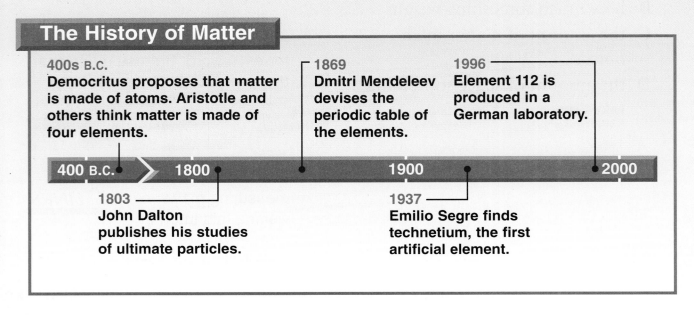

400s B.C.
Democritus proposes that matter is made of atoms. Aristotle and others think matter is made of four elements.

1869
Dmitri Mendeleev devises the periodic table of the elements.

1996
Element 112 is produced in a German laboratory.

400 B.C. 1800 1900 2000

1803
John Dalton publishes his studies of ultimate particles.

1937
Emilio Segre finds technetium, the first artificial element.

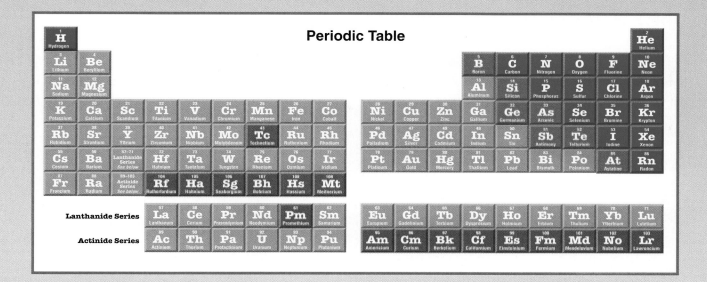

Periodic Table

his experiments, he inferred three things about atoms:

- Atoms of different elements have different weights.
- Two atoms of the same element are identical.
- An atom of one element can't be changed into an atom of a different element.

Making Sense of Elements

In the 1700s and 1800s, many scientists searched for new elements. As more and more elements were discovered, people began to look for an order. Could they predict the elements that hadn't been discovered yet?

In 1869 a Russian scientist named Dmitri Mendeleev studied each of the 63 known elements. He grouped the elements by their properties. He grouped all the metals together and

all the nonmetals together. Then he ordered the elements in each group by how much their atoms weighed. He organized his ordered groups in a table, called the periodic table. The table is arranged in rows and columns. Mendeleev left gaps in his table where none of the known elements fit. He predicted that these gaps would be filled as new elements were discovered. Today, more than 100 elements are listed on the periodic table.

Think About It

- Why did Mendeleev's periodic table let him predict new elements that hadn't been discovered yet?

Dorothy Crowfoot Hodgkin

CHEMIST

"You're finding what's there and then trying to make sense of what you find."

Dorothy Crowfoot Hodgkin won the Nobel Prize in chemistry in 1964. She was only the third woman ever to win it. By the time she won the award, she had spent more than 30 years studying insulin. Insulin is a chemical made in the body that allows us to use sugar for energy. The results of her studies helped fight diseases and save lives.

Hodgkin did most of her research at Oxford University in England. While there, she attended meetings of the research club. At these meetings she was able to communicate her ideas and research findings with other students and scientists.

Hodgkin loved studying how things were put together. She became interested in crystals. She used X rays to find the shapes of the crystals. She did much of her work before computers had been invented, so her research took a very long time. She used the first IBM computers to help do her calculations. Later, she sent her data to a professor in Los Angeles who had a faster computer. They used mail and telegrams to send information back and forth.

Hodgkin traveled around the world to meet and talk with other chemists. She continued to do research, teach, and travel throughout her life.

Think About It

1. How did not having a computer slow down Hodgkin's research?
2. How can communicating with others help solve a problem?

Insulin

Properties of Metals

Which metals have magnetic properties?

Materials

- magnet
- penny
- piece of aluminum foil
- straight pin
- scissors
- dime
- paper clip

	Objects
Magnetic	
Non-Magnetic	Objects

Procedure

1. Copy the chart onto a sheet of paper.

2. Place the magnet close to the penny. Does the penny stick to the magnet? Write down the results on your chart.

3. Repeat Step 2 for each of the other objects. Write down the results for each one on the chart.

Draw Conclusions

Study your completed chart. Are all metals attracted by a magnet? Which kinds are?

Mass of Liquids

Which of three liquids has the greatest mass?

Materials

- clear measuring cup
- water
- oil
- red vinegar

Procedure

1. Will water float on oil? Or will oil float on water? Predict which liquid will float on the other.

2. Pour some water into the measuring cup.

3. Add some oil. Observe what happens to the oil. Write down your observations. Was your prediction correct?

4. Will the vinegar float on the water? Make a prediction.

5. Pour some red vinegar into the measuring cup. Let it stand still for five minutes. Write down your observations.

Draw Conclusions

The lightest liquid floats on the others. List the liquids from lightest to heaviest.

Chapter 1 Review and Test Preparation

Vocabulary Review

Use the terms below to complete the sentences 1 through 9. The page numbers in ( ) tell you where to look in the chapter if you need help.

matter (E6)

physical property (E6)

solid (E11)

liquid (E12)

gas (E12)

atoms (E16)

evaporation (E18)

volume (E22)

mass (E24)

1. A ____ is matter that has a definite shape.

2. All matter is made of ____.

3. Stickiness is a ____ of matter.

4. ____ is the amount of matter in an object.

5. Everything that takes up space is ____.

6. The amount of space that matter takes up is its ____.

7. A ____ has particles that are not tightly connected.

8. A ____ has no definite shape and no definite volume.

9. When a liquid changes into a gas, the process is called ____.

Connect Concepts

Write the terms needed to complete the concept map.

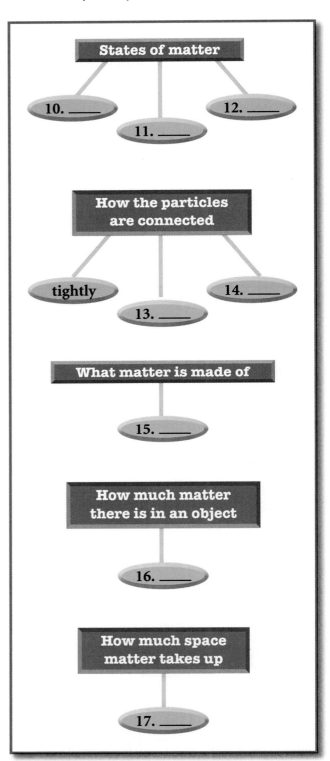

States of matter
- 10. ____
- 11. ____
- 12. ____

How the particles are connected
- tightly
- 13. ____
- 14. ____

What matter is made of
- 15. ____

How much matter there is in an object
- 16. ____

How much space matter takes up
- 17. ____

Check Understanding

Write the letter of the best choice.

18. There are two jars that are the same size. One is filled with peanut butter, and the other is filled with jelly. They have the same volume, but they may not have the same —

    A heat   C evaporation
    B mass   D gas

19. One physical property that a football and a soccer ball share is that both —

    F bounce   H fold
    G stretch   J crackle

20. Syrup pours because its atoms are —

    A tightly connected
    B not connected
    C loosely connected
    D split

21. A shallow pond can dry up because of —

    F ice
    G cold weather
    H heat and evaporation
    J snow falling during the winter

Critical Thinking

22. Explain what happens to a liquid when heat is added to it.

23. A solid has a definite shape. Sand can take the shape of its container. Then why is sand a solid?

Process Skills Review

Write *True* or *False*. If a statement is false, change the underlined words to make it true.

24. **Predicting** means explaining what underlined{happened in the past}.

25. **Measuring** is underline{using tools} to find the volume or mass of something.

26. **Observing** means underline{watching something for a second}.

Performance Assessment

Make Models

Make clay models of the particles in a solid, a liquid, and a gas. Make the models small, but be sure each one looks different. Use an index card to make a label for each model. Place the labels in front of the models.

Changes in Matter

When you put the silverware away, it's easy to separate the spoons from the forks. But if you tried to unscramble an egg, you'd have a pretty hard time. What changes mixtures so you can't separate them? In this chapter, you'll find out.

Vocabulary Preview

physical change
mixture
solution
chemical change

FAST FACT

When you cut yourself, blood looks like a thick red liquid. But blood is really a mixture of liquids and cells of different sizes. Here are some other things that you might not think of as mixtures.

Different Kinds of Mixtures

Kinds of Matter Mixed	Result
Carbon and iron	Steel
Water and gelatin	Jelly
Air and rock	Pumice
Fat and water	Milk
Ash and air	Smoke
Water and air	Fog

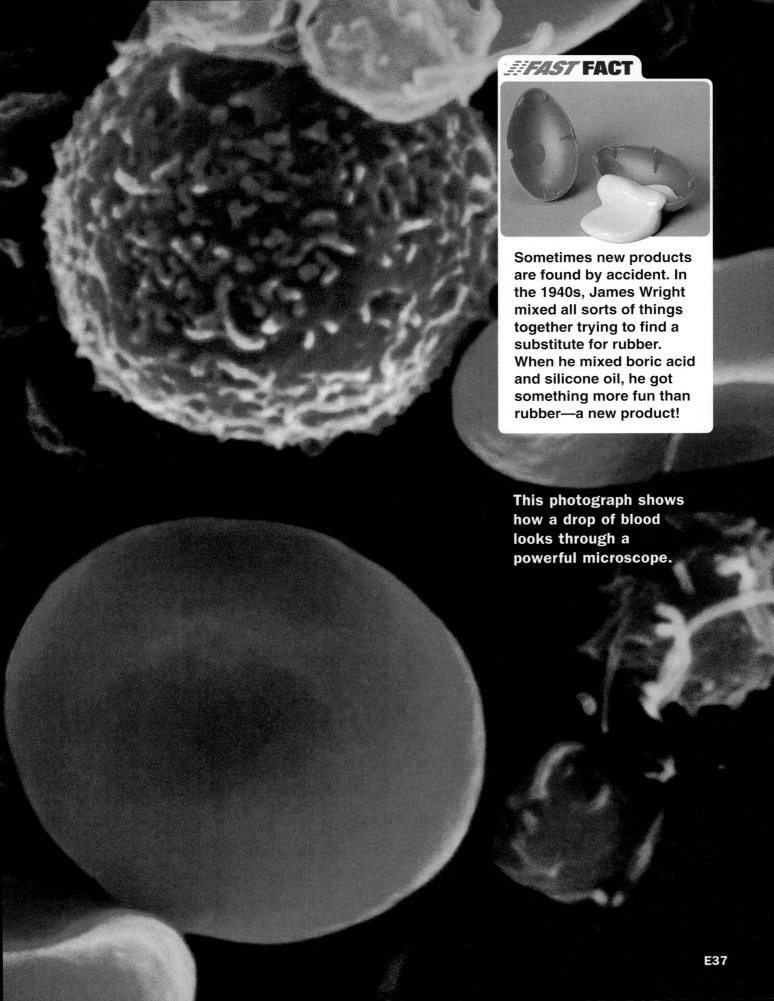

Sometimes new products are found by accident. In the 1940s, James Wright mixed all sorts of things together trying to find a substitute for rubber. When he mixed boric acid and silicone oil, he got something more fun than rubber—a new product!

This photograph shows how a drop of blood looks through a powerful microscope.

What Are Physical Changes?

In this lesson, you can . . .

INVESTIGATE how to separate mixtures.

LEARN ABOUT physical changes in matter.

LINK to math, writing, social studies, and technology.

Separate a Mixture

Activity Purpose In a mixture of sand, shells, twigs, and seaweed, you might want to separate the shells. You could do it easily with your hands. To separate other mixtures, you might need to use different methods or tools. **Plan and conduct an investigation** to discover methods for separating mixtures.

Materials

- 4 clear plastic cups
- 6 marbles
- water
- steel paper clips
- rice
- magnet
- measuring cup
- paper towels
- funnel

Activity Procedure

1 In one cup, make a mixture of marbles and water. Plan a way to separate the marbles from the water. Try it. **Record** your method and your results.

◀ Heat causes a physical change in the ice pop. It melts.

2 In another cup, make a mixture of marbles, paper clips, and rice. Plan a way to separate the mixture. Try it. **Record** your method and your results.

3 If your method doesn't work, plan a different way to separate the mixture. Try different methods until you find one that works. Try using the magnet. **Record** each method you try.

4 In another cup, mix $\frac{1}{4}$ cup of rice with 1 cup of water. How could you separate the rice from the water? **Record** your ideas.

Picture A

5 Make a filter with the paper towels and the funnel. **Predict** how this tool could be used to separate the mixture. Then use the filter to separate the mixture. (Picture A)

Draw Conclusions

1. When would it be easy to use only your hands to separate a mixture?

2. When might you need a tool to separate a mixture?

3. **Scientists at Work** Scientists often use charts to **record** the results of an investigation. How would setting up charts help you **plan and conduct an investigation**?

Investigate Further Make a mixture of sand and water. **Plan and conduct an investigation** to separate the mixture. Would a tool be useful? Which tool would you use?

Process Skill Tip

Scientists ask questions about the world around them. To find the answers, they **plan and conduct investigations**. First, they think about the question they want to answer. Then, they plan a way to answer the question. As they conduct the investigation, they **record** their results.

Physical Changes in Matter

FIND OUT

- how matter can change and still be the same
- about two kinds of mixtures

VOCABULARY

physical change
mixture
solution

Kinds of Physical Changes

When you wash your clothes, they get wet, soapy, and wrinkled. Even with all these changes, they are still your clothes. No new kinds of matter are formed. Changes to matter in which no new kinds of matter are formed are called **physical changes**.

Some physical changes make objects look very different. Paper can be cut, painted on, written on, torn, folded, and glued. Each time, the paper looks different, but it is still paper.

Changing the temperature can make matter change. Cooling makes liquid water change to ice. The ice has the same particles in it that the liquid water had. No new kinds of matter are formed.

✔ **What are some ways that matter can change and still be the same matter?**

People make paper so they can use it. ▼

One way people change paper is by giving it a different shape. ▶

◀ Another way people change paper is by cutting it into smaller pieces.

Mixtures

A **mixture** is a substance that contains two or more different types of matter. The types of matter in a mixture can be separated. After a mixture is separated, the matter is the same as it was before it was mixed.

In the investigation you made a mixture of rice, paper clips, and marbles. Then you separated the pieces back into separate piles of rice, paper clips, and marbles. Making a mixture is a physical change.

Separating the parts of a mixture is another physical change.

Some mixtures can be separated by hand. You separated the rice from the marbles with your hands. Some mixtures can be separated by evaporation or by condensation. In *evaporation* a liquid part of a mixture turns into a gas. This leaves the other parts behind. In *condensation* a gas in a mixture turns into a liquid. The liquid can be separated from the rest of the mixture.

✔ **What is a mixture?**

This alphabet soup is a mixture of broth, peas, pasta, carrots, and other vegetables.

Solutions

Have you ever put sugar in iced tea? After you stir the tea, you can't see the sugar anymore. You know the sugar is still there because you can taste it. This mixture of sugar and tea is called a solution. In a **solution** the particles of the different kinds of matter mix together evenly.

The different kinds of matter in a solution can't be separated by hand. But evaporation can separate some solutions. If you heat the iced tea or leave the glass out for a while, the water in the tea will evaporate. Then the sugar will be left.

✓ **What is a solution?**

THE INSIDE STORY

Solutions

This bright-blue substance is called copper sulfate. Watch what happens when it is mixed with water.

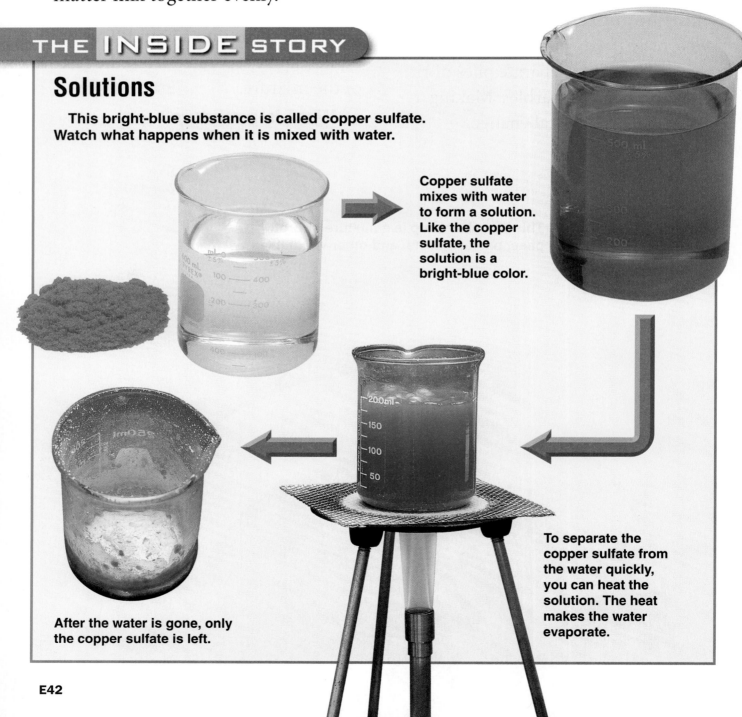

Copper sulfate mixes with water to form a solution. Like the copper sulfate, the solution is a bright-blue color.

To separate the copper sulfate from the water quickly, you can heat the solution. The heat makes the water evaporate.

After the water is gone, only the copper sulfate is left.

Summary

Matter can change size, shape, and state. Matter can be mixed. Changes to matter that don't form any new kinds of matter are called physical changes. A mixture contains two or more types of matter. A solution is a kind of mixture. In a solution the particles of the different kinds of matter are mixed evenly.

Review

1. What is a physical change?
2. Name three ways to cause a physical change in matter.
3. What is the difference between a mixture and a solution?
4. **Critical Thinking** Suppose you have a mixture of water and salt. You use evaporation to separate the water from the salt. Where does the water go?
5. **Test Prep** Which one is a solution?
   A marbles mixed in water
   B sugar mixed in water
   C clay, rocks, and twigs
   D rice mixed in water

◄ **Mixture**

LINKS

MATH LINK

Trail Mix Make a food mixture. Use a $\frac{1}{4}$-cup measuring cup and a 2-cup measuring cup. Measure $\frac{1}{4}$ cup each of raisins, dried banana chips, sunflower seeds, and pretzel circles. Put all these into the 2-cup measuring cup. How much trail mix do you have altogether?

WRITING LINK

Expressive Writing—Song Lyrics Almost all soups are mixtures. Choose a familiar tune and write song lyrics for a younger child about your favorite soup.

SOCIAL STUDIES LINK

Gold Rush Look up the California gold rush. Find out how people separated mixtures of water, sand, and rock to find gold.

TECHNOLOGY LINK

Visit the Harcourt Learning Site for related links, activities, and resources.
www.harcourtschool.com

LESSON 2

What Are Chemical Changes?

In this lesson, you can . . .

INVESTIGATE a change in matter.

LEARN ABOUT how new matter is formed.

LINK to math, writing, language arts, and technology.

Chemical Changes

Activity Purpose You mix flour, eggs, milk, and oil. Then you pour some of the mixture into a hot pan. Pancakes! The pancakes are a different kind of matter than the flour and eggs. Many changes happen to cause the new kind of matter to form. You can **observe** a new kind of matter being formed in this investigation.

Materials

- safety goggles
- cookie sheet
- large glass bowl
- measuring cup
- baking soda
- vinegar

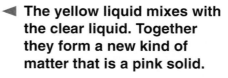

Activity Procedure

1 **CAUTION** **Put on your safety goggles.**

◄ The yellow liquid mixes with the clear liquid. Together they form a new kind of matter that is a pink solid.

2 Place the cookie sheet on the table. Place the bowl on the cookie sheet.

3 **Measure** $\frac{1}{4}$ cup of baking soda. Pour it into the bowl.

4 **Measure** $\frac{1}{4}$ cup of vinegar. Hold the cup with the vinegar in one hand. Use your other hand to fan some of the air from the cup toward your nose. Do not put your nose directly over the cup. (Picture A)

5 Pour the vinegar into the bowl.

6 **Observe** the matter in the bowl. **Record** what it looks like. Use the procedure from Step 4 to smell the matter in the bowl. Record what it smells like.

Picture A

Draw Conclusions

1. How is the material in the bowl like the baking soda and vinegar you started with? How is it different?

2. What can you **infer** about where the bubbles came from?

3. **Scientists at Work** Scientists **observe** changes. Then they **record** their observations. Describe the changes you observed in the bowl.

Investigate Further Mix warm water and a fresh packet of dry yeast. **Observe** the mixture. **Record** what you see. What can you **infer** about the changes you see?

Process Skill Tip

Scientists **observe** matter carefully. Sometimes they see things they don't understand right away. Sometimes they can use their experience to **infer** what those things mean. When you infer, you use your observations to form an opinion.

Chemical Changes in Matter

FIND OUT

- how new kinds of matter are formed
- some ways we use chemical changes every day

VOCABULARY

chemical change

Forming Different Kinds of Matter

Matter is always changing. Some changes are physical changes. In physical changes the kind of matter stays the same.

Some changes form new kinds of matter. Changes that form different kinds of matter are called **chemical changes**. In chemical changes the particles in the matter change. Cooking food makes new kinds of matter. Flour, eggs, milk, and oil turn into pancakes. The particles in the flour, eggs, milk, and oil change. The pancakes will never be just flour, eggs, milk, and oil again.

✔ **What is a chemical change?**

▲ This liquid looks like water. It is actually a solution with lead in it.

This is a solution with iodine in it. It also looks like water. ▶

When the two liquids are mixed, they form a yellow solid. This is an example of a chemical change. ▶

E46

Some Chemical Changes

Burning People burn things every day. Many people burn oil or gas to heat their homes. When things burn, different kinds of matter form. So burning is a chemical change. When wood burns, it combines with the oxygen in the air. The matter that forms includes smoke and ash. Another kind of matter forms that you can't see. It is a gas that mixes with the air.

Rusting Have you ever noticed orange-brown spots on the metal of a bike or a car? This orange-brown matter is rust. Rust forms when air and water mix with the iron in metal. The rust is a different kind of matter. It is flaky and soft. It is not strong like iron. When a metal gets rusty, it loses some of its strength. Often you can break the rusty part off. Rusting is a chemical change.

✔ **What are two common chemical changes?**

A chemical change is happening in this fire. The wood is combining with oxygen in the air to form new kinds of matter. ▼

The new bolt is shiny. The other bolts are old. The iron in the old bolts has rusted. It has combined with air and water to form a new kind of matter. ▼

▲ When wood burns, one of the new kinds of matter that forms is ash. The ash doesn't look like the wood.

Using Chemical Changes

Chemical changes go on all around us. We burn fuel to heat our homes. The engines of cars and buses burn fuel to make them move. Chemical changes happen when we cook food. Many of the materials in our clothes are made by chemical changes. Plants use chemical changes to make their food. The film in a camera goes through chemical changes to make photographs.

✔ **Name three chemical changes.**

1 First you take a picture.

2 The film inside a camera has chemicals on it. These chemicals change when light hits them. The changes are the beginning of your photograph.

3 This first process makes a negative. On a negative, the colors are backward. The negative is used to make a print.

4 A machine shines light through the negative and onto a sheet of paper. This sheet of paper is coated with chemicals. The paper is put through a chemical bath.

E48

Summary

Chemical changes cause new kinds of matter to form. Chemical changes can be very useful. We use chemical changes to cook. We use chemical changes to take pictures. Some chemical changes are harmful. Rust on metal makes the metal weak.

Review

1. What happens to particles of matter in a chemical change?
2. Name two common chemical changes.
3. Describe some ways we use chemical changes to help us.
4. **Critical Thinking** What is the difference between a chemical change and a physical change?
5. **Test Prep** Which of the following is a chemical change?
   A tearing
   B soaking
   C rusting
   D folding

4

LINKS

MATH LINK

A Fire Problem A log had a mass of 5 kilograms before it burned. After the fire was out, the ashes had a mass of 1 kilogram. What was the mass of the smoke and gas that were formed?

WRITING LINK

Narrative Writing—Story
Write the story of a forest fire for your teacher. Tell how the fire begins. Describe what is left of the forest when the fire is over.

LANGUAGE ARTS LINK

Many Uses of Fire Look up the word *fire* in a dictionary. Write two sentences that use the word. But use the word in ways that are different from the way *fire* is used in science. Explain what *fire* means in each sentence.

TECHNOLOGY LINK

To learn more about how matter that has undergone a chemical change can be used, watch *Recycled Roads* on the **Harcourt Science Newsroom Video.**

CNN
Turner
Le@rning

Plastic Bridges

Physical changes can be useful. When you fold a sheet of paper, you want it to change shape. And you want a plastic bag to change its shape to hold the groceries you buy at the store. But if a bridge you were driving on changed shape as much as the paper or the plastic bag, you'd be in trouble.

Choosing Materials

When engineers design and make something, they choose their materials carefully. They use materials that change in ways that are useful and don't change in ways that cause problems. When they want to build a bridge, they use materials that are strong. They look for materials that won't bend or break when cars and trucks drive over them. They might use steel, or concrete—or plastic.

Why Build Plastic Bridges?

People don't usually think of plastic when they think of bridges.

▲ Building a plastic bridge

plastic building material

Plastic bags get holes in them. Plastic milk bottles bend and break. Even the hard plastic used in toys and computers breaks. But scientists have developed a new kind of plastic that is strong enough to hold the weight of cars and trucks. It is a kind of composite, or a material made of several different things put together.

Composite plastic is as strong as steel, but it is much lighter. Bridges built with plastic can be put together and used in about a day. Bridges made with steel and concrete take much longer to build.

Weathering wears out bridges made of steel and concrete. Heat, cold, rain, ice, and wind slowly break them apart. Water can erode cement and make steel rust. But water and salt don't affect composite plastic. The plastic doesn't break down or rust.

Using Plastic in Bridges

Today plastic bridges are being tested in different places around the country. These bridges aren't made completely of plastic. They still have steel rails on the sides and concrete on the road surface. They look just like the bridges you're used to. But scientists hope they will last longer.

Plastic is also being used to fix old bridges. Plastic can be wrapped around parts of these bridges to add support. The plastic coating also keeps the bridges from being damaged by heat, cold, wind, water, and salt.

Think About It

1. Why do we still need to use concrete and steel to make bridges?

2. Why might you want to wrap plastic around the supporting parts of a building?

WEB LINK:
For Science and Technology updates, visit the Harcourt Internet site.
www.harcourtschool.com

Careers Civil Engineer

What They Do Civil engineers design buildings, bridges, roads, airports, and tunnels and make sure these things are safe to use.

Education and Training Civil engineers have at least a bachelor's degree in engineering. They study physics, chemistry, and math so that they can test and design structures.

Enrico Fermi
PHYSICIST

"I'm hungry. Let's go to lunch!"

Enrico Fermi was a man who lived on a schedule. It was noon and he was hungry. So work on his great experiment could wait awhile. That afternoon, December 2, 1942, his experiment succeeded and made it possible to develop the atomic bomb. The work of many scientists over several years had been completed.

Fermi became interested in atoms after reading about the research done by other scientists. In 1938 he was awarded the Nobel Prize in physics.

After Fermi, his wife, and their two children went to Sweden to accept the prize, they did not return to Italy. Fermi's wife, Laura, was Jewish. She

was in danger because of the prejudice against Jews in Italy. So the Fermi family came to the United States. Fermi taught at Columbia University. A few years later, he went to the University of Chicago, where many of his experiments took place.

In 1943 Fermi went to Los Alamos, New Mexico, to help develop the first atomic bomb. All of the major countries involved in World War II were racing to make this bomb. After the war ended, Fermi returned to the University of Chicago.

Think About It

1. Why did all the major countries in the war want to make an atomic bomb?
2. Why is it important for scientists to write about their discoveries?

Changes in Cooking

What happens to muffins as they bake?

Materials

- 1 box of muffin mix
- other needed ingredients
- mixing bowl
- spoon
- muffin pan

Procedure

1. Read and follow the directions on the box of muffin mix.

2. Halfway through the cooking time, open the oven or turn on the oven light and observe the muffins. Record your observations.

Draw Conclusions

What is happening to the muffins?

Making a Solution

Which works better, hot water or cold water?

Materials

- 2 small, heat-proof glass containers
- cold water
- spoon
- sugar
- clock with second hand
- warm water (from the tap)

Procedure

1. Fill one container with cold water.

2. Mix a spoonful of the sugar into the water. Stir until the sugar dissolves.

3. Watch the clock to see how long it takes. Record the number of seconds it takes.

4. Repeat Steps 1–3 using warm water.

Draw Conclusions

How were the results different? Why do you think they were different?

Chapter 2 Review and Test Preparation

Vocabulary Review

Choose a term below to match each definition. The page numbers in ( ) tell you where to look in the chapter if you need help.

physical change (E40)

mixture (E41)

solution (E42)

chemical change (E46)

1. Matter that contains two or more different things that can be separated

2. A change in which no new kinds of matter are formed

3. A change that makes new kinds of matter

4. A mixture in which the particles of the different kinds of matter mix together evenly

Connect Concepts

Complete the diagram below by listing three examples of physical change and two examples of chemical change.

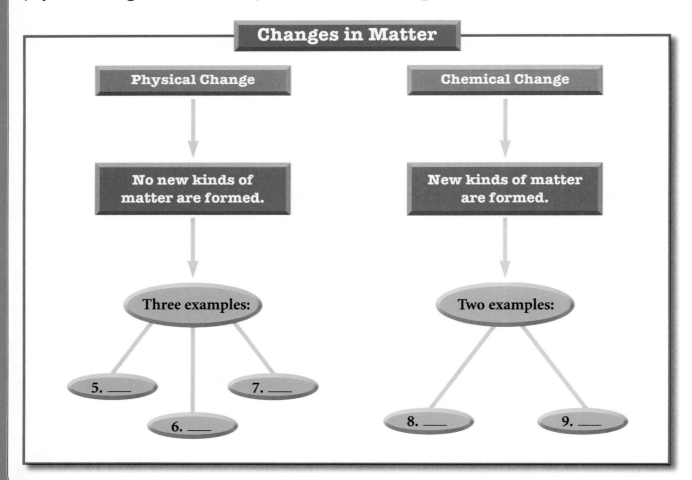

Changes in Matter

Physical Change → No new kinds of matter are formed. → Three examples:
5. ____
6. ____
7. ____

Chemical Change → New kinds of matter are formed. → Two examples:
8. ____
9. ____

Check Understanding

Write the letter of the best choice.

10. Which of the following involves a chemical change?
    A dissolving soap in water
    B cutting paper with scissors
    C burning paper
    D filling a balloon with air

11. Which of the following is a physical change?
    F mixing blueberries, strawberries, and raspberries
    G rusting of iron on a car
    H burning a log
    J cooking pancakes

12. When you add heat to ice to turn it into liquid water, you make a —
    A solution   C chemical change
    B mixture   D physical change

13. Which of the following is a solution?
    F twigs, leaves, and bugs
    G sugar and water
    H newspapers and magazines
    J milk and cereal

14. What new kind of matter forms when iron is mixed with air and water?
    A wood   C ice
    B rust   D ash

Critical Thinking

15. Think of the investigation you did with vinegar and baking soda. What happened that showed a gas was forming?

16. Suppose you leave a shovel out in the rain. Two weeks later there are orange-brown spots on it. Explain what has happened.

Process Skills Review

Write *True* or *False*. If the statement is false, change the underlined part to make it true.

17. A scientist who <u>wants to find an answer to a question</u> **plans and conducts an investigation.**

18. When you **observe** something, you <u>watch it carefully</u>.

19. When you **infer**, you <u>make a wild guess</u>.

Performance Assessment

Mixtures and Solutions

Work together with three or four other students. Your teacher will give you the following things: a pitcher of water, two cups, paper clips, safety pins, salt, a spoon, and unpopped popcorn. Make one mixture and one solution and correctly label each.

Unit Project Wrap Up

Here are some ideas for ways to wrap up your unit project.

Display at a Science Fair

Display the results of your project in a school science fair. Be prepared to explain how you identified and controlled variables in your experiments. Let volunteers conduct their own tests with materials you provide.

Draw a Billboard

Design a billboard advertisement for the best soap you tested. What claims could you make that you have evidence for?

Make an Ad Scrapbook

Collect advertisements that make claims that could be tested. Analyze the ads for proof for the claims.

Investigate Further

How could you make your project better? What other questions do you have? Plan ways to find answers to your questions. Use the Science Handbook on pages R2-R9 for help.

Exploring Energy and Forces

PHYSICAL SCIENCE

Exploring Energy and Forces

Unit Project | ## Shadow Show

Present a shadow show for another class. Collect a group of toys that move, and write an action story about them. Find some flashlights, and a light-colored sheet. Set up the sheet as a screen. Stand behind it, with the toys between you and the screen. Make shadows by shining the flashlights on the toys as they are moved and the story is read. Ask your audience to describe the forces that are moving the toys in your shadow show.

Vocabulary Preview

energy
thermal energy
heat
conductor
insulator
thermometer

Heat

Have you ever been to a crowded basketball game? The more the people move around, the hotter it gets. Matter acts in much the same way. Matter is made of little particles that move. The more the particles move, the hotter the matter gets.

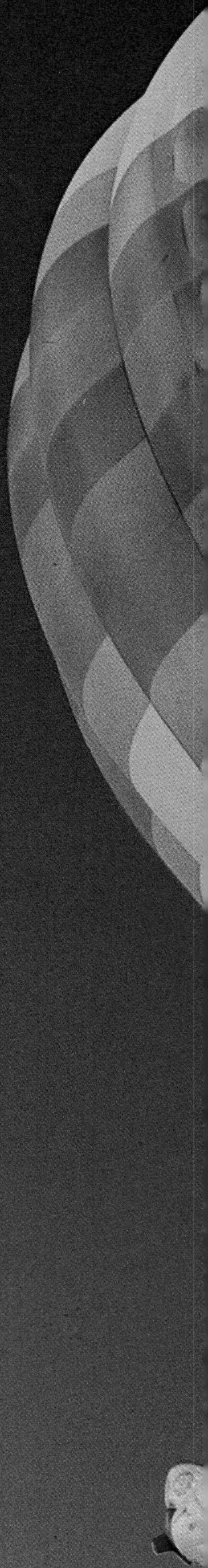

FAST FACT

Using heat can be lots of fun! Hot-air balloons are able to fly because hot air is pushed up by denser cold air. One of the first hot-air balloons flew in 1783. The first fliers weren't people. They were a sheep, a rooster, and a duck!

Have you ever wanted to know the temperature when you didn't have a thermometer? Next time this happens, just count the number of times a cricket chirps in one minute and use this table.

Cricket Chirp Thermometer

Number of Chirps per Minute	The Temperature
10	40°F
40	47°F
80	57°F
120	67°F
160	77°F
200	87°F
240	97°F

LESSON 1

What Is Heat?

In this lesson, you can . . .

INVESTIGATE a way to get thermal energy.

LEARN ABOUT thermal energy and heat.

LINK to math, writing, health, and technology.

Rubbing Objects Together

Activity Purpose Scientists use what they know to make statements about how the world works. Then they do tests to see if their statements are correct. The statements they test are called **hypotheses**. In this investigation you will make hypotheses about heat.

Materials

- metal button
- small piece of wool
- penny
- sheet of paper

Activity Procedure

1. Hold your bare hands together, palms touching. Do your hands feel cold, hot, sticky, or damp? **Record** what you **observe**.

◀ Standing close to a grill, you can feel the heat. It begins in the coals. Then the sides of the grill get hot. When the fire is ready for cooking, almost any part of the grill feels hot.

2 Make a **hypothesis**. What would you feel if you rubbed your hands together? **Record** your hypothesis.

3 Now rub your palms together very fast for about ten seconds. **Record** what you **observe**. (Picture A)

4 What might you feel if you rubbed the button with the wool? The penny with the paper? Form a **hypothesis** for each test. **Record** each one.

5 Rub the button with the wool for about ten seconds. Touch the button. Touch the wool. **Record** what you **observe**. (Picture B)

6 Then rub the penny with the paper for about ten seconds. Touch the penny. Touch the paper. **Record** what you **observe**.

Picture A

Picture B

Draw Conclusions

1. What changes did you **observe**? What actions did you perform that caused the changes you observed?

2. Were your **hypotheses** correct? If not, how could you change them based on what you learned?

3. **Scientists at Work** Scientists use their knowledge and experiences to help them **hypothesize**. What knowledge and experiences did you use in this investigation to help you hypothesize?

Process Skill Tip

A **hypothesis** is an *if . . . then* statement. It tells what will happen if something else happens. For example, suppose you noticed that you see bugs only in the summer. You could say *"If* it is summer, *then* there are bugs outside."

Thermal Energy

FIND OUT

• what thermal energy is

• what heat is

• what thermal energy can do

VOCABULARY

energy
thermal energy
heat

Energy

It's hot outside. My soup's cold. Don't touch the stove—it's hot. It's cold out—put on your coat. You've heard these things many times. You know what hot and cold feel like. But do you know what causes them? It's heat.

The story of heat begins with energy. **Energy** is the ability to cause change. There are many ways matter can change. A sheet of paper can be cut into pieces. Baking soda and vinegar can be mixed together to make a new kind of matter. But these changes don't happen by themselves. The paper doesn't cut itself. The baking soda and vinegar don't mix themselves. Energy has to be added to make the changes happen. Your energy cuts the paper. Your energy also mixes the baking soda and the vinegar. Energy in the baking soda and the vinegar makes the new kind of matter. There are many different kinds of energy. All kinds of energy cause changes in matter.

✔ **What is energy?**

You use energy to fold paper. Your energy changes the paper into a different shape. ▼

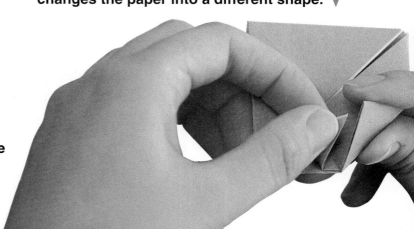

◄ The energy in the flame melts the candle wax. This energy makes the matter in the candle change states.

Thermal Energy

Even though you can't see them, the particles in all matter are always moving. The particles in solids move back and forth in place. The particles in liquids slide past each other. The particles in gases fly off in all directions. If you have ever moved a heavy chair across the living room, you know it takes a lot of energy. Moving anything from one place to another takes energy. Even moving the tiny particles in matter takes energy. The energy that moves the particles in matter is called **thermal energy**.

We feel thermal energy as heat. Something that is hot has more thermal energy than something that is cold. The particles in a hot stove are moving very fast. They have a lot of thermal energy. The particles in a bowl of cold soup are moving more slowly. They have less thermal energy.

✔ **What is thermal energy?**

A horseshoe is a solid. Its particles are packed tightly together, but they still move a little bit. ▶

A blacksmith puts the horseshoe into the fire. The thermal energy from the fire moves into the horseshoe. When the particles in the fire bump into the particles in the horseshoe, they make them start to move faster too. ▼

Heat

Thermal energy can move from one thing to another. Suppose you warm some cocoa on the stove. Then you pour the cocoa into a cup. When you touch the cup, it feels hot. Thermal energy moves from the hot cocoa to the cool cup. Then thermal energy moves from the warmed cup to your hand. The movement of thermal energy from one place to another is called **heat**.

When you touch a hot cup of cocoa, thermal energy moves from the cup to your hand. If you touch a cold glass of milk, thermal energy moves from your hand to the cold glass. Thermal energy always moves from a hot place to a cold place. It never moves from a cold place to a hot place.

✔ **What is heat?**

These children are blowing warm air onto their hands. Doing this keeps their hands warm on a chilly day. ▼

▲ Fire produces thermal energy. The thermal energy from the stove is used to cook food.

Ways to Make Things Hot

Every time two objects rub together, they produce thermal energy. In the investigation you rubbed your hands together. The particles in your left hand rubbed against the particles in your right hand. The rubbing made the particles in both hands move faster. So you felt heat.

Burning also produces thermal energy. When a gas stove is lighted, the energy stored in the gas particles changes into thermal energy. The thermal energy cooks your food.

Some materials produce thermal energy when they are mixed together. When iron oxide and aluminum are mixed together, they make a hot fire. The fire is so hot that it can even melt metals.

Some gardeners like to use natural materials to make the soil richer. They pile up leaves, soil, food scraps, and grass clippings. Tiny living things in the soil, called *bacteria*, "eat" the leaves and other matter. The bacteria change the mixture into a rich, dark soil-like material called *compost*. During this change, thermal energy is produced.

✔ **Name three ways to produce thermal energy.**

▲ Aluminum mixes with iron oxide to produce a lot of thermal energy.

▲ A gardener turns the compost pile. Turning mixes the bacteria. The more the bacteria "eat," the more thermal energy is produced.

Ways to Use Thermal Energy

You may not think about it, but you use thermal energy every day. It cooks your food. It keeps you warm. You probably use hot air to dry your clothes and hair. You wash your face with warm water. Factories use thermal energy to form metal parts for cars and refrigerators. On the Fourth of July, thermal energy helps give us fireworks. People could not live without thermal energy.

✔ **How do we use thermal energy?**

◄ This artist uses thermal energy to form glass into many shapes, such as this horse.

Factories use thermal energy to melt metal. ►

▲ A warm home lets you enjoy the snow.

Summary

Energy is the ability to cause matter to change. Thermal energy is the energy that moves the particles inside matter. Thermal energy that moves from one thing to another is called heat.

Review

1. How can you use energy?
2. What does thermal energy do to matter?
3. Name two ways thermal energy can be made.
4. **Critical Thinking** Why do we need thermal energy?
5. **Test Prep** Which is a good definition of heat?
   A ice melting
   B thermal energy that moves
   C fire
   D the energy that moves the particles in matter

LINKS

MATH LINK

Cooking A pie has to bake at 425°F for 15 minutes. Then it has to bake at 350°F for 45 minutes. What is the difference between the two temperatures?

WRITING LINK

Narrative Writing—Story
Write a story about a day without thermal energy. Read your story to a younger child.

HEALTH LINK

Keeping Warm People have used wool for centuries to keep warm. Find out four kinds of animals that we get wool from.

TECHNOLOGY LINK

Learn more about ways thermal energy can be used by watching *Solar Float* on the **Harcourt Science Newsroom Video**.

CNN
Turner
Le@rning

LESSON **2**

How Does Thermal Energy Move?

In this lesson, you can . . .

INVESTIGATE what kinds of objects get hot.

LEARN ABOUT three ways thermal energy moves.

LINK to math, writing, health, and technology.

What Gets Hot

Activity Purpose When you were little, you learned not to touch the stove. You had to learn this lesson to keep safe. Now that you are older, you can learn what kinds of things may get hot and what things almost never get hot. **Experiment** to find out.

Materials

- wooden spoon
- plastic spoon
- metal spoon
- 3 foam cups
- water
- ceramic mug
- plastic cup with handle
- metal cup with handle

Activity Procedure

1 Make charts like the ones shown to **record** your **observations**.

2 Touch the three spoons. Are they hot or cold? **Record** what you **observe**.

3 CAUTION **Be careful with hot water. It can burn you.** Fill three foam cups with hot tap water. Set them on the table in front of you. Put one spoon in each cup. Wait one minute.

◄ Two colored liquids are inside this lamp. They move because one liquid gets hotter than the other.

Spoons

Wooden	Plastic	Metal

Cups

Ceramic	Plastic	Metal

Picture A

4 Gently touch each spoon. Which one is hottest? **Record** how hot each spoon is. Use words like *cool, warm,* or *hot.* (Picture A)

5 Next, fill each cup with hot tap water. Wait one minute. Then gently touch the handle of each cup. Which one is hottest? (Picture B)

6 Use the words you wrote in Step 4 to **record** how hot each cup handle is.

Picture B

Draw Conclusions

1. Study your Spoons chart. Did all the spoons get hot? Which spoon got the hottest?

2. Look at both charts. Which material got hot in both experiments? How did the plastic items change in the hot water?

3. **Scientists at Work** As they test their ideas, scientists may change their **experiments** in small ways. Suppose you want to see if wood always stays cool when it is placed near heat. What kinds of wooden objects could you use in your experiment?

Process Skill Tip

Scientists wonder how things work. They form hypotheses to explain how things work. To test their hypotheses, they do experiments. An **experiment** is a kind of test done very carefully to find out new information.

The Movement of Thermal Energy

FIND OUT

- three ways thermal energy moves
- how to keep thermal energy from moving easily

VOCABULARY

conductor
insulator

Bumping Particles

In the investigation you put a metal spoon into hot water. At first the spoon was cool. But after it had been in the water, it got hot. Thermal energy moved from the hot water to the cool spoon.

There are three ways thermal energy can move from one place to another. The first way happens when things are touching each other.

When objects touch each other, their particles bump into each other. The particles in a hot object move faster than the particles in a cold object. The faster, hotter particles give some of their energy to the slower, cooler particles. Then the slower particles speed up and get hotter.

✔ **How does thermal energy move between objects that touch each other?**

The particles in the hot pancakes bump against the cold butter particles. They hit so hard that they shake the butter particles loose, and the butter melts. ▶

Conductors

Thermal energy moves very quickly in some materials. Metals are an example. Most cooking pots and pans are made of metal because these materials let thermal energy move easily. The energy has to move from the hot stove to the pan to the food. Then the thermal energy will cook the food. Materials in which thermal energy moves easily are called **conductors**.

✔ **What is a conductor?**

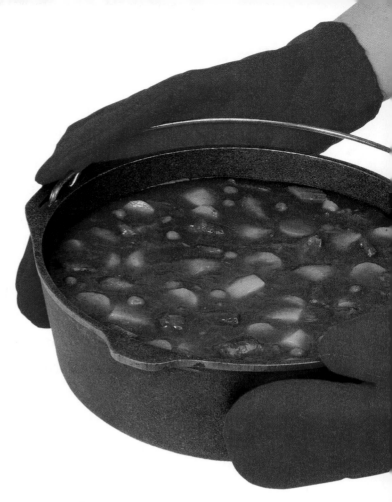

▲ The iron in the Dutch oven makes this a good cooking pot. The iron heats easily so the food can cook.

Insulators

Sometimes you don't want thermal energy to move from one object to another. Suppose you are using a metal cookie sheet to use the thermal energy in the oven to bake some cookies. But then you need to take the cookie sheet out of the oven. Now you need something to keep the thermal energy away from your hands! You need an insulator. An **insulator** is a material in which thermal energy can't move easily. Its particles don't move much when particles from a hot object bump into them. Oven mitts are good insulators.

✔ **What is an insulator?**

▲ This pizza holder does not take in thermal energy easily. The thermal energy from the pizza moves very slowly to the holder. The holder is an insulator.

Moving Liquids and Gases

The second way thermal energy moves from one place to another is in moving liquids and gases. The particles in liquids and gases can move from one place to another. Particles in hot liquids and gases often move to new places before they transfer thermal energy. In some homes, furnaces use fire to heat air. Then fans blow the hot air into the cold rooms in the house. The hot air from the furnace gives its thermal energy to the whole house.

Even when they're not pushed by fans, hot liquids and gases move. When a liquid or gas is heated, its particles spread out. This makes the hot liquid or hot gas lighter. Hot air is lighter than cold air. Cold air sinks to the floor, pushing the hot air up.

✔ **Why does hot air move up?**

▲ **In the desert the hot ground warms the air. The hot air is pushed up by cooler air. As the hot air moves, it makes things around it look wavy.**

Heat from the Sun

The third way thermal energy moves from one place to another happens when things aren't touching each other. When you feel warm standing in the sun, you are not touching the sun. So how do you get warm without touching something that is warm? Thermal energy that moves without touching anything is called *radiation*.

✔ **How can thermal energy move without touching anything?**

◄ **Energy from the sun warms the air and the Earth. We cannot touch the sun, but we can feel its heat.**

Animals and humans depend on the sun to keep warm. ►

Summary

When things touch each other, their particles bump and thermal energy moves between them. Conductors let thermal energy travel easily. Insulators are materials in which thermal energy doesn't move easily. Heated liquids and gases can move before they transfer their thermal energy. We get thermal energy from the sun without touching it.

Review

1. Describe the three ways thermal energy can move.

2. Is a potholder a conductor or an insulator? Explain.

3. Is the metal in a pot a conductor or an insulator? Explain.

4. **Critical Thinking** Animals that have wool keep warm because of their wool. A sweater or coat made of wool keeps you warm too. Why?

5. **Test Prep** Which is the best way to describe what happens to air when it gets warm?

    A Warm air sinks.

    B The particles in warm air get close to each other.

    C Warm air is pushed up by cooler air.

    D Warm air is very still.

LINKS

MATH LINK

A Problem Suppose the burner under a pot of water is turned on at 2:15 P.M. It begins to boil at 2:35 P.M. How long did it take the water to come to a boil?

WRITING LINK

Informative Writing—Explanation Some sports are often done in the warm sunshine. Write a paragraph for your teacher explaining why people who swim outdoors usually do so only when it's warm.

HEALTH LINK

Safety Rules People need thermal energy, but using it can be dangerous. Write two rules for staying safe in the kitchen when food is cooking on the stove.

TECHNOLOGY LINK

Visit the Harcourt Learning Site for related links, activities, and resources.
www.harcourtschool.com

WELCOME TO THE LEARNING SITE

How Is Temperature Measured?

In this lesson, you can . . .

 INVESTIGATE tools for measuring temperature.

 LEARN ABOUT ways to control thermal energy.

 LINK to math, writing, social studies, and technology.

 **INVESTIGATE**

Measuring Temperature

Activity Purpose Many people don't leave home in the morning without finding out what the temperature outside is. Knowing the temperature is especially handy for getting dressed! In this investigation you will find out how to **measure** temperature.

Materials
- 2 cups
- water
- thermometer

Activity Procedure
CAUTION

1 Make a chart like the one shown.

2 **CAUTION** **Be careful with hot water. It can burn you.** Fill one of the cups with cold tap water. Fill the other with hot tap water.

◄ **Thermometers come in many shapes and sizes. This one is used to measure body temperature.**

3 Put the thermometer into the cup of cold water. **Observe** what happens to the liquid in the thermometer. On your chart, **record** the temperature. (Picture A)

Water	Temperature
Cold water, Step 3	
Hot water, Step 4	
Cold water, Step 5	
Hot water, Step 6	

4 Put the thermometer into the cup of hot water. **Observe** what happens to the liquid in the thermometer. On your chart, **record** the temperature.

5 Put the thermometer back into the cup of cold water. **Observe** what happens to the liquid in the thermometer. On your chart, **record** the temperature.

Picture A

6 Wait one minute. Put the thermometer back into the cup of hot water. **Observe** what happens to the liquid in the thermometer. On your chart, **record** the temperature.

Draw Conclusions

1. What happened to the liquid inside the thermometer each time you put the thermometer in the hot water? What happened when you put it in the cold water?

2. Was the temperature of the hot water the same both times you **measured** it? What do you think caused you to get the measurements you got?

3. **Scientists at Work** Scientists **measure** carefully. Write directions for how to measure temperature by using a thermometer.

Process Skill Tip

Scientists look for answers to questions, but they do not ever make up the answers. To try to answer their questions, they **measure** with care. Then anyone who wants to check the answers can take the same measurements.

Measuring Temperature

FIND OUT

• **how to measure temperature**

• **ways to control thermal energy**

VOCABULARY

thermometer

Thermometers

In the investigation you used a thermometer. A **thermometer** is a tool used to measure how hot or cold something is. The liquid in your thermometer expanded when it got hot. It needed more space, so it moved up the tube. Many thermometers work this way. When the liquid cools, its particles don't move as fast. They get closer together. Then the liquid sinks down the tube.

Thermometers have numbers printed on them much like rulers do. Instead of inches or centimeters, they use scales called Fahrenheit and Celsius. By learning to read these scales, you can read the temperature from a thermometer.

✓ **How does a liquid thermometer work?**

▲ One kind of thermometer has the scale printed in a circle. It is a dial thermometer. It uses a metal coil instead of a liquid.

Scientists have measured the temperatures of many kinds of things. Some examples are shown here.

-200°C (-328°F) Air becomes liquid

-89°C (-128°F) Earth's lowest temperature

0°C (32°F) Freezing point of water

58°C (136°F) Earth's highest temperature

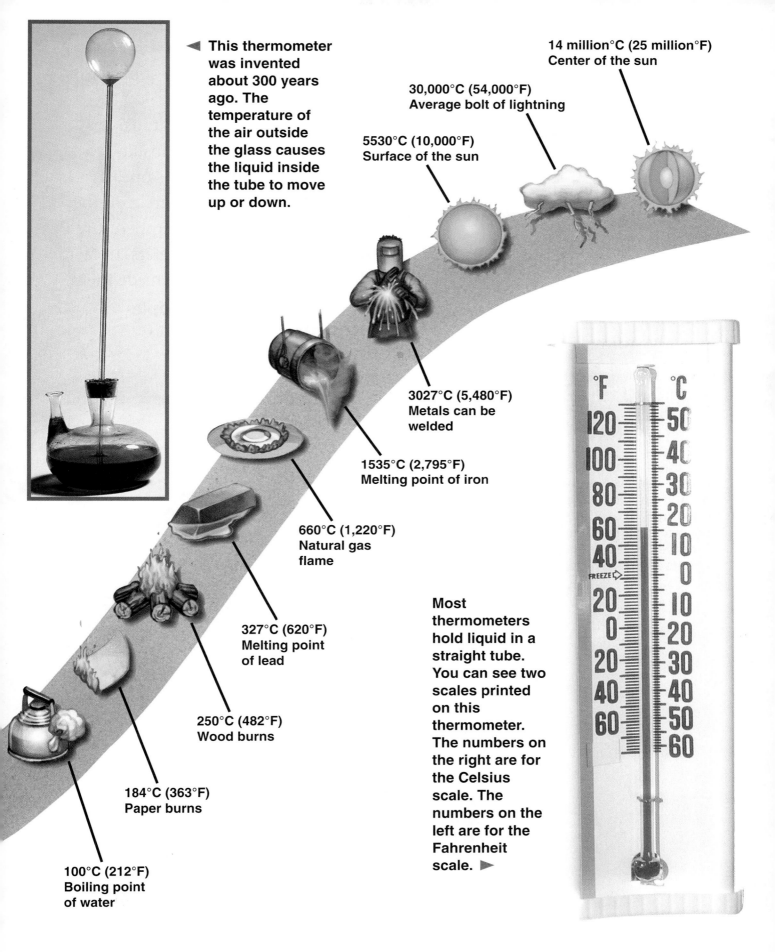

◀ This thermometer was invented about 300 years ago. The temperature of the air outside the glass causes the liquid inside the tube to move up or down.

14 million°C (25 million°F)
Center of the sun

30,000°C (54,000°F)
Average bolt of lightning

5530°C (10,000°F)
Surface of the sun

3027°C (5,480°F)
Metals can be welded

1535°C (2,795°F)
Melting point of iron

660°C (1,220°F)
Natural gas flame

327°C (620°F)
Melting point of lead

250°C (482°F)
Wood burns

184°C (363°F)
Paper burns

100°C (212°F)
Boiling point of water

Most thermometers hold liquid in a straight tube. You can see two scales printed on this thermometer. The numbers on the right are for the Celsius scale. The numbers on the left are for the Fahrenheit scale. ▶

Controlling Thermal Energy

Humans can die from being too cold or too hot. People's bodies need to stay at a certain temperature. We can live in cold weather and in hot weather because we have learned how to control heat.

One way we control heat is by wearing clothes. In hot weather we dress lightly. In cold weather we dress warmly. Animals adjust to different temperatures also. In the winter a dog's coat gets thicker. By summer its fur is thinner.

One way to control heat inside a building is to use a thermostat. Almost every building has one. It looks like a little box or circle on the wall. Thermostats have temperature scales, just like thermometers. In fact, they have thermometers inside them.

✔ **Name two ways people control heat.**

THE INSIDE STORY

Thermostats

A thermostat turns the furnace and the air conditioner off and on. Most large buildings, like schools, have several furnaces. Each furnace or air conditioner has its own thermostat.

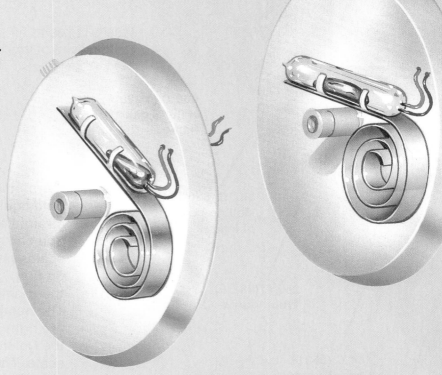

Inside this thermostat is a coiled piece of metal made of two different kinds of metals glued together. Each kind of metal gets bigger when it gets warm. But the metal on the bottom gets bigger faster than the metal on the top. So when the room gets warmer, the coil gets bigger. It turns on the switch for the air conditioner. Then the air conditioner can cool the room.

◄ **This thermostat is round. You can set it to the temperature you want in the room.**

Summary

Thermometers are used to measure temperature. In a liquid thermometer, thermal energy makes the liquid inside the tube move up. We can read the temperature on a scale next to the tube. A thermostat helps control the temperature inside a building.

Review

1. What does a thermometer do?
2. Why does a liquid thermometer work as it does?
3. What kinds of scales are used on thermometers?
4. **Critical Thinking** Why would you need to know what the temperature outside is?
5. **Test Prep** Two different kinds of metals make up thermostat coils because —

   A it's cheaper to make them using two metals

   B they look better that way

   C there is not enough of one kind of metal

   D one metal gets bigger faster than the other

LINKS

MATH LINK

Skip-Counting Look at the scale on a thermometer. Do you need to skip-count by 5s or by 10s to read it?

WRITING LINK

Informative Writing— Description Write a weather forecast for your class. Pretend you are on the TV news. Describe what the weather will be like for the next five days.

SOCIAL STUDIES LINK

Geography Use a world map or a globe to find two countries that have extremely cold winters. Find two tropical countries that are warm all year. Explain how you chose your countries.

TECHNOLOGY LINK

Learn more about measuring temperature by visiting this Internet Site.
www.scilinks.org/harcourt

SCi **LINKS**™
THE WORLD'S A CLICK AWAY

Technology Delivers
Hot Pizza

You know that thermal energy always moves from hot objects to cold objects. This means thermal energy moves from a hot pizza to the cooler air around it. In the process, the hot pizza gets cold. And who wants cold pizza?

We Want It Hot

A recent survey found that more than half of all take-out food was delivered to homes rather than picked up. Keeping pizza hot while the delivery person finds the right house is sometimes a problem. Customers want their food delivered fast, and they want it to arrive piping hot. Companies that deliver cold pizzas are soon out of business. So it's good news that science is helping pizza companies deliver your pizza hot to your door.

Thermal Retention

A new product is being used to keep take-out food hot. It is called the hot bag, and it keeps the heat of the food inside the container.

The hot bag is made with three layers of material. The inside liner, made of nylon and vinyl, reduces condensation. It also has a shiny silver color to reflect the heat of the food back inside the container.

The middle layer is a dense foam. This layer is the insulator for the bag. Thermal energy doesn't move easily through the foam. That means the heat is trapped inside the bag. The foam also prevents air from moving into or out of the bag. Even though the inside of the bag is hot, the outside of the bag remains cool and easy to handle.

The outside of the bag is made of heavy vinyl. This makes the bag waterproof. The hot-bag makers use strips of Velcro to seal the bag, keeping even more thermal energy in. The hot bag also has two small openings that allow steam to escape.

They keep the pizza crust from becoming soggy on its trip to your home.

Hot Delivery

The makers of the hot bag promise that food in this bag will remain at 80°C (176°F) for at least 15 minutes. After 30 minutes the temperature inside the bag may drop 5 to 8°C (about 10 to 15°F). But thanks to the new materials, the pizza remains 17°C (31°F) hotter than it would using the old way. The crust stays crisp, and the cheese stays gooey. Hot-bag manufacturers are always watching for new technology that can help them deliver your pizza just the way you like it—hot from the oven.

Think About It

1. What other types of fast-food companies could use the hot bag to help them in their deliveries?

2. Would these bags be helpful for delivering ice cream? Explain.

WEB LINK:
For Science and Technology updates, visit the Harcourt Internet site.
www.harcourtschool.com

foam

pizza

Our Pizza
Is the Greatest...
Fresh & Oven Hot
MADE WITH THE FINEST INGREDIENTS
Thank You For Your Patronage, Please Call Again

Percy Spencer

INVENTOR

Have you ever made popcorn in a microwave oven? That's how microwave ovens were invented in 1945. Percy Spencer was touring one of the laboratories at the Raytheon Company, where he worked. He was standing close to the power tube that drives a radar set. Suddenly he realized that the chocolate bar in his pocket was beginning to melt. He asked for some unpopped popcorn to test his theory that the machine could cook food.

Percy Spencer was awarded 120 patents during his lifetime. His patent for the microwave oven was given in 1952. The first microwave oven was more than 5 feet tall and weighed 750 pounds! It was designed for cooking large amounts of food in restaurants, on ocean liners, and on railroad cars.

Today microwaves are used to do many things besides heat food. Microwaves are used in radar. Some researchers are working to use microwaves to sterilize food. Some industries have begun using microwaves as well. Microwaves are used to bake the tiles that protect a space shuttle from heat when it returns to the Earth's atmosphere.

One of the most exciting possibilities is that microwaves might be used to treat some kinds of cancer. Cancer tissue begins to die at 109°F. Researchers hope they can use microwaves to kill the cancer and not harm the healthy tissue.

Think About It

1. How do you know that Percy Spencer was creative?
2. Have you ever had an unexpected discovery? What was it?

Testing Insulators

Is wool or sand a better insulator?

Materials

- 1 small coffee can with plastic lid
- 2 wool socks
- scissors
- 1 long lab thermometer
- clock with a second hand
- hair dryer
- 3 cups of sand

Procedure

1. Stuff the can with the socks. Put the lid on. Cut a small hole in the middle of the lid for the thermometer. Make sure the thermometer is surrounded by wool. After five minutes, read and record the temperature.

2. Start the hair dryer. Warm the outside of the can. Watch the thermometer and the clock. See how long it takes the temperature to go up 10°C.

3. Repeat using sand in the coffee can.

Draw Conclusions

Compare results. Which is the better insulator? How do you know?

Cooling Water

How long does it take for warm water to cool?

Materials

- 2 foam cups
- measuring cup
- 2 thermometers
- clock with a second hand
- warm water

Procedure

1. Fill one cup with 1 cup of warm water. Fill the other cup with $\frac{1}{2}$ cup of warm water.

2. In which cup will the water cool faster? Make a hypothesis to answer the question. Write down your hypothesis.

3. Make a chart to record temperatures. Record the starting temperature in each cup. Then record the temperature of each cup every minute until one cup of water reaches room temperature.

Draw Conclusions

Was your hypothesis correct? Explain.

Chapter 1 Review and Test Preparation

Vocabulary Review

Choose a term below to match each definition. The page numbers in ( ) tell you where to look in the chapter if you need help.

energy (F6)

thermal energy (F7)

heat (F8)

conductor (F15)

insulator (F15)

thermometer (F20)

1. The ability to cause change

2. Matter in which thermal energy doesn't move easily

3. The movement of thermal energy from one place to another

4. Matter in which thermal energy moves easily

5. A tool that measures temperature

6. The energy of the moving particles inside matter

Connect Concepts

Write the terms to complete the concept map.

hot   the sun   liquids   gases

particles   thermal energy   cold

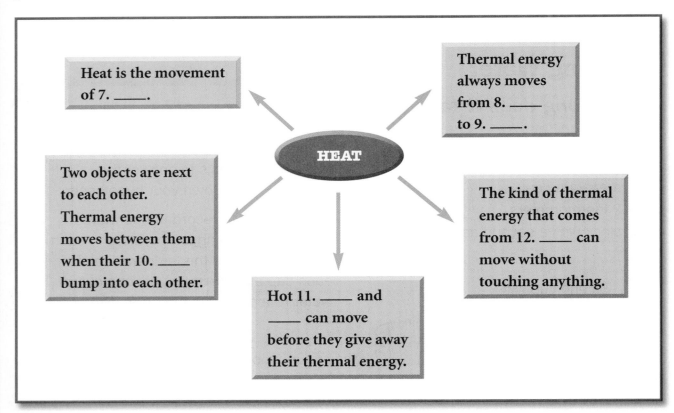

Heat is the movement of 7. _____.

Thermal energy always moves from 8. _____ to 9. _____.

HEAT

Two objects are next to each other. Thermal energy moves between them when their 10. _____ bump into each other.

Hot 11. _____ and _____ can move before they give away their thermal energy.

The kind of thermal energy that comes from 12. _____ can move without touching anything.

Check Understanding
Write the letter of the best choice.

13. Which is an insulator?
    A silver spoon
    B aluminum foil
    C stainless steel spoon
    D wooden spoon

14. Which is a conductor?
    F wooden spoon
    G oven mitt
    H aluminum foil
    J wool sweater

15. Heat from the sun gets to Earth by —
    A moving through liquids
    B moving through gases
    C moving without touching anything
    D bumping into Earth's particles

16. Moving anything from one place to another takes —
    F heat   H a thermometer
    G energy   J a thermostat

Critical Thinking

17. You take a dish out of a hot oven. Before you set the dish on the table, you put down a thick straw pad. Why?

18. You are holding an ice cube. Is thermal energy moving from your hand to the ice or from the ice to your hand? Explain.

Process Skills Review

19. Two people **measure** the temperature of the same cup of hot water. They use two different thermometers. One person says the temperature of the water is 40°C. The other says it is 50°C. What can cause the different answers?

20. What **experiment** could you do to find out why the temperatures in Question 19 were different?

21. It is July. The sun is shining. What **hypothesis** can you state about the temperature? How could you check your hypothesis?

Performance Assessment

Diagram a Thermometer

Water boils at 100°C and freezes at 0°C. Draw a picture of a liquid thermometer in a pot of boiling water. Draw a picture of the same thermometer in a pot of freezing water. Explain what happens to the thermometer when it moves from the boiling water to the freezing water.

Vocabulary Preview

reflection
refraction
absorption
prism

Light

Flick! Bounce, reflect, bounce! That's what happens to the light from a flashlight if you turn it on and shine it at your image in a mirror. The light goes so fast it seems to hit the mirror and you at the same instant you turn the flashlight on!

FAST FACT

We see stars as they were when their light left them. This table shows how long it takes the light from some space objects to reach us.

The Speed of Light		
Object in Space	**Distance from Earth**	**Light Reaches Us In**
Moon	384,462 km	$1\frac{1}{3}$ seconds
Venus	41.2 million km	$2\frac{1}{3}$ minutes
Sun	149.7 million km	$8\frac{1}{2}$ minutes
Alpha Centauri	40.2 trillion km	$4\frac{1}{3}$ years
Sirius	81.7 trillion km	$8\frac{1}{2}$ years
Andromeda Galaxy	21.2 billion billion km	$2\frac{1}{4}$ million years

Andromeda Galaxy

How Does Light Behave?

In this lesson, you can . . .

INVESTIGATE how light travels.

LEARN ABOUT things light can do.

LINK to math, writing, drama, and technology.

INVESTIGATE

How Light Travels

Activity Purpose You can make shadows with your hands because of the way light travels. In this investigation you will **observe** how light travels.

Materials
- 3 index cards
- ruler
- pencil
- clay
- small, short lamp without a lampshade

Activity Procedure

1. Make a large X on each card. To draw each line, lay the ruler from one corner of the card to the opposite corner. (Picture A)

▲ **Shadow puppets can be fun.**

2 On each card, make a hole at the place where the lines of the X cross. Use the pencil to make the holes.

3 Use the clay to make a stand for each card. Make sure the holes in the cards are the same height. (Picture B)

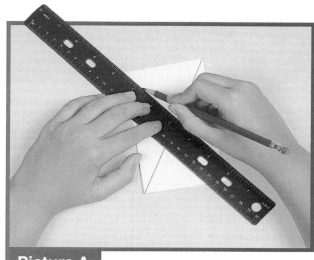

Picture A

4 Turn on the light. Look through the holes in the cards. Move the cards around on the table until you can see the light bulb through all three cards at once. Draw a picture showing where the light is and where the cards are.

5 Move the cards around to new places on the table. Each time you move the cards, draw a picture showing where the cards are. Do not move the light! **Observe** the light through the holes each time.

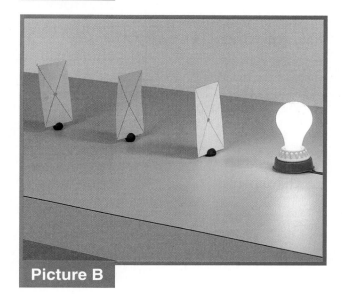

Picture B

Draw Conclusions

1. Where were the cards when you were able to see the light?

2. Were there times you couldn't see the light? Where were the cards then?

3. **Scientists at Work** Scientists **observe** carefully and then **record** what they observe. Often they draw pictures to **communicate** what they observe. Did drawing pictures help you describe what you saw? Explain.

Process Skill Tip

Scientists can learn many things about the world just by **observing**. Then they **record** what they see. After they observe the same thing many times, they **communicate** by telling other scientists what they have observed.

Light

FIND OUT

- **what makes shadows**
- **how mirrors work**
- **why things look funny through water**

VOCABULARY

reflection
refraction
absorption

Light Energy

You know that energy is the ability to cause things to change. The energy in a fire changes a sheet of paper into ashes. The heat from a fire can change your hands from cold to warm. Bacteria use energy to change a dead log into soil for plants.

Light is also a kind of energy. Light energy can make many changes. Without light energy, you could not see anything. Light energy gives things colors. The sun shines on the soil, and plants grow. Light energy can make cars move. In space, light energy powers satellites and space stations. Doctors use the light energy of lasers to perform some operations.

✔ **What are three changes light energy can cause?**

◀ Plants can't live without light. Plants use the sun's light to make food.

▲ Scientists are finding new ways to use the sun's energy. Some new cars use light energy instead of gas.

◄ **The sun provides energy to Earth.**

Shadows

When you put your hand in front of a lamp, you make a shadow on the wall. The shadows move and change shape as you move your hand. Shadows move and change because of the way light travels.

Light travels in straight lines. When you put your hand in front of a lamp, some of the straight lines of light hit your hand. The shadow on the wall shows where the light is blocked by your hand. When you move your hand, the shadow moves because your hand blocks different lines of light.

In the investigation you could see the light bulb only when the holes in the three cards were in a straight line. When one of the holes wasn't in line with the others, it blocked the line of light. How did this show that light travels in a straight line?

When you stand in the sun, you block some of the lines of sunlight. As the sun moves in the sky, you block different lines of light. When the sun is low in the sky, in the morning and in the afternoon, your shadow is long. When the sun is high overhead, your shadow is short.

✔ **How does light travel?**

▲ Shadows caused by sunlight are long in the morning. These shadows always point away from the sun.

▲ In the afternoon the sun is in a different place. Now the shadow points another way, but it still points away from the sun.

Bouncing Light

Look in a mirror. What do you see? You probably see yourself and some of the things around you. You are looking in front of you at the mirror. But the things you see in the mirror are next to you or even behind you. How is this possible?

Hold a lamp in front of a mirror, and you will see the lamp in the mirror. The light from the lamp moves in a straight line to the mirror. When it hits the mirror, it bounces off. It is still traveling in a straight line. But now it's going in a new direction. It is coming straight back to you. The bouncing of light off an object is called **reflection** (rih•FLEK•shuhn). You see objects in a mirror because their light is reflected straight back to you.

◄ When light bounces off a mirror, the light changes direction. The letters on the sign are backward. This is because a mirror reverses an image from left to right.

Light travels in straight lines. Even if it bounces off many mirrors, you can still see the object. If the mirrors are lined up exactly right, you can see many reflections of the object. ▼

Light bouncing off a smooth surface gives an image you can see. A mirror is very smooth. So are shiny metal and still water. You can see yourself in these things. But most things aren't as smooth as mirrors.

Most things are bumpy. When light hits a bumpy surface, each straight line of light goes off in a different direction. Then you don't see any image.

✔ **What is reflection?**

◀ If the water is rippling, each wave reflects light in a different direction. Since the light is traveling in so many directions, it is hard to see a clear picture on the surface of the water.

The water on the lake is so still that it acts like a mirror. ▼

Bending Light

Light doesn't bounce off every surface. There are some things light goes through. That's why you can see through air, water, and glass.

Light travels at different speeds in air, water, and glass. So when light goes from one thing to another, such as from air to glass, it changes speed. Any time light goes from one kind of matter to another, it changes speed. If light hits the new matter straight on, it keeps going straight. But if light hits the new matter at a slant, the light bends. The bending of light when it moves from one kind of matter to another is called **refraction** (rih•FRAK•shuhn).

Light moving from air to glass is like a skater moving from a sidewalk to the grass. If the skater is going straight into the grass, both front wheels hit the grass at the same time. The skater slows down because grass is softer than concrete. But he or she continues to go straight. If the skater does not go straight into the grass, one wheel hits the grass first. The other is still on the sidewalk. The wheel that hits the grass first slows down first. This makes the skater change direction.

✔ **What is refraction?**

Half of this toy diver is in the water. You see the bottom half through the water. The light bends when it hits the water. You see the top half through air. This light isn't bending. So the toy diver looks as if it is broken in two. ▼

Light travels through air and glass. This light hits the glass straight on and keeps going straight. ▶

Here the light hits the glass at an angle. This time the light bends and changes direction. ▼

Here the light is refracted three times. So the pencil looks as if it is broken into four pieces. ▼

Stopping Light

You have learned that you can see through air, water, and glass. Light travels through these forms of matter. But most matter doesn't let light pass. When light hits a wall, the wall stops, or absorbs, the light. Stopping light is called **absorption** (ab•SAWRP•shuhn). Have you ever watched rain falling on grass? The soil absorbs the water. Most matter absorbs light in the same way.

When light hits most objects, some of the light bounces off and the rest is absorbed. Smooth, shiny objects reflect almost all the light that hits them. Other objects absorb most of the light that hits them and reflect the rest. If an object doesn't produce its own light, what you see when you look at it is the light that bounces off it.

✔ **What is absorption?**

▲ Light travels through this glass window because it is *transparent*. You can see a clear image of the girl through the window. Light also travels through the thin curtain. Matter that lets only some light through is called *translucent*. Light can't travel through the dark curtains. A material that doesn't let light through is *opaque*.

Summary

Light energy can cause things to change. Light travels in a straight line unless it bumps into something. An object that stops light can cause a shadow. Some objects let light pass through them. When light hits an object, it can be reflected, refracted, or absorbed.

Review

1. What does a mirror do?
2. At about what time of day is your shadow shortest?
3. What word describes stopping light so that it is not reflected or refracted?
4. **Critical Thinking** You stick your hand into an aquarium to get something out. Why does your hand look as if it is cut off from your arm?
5. **Test Prep** Which is an example of light energy being used?
   A water boiling
   B a seed sprouting
   C a ball bouncing
   D a girl lifting a chair

LINKS

MATH LINK

Elapsed Time Suppose the sun rises at 6:15 A.M. and sets at 7:15 P.M. How many hours of daylight are there?

WRITING LINK

Informative Writing— Description Write a short story for your classmates that describes a building reflected in a puddle. Include one description for when the water is smooth and one for when the water is rippling.

DRAMA LINK

Shadow Puppets Make a screen out of a cloth sheet. Shine a light behind it. Make shadow animals on the sheet. Use them to tell a story to the class.

TECHNOLOGY LINK

Learn more about how light can be used by watching *Using Natural Light* on the **Harcourt Science Newsroom Video.**

LESSON 2

How Are Light and Color Related?

In this lesson, you can . . .

INVESTIGATE rainbows.

LEARN ABOUT light and color.

LINK to math, writing, art, and technology.

INVESTIGATE

Making a Rainbow

Activity Purpose The world is a colorful place. You know that you can see colors only when the light is shining. In the dark you can't see color. So is color in the objects or in the light? In this investigation you can **observe** where colors come from.

Materials
- small mirror
- clear glass
- water
- flashlight

Activity Procedure

1 Gently place the mirror into the glass. Slant it up against the side.

2 Fill the glass with water. (Picture A)

3 Set the glass on a table. Turn out the lights. Make the room as dark as possible.

◀ **You can get all the colors of the rainbow in a box of colored pencils.**

F42

Picture A

Picture B

4 Shine the flashlight into the glass of water. Aim for the mirror. Adjust your aim until the light hits the mirror. If necessary, adjust the mirror in the water. Make sure the mirror is slanted.

5 **Observe** what happens to the light in the glass. Look at the light where it hits the ceiling or the wall. **Record** what you observe. (Picture B)

Draw Conclusions

1. What did the light look like as it went into the glass?

2. What did the light look like after it came out of the glass?

3. **Scientists at Work** Scientists **draw conclusions** based on what they **observe**. What conclusions can you draw about where color comes from?

Investigate Further Change the angles of the mirror and the flashlight. Which setup gives the best result? Draw a picture of the best arrangement.

Process Skill Tip

You **draw conclusions** when you have gathered data by observing, measuring, and using numbers. Conclusions tell what you have learned.

Light and Color

FIND OUT

- **how many colors are in light**
- **what makes a rainbow**

VOCABULARY

prism

Prisms

Have you ever drawn a picture of the sun? Did you color it yellow? People often do. But sunlight is really made of many different colors. Yellow is only one of them. The sunlight you see is really white light. White is the color of all the sun's colors mixed together.

Different colors of light travel at different speeds in water and in glass. So when white light moves from air to glass or from air to water, the different colors of light bend at different angles. They separate into each individual color.

In the investigation you used water and a mirror to break white light into different colors. Scientists use glass triangle prisms to experiment with light. A **prism** (PRIZ•uhm) is a solid object that bends light. When white light hits the prism, each color of light bends at a different angle. Light that passes through a prism separates into a rainbow.

✔ **What is a prism?**

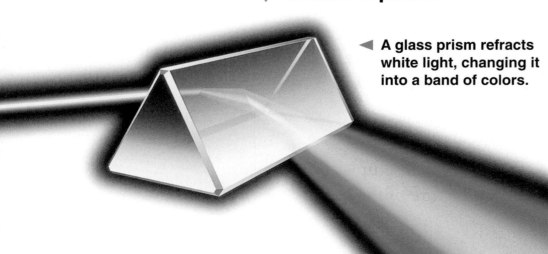

◀ A glass prism refracts white light, changing it into a band of colors.

How Rainbows Form

You can sometimes see a rainbow in the sky during a summer rain when the sun is out.

Each drop of falling water is like a tiny prism. So sunlight passes through all the raindrops, and the light rays bend. This bending separates the light into its colors, and you see a rainbow.

When white light separates, its colors always appear in the same order. The order is red, orange, yellow, green, blue, and violet.

Adding Colors

A prism breaks white light into colors. You can also add colors together. When you add different colored lights together, they form other colors. Shining a red light and a green light onto the same spot will make a yellow light. Shining a blue light and a red light onto the same spot will make a purple light. You can add red light, blue light, and green light in different ways to make all other colors.

✔ **What is one method for making colors?**

Seeing Colors

All the colors of light, called white light, hit every object you see. Most objects absorb most of the light, but not all of it. The light that is not absorbed is reflected and is the color you see. For example, green grass absorbs all of the white light except the green part. The green part reflects back to your eyes, and you see green grass.

✔ **Why do you see color?**

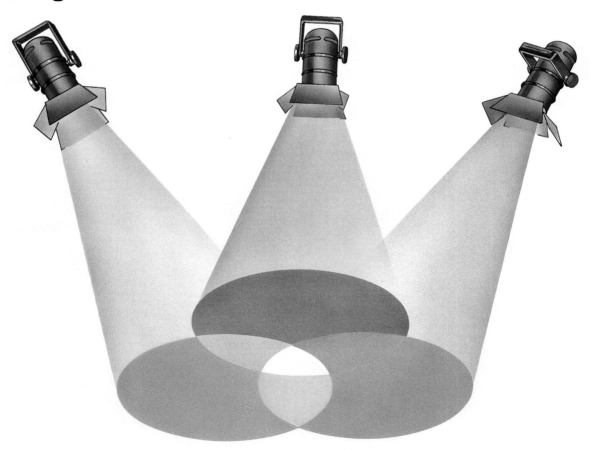

Three basic light colors are red, blue, and green. They will form all other colors. Adding all three of these colors will give white light.

The red rose absorbs all parts of white light except red. Red light is reflected, and we see a red flower.

Summary

White light is made up of many colors mixed together. A prism separates the colors. Raindrops act like prisms to form rainbows. You can make colors by adding different colored lights. The colors of objects you see are the colors of light that the objects reflect.

Review

1. Describe how a prism works.
2. Name the colors that make up white light.
3. What happens if you add different colors of light?
4. **Critical Thinking** Why don't you see a rainbow during most rainstorms?
5. **Test Prep** Which light colors are absorbed by a yellow tulip?
   - **A** red, orange, and yellow
   - **B** red, orange, green, blue, and violet
   - **C** violet, orange, green, and yellow
   - **D** yellow, red, blue, and green

LINKS

MATH LINK

Solid Figures The bases of a triangular prism are triangles. What are the bases of a rectangular prism?

WRITING LINK

Informative Writing— Narration Find five different words that describe colors of red. Write a paragraph for your teacher describing a scene that includes each of these colors.

ART LINK

Color Wheel Find out what a color wheel is and how an artist might use one. Draw one, and explain it to a classmate.

TECHNOLOGY LINK

Visit the Harcourt Learning Site for related links, activities, and resources.
www.harcourtschool.com

WELCOME TO **THE LEARNING SITE**

DISCOVERING LIGHT AND OPTICS

We use our eyes to see. A curved lens inside the eye bends light, focusing an image on the retina. This image is sent to the brain, which interprets the image.

Using Lenses

Lenses in tools such as microscopes, telescopes, and even eyeglasses work the same way. All lenses have at least one curved surface. The curve of the lens bends and focuses the light. The image formed by the lens might be smaller than, larger than, or the same size as the original object.

People have worn eyeglasses for hundreds of years. The Italian explorer Marco Polo saw people in China wearing glasses around 1275. After books became common in the late 1400s, glasses became common for reading. During the 1600s, people discovered that using lenses would correct nearsightedness. Nearsighted people have difficulty seeing objects far away. More than 125 million people in the United States now wear glasses or contact lenses.

The History of Optics

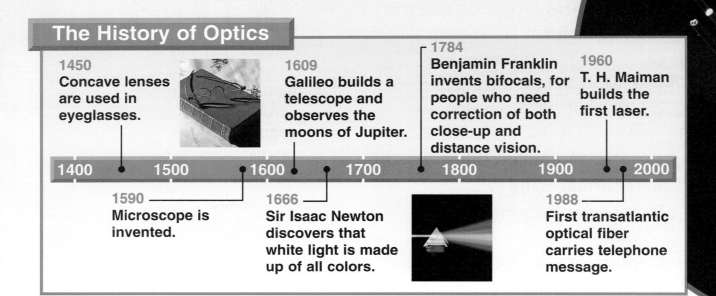

1450
Concave lenses are used in eyeglasses.

1609
Galileo builds a telescope and observes the moons of Jupiter.

1784
Benjamin Franklin invents bifocals, for people who need correction of both close-up and distance vision.

1960
T. H. Maiman builds the first laser.

1400   1500   1600   1700   1800   1900   2000

1590
Microscope is invented.

1666
Sir Isaac Newton discovers that white light is made up of all colors.

1988
First transatlantic optical fiber carries telephone message.

Lasers—Light in a Straight Line

If you've ever shone a flashlight into a dark room, you've seen a property of most light beams. The beams spread apart as they leave their source. Lasers turn a regular beam of light into a narrow, straight beam of bright light. Laser light is very focused and has only one color.

Laser light is used in many ways. Lasers are used to scan bar codes on products. Laser light has been bounced off the moon to accurately measure its distance from Earth.

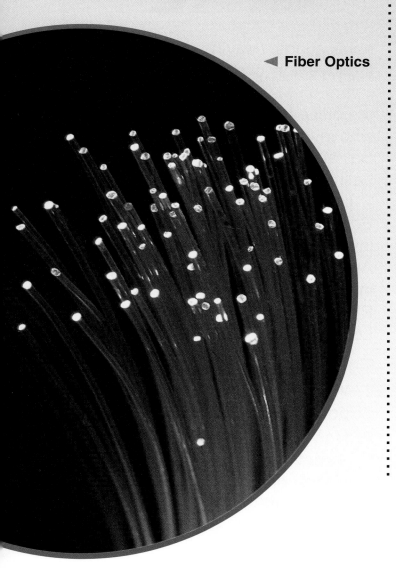

◀ **Fiber Optics**

Physicians use lasers to do surgery. The most common use of lasers is in compact disc (CD) players. A laser beam cuts information onto the discs. The narrow beam allows a disc to hold more information than a tape. Lasers are then used to read and play back the recorded information. Besides music, entire encyclopedias have been put on CDs.

Telephones have long used electric current and copper wire to carry messages. Flashes of light can be used to send messages, too. Laser beams can carry many different messages along very thin glass fibers called optical fibers. Many fibers, each carrying a different message, can be squeezed into a single cable. Fiber-optic telephone lines are now used between many cities. Lines were laid across the Atlantic and Pacific Oceans in the late 1980s.

Fiber optics are also used in medicine to make surgery easier. Doctors can use the fibers to see inside the body while making only small cuts—or no cuts at all.

Think About It

1. How can lenses change an image?
2. What are two uses of optical fibers?

Lewis Howard Latimer

INVENTOR, ENGINEER

Every time you turn on an electric light, you can thank Lewis Latimer. His many inventions helped improve the first light bulb, which had been made by Thomas Edison. And if you've ever screwed a light bulb into a socket, you have used one of Latimer's inventions. He designed the threads of the socket. His model was made of wood, but we still use his idea.

Latimer was the youngest son of escaped slaves. He had to leave school when he was ten to earn money for the family. He never stopped learning, though. He taught himself mechanical drawing by watching the men in the office where he worked. They made detailed drawings of inventions for patent

applications. (Having a patent means the inventor "owns" the idea and the invention.) Latimer's office was near the office of Alexander Graham Bell, who invented the telephone. When Bell applied for a patent, he asked Latimer to make the drawing.

Later Latimer worked with the Edison Pioneers, a group of 80 inventors. He was the only African American in the group. He helped install lighting systems in New York, Philadelphia, Montreal, and even London.

Think About It

1. What do inventing and writing poetry have in common?
2. How is teaching yourself something, perhaps by watching others, different from learning in a classroom?

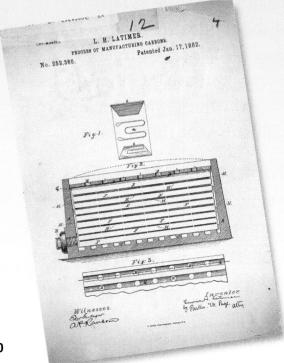

Colors

What colors are reflected off different colors of paper?

Materials
- glue
- strips of colored construction paper
- prism

Procedure

1 Glue strips of construction paper together in the order of the colors of the rainbow: red, orange, yellow, green, blue, and violet.

2 Use a prism to separate the colors in sunlight. Aim the colors from the prism at the different colors of construction paper.

3 Observe how the light from the prism is reflected by the different colors of construction paper.

Draw Conclusions

What colors from the prism are reflected from the green piece of construction paper? Explain.

Make a Periscope

How can you see around a corner?

Materials
- glue
- aluminum foil
- 2 index cards
- shoe box
- black construction paper

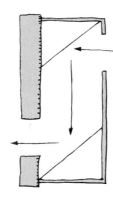

Procedure

1 Glue aluminum foil, shiny side out, to the index cards to make mirrors. Make the foil as smooth as possible.

2 Line the inside of the box with black paper. Cut out a hole in the bottom of the box, about 3 cm from one end. Cut a hole in the lid about 3 cm from one end.

3 Fold the ends of the aluminum foil mirrors to make tabs. Then glue the aluminum-foil mirrors to the inside of the box as shown.

4 Put the lid back on the box, and look through your periscope.

Draw Conclusions

How could you use a periscope to see around a corner?

Vocabulary Review

Use the terms below to complete the sentences 1 through 4. The page numbers in ( ) tell you where to look in the chapter if you need help.

reflection (F36)   **absorption** (F40)
refraction (F38)   **prism** (F44)

1. The bending of light is called ____.

2. A ____ breaks white light into colors.

3. The bouncing of light off objects is called ____.

4. Stopping light and holding it in is ____.

Connect Concepts

Follow the path of light as it travels. Use the terms in the Vocabulary Review to complete the concept map.

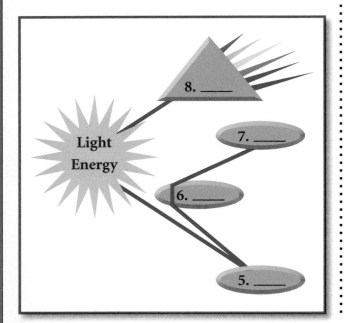

Check Understanding

Write the letter of the best choice.

9. Suppose you drop a penny into a shallow pool of water. You try to grab it but cannot seem to get your fingers in the right place. This happens because of —
   A reflection
   B absorption
   C refraction
   D light energy

10. Suppose you are standing at a pond. Your friend tries to sneak up on you, but you see him coming. You see him in the pond because of —
   F refraction
   G reflection
   H noise in the grass
   J absorption

11. White light is really —
   A all colors of light mixed
   B a mixture of yellow and white light
   C bright in the morning
   D a mixture of red and green light

12. Light travels —
 F through walls
 G around objects
 H in straight lines
 J in a curvy pattern

Critical Thinking

13. A skylight has water drops on it from a rainstorm. The sun comes out, and you see a rainbow on the wall. What is happening?

14. Describe how you could use a mirror to signal your friend in the house across the street.

15. You go to see a play. The light on the stage is yellow. You look up at the lights. They are red and green. Explain.

16. For art class, your teacher has you draw a bowl of fruit. The bowl contains a red apple, an orange, and a banana. After you have finished, your teacher puts a green spotlight on the fruit and asks you to draw it again. Why do you need to draw a new picture?

Process Skills Review

Write *True* or *False*. If the statement is false, correct it to make it true.

17. When you **observe** what is happening in an experiment, you use only your eyes.

18. Scientists sometimes draw pictures to explain their experiments.

Performance Assessment

Make a Model Prism

With a partner, use construction paper to make a large model of a prism breaking a ray of white light into its colors. Be sure to show the colors in the right order. Label each color. Make a hole in the model and add some string so it can be hung up in the classroom. You will need construction paper, glue, scissors, string, and a pencil.

Vocabulary Preview

force
motion
speed
gravity
weight
work
simple machine
lever
inclined plane

Forces and Motion

Do you ever wonder if you could throw a ball so fast that it wouldn't fall back to Earth? It takes a lot of energy to overcome gravity. Gravity is the force that pulls things back to Earth's surface. Rockets are the only human-made things that have been able to escape Earth's gravity and make it into space.

FAST FACT

You may never travel fast enough to escape Earth's gravity. But how fast can you go? A race car goes about 354 kilometers (220 mi) per hour. To go the 4715 kilometers (2,930 mi) between New York and San Francisco, it would take a race car $13\frac{1}{2}$ hours!

Time to Travel from New York to San Francisco

Object	Speed	Time
8-year-old runner	19 kph	248 hours
Propeller plane	483 kph	$9\frac{3}{4}$ hours
Supersonic jet	2,173 kph	2 hours
Space shuttle	40,233 kph	7 minutes
Fast meteoroid	241,395 kph	1 minute
Light	299,330 km per second	0.016 second

FAST FACT

To throw a ball that didn't come back down, you'd have to throw it at a speed of at least 40,000 kilometers per hour (24,856 mph)! A good fastball pitcher can throw a baseball at about 161 kilometers per hour (100 mph).

How Do Forces Cause Motion?

In this lesson, you can . . .

 INVESTIGATE how forces are measured.

 LEARN ABOUT how forces act.

 LINK to math, writing, social studies, and technology.

Measuring Pushes and Pulls

Activity Purpose

Suppose you pull an empty wagon down the street. Then a friend gets in the wagon, and you pull again. The second time, you have to pull a lot harder. Scientists use a tool called a spring scale to **measure** pulls. In this investigation you will use a spring scale to measure pulls.

Materials

- spring scale
- 2 pieces of string
- 2 wooden blocks

Activity Procedure

1. Work with a partner. One of you should hold one end of the spring scale while the other gently pulls on the hook. Read the number on the scale. The number is in newtons. Newtons measure pushes and pulls. **Record** the number. (Picture A)

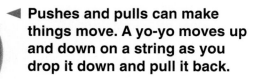

◄ Pushes and pulls can make things move. A yo-yo moves up and down on a string as you drop it down and pull it back.

2 Tie one piece of string around one of the wooden blocks. Tie the other end of the string to the hook on the scale.

3 Begin to pull on the spring scale. Pull as hard as you can without making the block move. **Record** the number on the scale.

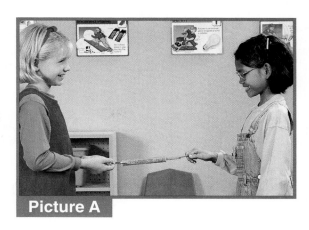
Picture A

4 Now pull hard enough to make the block move. **Record** the number on the scale. Carefully pull the block across the room. Watch the scale. Make sure the number doesn't change as you pull. (Picture B)

5 Repeat Step 4. This time, pull so that the number on the scale changes. **Record** your observations.

6 Tie the second wooden block to the first one. Repeat Steps 3 through 5. **Record** your observations.

Picture B

Draw Conclusions

1. How many newtons did it take to pull on the block without moving it? How many newtons did you use to move the block in Step 4?

2. How did you pull differently in Steps 4 and 5?

3. How did your results change when you added the second block?

4. **Scientists at Work** Scientists make charts to help them **interpret data**. Make a chart to organize the data you collected in this investigation.

Forces and Motion

FIND OUT

- **how motion begins**
- **how to find speed**
- **what gravity is**

VOCABULARY

force
motion
speed
gravity
weight

Forces

A **force** is a push or a pull. You push on a door. You pull on a wagon. Each push or pull is a force. There are many different forces. The force of the wind pushes sailboats and windmills. Forces in car engines can pull cars down the street.

In the investigation you pulled a wooden block. You used a spring scale to measure how hard you pulled. The spring scale measured the amount of force you used. The amount of force you have to use to move an object depends on its mass. The more mass something has, the more force you have to use to make it move. In the investigation you added a second block. How did that change the amount of force it took to move the blocks?

✔ **What is a force?**

◄ This boy is pushing the snowball. The push of the boy is a force.

This girl is pulling a wagon. The pull of the girl is a force. ►

Motion

Birds fly across the sky. Insects crawl across the ground. Leaves move back and forth in the breeze. The wheels on a bicycle go around in a circle. All these things are in motion. **Motion** is a change in position.

Every time you see something in motion, you know a force somewhere got it going. Every motion is started by a force. And every motion is stopped by a force. Once something is in motion, it will move until some force stops it.

✔ **What is motion?**

▲ Look at the picture of the river and the city. Each streak of light shows that an object is moving. What other motion can you see?

The speed of something tells how fast it is moving. Some things can move much faster than others. ▼

Person biking
60 kmh
(37 mph)

Person walking
5 kmh
(3 mph)

Race horse
70 kmh
(43 mph)

Snail
$\frac{5}{100}$ **kilometers per hour (kmh)**
($\frac{3}{100}$ **miles per hour mph)**

Motion

Suppose you want to move a soccer ball down the field. To start the ball moving, you have to apply a force. You give the ball a push with your foot. The ball starts moving. Now suppose you want to stop the ball. Again you have to apply a force. You have to put your foot up and push on the ball to stop it. If you don't stop the ball, it will keep rolling until some other force stops it.

Not all forces stop or start motion. Suppose you and a friend push on a box. You push one way. Your friend pushes the opposite way. The forces on the box are balanced, so the box doesn't move. But if another person starts pushing on your side, the

forces aren't balanced anymore. Now the box moves.

✔ **Why does a rolling ball stop rolling?**

When this clown rides her unicycle, the forces pushing on the left side are the same as the forces pushing on the right side. This keeps her from falling sideways. ▼

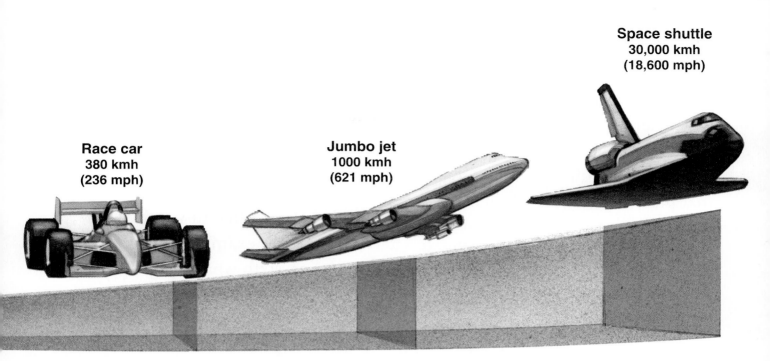

Race car
380 kmh
(236 mph)

Jumbo jet
1000 kmh
(621 mph)

Space shuttle
30,000 kmh
(18,600 mph)

Speed

Glaciers are large sheets of ice that move very slowly. They move less than 30 centimeters (about 1 ft) a day. A train can move much faster. A train can move more than 2000 kilometers (about 1,200 mi) in a day. The measure of how fast something moves over a certain distance is its **speed**. Something that moves a greater distance in the same amount of time has greater speed.

To find speed, you divide the distance you go by the time it takes you to get there. It's about 440 miles from Washington, D.C., to Boston. If you drive it by car in 8 hours, your speed is 440 miles divided by 8 hours, which is 55 miles per hour. An airplane can make the same trip in about 2 hours. The speed of the airplane is 880 miles divided by 2 hours, which is 440 miles per hour. Which has the greater speed, the car or the airplane?

✔ **What is speed?**

Glaciers move slowly. ▼

Gravity

There is a force that pulls us and everything around us down. That's why when you drop something, it falls down. The force is called gravity. **Gravity** (GRAV•ih•tee) is the force that pulls objects toward each other. All objects are acted on by gravity.

The more mass two things have, the more gravity pulls them toward each other. Earth has a very large mass, so the pull between objects and Earth is large. The moon has less mass than Earth. The pull between the moon and objects is about one-sixth of what it is on Earth.

Weight (WAYT) is a measure of the pull of gravity on an object. On Earth you have one weight. But if you were to go somewhere with a different amount of gravity, you would have a different weight. On the moon, for example, you would weigh one-sixth what you weigh on Earth.

✔ **What is weight?**

Gravity is the force that pulls objects toward Earth. On Earth, all things fall toward the ground. ▼

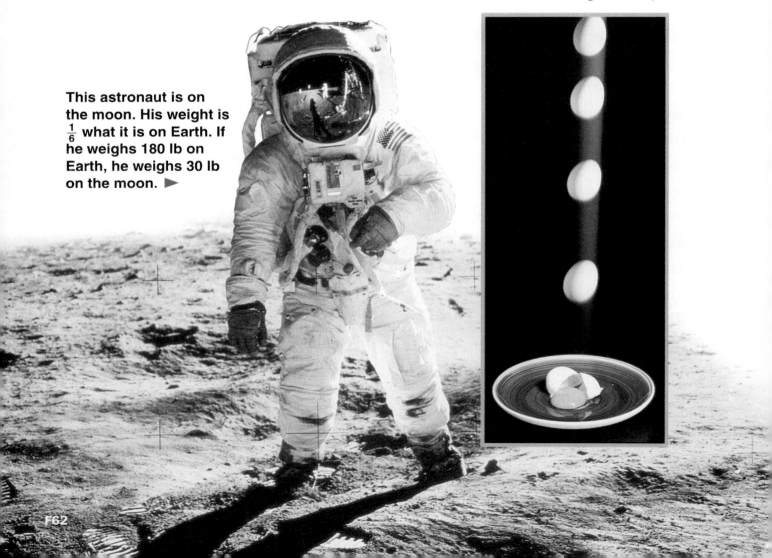

This astronaut is on the moon. His weight is $\frac{1}{6}$ what it is on Earth. If he weighs 180 lb on Earth, he weighs 30 lb on the moon. ▶

Summary

A force is a push or a pull. Motion is a change in position. All motion is caused by forces. Gravity is the force that pulls objects toward each other. Earth's gravity is so strong that it causes all things near Earth to fall toward Earth. Weight is a measure of gravity's pull on an object.

Review

1. What is force?
2. What happens if you start something moving and no force stops it?
3. What two things do you need to know to tell how fast something is moving?
4. **Critical Thinking** What would happen to a rock in a garden if no forces were ever applied to it?
5. **Test Prep** Which sentence is the best definition of *weight*?

    A Weight measures how big something is.

    B Weight measures how fast something can travel.

    C Weight measures the pull of gravity on an object.

    D Weight measures the height of an object.

LINKS

MATH LINK

Subtraction Story A cheetah can run as fast as 70 mph. A zebra can run 40 mph. How much faster can a cheetah run?

WRITING LINK

Expressive Writing—Poem Write a short poem for your classmates, describing how the force of the wind moves the leaves on a plant.

SOCIAL STUDIES LINK

History of the Metric System Find out where the metric system came from. Who invented it? What is the metric unit that measures force?

TECHNOLOGY LINK

To learn more about forces and motion, watch *Big Machine Summer* on the **Harcourt Science Newsroom Video.**

CNN Turner Le@rning

What Is Work?

In this lesson, you can . . .

INVESTIGATE the scientific definition of *work*.

LEARN ABOUT what work is.

LINK to math, writing, language arts, and technology.

INVESTIGATE

Measuring Work

Activity Purpose Scientists say that whenever you move an object, you do work. When you make your bed, put books onto shelves, or take out the trash, you do work. In this investigation you will gather information about work. Then you will **infer** how work is related to force.

Materials

- mug
- spring scale
- meterstick
- shoe with laces
- hat
- stapler
- string

Activity Procedure

1 Make a table like the one shown.

2 Hook the mug onto the spring scale. Work with a partner. One of you should hold the meterstick on the table, with the 1-cm mark toward the bottom. The other person should rest the mug on the table next to the meterstick. (Picture A)

◀ A forklift can lift heavy loads. It is made to do work.

Distance x Force = Work			
Object	Distance (centimeters)	Force (newtons)	Work (newton-centimeters)

3 Gently lift the scale, and pull the mug off the table. Keep the scale and the mug next to the meterstick. **Record** the height you lifted the mug. (Picture B)

4 Read the number of newtons on the spring scale. **Record** the number.

5 Multiply the number of newtons you used times the distance you moved the mug. This is the amount of work that was done. **Record** this number in your table under the heading *Work*.

6 Repeat Steps 2 through 5, using each of the other objects. You may need to use the string to attach the objects to the spring scale. Lift each object the same distance you lifted the mug.

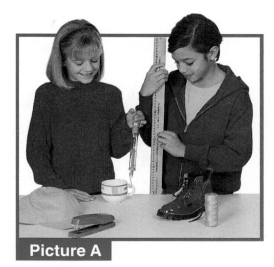
Picture A

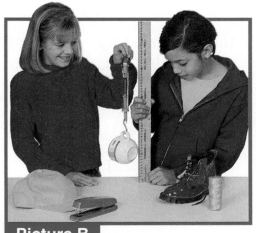
Picture B

Draw Conclusions

1. Which object took the most force to lift? Which object took the least force to lift?

2. Describe the math you did in the chart.

3. In this investigation one of the measurements was kept the same. Which one was it?

4. **Scientists at Work** Scientists **infer** from data. Look at the data you collected. Infer how work is related to force.

Process Skill Tip

Scientists **infer** from data they collect when they **experiment**. After they make inferences, they continue experimenting to see if they are right.

Work

Doing Work

For scientists the word *work* has a specific meaning. **Work** is the measure of force it takes to move an object a certain distance. In the investigation you did work when you lifted a mug off the table. Scientifically, you do work when you plant flowers, ride your bike, or help put away groceries. In each of these activities, you use a force to make something move. You don't do work when you push on a door and can't get it open. If you and a friend push against a box as hard as you can but the box doesn't move, you aren't doing any work.

This boy is pushing as hard as he can against a wall. He's not doing any work, though, because the wall doesn't move. ▼

▲ This time he pushes on a door. The door moves. Now he's doing work.

F66

To figure out how much work is done, scientists multiply the force needed to move the object times the distance the object moves. If you use 3 newtons of force to pull a wagon 10 meters, you do 30 newton-meters of work.

✔ **What is work?**

Summary

In science, work is done when a force moves an object. If the object doesn't move, no work is done. To figure out the amount of work done, scientists multiply the force that is used times the distance the object moves.

Review

1. At the beginning of this lesson there is a picture of a forklift. Is it doing work? How do you know?

2. To a scientist, what is work?

3. How do scientists find the amount of work done?

4. **Critical Thinking** Describe a scene in which someone is using force but is not doing work.

5. **Test Prep** For which activity would you be doing work?
   A watching TV
   B pushing on a box that doesn't move
   C reading a page in a book
   D raking leaves

LINKS

MATH LINK

How Much Work? Marie used 3 newtons to move a chair 2 meters. Latifa used 2 newtons to lift her kitten 1 meter. Who did more work?

WRITING LINK

Informative Writing—How-To Write step-by-step instructions for your brother in first grade. Tell him how to do some kind of work. It might be how to hit a ball or how to make a bed. Be creative or funny.

LANGUAGE ARTS LINK

Many Meanings Write four sentences using the word *work*. Make two sentences with the scientific meaning and two sentences with the everyday meaning.

TECHNOLOGY LINK

Visit the Harcourt Learning Site for related links, activities, and resources.
www.harcourtschool.com

WELCOME TO THE LEARNING SITE

What Are Simple Machines?

In this lesson, you can . . .

INVESTIGATE
how simple machines help us do work.

LEARN ABOUT
kinds of simple machines.

LINK to
math, writing, social studies, and technology.

INVESTIGATE

Moving Up

Activity Purpose People often get help when they do work. Sometimes they ask friends to help. Sometimes they use machines to help. In this investigation you will **compare** two ways of doing work.

Materials
- string
- spring scale
- toy car
- chair
- meterstick
- wooden board (about 1 m long)
- masking tape

Activity Procedure

1 Using the string, attach the spring scale to the toy car. With the spring scale, slowly lift until the bottom of the car is at the same level as the seat of the chair. Read the spring scale, and **record** the number. (Picture A)

3 Use the meterstick to **measure** how high you lifted the car. **Record** this number, too.

◄ A nutcracker is an example of a simple machine called a lever. It makes work—in this case cracking nuts—seem easier to do.

Picture A

3 Prop up one end of the board on the seat of the chair. Tape the board to the floor so the board does not move. (Picture B)

4 Now place the toy car at the bottom of the board. Slowly pull the car to the top of the board at a steady rate. As you pull, read the force on the spring scale. **Record** it.

5 **Measure** the distance you pulled the car up the board. **Record** it.

Draw Conclusions

1. Multiply the force you **measured** by the distance you moved the toy car. How much work did you do without the board? How much work did you do with the board?

2. **Compare** the force used without the board to the force used with the board. Which method used less force?

3. **Compare** the distance the car moved each time. Which method used less distance?

4. **Scientists at Work** Scientists often **compare** their data. Compare your answers to Question 1 to the answers of your classmates. What did you find out?

Investigate Further Repeat the activity using boards of several different lengths. **Record** the results. Did you use less force with longer boards or with shorter ones?

Picture B

Process Skill Tip

Scientists look at the data they collect. They want to see what it means. Sometimes they have to **compare** two pieces of data. This means they look at the pieces of data to see how they are alike and how they are different.

Machines

FIND OUT

• what a simple machine is

• names of simple machines

VOCABULARY

simple machine
lever
inclined plane

Simple Machines

A **simple machine** is a tool that helps people do work. It doesn't change the amount of work. It just makes the work seem easier. Some simple machines reduce the amount of force you have to use. Other simple machines change the direction of the force you use. Some simple machines do both.

There are six simple machines. These machines are the lever, the pulley, the wheel and axle, the inclined plane, the wedge, and the screw. The board you used in the investigation was an inclined plane. When you pull something up an inclined plane, you use less force than you use to pick it straight up. But you have to move it a longer distance with the inclined plane. A pulley changes the direction of the force. As you pull down on one end of the rope, you lift up whatever is attached to the other end. Because of gravity, pulling down is easier than pulling up.

✔ **What is a simple machine?**

A **lever** (LEV·er) is a bar that moves on or around a fixed point. For a seesaw, the board you sit on is the bar. The fixed point is the stand. You can go up and down on the seesaw as it moves on the stand. ▶

A pulley is used on a flagpole to raise and lower the flag. A pulley is a rope over a wheel. It changes the direction of the force you use. When you pull down on one end of the rope, the object attached to the other end moves up. ▶

◀ A wedge, such as this doorstop, is two inclined planes stuck back to back.

An **inclined plane** (IN•klynd PLAYN) is a flat surface set at an angle to another surface. It has many uses. Here it is used as a ramp for wheelchairs. ▼

▲ Look closely at a screw. It has an inclined plane winding around it. A screw is like an inclined plane wrapped around a pencil.

Scissors

Several simple machines put together make a compound machine. A pair of scissors is made up of two wedges and two levers. Look closely. Each blade is a wedge. The very narrow edges of the wedges meet and can cut through paper or fabric.

To make the blades meet every time, you need another machine. Each wedge moves around a bolt in the center. This bolt turns the wedges into levers.

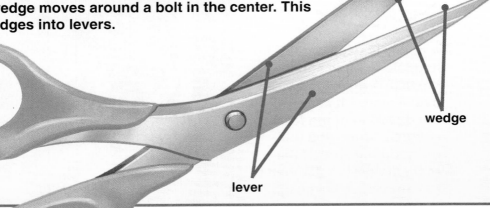

wedge

lever

In a wheel and axle, the wheel is larger than the axle. It takes less force to move the wheel than it does to move the axle. But when the wheel makes a circle, it goes a longer distance than the axle. ▼

Summary

Simple machines do not change the amount of work, but they make work seem easier. They reduce the amount of force you use or change the direction of the force. They can be used by themselves, or they can be parts of more complicated machines.

Review

1. Name two ways simple machines can make work seem easier.

2. What kind of simple machine is a ramp?

3. When you turn a wheel and axle, which moves farther, the wheel or the axle?

4. **Critical Thinking** A hand-cranked can opener contains a wheel and axle, a wedge, and two levers. Tell what part of a can opener each of these is.

5. **Test Prep** Which simple machine is a kind of inclined plane?
   A wheel and axle
   B pulley
   C screw
   D lever

LINKS

MATH LINK

A Word Problem Evan used 2 newtons of force to roll a rock 6 meters up a ramp. Janet attached the same rock to a pulley and used 6 newtons of force to raise it 2 meters. Who did more work?

WRITING LINK

Informative Writing—Description Write a paragraph describing a machine you have designed to make it easier to carry your books to school.

SOCIAL STUDIES LINK

Log Cabins How were log cabins built? In a group, talk about how the logs had to be cut and lifted into place. Decide which simple machines the pioneers may have used.

TECHNOLOGY LINK

Learn more about simple machines and how they work by investigating *Simple Machines* on **Harcourt Science Explorations CD-ROM.**

PROGRAMMABLE
Toy Building Bricks

At first they were just plastic building blocks. Now you can use them to build simple machines that think on their own.

Why a Programmable Brick?

The official reason for making programmable bricks is that students can learn by using them. The real reason may be that it's fun.

It was surely fun to use plastic building blocks to make toy bridges and skyscrapers. But people wanted to do more with them. So scientists have made blocks that can be put together to make motors and other devices. These blocks are called bricks. It seems reasonable that the next thing they would do is make programmable bricks. Now you can make machines that you can program to move, act, and even think.

How Does It Work?

The programmable brick has places to plug in sensors that can "see" and "touch." There are also places to plug in motors and devices that make sounds, such as bells and whistles. The brick also has a transmitter like the one on your TV

remote control. So it can send signals to and receive signals from your computer.

The brick has a tiny processor that can handle 1,000 commands per second. You use your computer to program the brick. For example, you can program the brick to send a message to a motor to go backward or forward when the brick's sensor touches something.

What Can You Do with a Programmable Brick?

You can use the programmable brick to make a clever toy. Or you can use it to make an instrument that gathers data. For example, you can build an instrument that senses when you enter a room and turns on the light for you. Or you can build a robot similar to the Mars rover. You can program your rover to go around obstacles as it moves. Then you can send it to explore the house or back yard.

Two elementary school students used a programmable brick to make a device that took a picture every time a bird landed on their bird feeder. That way they could see what types of birds came to eat there.

The programmable brick was made to be used in robotics projects by students in elementary school,

junior high school, and high school. But that doesn't mean you can't have fun with it. With a little work and imagination, you might make a working model of a horse. Or you might build a robot that plays hockey!

Think About It

1. What other types of robot do you think you could make with a programmable brick?
2. How might a programmable brick be used to make a burglar alarm?

WEB LINK:
For Science and Technology updates, visit the Harcourt Brace Internet site.
www.harcourtschool.com

Careers   Toy Designer

What They Do
Toy designers use their imagination to invent new toys that people will want to buy. They need to know how to make toys that are safe, last a long time, and are easy to take care of.

Education and Training Some colleges offer courses in toy design. Toy design is a part of a degree in industrial design.

Christine Darden

ENGINEER

"Most of what you obtain in life will be because of your discipline. Discipline is perhaps more important than ability."

One of Christine Darden's childhood loves was fixing things. If her bicycle was broken, she tried to fix it herself. In high school, Darden knew that she wanted to study math.

After teaching math for several years, Darden went back to school herself. She began working as a mathematician at the National Aeronautics and Space Administration (NASA). There she became fascinated by the work that the engineers were doing.

Darden wanted to study engineering, but NASA didn't approve of the idea at first. It is not easy to switch fields of study. Finally, she persuaded NASA, and she returned to school where she earned a degree in engineering.

Darden is now working with others to make a plane that flies faster than the speed of sound but doesn't cause a sonic boom. Because of the noise they make, planes that fast are banned in the United States.

Darden was given the 1992 Women in Science and Engineering (WISE) Award. Every year WISE honors three women who have done important work in science and engineering.

Think About It

1. Which do you think is more important—finding a job easily or doing the work you love to do?
2. How did Christine Darden show her determination?

Movement from Air

How can you move a Ping Pong ball with your breath?

Materials

- Ping Pong ball
- 3 straws
- colorful tape

Procedure

1 Work in groups of three. Each person needs a straw. Clear a space on the floor. With tape, mark a course on the floor. Make sure the course has some twists and turns in it.

2 Put the Ping Pong ball at the beginning of the course. With your partners, blow on the ball to make it follow the path.

Draw Conclusions

From which angle did you blow to make the ball move farthest? Which made the ball move farther, blowing softly or blowing hard? Which made the ball move farther, blowing steadily or blowing in short puffs?

Measuring Weight

How can you make your own spring scale?

Materials

- paper cup
- a large, heavy rubber band
- 2 rulers
- string
- tape
- objects

Procedure

1 With your pencil, punch two small holes on each side of the paper cup. Place the rubber band as shown. Thread a piece of string through each pair of holes in the cup and tie the cup to the rubber band.

2 Hold the ruler straight, and have your partner use another ruler to measure the length of the rubber band from the top of the cup to the ruler.

3 Compare the weights of different objects by putting them in the cup and measuring the length of the rubber band.

Draw Conclusions

How is the length of the rubber band related to the weight of the objects put in the cup?

Chapter 3 Review and Test Preparation

Vocabulary Review

Choose a term below to match each definition. The page numbers in ( ) tell you where to look in the chapter if you need help.

force (F58)

motion (F59)

speed (F61)

weight (F62)

gravity (F62)

work (F66)

simple machine (F70)

lever (F70)

inclined plane (F71)

1. How fast an object moves from one position to another

2. A flat surface set at an angle to another surface

3. A change in position

4. A force that pulls all objects toward each other

5. A tool that helps people do work

6. A bar that moves on or around a fixed point

7. A push or a pull

8. A measure of the pull of gravity on an object

9. Measure of a force moving an object

Connect Concepts

Study the diagram. Then use terms from the chapter to complete the sentences.

10. Your push on the truck is a ____.

11. The length of the ramp is the ____ the truck must move.

12. The distance the truck moves divided by the time it takes is the truck's ____.

13. The simple machine the truck is moving up is an ____.

14. The force to push the truck times the distance the truck moves is the ____ done to push the truck up the ramp.

Check Understanding

Write the letter of the best choice.

15. A rock sat on the edge of a cliff. One day the rock fell off. The force that caused this motion was probably —

    A energy   **C** work

    B a pulley   **D** gravity

16. Workers at an airport put suitcases on an airplane. They use a moving ramp. What kind of simple machine is it?

   F an inclined plane   **H** a wedge
   G a screw   **J** a pulley

17. A jet flies at 550 mph. This is a measure of —

   A height   **C** fuel
   B speed   **D** weight

18. Alice uses 2 newtons of force to push her little sister's stroller 5 meters. How much work does she do?

   F 2 newton-meters
   G 5 newton-meters
   H 7 newton-meters
   J 10 newton-meters

Critical Thinking

19. Suppose you use a screwdriver to pry the top off a can. Explain which kinds of simple machines you use and how they work for this job.

20. Anthony moved dirt all day with a wheelbarrow. He moved it 20 meters from the vegetable garden to the flower garden. Max sat in his room and studied science. Who would scientists say did more work? Why?

Process Skills Review

21. A red car and a blue car both travel to a town 60 miles away. The red car gets there first. What can you **infer** about the speeds of the two cars?

22. You tried four different ways to lift a bag of sand 1 meter. With the pulley, you used 5 newtons of force. You used 3 newtons when you dragged the bag up the inclined plane. When you pushed the bag up with the lever, you used 2 newtons of force. And when you picked it up by yourself, you used 5 newtons of force. Make a table to help you **interpret the data. Compare** the methods. Tell which used the most force and which used the least force.

Performance Assessment
Motion and Work

  A. Using a book on your desk, show a force causing motion. Identify the force.

  B. Using the book again, show a force that doesn't cause motion. Was work done in **A**, in **B**, or in both?

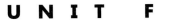

Unit Project Wrap Up

Here are some ideas for ways to wrap up your unit project.

Write a Program

Write a program for your shadow show. Include a short summary of the story. Tell about the different kinds of forces and energy used in the show.

Invent a Toy

Invent a toy that has moveable parts. Your toy should have at least one part that is a simple machine. Draw a diagram of your invention, and label the simple machine.

Make a Booklet

Fold and staple paper into a booklet. Write the name of a simple machine on the top of each page. Look through magazines for pictures of items that have simple machine parts. Cut out the pictures and glue them on the right pages of your booklet.

Investigate Further

How could you make your project better? What other questions do you have about energy and forces? Plan ways to find answers to your questions. Use the Science Handbook on pages R2-R9 for help.

References

Science Handbook

Planning an Investigation

When scientists observe something they want to study, they use scientific inquiry to plan and conduct their study. They use science process skills as tools to help them gather, organize, analyze, and present their information. This plan will help you work like a scientist.

Step 1—Observe and ask questions.

Which food does my hamster eat the most of?

- Use your senses to make observations.
- Record a question you would like to answer.

Step 2—Make a hypothesis.

My hypothesis: My hamster will eat more sunflower seeds than any other food.

- Choose one possible answer, or hypothesis, to your question.
- Write your hypothesis in a complete sentence.
- Think about what investigation you can do to test your hypothesis.

Step 3—Plan your test.

I'll give my hamster equal amounts of three kinds of foods, then observe what she eats.

- Write down the steps you will follow to do your test. Decide how to conduct a fair test by controlling variables.
- Decide what equipment you will need.
- Decide how you will gather and record your data.

Step 4 — Conduct your test.

I'll repeat this experiment for four days. I'll meaure how much food is left each time.

- Follow the steps you wrote.
- Observe and measure carefully.
- Record everything that happens.
- Organize your data so that you can study it carefully.

Step 5 — Draw conclusions and share results.

My hypothesis was correct. She ate more sunflower seeds than the other kinds of foods.

- Analyze the data you gathered.
- Make charts, graphs, or tables to show your data.
- Write a conclusion. Describe the evidence you used to determine whether your test supported your hypothesis.
- Decide whether your hypothesis was correct.

Investigate Further

I wonder if there are other foods she will eat . . .

Using Science Tools

Using a Hand Lens

1. Hold the hand lens about 12 centimeters (5 in.) from your eye.

2. Bring the object toward you until it comes into focus.

Using a Thermometer

1. Place the thermometer in the liquid. Never stir the liquid with the thermometer. Don't touch the thermometer any more than you need to. If you are measuring the temperature of the air, make sure that the thermometer is not in line with a direct light source.

2. Move so that your eyes are even with the liquid in the thermometer.

3. If you are measuring a material that is not being heated or cooled, wait about two minutes for the reading to become stable, or stay the same. Find the scale line that meets the top of the liquid in the thermometer, and read the temperature.

4. If the material you are measuring is being heated or cooled, you will not be able to wait before taking your measurements. Measure as quickly as you can.

Caring for and Using a Microscope

Caring for a Microscope

- Carry a microscope with two hands.
- Never touch any of the lenses of a microscope with your fingers.

Using a Microscope

1. Raise the eyepiece as far as you can using the coarse-adjustment knob. Place your slide on the stage.

2. Start by using the lowest power. The lowest-power lens is usually the shortest. Place the lens in the lowest position it can go to without touching the slide.

3. Look through the eyepiece, and begin adjusting it upward with the coarse-adjustment knob. When the slide is close to being in focus, use the fine-adjustment knob.

4. When you want to use a higher-power lens, first focus the slide under low power. Then, watching carefully to make sure that the lens will not hit the slide, turn the higher-power lens into place. Use only the fine-adjustment knob when looking through the higher-power lens.

You may use a Brock microscope. This sturdy microscope has only one lens.

1. Place the object to be viewed on the stage.

2. Look through the eyepiece, and raise the tube until the object comes into focus.

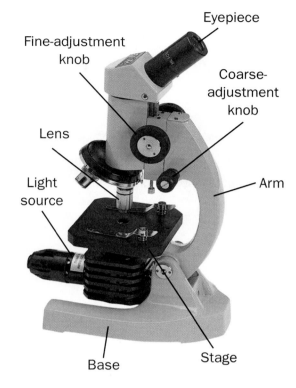

A Light Microscope

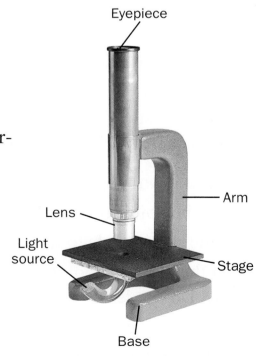

A Brock Microscope

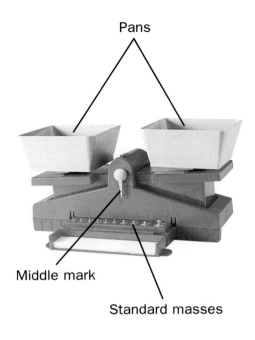

Pans

Middle mark

Standard masses

Using a Balance

1. Look at the pointer on the base to make sure the empty pans are balanced. Place the object you wish to measure in the left-hand pan.

2. Add the standard masses to the other pan. As you add masses, you should see the pointer move. When the pointer is at the middle mark, the pans are balanced.

3. Add the numbers on the masses you used. The total is the mass in grams of the object you measured.

Using a Spring Scale

Measuring an Object at Rest

1. Hook the spring scale to the object.

2. Lift the scale and object with a smooth motion. Do not jerk them upward.

3. Wait until any motion of the spring comes to a stop. Then read the number of newtons from the scale.

Measuring an Object in Motion

1. With the object resting on a table, hook the spring scale to it.

2. Pull the object smoothly across the table. Do not jerk the object.

3. As you pull, read the number of newtons you are using to pull the object.

Measuring Liquids

1. Pour the liquid you want to measure into a measuring container. Put your measuring container on a flat surface, with the measuring scale facing you.

2. Look at the liquid through the container. Move so that your eyes are even with the surface of the liquid in the container.

3. To read the volume of the liquid, find the scale line that is even with the surface of the liquid.

4. If the surface of the liquid is not exactly even with a line, estimate the volume of the liquid. Decide which line the liquid is closer to, and use that number.

Beaker   **Graduate**

Using a Ruler or Meterstick

1. Place the zero mark or end of the ruler or meterstick next to one end of the distance or object you want to measure.

2. On the ruler or meterstick, find the place next to the other end of the distance or object.

3. Look at the scale on the ruler or meterstick. This will show the distance or the length of the object.

Using a Timing Device

1. Reset the stopwatch to zero.

2. When you are ready to begin timing, press *Start*.

3. As soon as you are ready to stop timing, press *Stop*.

4. The numbers on the dial or display show how many minutes, seconds, and parts of seconds have passed.

Using a Computer

Writing Reports

To write a report with a computer, use a word processing software program. After you are in the program, type your report. By using certain keys and the mouse, you can control how the words look, move words, delete or add words and copy them, check your spelling, and print your report.

Save your work to the desktop or hard disk of the computer, or to a floppy disk. You can go back to your saved work later if you want to revise it.

There are many reasons for revising your work. You may find new information to add or mistakes you want to correct. You may want to change the way you report your information because of who will read it.

Computers make revising easy. You delete what you don't want, add the new parts, and then save. You can also save different versions of your work.

For a science lab report, it is important to show the same kinds of information each time. With a computer, you can make a general format for a lab report, save the format, and then use it again and again.

Making Graphs and Charts

You can make a graph or chart with most word processing software programs. You can also use special software programs such as Data ToolKit or Graph Links. With Graph Links you can make pictographs and circle, bar, line, and double-line graphs.

First, decide what kind of graph or chart will best communicate your data. Sometimes it's easiest to do this by sketching your ideas on paper. Then you can decide what format and categories you need for your graph or chart. Choose that format for the program. Then type your information. Most software programs include a tutor that gives you step-by-step directions for making a graph or chart.

Doing Research

Computers can help you find current information from all over the world through the Internet. The Internet connects thousands of computer sites that have been set up by schools, libraries, museums, and many other organizations.

Get permission from an adult before you log on to the Internet. Find out the rules for Internet use at school or at home. Then log on and go to a search engine, which will help you find what you need. Type in keywords, words that tell the subject of your search. If you get too much information that isn't exactly about the topic, make your keywords more specific. When you find the information you need, save it or print it.

Harcourt Science tells you about many Internet sites related to what you are studying. To find out about these sites, called Web sites, look for Technology Links in the lessons in this book.

If you need to contact other people to help in your research, you can use e-mail. Log into your e-mail program, type the address of the person you want to reach, type your message, and send it. Be sure to have adult permission before sending or receiving e-mail.

Another way to use a computer for research is to access CD-ROMs. These are discs that look like music CDs. CD-ROMs can hold huge amounts of data, including words, still pictures, audio, and video. Encyclopedias, dictionaries, almanacs, and other sources of information are available on CD-ROMs. These computer discs are valuable resources for your research.

Measurement Systems

SI Measures (Metric)

Temperature
Ice melts at 0 degrees Celsius (°C)
Water freezes at 0°C
Water boils at 100°C

Length and Distance
1000 meters (m) = 1 kilometer (km)
100 centimeters (cm) = 1 m
10 millimeters (mm) = 1 cm

Force
1 newton (N) = 1 kilogram $\times$
   meter/second/second (kg-m/s^2)

Volume
1 cubic meter (m^3) = 1m $\times$ 1m $\times$ 1m
1 cubic centimeter (cm^3) =
   1 cm $\times$ 1 cm $\times$ 1 cm
1 liter (L) = 1000 milliliters (mL)
1 cm^3 = 1 mL

Area
1 square kilometer (km^2) =
   1 km $\times$ 1 km
1 hectare = 10 000 m^2

Mass
1000 grams (g) = 1 kilogram (kg)
1000 milligrams (mg) = 1 g

Rates (Metric and Customary)
kmh = kilometers per hour
m/s = meters per second
mph = miles per hour

Customary Measures

Volume of Fluids
8 fluid ounces (fl oz) = 1 cup (c)
2 c = 1 pint (pt)
2 pt = 1 quart (qt)
4 qt = 1 gallon (gal)

Temperature
Ice melts at 32 degrees
   Fahrenheit (°F)
Water freezes at 32°F
Water boils at 212°F

Length and Distance
12 inches (in) = 1 foot (ft)
3 ft = 1 yard (yd)
5,280 ft = 1 mile (mi)

Weight
16 ounces (oz) = 1 pound (lb)
2,000 pounds = 1 ton (T)

Health Handbook

Bicycle Safety

A Safe Bike

You probably know how to ride a bike, but do you know how to make your bike as safe as possible? A safe bike is the right size for you. When you sit on your bike with the pedal in the lowest position, you should be able to rest your heel on the pedal. Your body should be 2 inches (about 5 cm) above the support bar that goes from the handlebar stem to the seat support when you are standing astride your bike with both feet flat on the ground. After checking for the right size, check your bike for the safety equipment shown below. How safe is *your* bike?

headlight

horn

white front reflector

red rear reflector

clear reflector

pedal reflectors

clear reflector

Your Bike Helmet

About 400,000 children are involved in bike-related crashes every year. That's why it's important to *always* wear your bike helmet. Wear your helmet flat on your head. Be sure it is strapped snugly so that the helmet will stay in place if you fall. If you do fall and strike your helmet on the ground, replace it, even if it doesn't look damaged. The padding inside the helmet may be crushed, which reduces the ability of the helmet to protect your head in the event of another fall. Look for the features shown here when purchasing a helmet.

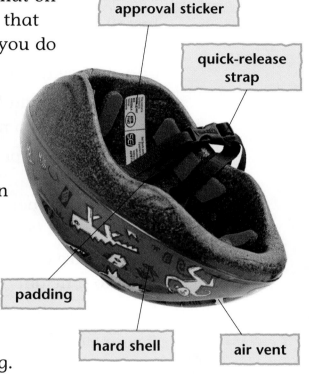

approval sticker

quick-release strap

padding

hard shell

air vent

Safety on the Road

Here are some tips for safe bicycle riding.

- Check your bike every time you ride it. Is it in safe working condition?
- Ride in single file in the same direction as traffic. Never weave in and out of parked cars.
- Before you enter a street, **STOP. Look** left, then right, then left again. **Listen** for any traffic. **Think** before you go.
- Walk your bike across an intersection. **Look** left, then right, then left again. Wait for traffic to pass.
- Obey all traffic signs and signals.
- Do not ride your bike at night without an adult. Be sure to wear light-colored clothing and use reflectors and front and rear lights for night riding.

Fire Safety

Fires cause more deaths than any other type of disaster. But a fire doesn't have to be deadly if you prepare your home and follow some basic safety rules.

- Install smoke detectors outside sleeping areas and on every other floor of your home. Test the detectors once a month and change the batteries twice a year.

- Keep a fire extinguisher on each floor of your home. Check them monthly to make sure they are properly charged.

- Make a fire escape plan. Ideally, there should be two routes out of each room. Sleeping areas are most important, as most fires happen at night. Plan to use stairs only, as elevators can be dangerous in a fire.

- Pick a place outside for everyone to meet. Choose one person to go to a neighbor's home to call 911 or the fire department.

- Practice crawling low to avoid smoke.

- If your clothes catch fire, follow the three steps shown here.

1. STOP

2. DROP

3. ROLL

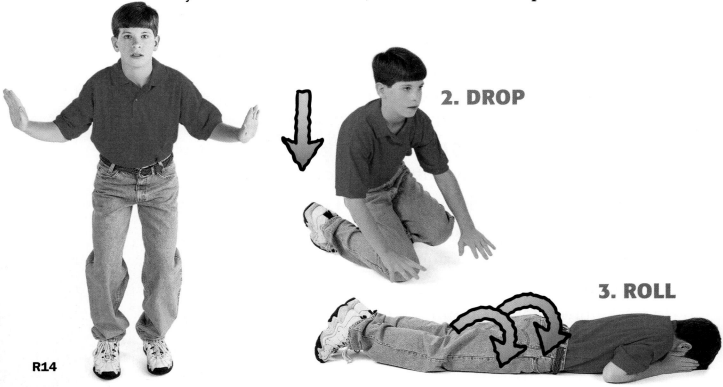

Earthquake Safety

An earthquake is a strong shaking or sliding of the ground. The tips below can help you and your family stay safe in an earthquake.

Before an Earthquake	During an Earthquake	After an Earthquake
• Attach tall, heavy furniture, such as bookcases, to the wall. Store the heaviest items on the lowest shelves. • Check for fire risks. Bolt down gas appliances, and use flexible hosing and connections for both gas and water lines. • Strengthen and anchor overhead light fixtures to help keep them from falling.	• If you are outdoors, stay outdoors and move away from buildings and utility wires. • If you are indoors, take cover under a heavy desk or table, or in a doorway. Stay away from glass doors and windows and from heavy objects that might fall. • If you are in a car, drive to an open area away from buildings and overpasses.	• Keep watching for falling objects as aftershocks shake the area. • Check for hidden structural problems. • Check for broken gas, electric, and water lines. If you smell gas, shut off the gas main. Leave the area. Report the leak.

Storm Safety

- **In a Tornado** Take cover in a sheltered area away from doors and windows. An interior hallway or basement is best. Stay in the shelter until the danger has passed.

- **In a Hurricane** Prepare for high winds by securing objects outside or bringing them indoors. Cover windows and glass with plywood. Listen to weather bulletins for instructions. If asked to evacuate, proceed to emergency shelters.

- **In a Winter Storm or Blizzard** Stock up on food that does not have to be cooked. Dress in thin layers that help trap the body's heat. Pay special attention to the head and neck. If you are caught in a vehicle, turn on the dome light to make the vehicle visible to search crews.

First Aid

For Choking . . .

The tips on the next few pages can help you provide simple first aid to others and yourself. Always tell an adult about any injuries that occur.

If someone else is choking . . .

1. Recognize the Universal Choking Sign—grasping the throat with both hands. This sign means a person is choking and needs help.

2. Put your arms around his or her waist. Make a fist and put it above the person's navel. Grab your fist with your other hand.

3. Pull your hands toward yourself and give five quick, hard, upward thrusts on the choker's belly.

If you are choking when alone . . .

 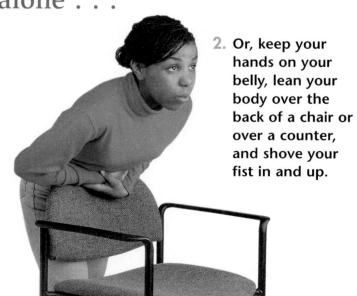

1. Make a fist and place it above your navel. Grab your fist with your other hand. Pull your hands up with a quick, hard thrust.

2. Or, keep your hands on your belly, lean your body over the back of a chair or over a counter, and shove your fist in and up.

For Bleeding . . .

If someone else is bleeding . . .

Wash your hands with soap, if possible.

Put on protective gloves, if available.

Wash small wounds with soap and water. Do *not* wash serious wounds.

Place a clean gauze pad or cloth over the wound. Press firmly for ten minutes. Don't lift the gauze during this time.

If you don't have gloves, have the injured person hold the cloth in place with his or her own hand.

If after ten minutes the bleeding has stopped, bandage the wound. If the bleeding has not stopped, continue pressing on the wound and get help.

If you are bleeding . . .

- Follow the steps shown above. You don't need gloves to touch your own blood.

- Be sure to tell an adult about your injury.

First Aid

For Nosebleeds . . .

- Sit down, and tilt your head forward. Pinch your nostrils together for at least ten minutes.
- You can also put an ice pack on the bridge of your nose.
- If your nose continues to bleed, get help from an adult.

For Burns . . .

Minor burns are called first degree burns and involve only the top layer of skin. The skin is red and dry and the burn is painful. More serious burns are called second or third degree burns. These burns involve the top and lower layers of skin. Second degree burns cause blisters, redness, swelling, and pain. Third degree burns are the most serious. The skin is gray or white and looks burned. All burns need immediate first aid.

Minor Burns

- Run cool water over the burn or soak it in cool water for at least five minutes.
- Cover the burn with a clean, dry bandage.
- Do *not* put lotion or ointment on the burn.

More Serious Burns

- Cover the burn with a cool, wet bandage or cloth. Do *not* break any blisters.
- Do *not* put lotion or ointment on the burn.
- Get help from an adult right away.

For Insect Bites and Stings . . .

- Always tell an adult about bites and stings.
- Scrape out the stinger with your fingernail.
- Wash the area with soap and water.
- Ice cubes will usually take away the pain from insect bites. A paste made from baking soda and water also helps.

▲ deer tick

- If the bite or sting is more serious and is on the arm or leg, keep the leg or arm dangling down. Apply a cold, wet cloth. Get help immediately!
- If you find a tick on your skin, remove it. Crush it between two rocks. Wash your hands right away.
- If a tick has already bitten you, do not pull it off. Cover it with oil and wait for it to let go, then remove it with tweezers. Wash the area and your hands.

For Skin Rashes from Plants . . .

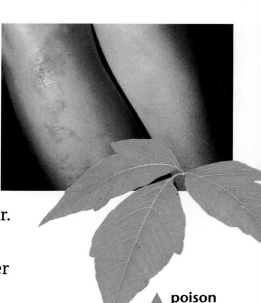

Many poisonous plants have three leaves. Remember, "Leaves of three, let them be." If you touch a poisonous plant, wash the area. Put on clean clothes and throw the dirty ones in the washer. If a rash develops, follow these tips.

- Apply calamine lotion or a baking soda and water paste. Try not to scratch. Tell an adult.

▲ poison ivy

- If you get blisters, do *not* pop them. If they burst, keep the area clean and dry. Cover with a bandage.
- If your rash does not go away in two weeks or if the rash is on your face or in your eyes, see your doctor.

Being Safe at Home

When Home Alone

Everyone stays home alone sometimes. When you stay home alone, it's important to know how to take care of yourself. Here are some easy rules to follow that will help keep you safe when you are at home by yourself.

Do These Things

- Lock all the doors and windows. Be sure you know how to lock and unlock all the locks.

- If someone calls who is nasty or mean, hang up. Your parents may not want you to answer the phone at all.

- If you have an emergency, call 911 or 0 (zero) for the operator. Describe the problem, give your full name, address, and telephone number. Follow all instructions given to you.

  - If you see anyone hanging around outside, tell an adult or call the police.

  - If you see or smell smoke, go outside right away. If you live in an apartment, do not take the elevator. Go to a neighbor's home and call 911 or the fire department immediately.

- Entertain yourself. Time will pass more quickly if you are not bored. Try not to spend your time watching television. Instead, work on a hobby, read a book or magazine, do your homework, or clean your room. Before you know it, an adult will be home.

Do NOT Do These Things

- Do NOT use the stove, microwave, or oven unless an adult family member has given you permission, and you are sure about how to use these appliances.

- Do NOT open the door for anyone you don't know or for anyone who is not supposed to be in your home.
  - If someone rings the bell and asks to use the telephone, tell the person to go to a phone booth.
  - If someone tries to deliver a package, do NOT open the door. The delivery person will leave the package or come back later.
  - If someone is selling something, do NOT open the door. Just say, "We're not interested," and nothing more.

- Do NOT talk to strangers on the telephone. Do not tell anyone that you are home alone. If the call is for an adult family member, say that they can't come to the phone right now and take a message. Ask for the caller's name and phone number and deliver the message when an adult family member comes home.

- Do NOT have friends over unless you have gotten permission from your parents or other adult family members.

Being Physically Active

Planning Your Weekly Activities

Being active every day is important for your overall health. Physical activity helps you manage stress, maintain a healthful weight, and strengthen your body systems. The Activity Pyramid, like the Food Guide Pyramid, can help you choose a variety of activities in the right amounts to keep your body strong and healthy.

The Activity Pyramid

Sitting for more than thirty minutes at a time: Only Once in a While

Light Exercise: Two to Three Times a Week

Flexibility and Strength: Two to Three Times a Week

Twenty-plus minutes of continuous aerobic activity: Three to Five Times a Week

Stay active: Every Day

Guidelines for a Good Workout

There are three things you should do every time you are going to exercise—warm up, work out, and cool down.

Warm-Up When you warm up, your heart rate, breathing rate, and body temperature increase and more blood flows to your muscles. As your body warms up, you can move more easily. People who warm up are less stiff after exercising, and are less likely to have exercise-related injuries. Your warm-up should include five minutes of stretching, and five minutes of low-level exercise.

Workout The main part of your exercise routine should be an aerobic exercise that lasts 20 to 30 minutes. Aerobic exercises make your heart, lungs, and circulatory system stronger.

Some common aerobic exercises are shown on pages R26–R27. You may want to mix up the types of activities you do. This helps you work different muscles, and provides a better workout over time.

Cool-Down When you finish your aerobic exercise, you need to give your body time to cool down. Start your cool-down with three to five minutes of low-level activity. End with stretching exercises to prevent soreness and stiffness.

Being Physically Active

Warm-Up and Cool-Down Stretches

Before you exercise, you should warm up your muscles. The warm-up exercises shown here should be held for at least fifteen to twenty seconds and repeated at least three times.

At the end of your workout, spend about two minutes repeating some of these stretches.

▲ **Shoulder and Chest Stretch** HINT—Pulling your hands slowly toward the floor gives a better stretch. Keep your elbows straight, but not locked!

▶ **Hurdler's Stretch** HINT—Keep the toes of your extended leg pointed up.

◀ **Sit-and-Reach Stretch** HINT—Remember to bend at the waist. Keep your eyes on your toes!

▲ **Upper Back and Shoulder Stretch**
HINT—Try to stretch your hand down
so that it rests flat against your back.

▼ **Thigh Stretch** HINT—
Keep both hands flat on
the ground. Lean as far
forward as you can.

▲ **Calf Stretch** HINT—Keep
both feet on the floor during
this stretch. Try changing the
distance between your feet.
Is the stretch better for you
when your legs are closer
together or farther apart?

Tips for Stretching

- Never bounce when stretching.
- Hold each stretch for fifteen to twenty seconds.
- Breathe normally. This helps your body get the oxygen it needs.
- Do NOT stretch until it hurts. Stretch only until you feel a slight pull.

Being Physically Active

Building a Strong Heart and Lungs

Aerobic activities cause deep breathing and a fast heart rate for at least twenty minutes. These activities help both your heart and your lungs. Because your heart is a muscle, it gets stronger with exercise. A strong heart doesn't have to work as hard to pump blood to the rest of your body. Exercise also allows your lungs to hold more air. With a strong heart and lungs, your cells get oxygen faster and your body works more efficiently.

▲ **Swimming** Swimming is great for your endurance and flexibility. Even if you're not a great swimmer, you can use a kickboard and have a great time and a great workout just kicking around the pool. Be sure to swim only when a lifeguard is present.

◄ **In-line Skating** Remember to always wear a helmet when skating. Always wear protective pads on your elbows and knees, and guards on your wrists, too. Learning how to skate, stop, and fall correctly will make you a safer skater.

▼ **Walking** A fast-paced walk is a terrific way to build your endurance. The only equipment you need is supportive shoes. Walking with a friend can make this exercise a lot of fun.

▲ **Jumping Rope** Jumping rope is one of the best ways to increase your endurance. Remember to always jump on an even surface and always wear supportive shoes.

▼ **Bicycling** Bicycling provides good aerobic activity *and* a great way to see the outdoors. Be sure to learn and follow bicycle safety rules. And *always* remember to wear your helmet!

Good Nutrition

The Food Guide Pyramid

No one food or food group supplies everything your body needs for good health. That's why it's important to eat foods from all the food groups. The Food Guide Pyramid can help you choose healthful foods in the right amounts. By choosing more foods from the groups at the bottom of the pyramid and fewer foods from the group at the top, you will eat the foods that provide your body with energy to grow and develop.

Fats, oils, and sweets
Eat sparingly.

Meat, poultry, fish, dry beans, eggs, and nuts 2–3 servings

Milk, yogurt, and cheese
2–3 servings

Fruits
2–4 servings

Vegetables
3–5 servings

Breads, cereals, rice, and pasta 6–11 servings

Estimating Serving Sizes

Choosing a variety of foods is only half the story. You also need to choose the right amounts. The table below can help you estimate the number of servings you are eating of your favorite foods.

Food Group	Amount of Food in One Serving	Some Easy Ways to Estimate Serving Size
Bread, Cereal, Rice, Pasta Group	1 ounce ready-to-eat (dry) cereal	large handful of plain cereal or a small handful of cereal with raisins and nuts
	1 slice bread, $\frac{1}{2}$ bagel	
	$\frac{1}{2}$ cup cooked pasta, rice, or cereal	ice cream scoop
Vegetable Group	1 cup of raw, leafy vegetables	about the size of a fist
	$\frac{1}{2}$ cup other vegetables, cooked or raw, chopped	
	$\frac{3}{4}$ cup vegetable juice	
	$\frac{1}{2}$ cup tomato sauce	ice cream scoop
Fruit Group	medium apple, pear, or orange	a baseball
	$\frac{1}{2}$ large banana or one medium banana	
	$\frac{1}{2}$ cup chopped or cooked fruit	
	$\frac{3}{4}$ cup of fruit juice	
Milk, Yogurt, and Cheese Group	$1\frac{1}{2}$ ounces of natural cheese	two dominoes
	2 ounces of processed cheese	$1\frac{1}{2}$ slices of packaged cheese
	1 cup of milk or yogurt	
Meat, Poultry, Fish, Dry Beans, Eggs, and Nuts Group	3 ounces of lean meat, chicken, or fish	about the size of your palm
	2 tablespoons peanut butter	
	$\frac{1}{2}$ cup of cooked dry beans	
Fats, Oils, and Sweets Group	1 teaspoon of margarine or butter	about the size of the tip of your thumb

Preparing Foods Safely

Fight Bacteria

You probably already know to throw away food that smells bad or looks moldy. But food doesn't have to look or smell bad to make you ill. To keep your food safe and yourself from becoming ill, follow the steps outlined in the picture below. And remember—when in doubt, throw it out!

FIGHT BAC!

Keep Food Safe From Bacteria

CLEAN Wash hands and surfaces often.

SEPARATE Don't cross-contaminate.

CHILL Refrigerate promptly.

COOK Cook to proper temperatures.

BAC

TM

Food Safety Tips

Tips for Preparing Food

- Wash hands in warm, soapy water before preparing food. It's also a good idea to wash hands after preparing each dish.
- Defrost meat in the microwave or the refrigerator.
- Keep raw meat, poultry, fish, and their juices away from other food.
- Wash cutting boards, knives, and countertops immediately after cutting up meat, poultry, or fish. Never use the same cutting board for meats and vegetables without washing the board first.

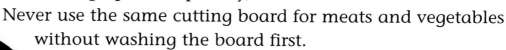

Tips for Cooking Food

- Cook all food completely, especially meat. Complete cooking kills the bacteria that can make you ill.
- Red meats should be cooked to a temperature of 160°F. Poultry should be cooked to 180°F. When done, fish flakes easily with a fork.
- Never eat food that contains raw eggs or raw egg yolks, including cookie dough.

Tips for Cleaning Up the Kitchen

- Wash all dishes, utensils, and countertops with hot, soapy water. Use a soap that kills bacteria, if possible.
- Store leftovers in small containers that will cool quickly in the refrigerator. Don't leave leftovers on the counter to cool.

Sense Organs

Eye

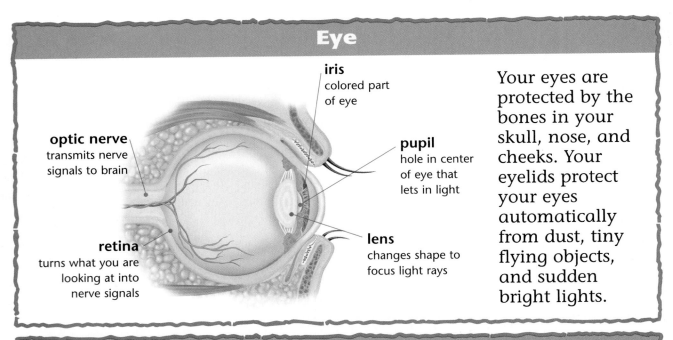

iris
colored part
of eye

optic nerve
transmits nerve
signals to brain

pupil
hole in center
of eye that
lets in light

retina
turns what you are
looking at into
nerve signals

lens
changes shape to
focus light rays

Your eyes are protected by the bones in your skull, nose, and cheeks. Your eyelids protect your eyes automatically from dust, tiny flying objects, and sudden bright lights.

Ear

Earwax is made inside your ears to help keep them clean. Dust, dirt, and germs stick to the earwax instead of going farther into your ear. When you move your mouth by chewing and talking, old wax works its way to your outer ear.

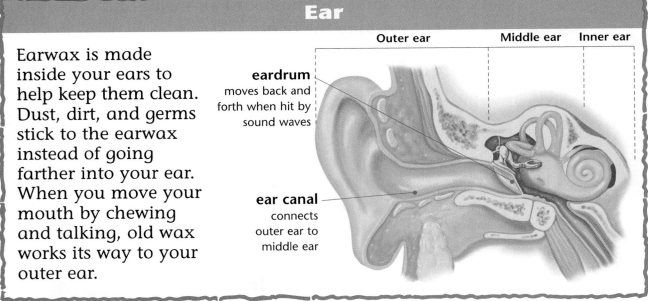

Outer ear   Middle ear   Inner ear

eardrum
moves back and
forth when hit by
sound waves

ear canal
connects
outer ear to
middle ear

Caring for Your Eyes and Ears

- Have your eyesight (vision) checked every year.

- Wear safety glasses when participating in activities that can be dangerous to the eyes, such as sports and mowing grass.

- Wash in, around, and behind your outer ear. Do not try to clean your ear canal with cotton-tip sticks or other objects.

Nose

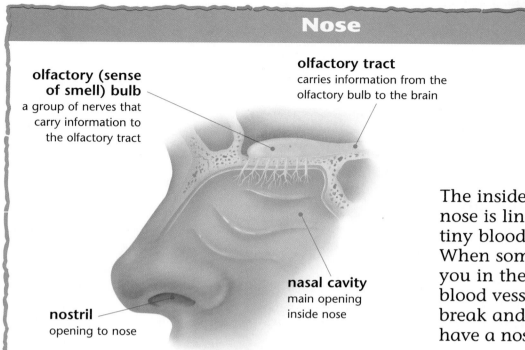

olfactory (sense of smell) bulb
a group of nerves that carry information to the olfactory tract

olfactory tract
carries information from the olfactory bulb to the brain

nasal cavity
main opening inside nose

nostril
opening to nose

The inside of your nose is lined with tiny blood vessels. When something hits you in the nose, these blood vessels can break and you can have a nosebleed.

Caring for Your Nose, Tongue, and Skin

- If you get a nosebleed, sit, lean forward slightly, and pinch just below the bridge of your nose for ten minutes. Breathe through your mouth.

- When you brush your teeth, brush your tongue too.

- Always wear sunscreen when you are in the sun.

Tongue

Germs live on your tongue and in other parts of your mouth. Germs can harm your teeth and give you bad breath.

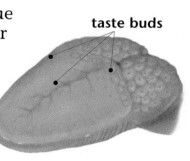

taste buds

Skin

protective outer layer

strong, springy middle layer

fatty lower layer

Your skin protects your insides from the outside world. It keeps fluids you need inside your body and fluids you don't need, such as swimming pool water, outside your body.

Skeletal System

Each of your bones has a particular shape and size that allow it to do a certain job. You have bones that are tiny, long, wide, flat, and even curved. The job of some bones is to protect your body parts.

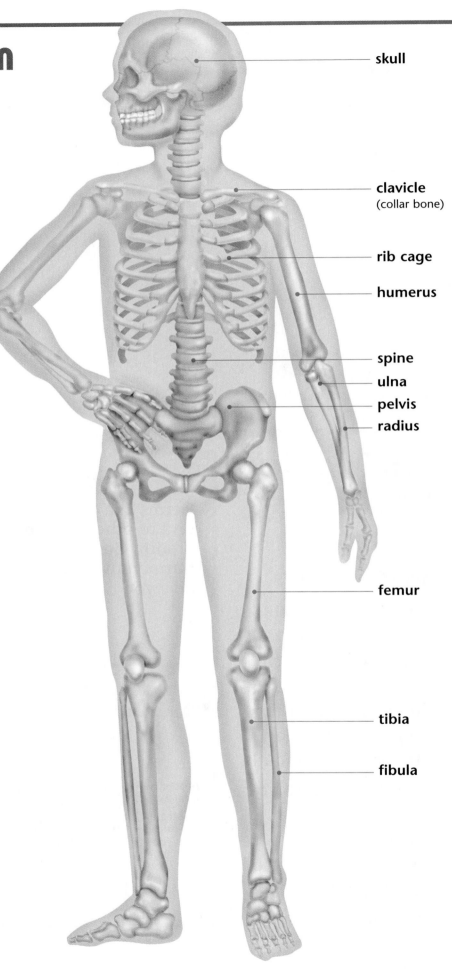

skull

clavicle
(collar bone)

rib cage

humerus

spine

ulna

pelvis

radius

femur

tibia

fibula

Bones that Protect

Rib Cage Your rib bones form a cage that protects your heart and lungs from all sides. Your ribs are springy. When something strikes you in the chest, your ribs push the object away instead of letting it hit your heart and lungs.

Your ribs are connected to your breastbone (sternum) by springy material called cartilage. The springy connection lets your ribs move up and down. This happens when your rib cage gets bigger and smaller as you breathe in and out.

Skull The bones in your head are called your skull. Some of the bones in your skull protect your brain. The bones in your face are part of your skull too.

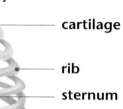

cartilage

rib

sternum

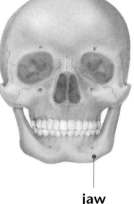

jaw

Caring for Your Skeletal System

• Calcium helps bones grow and makes them strong. Dairy products like milk, cheese, and yogurt contain calcium. Have 2–3 servings of dairy products every day.

• Exercise also makes your bones strong. When bones aren't used, they can become brittle and may break.

Activities

1. Look at the picture of the skeleton. Name a long bone. Name a short bone. Name a curved bone.

2. Put a tomato inside a wire cage. Gently throw a wad of paper at the cage. What happens? The cage protects the tomato in the same way your ribs protect your heart.

3. Measure around your rib cage with a string. How big is it when you breathe in? How big is it when you breathe out? Which measurement is greater?

Muscular System

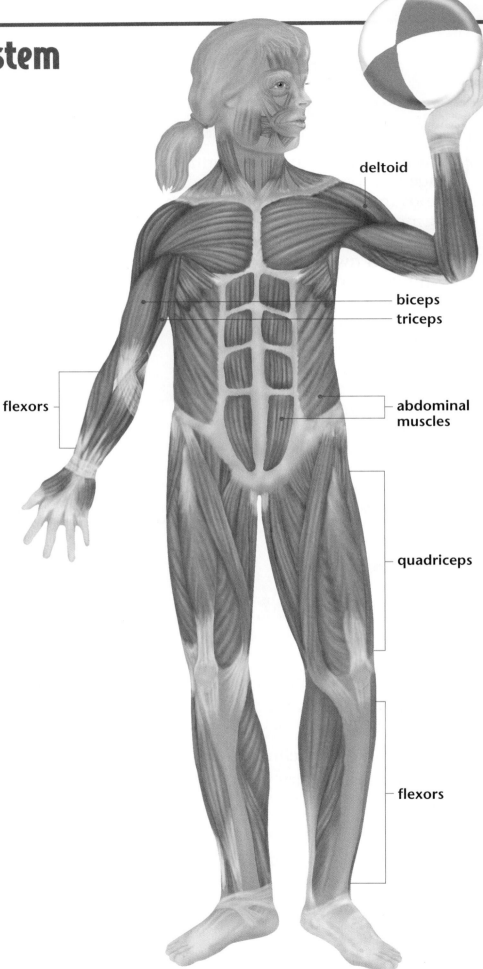

ike your bones, each muscle in your body does a certain job. Muscles in your thumb help you hold things. Muscles in your neck help you turn your head. Muscles in your arms help you pull or lift objects.

deltoid

biceps

triceps

flexors

abdominal muscles

quadriceps

flexors

How Muscles Move Your Body

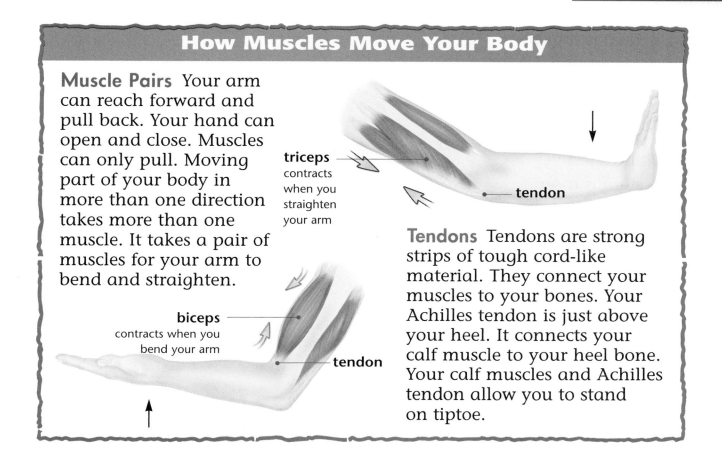

Muscle Pairs Your arm can reach forward and pull back. Your hand can open and close. Muscles can only pull. Moving part of your body in more than one direction takes more than one muscle. It takes a pair of muscles for your arm to bend and straighten.

triceps contracts when you straighten your arm

tendon

biceps contracts when you bend your arm

tendon

Tendons Tendons are strong strips of tough cord-like material. They connect your muscles to your bones. Your Achilles tendon is just above your heel. It connects your calf muscle to your heel bone. Your calf muscles and Achilles tendon allow you to stand on tiptoe.

Caring for Your Muscular System

- Exercise makes your muscles stronger.
- Stretching before you exercise makes muscles and tendons more flexible and less likely to get hurt.

Activities

1. Tie your shoe without using your thumb. What happens?

2. Pull up on a desk with one hand. With your other hand, feel which arm muscle is working. Now push on the desk. Which arm muscle is working?

3. Ask a friend to push down on your arms for one minute while you push up as hard as you can. When your friend lets go, what happens?

Digestive System

Food is broken down and pushed through your body by your digestive system. Your digestive system is a series of connected parts that starts with your mouth and ends with your large intestine.

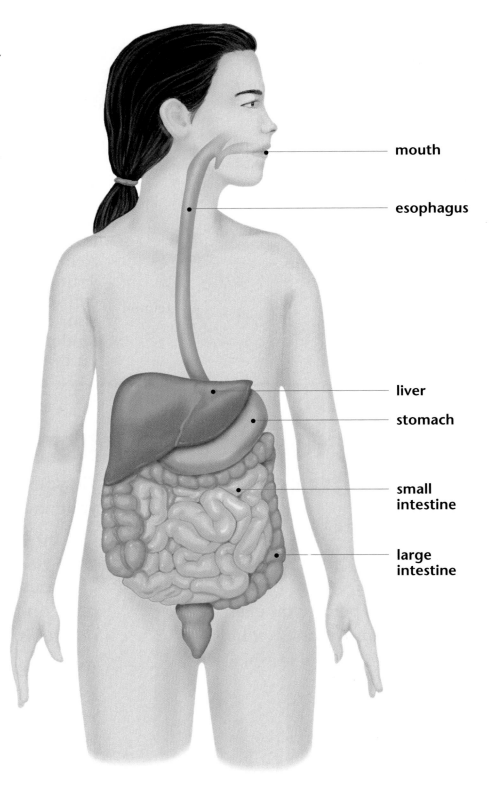

mouth

esophagus

liver

stomach

small intestine

large intestine

From Mouth to Stomach

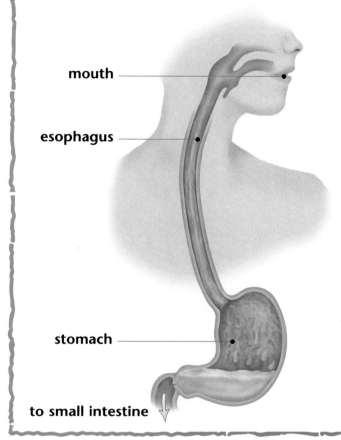

mouth

esophagus

stomach

to small intestine

Esophagus Your esophagus, or food tube, is a tube that connects your mouth to your stomach. After you swallow a bite of food, muscles in your esophagus push the food into your stomach.

Stomach Your stomach is filled with acid that helps dissolve food. The stomach walls are strong muscles that mix food with the acid. The stomach walls are protected from the acid by a thick layer of mucus. From your stomach, food moves to the small intestine and then to the large intestine.

Caring for Your Digestive System

- Chew everything you eat carefully. Well-chewed food is easier to digest.
- Do not overeat. Overeating can cause a stomachache.

Activities

1. Measure 25 feet (about 8 m) on the floor. This is how long your digestive system is.

2. Cut a narrow balloon so that it is open on both ends. Put a wad of paper in one end. Squeeze the outside of the balloon to push the paper through and out the other end. This is similar to how your esophagus pushes food to your stomach.

Circulatory System

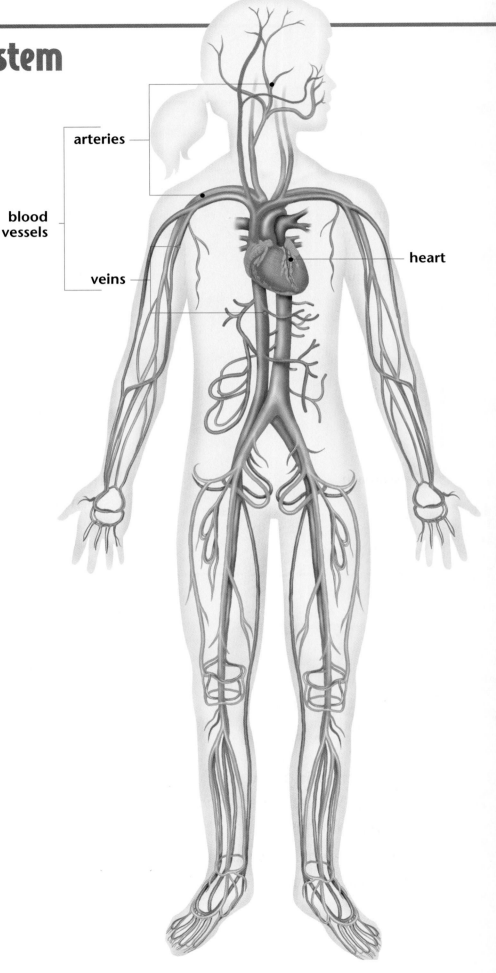

Food and oxygen travel through your circulatory system to every cell in your body. Blood moves nutrients throughout your body, fights infection, and helps control your body temperature. Your blood is made up mostly of a watery liquid called plasma.

arteries

blood vessels

veins

heart

Blood Vessels

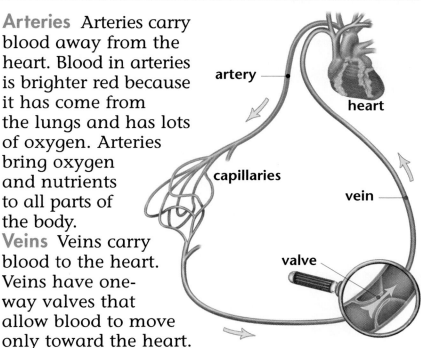

Arteries Arteries carry blood away from the heart. Blood in arteries is brighter red because it has come from the lungs and has lots of oxygen. Arteries bring oxygen and nutrients to all parts of the body.

Veins Veins carry blood to the heart. Veins have one-way valves that allow blood to move only toward the heart.

Capillaries Capillaries are very small pathways for blood. When blood flows through capillaries, it gives oxygen and nutrients to the cells in your body. Blood also picks up carbon dioxide and other waste.

Caring for Your Circulatory System

- Never touch another person's blood.
- Eat a healthy, balanced diet throughout your life to keep excess fat from blocking the blood flowing through your arteries.
- Get regular exercise to keep your heart strong.

Activities

1. Take the bottom out of a paper cup. Bend the top together like a clamshell. Hold the cup and drop a marble through from the bottom. Now try to drop one into the top. The clamshell-shaped cup is like the one-way valve in a vein.

2. Find the blue lines under the skin on your wrist. These are veins. Press gently and stroke along the lines toward your elbow. Now stroke toward your hand. What do you see?

Respiratory System

Your body uses its respiratory system to get oxygen from the air and get rid of excess carbon dioxide. Your respiratory system is made up of your nose and mouth, your trachea (windpipe), your two lungs, and your diaphragm—a dome-shaped muscle under your lungs.

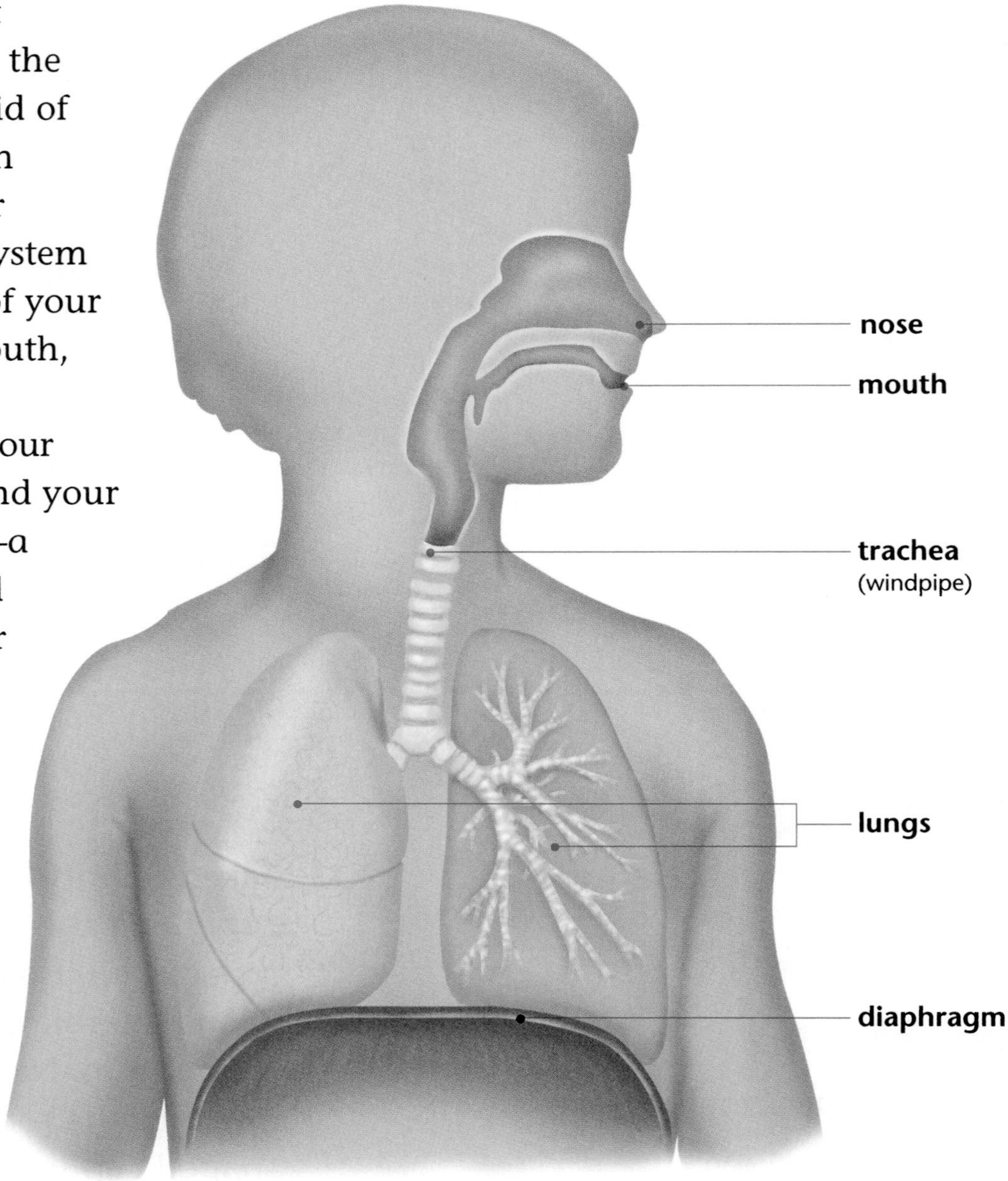

nose

mouth

trachea
(windpipe)

lungs

diaphragm

Breathing

When you inhale, or breathe in, air enters your mouth and nose and goes into your trachea. Your trachea connects your nose and mouth to your lungs. Your trachea divides into two smaller tubes that go to your lungs. Your lungs fill with air. When you exhale, or breathe out, your diaphragm pushes upward. Air is forced up your trachea and out your mouth and nose.

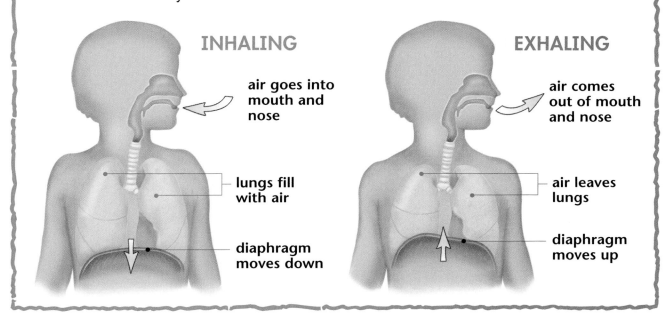

INHALING

air goes into mouth and nose

lungs fill with air

diaphragm moves down

EXHALING

air comes out of mouth and nose

air leaves lungs

diaphragm moves up

Caring for Your Respiratory System

- Exercise. When you exercise your body, you exercise your respiratory system too. Your muscles use more oxygen, so you breathe faster and deeper.

- Get enough sleep to help your resistance to colds.

Activities

1. Sit in a chair and count how many breaths you take in 30 seconds. Then exercise for two minutes. When you stop, count how many breaths you take in 30 seconds. Do you breathe more while sitting or after exercise?

2. Put your hand on your bellybutton and take a deep breath in and out. How does your hand move?

Nervous System

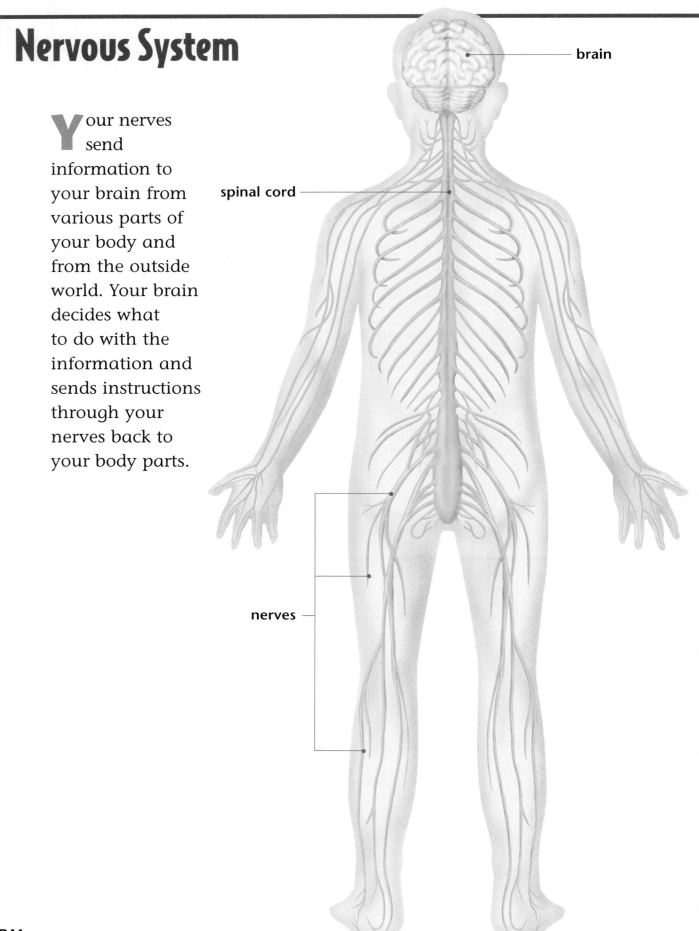

brain

spinal cord

Your nerves send information to your brain from various parts of your body and from the outside world. Your brain decides what to do with the information and sends instructions through your nerves back to your body parts.

nerves

Your Brain

Your brain is about two pounds of wrinkled, pinkish-gray material. It's protected by your skull and cushioned by a thin layer of liquid. The brain's main connection to the body is the spinal cord.

Different parts of the brain send signals to different parts of your body. For example, the part right behind your forehead tells your body how to move. The area near the base of your neck controls your breathing and heartbeat. If you are left-handed, the right half of your brain controls your handwriting.

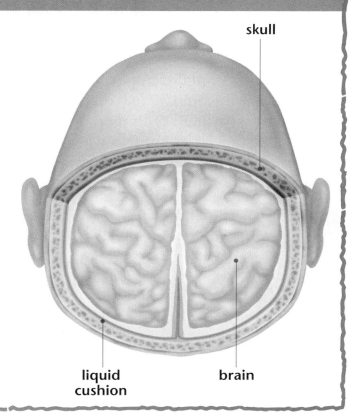

skull

liquid cushion

brain

Caring for Your Nervous System

- Many injuries to the brain are caused by car crashes. Wear your safety belt and sit in the backseat when you are in the car.

- Always wear a helmet when you ride your bike, skate, or use a skateboard.

Activities

1. Make a list of signals your nerves are sending to your brain right now. Also list instructions your brain is sending to your nerves.

2. Read a paragraph out of a book while the television is on. Do you know what the paragraph was about? Do you know what happened on television?

3. Write your name with your opposite hand ten times. Does your writing improve?

Glossary

This Glossary contains important science words and their definitions. Each word is respelled as it would be in a dictionary. When you see the ′ mark after a syllable, pronounce that syllable with more force than the other syllables. The page number at the end of the definition tells where to find the word in your book. The boldfaced letters in the examples in the Pronunciation Key that follows show how these letters are pronounced in the respellings after each glossary word.

PRONUNCIATION KEY

a	**a**dd, m**a**p	m	**m**ove, see**m**	u	**u**p, d**o**ne
ā	**a**ce, r**a**te	n	**n**ice, ti**n**	û(r)	b**ur**n, t**er**m
â(r)	**c**are, **air**	ng	ri**ng**, so**ng**	yo͞o	**f**use, **few**
ä	p**a**lm, f**a**ther	o	**o**dd, h**o**t	v	**v**ain, e**v**e
b	**b**at, ru**b**	ō	**o**pen, s**o**	w	**w**in, a**w**ay
ch	**ch**eck, cat**ch**	ô	**or**der, j**aw**	y	**y**et, **y**earn
d	**d**og, ro**d**	oi	**oi**l, b**oy**	z	**z**est, mu**s**e
e	**e**nd, p**e**t	ou	p**ou**t, n**ow**	zh	vi**s**ion, plea**s**ure
ē	**e**qual, tr**ee**	o͝o	t**oo**k, f**u**ll	ə	the schwa, an
f	**f**it, hal**f**	o͞o	p**oo**l, f**oo**d		unstressed vowel
g	**g**o, lo**g**	p	**p**it, sto**p**		representing the
h	**h**ope, **h**ate	r	**r**un, poo**r**		sound spelled
i	**i**t, g**i**ve	s	**s**ee, pa**ss**		*a* in *above*
ī	**i**ce, wr**i**te	sh	**s**ure, ru**sh**		*e* in *sicken*
j	**j**oy, le**dg**e	t	**t**alk, si**t**		*i* in *possible*
k	**c**ool, ta**k**e	th	**th**in, bo**th**		*o* in *melon*
l	**l**ook, ru**l**e	t̶h̶	**th**is, ba**th**e		*u* in *circus*

Other symbols:
- • separates words into syllables
- ′ indicates heavier stress on a syllable
- ′ indicates light stress on a syllable

absorption [ab•sôrp′shən] The stopping of light **(F40)**

amphibian [am•fib′ē•ən] An animal that begins life in the water and moves onto land as an adult **(A50)**

anemometer [an′ə•mom′ə•tər] An instrument that measures wind speed **(D40)**

asteroid [as′tər•oid] A chunk of rock that orbits the sun **(D64)**

atmosphere [at′məs•fir′] The air that surrounds Earth **(D30)**

atom [at′əm] The basic building block of matter **(E16)**

axis [ak′sis] An imaginary line that goes through the North Pole and the South Pole of Earth **(D68)**

barrier island [bar′ē•ər i′lənd] A landform; a thin island along a coast **(C35)**

bird [bûrd] An animal that has feathers, two legs, and wings **(A45)**

canyon [kan′yən] A landform; a deep valley with very steep sides **(C35)**

chemical change [kem′i•kəl chānj′] A change that forms different kinds of matter **(E46)**

chlorophyll [klôr′ə•fil′] The substance that gives plants their green color; it helps a plant use energy from the sun to make food **(A20)**

clay [klā] A type of soil made up of very small grains; it holds water well **(C69)**

coastal forest [kōs′təl fôr′ist] A thick forest with tall trees that gets a lot of rain and does not get very warm or cold **(B15)**

comet [kom′it] A large ball of ice and dust that orbits the sun **(D64)**

community [kə•myōō′nə•tē] All the populations of organisms that live in an ecosystem **(B7)**

condensation [kon′dən•sā′shən] The changing of a gas into a liquid **(D17)**

conductor [kən•duk′tər] A material in which thermal energy moves easily **(F15)**

coniferous forest [kō•nif′ər•əs fôr′ist] A forest in which most of the trees are conifers (cone-bearing) and stay green all year **(B16)**

conservation [kon′ser•vā′shən] The saving of resources by using them carefully **(C76)**

constellation [kon′stə•lā′shən] A group of stars that form a pattern **(D84)**

consumer [kən•sōōm′ər] A living thing that eats other living things as food **(B43)**

contour plowing [kon′tōōr plou′ing] A type of plowing for growing crops; creates rows of crops around the sides of a hill instead of up and down **(C76)**

core [kôr] The center of the Earth **(C8)**

crust [krust] The solid outside layer of the Earth **(C8)**

deciduous forest [dē•sij′ōō•əs fôr′ist] A forest in which most of the trees lose and regrow their leaves each year **(B13)**

decomposer [dē′kəm•pōz′er] A living thing that breaks down dead organisms for food **(B44)**

desert [dez′ərt] An ecosystem where there is very little rain **(B20)**

earthquake [ûrth′kwāk′] The shaking of Earth's surface caused by movement of the crust and mantle **(C48)**

ecosystem [ek′ō•sis′təm] The living and nonliving things in an environment **(B7)**

energy [en′ər•jē] The ability to cause change **(F6)**

energy pyramid [en′ər•jē pir′ə•mid] A diagram that shows that the amount of useable energy in an ecosystem is less for each higher animal in the food chain **(B50)**

environment [in•vī′rən•mənt] The things, both living and nonliving, that surround a living thing **(B6)**

erosion [i•rō′zhən] The movement of weathered rock and soil **(C42)**

estuary [es′chōō•er′•ē] A place where fresh water from a river mixes with salt water from the ocean **(D12)**

evaporation [ē•vap′ə•rā′shən] The process by which a liquid changes into a gas **(D17, E18)**

fish [fish] An animal that lives its whole life in water and breathes with gills **(A52)**

flood [flud] A large amount of water that covers normally dry land **(C50)**

food chain [fōōd′ chān′] The path of food from one living thing to another **(B48)**

food web [fōōd′ web′] A model that shows how food chains overlap **(B54)**

force [fôrs] A push or a pull **(F58)**

forest [fôr′ist] An area in which the main plants are trees **(B12)**

fossil [fos′əl] Something that has lasted from a living thing that died long ago **(C20)**

fresh water [fresh′ wôt′ər] Water that has very little salt in it **(B26)**

front [frunt] A place where two air masses of different temperatures meet **(D37)**

gas [gas] A form of matter that does not have a definite shape or a definite volume **(E12)**

germinate [jûr′mə•nāt′] When a new plant breaks out of the seed **(A13)**

gills [gilz] A body part found in fish and young amphibians that takes in oxygen from the water **(A51)**

glacier [glā′shər] A huge sheet of ice **(C44)**

gravity [grav′i•tē] The force that pulls objects toward each other **(F62)**

groundwater [ground′wôt′ər] A form of fresh water that is found under Earth's surface **(D8)**

habitat [hab′ə•tat′] The place where a population lives in an ecosystem **(B7)**

heat [hēt] The movement of thermal energy from one place to another **(F8)**

humus [hyo͞o′məs] The part of the soil made up of decayed parts of once-living things **(C62)**

igneous rock [ig′nē•əs rok′] A rock that was once melted rock but has cooled and hardened **(C12)**

inclined plane [in•klīnd′ plān′] A simple machine made of a flat surface set at an angle to another surface **(F71)**

inexhaustible resource [in′eg•zôs′tə•bəl rē′sôrs] A resource such as air or water that can be used over and over and can't be used up **(C94)**

inherit [in•her′it] To receive traits from parents **(A38)**

insulator [in′sə•lāt′ər] A material in which thermal energy does not move easily **(F15)**

interact [in′tər•akt′] When plants and animals affect one another or the environment to meet their needs **(B42)**

landform [land′fôrm′] A natural shape or feature of Earth's surface **(C34)**

leaf [lēf] A plant part that grows out of the stem; it takes in the air and light that a plant needs **(A7)**

lever [lev′ər] A bar that moves on or around a fixed point **(F70)**

liquid [lik′wid] A form of matter that has volume that stays the same, but can change its shape **(E12)**

loam [lōm] A type of topsoil that is rich in minerals and has lots of humus **(C70)**

lunar eclipse [lōō′nər i•klips′] The hiding of the moon when it passes through the Earth's shadow **(D78)**

mammal [mam′əl] An animal that has fur or hair and is fed milk from its mother's body **(A42)**

mantle [man′təl] The middle layer of the Earth **(C8)**

mass [mas] The amount of matter in an object **(E24)**

matter [mat′ər] Anything that takes up space **(E6)**

metamorphic rock [met′ə•môr′fik rok′] A rock that has been changed by heat and pressure **(C12)**

mineral [min′ər•əl] An object that is solid, is formed in nature, and has never been alive **(C6)**

mixture [miks′chər] A substance that contains two or more different types of matter **(E41)**

motion [mō′shən] A change in position **(F59)**

mountain [moun′tən] A landform; a place on Earth's surface that is much higher than the land around it **(C35)**

nonrenewable resource [non′ri•nōō′ə•bəl rē′sôrs] A resource, such as coal or oil, that will be used up someday **(C96)**

orbit [ôr′bit] The path an object takes as it moves around another object in space **(D58)**

phases [fāz•əz] The different shapes the moon seems to have in the sky when observed from Earth **(D76)**

photosynthesis [fōt′ō•sin′thə•sis] The food-making process of plants **(A20)**

physical change [fiz′i•kəl chānj] A change to matter in which no new kinds of matter are formed **(E40)**

physical property [fiz′i•kəl prop′ər•tē] Anything you can observe about an object by using your senses **(E6)**

plain [plān] A landform; a flat area on Earth's surface **(C35)**

planet [plan′it] A large body of rock or gas that orbits the sun **(D58)**

plateau [pla•tō′] A landform; a flat area higher than the land around it **(C35)**

population [pop′yoo•lā′shən] A group of the same kind of living thing that all live in one place at the same time **(B7)**

precipitation [prē•sip′ə•tā′shən] The water that falls to Earth as rain, snow, sleet, or hail **(D18)**

predator [pred′ə•tər] An animal that hunts another animal for food **(B54)**

prey [prā] An animal that is hunted by a predator **(B54)**

prism [priz′əm] A solid, transparent object that bends light into colors **(F44)**

producer [prə•doos′ər] A living thing that makes its own food **(B43)**

recycle [rē•sī′kəl] To reuse a resource to make something new **(C100)**

reflection [ri•flek′shən] The bouncing of light off an object **(F36)**

refraction [ri•frak′shən] The bending of light when it moves from one kind of matter to another **(F38)**

renewable resource [ri•noo′ə•bəl rē′sôrs] A resource that can be replaced in a human lifetime **(C94)**

reptile [rep′til] A land animal that has dry skin covered by scales **(A55)**

resource [rē′sôrs] A material that is found in nature and that is used by living things **(C88)**

revolution [rev′ə•loo′shən] The movement of one object around another object **(D68)**

rock [rok] A solid made of minerals **(C8)**

rock cycle [rok′ sī′kəl] The process in which one type of rock changes into another type of rock **(C14)**

root [root] The part of a plant that holds the plant in the ground and takes in water and minerals from the soil **(A7)**

rotation [rō•tā′shən] The spinning of an object on its axis **(D68)**

salt water [sôlt′ wôt′ər] Water that has a lot of salt in it **(B26)**

scales [skālz] The small, thin, flat plates that help protect the bodies of fish and reptiles **(A52)**

sedimentary rock [sed′ə•men′tər•ē rok′] A rock formed from material that has settled into layers and been squeezed until it hardens into rock **(C12)**

seed [sēd] The first stage in the growth of many plants **(A12)**

seedling [sēd′ling] A young plant **(A13)**

simple machine [sim′pəl mə•shēn′] A tool that helps people do work **(F70)**

soil [soil] The loose material in which plants can grow in the upper layer of Earth **(C62)**

solar eclipse [sō′lər i•klips′] The hiding of the sun that occurs when the moon passes between the sun and Earth **(D80)**

solar system [sō′lər sis′təm] The sun and the objects that orbit around it **(D58)**

solid [sol′id] A form of matter that takes up a specific amount of space and has a definite shape **(E11)**

solution [sə•lōō′shən] A mixture in which the particles of two different kinds of matter mix together evenly **(E42)**

speed [spēd] The measure of how fast something moves over a certain distance **(F61)**

star [stär] A hot ball of glowing gases, like our sun **(D84)**

stem [stem] A plant part that connects the roots with the leaves of a plant and supports the plant above ground; it carries water from the roots to other parts of the plant **(A7)**

strip cropping [strip′ krop′ing] A type of planting that uses strips of thick grass or clover between strips of crops **(C76)**

telescope [tel′ə•skōp′] An instrument used to see faraway objects **(D88)**

temperature [tem′pər•ə•chər] The measure of how hot or cold something is **(D36)**

thermal energy [thûr′məl en′ər•jē] The energy that moves the particles in matter **(F7)**

thermometer [thûr•mom′ə•tər] A tool used to measure temperature **(F20)**

topsoil [top′soil′] The top layer of soil made up of the smallest grains and the most humus **(C63)**

trait [trāt] A body feature that an animal inherits; it can also be some things that an animal does **(A38)**

tropical rain forest [trop′i•kəl rān′fôr′ist] A hot, wet forest where the trees grow very tall and their leaves stay green all year **(B14)**

valley [val′ē] A landform; a lowland area between higher lands, such as mountains **(C35)**

volcano [vol•kā′nō] An opening in Earth's surface from which lava flows **(C49)**

volume [vol′yoom] The amount of space that matter takes up **(E22)**

water cycle [wôt′ər sī′kəl] The movement of water from Earth's surface into the air and back to the surface again **(D19)**

weather [weth′ər] The happenings in the atmosphere at a certain time **(D32)**

weather map [weth′ər map′] A map that shows weather data for a large area **(D46)**

weathering [weth′ər•ing] The process by which rock is worn down and broken apart **(C40)**

weight [wāt] The measure of the pull of gravity on an object **(F62)**

wind [wind] The movement of air **(D40)**

work [wûrk] The measure of force that it takes to move an object a certain distance **(F66)**

Ulna, R34
Umpqua Research Company, D21
Understory, B15
Uranus, D58–59
    facts about, D63
Ursa Major, D84

Valles Marineris, Mars, D54
Valley, C35
Valley glaciers, C44
Valve, R41
Veins, R40, R41
Venus, D58–59
    facts about, D60
Verdi **(Cannon),** A57
Very Large Array telescope, D95
Volcanoes, C13, C46, C49–50, E18
    Hawaiian, C54
    types of, C54
Volume
    defined, E22
    and mass compared, E28
    measuring, E22–23

Wall, Diana, C80
Warm front, D46
Waste (chart), C100

Water
    amounts of salt and fresh, D7
    forms of, D16–17
    importance of, D6–7
    as resource, C88
    in space, D21
    uses of, D3
    wasting, D2
    and weathering, C41
Water cycle, D16–19
Water filters, D20–21
Water hole, African, A35
Water treatment plant, D11
Water vapor, D16, D17
Weather, D32
    gathering data, D44–45
    measuring, D36–41
Weather balloons, D45
Weather forecasting, D44–47
Weather fronts, D37, D46
Weather maps, D46
Weather researcher, D49
Weather satellites, D44
Weather station, D44
    symbols used by, D46, D47
Weather vanes, D34
Weathering, C40–41
Weaverbird, A45
Wedge, F70, F72
Weighing scale, E20
Weight, F62
Wells, C90
West Chop Lighthouse, MA, C31
Wetness, E8
Whales, A44
Wheel and axle, F70, F72
White light, F46
    colors of, F45
Wildfires **(Armbruster),** B9

Wind, D32
    measuring, D40
Wings, A45
Women in Science and Engineering (WISE) Award, F76
Work, F66–67
Workout, guidelines for, R23–25
World Health Organization, D20–21
Wright, James, E37

Xeriscaping, A25

Yellowstone National Park, B8
Yellow tang, A53

Zinc, C7

Photography Credits - Page placement key: (t) top, (c) center, (b) bottom, (l) left, (r) right, (bg) background, (i) inset

Cover Background, Charles Krebs/Tony Stone Images; Inset, Jody Dole.

Unit A - A1 (bg) Thomas Brase/Tony Stone Images; (i) Denis Valentine/The Stock Market; A2-A3 (bg) Joe McDonald/Bruce Coleman; A3 (i) Marilyn Kazmers/Deminsky Photo Associates; A4 Ed Young/AGStock USA; A6 (l) Anthony Edgeworth/The Stock Market; (r) Chris Vincent/The Stock Market; A6-A7 (bg) Barbara Gerlach/Dembinsky Photo Associates; A7 (t) Wendy W. Cortesi; A8 (t) Runk/Schoenberger/Grant Heilman Photography; (c) Runk/Schoenberger/Grant Heilman Photography; (bl) Renee Lynn/Photo Researchers; (br) Dr. E.R. Degginger/Color-Pic; A9 Runk/Schoenberger/Grant Heilman Photography; A10 Runk/Schoenberger/Grant Heilman Photography; A12 (l) Bonnie Sue/Grant Heilman/Photo Researchers; (li) Klaus Paysan/Peter Arnold, Inc.; (r) Runk/Schoenberger/Grant Heilman Photography; A13 (t) Ed Young/AgStock USA; (b) Dr. E. R. Degginger/Color-Pic; A14 (tr) Richard Shiell/Dembinsky Photo Associates; (bl) Robert Carr/Bruce Coleman, Inc.; (br) Scott Sinklier/AGStock USA; A16 (t) Thomas D. Mangelsen/Peter Arnold, Inc.; (c) E.R. Degginger/Natural Selection Stock Photography; (bl) Randall B. Henne/Dembinsky Photo Associates; (br) Stan Osolinski/Dembinsky Photo Associates; A17 (t) Scott Camazine/Photo Researchers; A17 William Harlow/Photo Researchers; A18 Christi Carter/Grant Heilman Photography; A20 Runk/Schoenberger/Grant Heilman Photography; A22 (t) DiMaggio/Kalish/The Stock Market; A22 (l) Jan-Peter Lahall/Peter Arnold, Inc.; (br) Holt Studios/Nigel Cattlin/Photo Researchers; A23 Robert Carr/Bruce Coleman, Inc.; A24 Richard Shiell; A25 J. Sapinsky/The Stock Market; A26 (tr) Corbis; A30-A31 (bkgd) Art Wolfe/Tony Stone Images; A31 (tr) Astrid & Hanns Frieder Michler/Science Photo Library/Photo Researchers; A32 (1) Rosemary Calvert/Tony Stone Images; (1) Ralph A. Reinhold/Animals Animals; (2) Johnny Johnson/ Tony Stone Images; (3) Mike Severns/ Tom Stack & Associates; (4) Fred Whitehead/Animals Animals; (5) Art Wolfe/ Tony Stone Images; (6) J.C. Stevenson/Animals Animals; A34-A35 Doug Perrine/Innerspace Visions; A35 (t) Ronald Hellstrom/Bruce Coleman, Inc.; (c) Stan Osolinski/Tony Stone Images; A37 (b) Mike Severns/Tony Stone Images; (lc) Kevin Schafer/Tony Stone Images; (bl) Marilyn Kazmers/Peter Arnold, Inc.; (r) Keren Su/Tony Stone Images; A38 (t) Rudie Kuiter/Innerspace Visions; (c) Fred Bruemmer/Peter Arnold, Inc.; (b) Art Wolfe/Tony Stone Images; A39 Phil A. Dotson/Photo Researchers; A40 Brian Stablyk/Tony Stone Images; A43 (t) Paul Metzger/Photo Researchers; (b) Frans Lanting/Minden Pictures; A44 (t) Stephen Dalton/Photo Researchers; (c) Tom McHugh/Photo Researchers; (cr) Evelyn Gallardo/Peter Arnold, Inc.; (c) The Photo Library-Sydney/Gary Lewis/Photo Researchers; (br) Francois Gohier/Photo Researchers; A45 (t) Theo Allofs/Tony Stone Images; (blue jay) Wayne Lankinen/Bruce Coleman, Inc.; (macaw) M. Mastrorillo/The Stock Market; (emperor penguin) Kjell B. Sandved/Photo Researchers; (ostrich) Leonard Lee Rue III/Photo Researchers; (bee humming bird) Robert A. Tyrrell Photography; (peacock) Tom McHugh/Photo Researchers; A46 (t) Manfred Danegger/Tony Stone Images; (cl) John Cancalosi/Peter Arnold, Inc.; (b) Bill Ivy/Tony Stone Images; (br) Stan Osolinski/The Stock Market; A48 (c) O.S.F./ Animals Animals; (b) Tim Davis/Tony Stone Images; A50 (tl) Nuridsany et Perennou/Photo Researchers; (r) E.R. Degginger/Tony Stone Images; A52 (t) Joseph T. Collins/Photo Researchers; A52 (t) David M. Schleser/Nature's Images; (c) Andrea & Antonella Ferrari/Innerspace Visions; A52-A53 Kelvin Aitken/Peter Arnold, Inc.; A53 (t) Zig Leszczynski/Animals Animals; (c) Kelvin Aitken/Peter Arnold, Inc.; (br) Tom McHugh/Steinhart Aquarium/Photo Researchers; A54(r) Kim Taylor/Bruce Coleman, Inc.; (c) Fred Bavendam/Minden Pictures; (b) Fred Bavendam/Minden Pictures; A55 (t) Zig Leszczynski/Animals Animals; (b) Suzanne L. Collins & Joseph T. Collins/Photo Researchers; (bli) Dwight R. Kuhn; A56 (t) Jany Sauvanet/Photo Researchers; (c) G.E. Schmida/Fritz/Bruce Coleman, Inc.; A56-A57 (b) Tom & Pat Leeson/Photo Researchers; A57 Schafer & Hill/Tony Stone Images; A58 (t) Tom Brakefield/Bruce Coleman, Inc.; (c) Dr. E. R. Degginger/Color-Pic; (b) Michael Holford; A59 Emory Kristof/National Geographic Image Collection; A60 (t) Bertha G. Gomez; (bl) Michael Fogden/bruce Coleman, Inc.

Unit B - B1 (bg) Derek Redfearn/The Image Bank; (i) George E. Stewart/Dembinsky Photo Association; B2-B3 (bg) Sven Linoblad/Photo Researchers; B2 (i) Wayne P. Armstrong; B4 Hans Pfletschinger/Peter Arnold, Inc.; B6 (t) Dwight R. Kuhn; (r) Michael Durham/ENP Images; B7 Frank Krahmer/Bruce Coleman, Inc.; B8 (tl) Jeff and Alexa Henry/Peter Arnold, Inc.; (r) Jeff and Alexa Henry/Peter Arnold, Inc.; (b) Christoph Burki/Tony Stone Images; B10 Kennan Ward/The Stock Market; B13 (all) James P. Jackson/Photo Researchers; B14 Zefa Germany/The Stock Market; B15 Janis Burger/Bruce Coleman Inc.; B16 (r) Michael Quinton/Minden Pictures; B16-B17 (b)Grant Heilman Photography; B18 J.C. Carton/Bruce Coleman, Inc.; B20 (t) Wolfgang Kaehler Photography; (r) James Randklev/Tony Stone Images; B21 Dr. E.R. Degginger/Color-Pic; B22 (l) Paul Chesley/Tony Stone Images; (r) Jen & Des Bartlett/Bruce Coleman, Inc.; B23 Lee Rentz/Bruce Coleman, Inc.; B24 Leo De Wys Inc.; (r) R.N. Mariscal/Bruce Coleman, Inc.; (b) Dr. E.R. Degginger/Color-Pic; (r) Naitar E. Harvey, APSA/National Audubon Society/Photo Researchers; B28 Flip Nicklin/Minden Pictures; B29 (t) Norbert Wu/Peter Arnold, Inc.; (b) Norbert Wu/Peter Arnold, Inc.; B30 (t) Gary Meszaros/Bruce Coleman, Inc.; (bli) Stevan Stefanovic/Okapia/Photo Researchers; (bci) Dwight R. Kuhn; (bri) Phil Degginger/Color-Pic; B30-B31 (b) Jeff Greenberg/Photo Researchers; B32 (b) Courtesy of Jane Weaver/Parie Project/L. A. Gililard Elementary; (ti) Globe-NASA/ Goddard Scientific Visualization Studio; B33 Derke/O'Hara/Tony Stone Images; B34 (tr) The Marjorie N. Boyer Trust; (bl) Anthony Mercieca/ Photo Researchers; B38-B39 Luiz C. Marigo/Peter Arnold, Inc.; B39 (br) Roland Seitre/Peter Arnold, Inc.; B40 (t) Roy Morsch/The Stock Market; (c) Norbert Wu/Tony Stone Images; (r) Rosemary Calvert/Tony Stone Images; B41 (bl) Stan Osolinski/The Stock Market; (c) R. Kopfle/KOPFL/Bruce Coleman; (br) Michael Durham/ENP Images; B42 (bg) Hans Reinhard/Bruce Coleman, Inc.; (li) Dwight R. Kuhn; (ri) Dr. Paul A. Zahl/Photo Researchers; B43 (t) Wolfgang Kaehler Photography; (b) Rob Hadlow/Bruce Coleman, Inc.; B44 (t) Stephen Dalton/Photo Researchers; (c) Andrew Syred/Science Photo Library/Photo Researchers; (b) Stephen Krasemann/Tony Stone Images; B46 Laurie Campbell/Tony Stone Images; B48 Dwight R. Kuhn; B47 (t) Paul E. Taylor/Photo Researchers; (c) Holt Studios/Photo Researchers; (b) Breck P. Kent/Animals Animals; B51 Mitsuaki Iwago/Minden Pictures; B52 Erwin and Peggy Bauer/Bruce Coleman, Inc.; B54-B55 Michael Durham/ENP Images; B57 Jane Burton/Bruce Coleman, Inc.; B58 (c) LASCAUX Caves II, France/Explorer, Paris/Superstock; (c) Fred Bruemmer/Peter Arnold; (c) Tom Brakefield/Bruce Coleman; B60 (tl) Leah Edelstein-Keshet/University of British Columbia; (bl) Fred McConnaughey/Photo Researchers.

Unit C Other - C1(bg) Richard Price/FPG International; (i) Martin Land/Science Photo Library/Photo Researchers; C2-C3 (bg) E. R. Degginger; C2 (bc) A.J. Copley/Visuals Unlimited; C3 (ri) Paul Chesley/Tony Stone Images; C4 (b) The Natural History Museum, London; C6 (tl), (ct), (cb) Dr. E. R. Degginger/Color-Pic; (r) E. R. Degginger/Bruce Coleman, Inc.; (bl) Mark A. Schneider/Dembinsky Photo Associates; C6-C7 (b) Chromosohm/Joe Sohm/Photo Researchers; C7 (tr) Blair Seitz/Photo Researchers; (tri), (bli) Dr. E. R. Degginger/Color-Pic; C8 (t) Barry Runk/Grant Heilman Photography; (ct) Dr. E. R. Degginger/Color-Pic; (b) Dr. E. R. Degginger/Color-Pic; (cb) Barry L. Runk/Grant Heilman Photography; C8-9 (b) Robert Pettit/Dembinsky Photo Associates; C10 Tom Bean/Tom & Susan Bean, Inc.; C12 Jim Steinberg/Photo Researchers; C12-C13 (bg) G. Brad Lewis/Photo Resource Hawaii; C14 (l), (tr) Dr. E. R. Degginger/Color-Pic; C14 (br) Aaron Haupt/Photo Researchers; C15 (tl) Robert Pettit/Dembinsky Photo Associates; (tr) Charles R. Belinky/Photo Researchers; (bl), (bc), (br) Dr. E. R. Degginger/Color-Pic; C16 (t) Roger Du Buisson/The Stock Market; (c) Jay Mallin Photos; C16-C17 (b) Ed Wheeler/The Stock Market; C18 Stephen Wilkes/The Image Bank; C21 (t) William E. Ferguson; (bl) Kerry T. Givens/Bruce Coleman, Inc.; C22 (t) AP Photo/Dennis Cook; (b) M. Timothy O'Keefe/Bruce Coleman, Inc.; C24 (t) Francois Gohier/Photo Researchers; (b) The National History Museum/London; C25 Stan Osolinski; C26 (tr) Jean Miele/Lamont-Doherty Earth Observatory of Columbia University; C30-C31 (bg) John Warden/Tony Stone Images; C31 (bl) Harold Naideau/The Stock Market; C32 G. Alan Nelson/Dembinsky Photo Associates; C33 (b) Superstock; C34-35 (b) Darrell Gulin/Dembinsky Photo Associates; C35 (t) Michael Hubrich/Dembinsky Photo Associates; (c) Mark E. Gibson; C36 (t) Breck P. Kent/Earth Scenes; C36-37 (b) Paraskevas Photography; C38 Mark E. Gibson; C40 (bl) Dr. E. R. Degginger/Color-Pic; C40 (bc) Mark A. Schneider/Dembinsky Photo Associates; C40-C41 (br-b) Rod Planck/Dembinsky Photo Associates; (c) John Gerlach/Dembinsky Photo Associates; C42 (t) Georg Gerster/Photo Researchers; (c) NASA Photo/Grant Heilman Photography; C42-C43 (b) C.C. Lockwood/Earth Scenes; C43 (t)

Mark E. Gibson; C46 Ken Sakamoto/Black Star; C48 (l) David Parker/SPL/Photo R[...] AP/Wide World Photos; C49 (l) AP/Wide World Photos; (r) AP Photo/Wide World [...] Will & Deni McIntyre/Photo Researchers; C50-C51 AP/Wide World Photos; C52 [...] Hall/Woodfin Camp & Associates; (i) Laura Riley/Bruce Coleman; C53 J. Aronovsk[...] Images/The Stock Market; C54 (tr) Courtesy of Scott Rowland; (bl) Dennis Oda/Ton[...] Images; C58-C59 (b) Lynn M. Stone/Bruce Coleman, Inc.; C59 (br) NASA; C60 An[...] Duncan/Tom Stack & Associates; C63 (all) Bruce Coleman, Inc.; C64 Grant Heilman[...] man Photography; C68-C69 (b) Gary Irving/Panoramic Images; C68 (l) Barry L. Runk/Grant Heilman Photography; C69 (li), (ri) Barry L. Runk/Grant Heilman Photography; C70-C71 (b) Larry Lefever/Grant Heilman Photography; C72 Andy Sacks/Tony Stone Images; C74 USDA - Soil Conservation Service; C74-C75 (b) Dr. E.R. Degginger/Color-Pic; C75 (t) James D. Nations/D. Donne Bryant; (tli) Gunter Ziseler/Peter Arnold, Inc.; (tri) S.A.M./Wolfgang Kaehler Photography; (bli) Walter H. Hodge/Peter Arnold, Inc.; (bri) Jim Steinberg/Photo Researchers; C76 (t) Thomas Hovland from Grant Heilman Photography; (b) B.W. Hoffmann/AGStock USA; C78 (b) Randall B. Henne/Dembinsky Photo Associates; (t) Russ Munn/AgStock USA; C79 Bruce Hands/Tony Stone Images; C80 (tr) Courtesy of Diana Wall, Colorado State University; (b) Oliver Mickes/Ottawa/Photo Researchers; C84-C85 (bg) Kirby, Richar OSF/Earth Scenes; C86 Bob Daemmrich/Bob Daemmrich Photography, Inc.; C88 (l) Peter Correz/Tony Stone Images; (c) Mark E. Gibson; C88-C89(b) Bill Lea/Dembinsky Photo Associates; C90 (t) Chris Rogers/Rainbow/PNI; (c) Yoav Levy/Phototake/PNI; C91 Rob Badger Photography; C92 (bl) Christie's Images, London/Superstock; (br) Jeff Greenberg / Photo Researchers; (bc) Joyce Photographics / Photo Researchers; (tr) Mary Ann Kulla/ The Stock Market; C93 (bl) Alan L. Detrick / Photo Researchers; (bc) Archive Photos; (br) David Barnes /The Stock Market; (br) Gary Retherford/ Photo Researchers; C94-C95 Jeff Greenberg/Visuals Unlimited; C95 (tl) Wolfgang Fischer/Peter Arnold, Inc.; (r) Wolfgang Fischer/Peter Arnold, Inc.; (c) Craig Hammell/The Stock Market; C96 (t) Barbara Gerlach/Dembinsky Photo Associates; (b) Brownie Harris/The Stock Market; C97 Chris Rogers/The Stock Market; C98 Michael A. Keller/The Stock Market; C100-C101 (b) Ray Pfortner/Peter Arnold, Inc.; C103 William E. Ferguson; C104-C105 Blaine Harrington III/The Stock Market; C106 James King-Holmes/Science Photo Library/ Photo Researchers; C107 (bl) Wellman Fibers Industry; (r) Gabe Palmer/The Stock Market; C108 (tr) Susan Sterner/HRW; (bl) Kristin Finnegan/Tony Stone Images.

Unit D Other - D1(bg) Pal Hermansen/Tony Stone Images; (i) Earth Imaging/Tony Stone Images; D2-D3 (bg) Zefa Germany/The Stock Market; D3 (tr) Michael A. Keller/The Stock Market; (br) Steven Needham/Envision; D4 J. Shaw/Bruce Coleman, Inc.; D5 (b) NASA; D6 (t) Yu Somov; S. Korytnikov/Sovfoto/Eastfoto/PNI; (r) Christopher Arend/Alaska Stock Images/PNI; D7 Grant Heilman Photography; D8-D9 Dr. Eckart Pott/Bruce Coleman, Inc.; D10 N.R. Rowan/The Image Works; D12-D13 Mike Price/Bruce Coleman, Inc.; D13 David Job/Tony Stone Images; D14 John Beatty/Tony Stone Images; D17 (l) Grant Heilman Photography; (r) Darrell Gulin/Tony Stone Images; D20 NASA; D21 Ben Osborne/Tony Stone Images; D22 (tr) Polytehnic State University; (b) NASA; D26-D27 Andrea Booher/Tony Stone Images; D27 NASA/Science Photo Library/Photo Researchers; D28 Joe Towers/The Stock Market; D30 Rich Iwasaki/Tony Stone Images; D32 (t) Peter Arnold; (c) Warren Faidley/International Stock Photography; (b) Stephen Simpson/FPG International; D33 E.R. Degginger/Bruce Coleman, Inc.; D34 Ray Pfortner/Peter Arnold, Inc.; D37 (t) Ralph H. Wetmore, II/Tony Stone Images; (b) Joe McDonald/Earth Scenes; D38 (t) Tom Bean; (b) Adam Jones/Photo Researchers; D42 Warren Faidley/International Stock Photography; D44 (l) Superstock; (r) David Ducros/Science Photo Library/Photo Researchers; D45 (both) © 1998 AccuWeather; D45 New Scientist Magazine; D49 Dwayne Newton/PhotoEdit; D50 (tr) Courtesy June Bacon-Bercey; (bl) David R. Frazier/Photo Researchers; D54-D55 David Hardy/Science Photo Library/Photo Researchers; D55 (tc) European Space Agency/Science Photo Library/Photo Researchers; D60 (t) U.S. Geological Survey/Science Photo Library/Photo Researchers; D60 (b) NASA; D60, D61, D62 (bg) Jerry Schad/Photo Researchers; D61 (t) Nationcal Oceanic and Atmospheric Administration; D61 (b) David Crisp and the WFPC2 Science Team (Jet Propulsion Laboratory/California Institute of Technology); D62 (t), (b) NASA; D63 (t) Erich Karkoschka (University of Arizona Lunar & Planetary Lab) and NASA; (c) NASA; (b) Nasa/Science Source/Photo Researchers; D64 J. Spurr/Bruce Coleman, Inc.; D65 Royer, Ronald/Science Photo Library/Photo Researchers; D66 Renee Lynn/Photo Researchers; D69 (l) Dr. E. R. Degginger/Color-Pic; (r) Dr. E. R. Degginger/Color-Pic; D72 (t) Joseph Nettis/Photo Researchers; (b) John Elk III/Bruce Coleman, Inc.; D74 NASA; D77 (all) Telegraph Colour Library/FPG International; D78-D79 Margaret Miller/Photo Researchers; D79 (t) Pekka Parviainen/Science Photo Library/Photo Researchers; (b) George East/Science Photo Library/Photo Researchers; D80 Dr. Fred Espenak/Science Photo Library/Photo Researchers; D88 Merritt Vincent/PhotoEdit; D90 (l) Rob Talbot/ Tony Stone Images; (r) Stephen Graham/Dembinsky Photo Associates; D91 NASA; D92 (both) NASA.

Unit E Other - E1(bg) Steve Barnett/Liaison International; (i) StockFood America/Lieberman; E2-E3 Chris Noble/Tony Stone Images; E3 Kent & Donna Dannen; E6 John Michael/International Stock Photography; E7 (r) R. Van Nostrand/Photo Researchers; E8 (tr) Mike Timo/Tony Stone Images; E9 (t) Daniel J. Cox/Tony Stone Images; (ti) Goknar/Vogue/Superstock; E10 (br) John Michael/International Stock Photography; (bc) William Cornett/Image Excellence Photography; E11 (tr) Lee Foster/FPG International; (br) Paul Silverman/Fundamental Photographs; E12 (t) William Johnson/Stock, Boston; E12-E13 (b) Robert Finken/Photo Researchers; E14 S.J. Krasemann/Peter Arnold, Inc.; E16 (ri) Dr. E. R. Degginger/Color-Pic; E17 (l) Charles D. Winters/Photo Researchers; (br) Spencer Gran/PhotoEdit; E18-E19 Peter French/Pacific Stock; E20 J. Sebo/Zoo Atlanta; E25 (r) Robert Pearcy/Animals Animals; E25 (cl) Ron Kimball Photography; E26 (tr) Jim Harrison/Stock, Boston; E32 (tr) Corbis; (bl) Alfred Pasieka/Science Photo Library/Photo Researchers; E36-E37 (bg)Dr. Dennis Kunkel/Phototake; E38 Robert Ginn/PhotoEdit; E42 (tl), (tr) Dr. E. R. Degginger/Color-Pic; (bl) Tom Pantages; E44 Chip Clark; E46 (l) Tom Pantages; (c) Tom Pantages; E47 (tl) John Lund/Tony Stone Images; E50 John Gaudio; E51 Michael Newman/Photo Edit; E52 (tr) Los Alamos National Laboratory/Photo Researchers; (bl) US Army White Sands Missile Range.

Unit F - F1 (bg) Simon Fraser/Science Photo Library/Photo Researchers; (i) Nance Trueworthy/Liaison International; F2 (bg) April Riehm; (tr) M. W. Black/Bruce Coleman, Inc.; F6 (bl) Mary Kate Denny/PhotoEdit; (br) Gary A. Conner/PhotoEdit; F7 (bl) Camerique, Inc./The Picture Cube; (br) Stephen Saks/The Picture Cube; F8 (cr) Pat Field/Bruce Coleman, Inc.; (bl) Mark E. Gibson; F9 (l) Dr. E. R. Degginger/Color-Pic; (r)Ryan and Beyer/Allstock/PNI; F10 (b) John Running/Stock Boston; (cl) Joseph Nettis/Photo Researchers; F11 (t) Jeff Schultz/Alaska Stock Images; F16 (t) Buck Ennis/Stock, Boston; (b) J.C. Carton/Bruce Coleman, Inc.; F21 (tl) Michael Holford Photographs; (br) Spencer Grant/PhotoEdit; F25 Marco Cristofori/ The Stock Market; F26 (tr) Corbis; (bl) Shaun Egan/Tony Stone Images; F30-F31 (bg) Jerry Lodriguss/Photo Researchers; F31 (br) Picture PerfectUSA; F32 (t) James M. Mejuto/Photo Researchers; F34 (tl) Mark E. Gibson; (br) Bob Daemmrich/Stock, Boston; F36 (b) Myrleen Ferguson/PhotoEdit; F37 (b), (tl) Jan Butchofsky/Dave G. Houser; F39 (tr), (c) Richard Megna/Fundamental Photographs; F42 (b) Randy Duchaine/The Stock Market; F44 (b) Tom Skrivan/The Stock Market; F45 (tr) David Woodfall/Tony Stone Images; F47 (t) Roy Morsh/The Stock Market; F48 (l) Ed Eckstein for The Franklin Institute Science Museum; (r) Peter Angelo Simon/The Stock Market; F48-F49 Paul Silverman/ Fundamental Photography; F54-F55 (bg) Superstock; (br) David Madison/Bruce Coleman, Inc.; F58 (cl) John Running/Stock, Boston; (b) David Young-Wolff/PhotoEdit; F59 H. Mark Weidman; F60 (t) D & I McDonald/The Picture Cube; F62 (b) Nasa/The Stock Market; (cr) Richard Megna/Fundamental Photographs; F64 (b) Edith G. Haun/Stock, Boston; F70 (b) Amy C. Etra/PhotoEdit; F71 (t) Tony Freeman/PhotoEdit; F72 (b) Dave G. Houser; F74 Webb Chappell; F75 John Lei/Omni-Photo Communications; F76 (tr) NASA/Langley Research Center; (bl) Valder/Tormey/International Stock.

Health Handbook - R15 Palm Beach Post; R19 (tr) Andrew Speilman/Phototake; (c) Martha McBride/Unicorn; (br) Larry West/FPG International; R21 Superstock; R26 (c) Index Stock; R27 (tl) Renne Lynn/ Tony Stone Images; (tr) David Young-Wolff/PhotoEdit.

All Other photographs by Harcourt photographers listed below, © Harcourt: Weronica Ankarorn, Bartlett Digital Photography, Victoria Bowen, Eric Camdem, Digital Imaging Group, Charles Hodges, Ken Karp, Ken Kinzie, Ed McDonald, Sheri O'Neal, Terry Sinclair.

Illustration Credits - Craig Austin A53; Graham Austin B56; John Butler A42; Rick Courtney A20, A51, B14, B55, C22, C40, C41, C62, C64; Mike Dammer A27, A61, B35, B61, C27, C55, C81, C109, D23, D51, D93, E35, E53, F27, F51, F77; Dennis Davidson D58; John Edwards D9, D17, D18, D31, D37, D39, D40, D59, D64, D68, D69, D70, D71, D76, D77, D78, D80, E17, D10, F45, F60; Wendy Griswold-Smith A37; Lisa Frasier F78; Geosystems C34, C42, C44, C103, D12, D46; Wayne Hovice B28; Tom Powers C8, C13, C20, C34, C50, C102; John Rice D16, B7, B21, B50; Ruttle D36, D7; Rosie Saunders A15; Shough C90, F22, F46, F71, F72.